TEARS BEFORE BEDTIME

E. R. RHODES

Publisher's Cataloging-In-Publication Data
(Prepared by The Donohue Group, Inc.)

Names: Rhodes, E. R. (Eric Robert), 1927- author.
Title: Tears before bedtime / E.R. Rhodes.
Description: 2018 edition. | [Delaware, Ontario, Canada] : [E.R. Rhodes], [2018]
Identifiers: ISBN 9781775306016 (paperback) | ISBN 9781775306009 (ebook)
Subjects: LCSH: Rhodes, E. R. (Eric Robert), 1927- | World War, 1939-1945--Personal narratives, British. | Teenage soldiers--England--Biography. | Great Britain. Royal Navy--Biography. | Prisoner-of-war camps--Thailand. | LCGFT: Personal narratives. | Autobiographies.
Classification: LCC D811.R482 A3 2018 (print) | LCC D811.R482 (ebook) | DDC 940.54/8141--dc23

TEARS
BEFORE
BEDTIME

Author's Note

Dear Reader,

My life has been full of adventure, laughter, and heartbreak. I've lost people, found people, and loved people. And I've written this book in their honor. It is a true account of my experiences before and after WWII, both in and out of the military. I have remembered it all to the best of my ability and put it down on paper in as pure a form as possible.

I've taken great strides to ensure my writing accurately reflects the relevant eras, geographical locations, and cultural norms included in the book. As a result, you will come across some derogatory comments, slurs, and behaviors that may be offensive to a modern-day reader. The usage of such language is not intended to be distasteful or unkind; it is merely meant for authenticity.

I hope you enjoy reading the story of my life. It's a pleasure to share it with you.

– E.R. Rhodes

For Vera, the dearest part of me.

Chapter One

Summer's dog days are over. I've mixed emotions as the train chugs into the station. Camp's been fantastic, the teachers terrific, and their handling of three dozen rowdy boys, valiant. The brakes squeal, bringing us to a shuddering halt. Tumbling from the carriage, we're jostled into line for a headcount. Pleased we're all present, Billy Williamson, our long-suffering leader, cuts us loose.

Charlie, my eldest brother, ruffles my hair. "Looks like you've been down in a coal mine."

My other brother, Fred, who is much sturdier than Charlie, greets me by punching my arm. "Hoped you'd be away longer. It's peaceful without you."

He's not joking. We're brothers and love each other but argue nonstop. Dad lumbers up. He's big, especially in his heart. I feel my ribs protest as he drags me into a hard embrace.

Mother, waiting for the antics to cease, isn't thrilled at the sight of her youngest son. "You're a disgrace. Tuck in that shirt and pull up those socks." I obey while she produces a damp handkerchief to wipe my face. It feels like she's beating an egg. "Whatever will the neighbours think?"

I couldn't care less but settle for cowardice. "I missed you, too, Mother."

A smile touches her eyes but quickly escapes. "Have you any money left? Silly me, is the moon made of green cheese?" And without waiting for an answer, she selects her next victims. "Come along, you lot. I've supper to cook, and he needs a scrub in the tub. One could grow potatoes in those ears."

It serves them right; they vanish the instant Mother starts nagging me. Delighted, I snatch the chance to discuss my holiday in spite of Fred's nitpicking. There are a couple of snot-nosed kids leaning on Dad's car. "We're keeping an eye on it, Mister!" they holler.

Dad tosses each a penny and watches their mad dash to the roasted-chestnut cart. Sighing at such extravagance, though smiling, Mother opens the car's rear door, ushering Fred to one side, me to the other, then sits between us. She's nobody's fool.

Charlie's riding shotgun tonight, although he can drive. Saturday evening in the madding crowd is hectic. It's slow-going down the Bull Ring, weaving around late-night shoppers searching for last-minute bargains. Except for fists thumping on the car's roof and lewd suggestions what to do with the horn, we safely reach the bottom. Finally, clear of the mayhem, we pick up speed, and everybody returns to their favourite topic: the imminent threat of war. Yesterday, Germany invaded Poland.

"The Poles don't stand a snowball's chance in hell," Dad says.

Mother's optimistic. "It's only a storm in a teacup," she insists, though clearly worried Charlie will be conscripted.

I hope she's right and we quickly defeat these thugs, although my motives are purely selfish. Plans to evacuate kids to the countryside are taking place. Thanks to Charlie, I'd been allowed to go to camp. Next time I may not be so lucky. If Hitler doesn't see sense and ignores Great Britain's ultimatum, we'll be at war.

Granddad always says, *Don't fret about things you can't fix.*

It's sound advice, and I'm too tired to join the discussion anyway. A month under canvas was an eye-opener and no place for shrinking violets; it was filled with backaches and bruised egos. Yet even the frailest flowers blossomed.

"Anyone unhappy, we can soon pack you off home," Billy declares.

I poke Tommy Bishop. "Speak up. You're always moaning."

"You've something to say, Roberts?" our leader asks.

"No, sir, I'm having a great time. Anyhow, I've no strength to raise my arm after digging those bogs."

"Glad you're paying attention. My colleagues and I intend to make men out of you." And he rambles on about democracy, freedom of speech, and the whole nine yards.

We're saved by the bell and the duty cook yelling, "Come and get it!" while hammering a tin tray with a huge ladle. Madness ensues as we break ranks to grab plates and mugs; the shouting and shoving get worse every second.

Shaking off the mists of sleep, I open my eyes. Mother's savagely poking my ribs while Fred's shouting, "Wake up Dozy-Locks. We're home!"

Chapter Two

A golden glow floods the room and a gentle breeze ripples the lace curtains while cotton-ball clouds drift across the bluest sky. God has certainly fashioned another glorious day.

Hopping out of my bed, I trill, "Good morning, birds, beasts, flowers, and trees."

"Drop dead," a muffled voice groans.

"Glad tidings to you also. May the bird of paradise fly up your nose."

Fred's never bright this early in the day, so I escape to the bathroom for a quick wash before he throws something. The serious scrub will come later when I gussy up for church. Sabbath's the one day we eat together. Mostly, we're ships that pass in the night. I'm greeted with frosty stares; my kin looks ravenous.

"We thought you'd died. Did you sleep well?" Mother asks.

"Yes, thank you. Like a log. Woke up in the fireplace."

Dad groans. "Is it going to be one of those days?"

"You could be lucky."

Charlie waves his knife and fork. "My belly thinks my throat's cut."

Dad agrees, folds the newspaper, and climbs from his armchair.

"We cannot eat, sir. Number-two son still lying in a pit and snoring like a pig."

"Lazy little sod. If he's not here in five minutes, we'll start without him."

"Good idea," Charlie says. "We'll share his breakfast and tell him later."

Mother pops her cork. "Albert, you should be ashamed, swearing on God's day, and I'm disconcerted with you, too, Charles."

I'm wondering what's in store for me as her frown turns to laughter. Standing in the doorway is something the cat might have found in the garden, yet we know it's Fred by the plaid dressing gown Mother bought years ago. His hair resembles a chimney sweep's brush, and his eyes are like pee-holes in the snow. It's a face only a mother could love.

Fred's solemn on a good day, and he has a short fuse. I wait for sparks; he doesn't disappoint. "Why didn't somebody bloody wake me? I'm going to Earlswood Lakes. My mates will be here any minute."

Mother's eyebrows nearly hit the ceiling. Dad tells him to mind his mouth.

Despite his tardiness, Fred consumes a huge breakfast while constantly whining. Mother tries soothing ruffled feathers as Charlie, and I sing "Nobody Loves Me." Fred does not stay mad long. Underneath his hard surface is a good-natured young man struggling to conquer the world.

The house is quieter once Fred's gone with a saddlebag full of sandwiches. But Mother is displeased her Sunday schedule's been thwarted. Dad has to meet a cricket team from London and can't take us to church, plus Charlie's off fishing. Mother thaws a tad when learning his friend's parents are collecting us. "Maybe Jack will bring the Mercedes, and I'll go in style," she chirrups.

I've heard the tale often. As a child, Mother was taken to church every Sunday by horse and carriage. People raised their hats, bowed, and curtsied as they passed.

It's peaceful with the other boys gone. We've the house to ourselves. In under an hour, the whole place is cleaned spotless, and the best is yet to come. Westminster doorbell chimes boom through the house. Mother insists they add a touch of class, though Dad claims it's like living in the Houses of Parliament.

Mr Barrett stands back, watching his blonde, blue-eyed wife, Cheryl, smother me with kisses. I even suffer a sloppy, warm kiss from their daughter, Anita, but my horrified look is purely for the adults' benefit. The adults don't understand our unique world. The spirited twelve-year-old and I have shared our toys, joys, tears, and the deepest secrets of our souls. Her dad's greeting is hearty, too, and I've been gone only a month.

Mother exchanges daft air kisses with Cheryl and pats Anita's head. She then waits for Mr Barrett's attention. She's fond of him and often says he's a knight in shining armour. She says Dad's a rough diamond.

We watch with glee. Mr Barrett is handsome and charming. Emerging from the clinch, Mother's flushed and smiling. It looks good on her.

Cheryl breaks the spell. "Better get your bum in gear, Dolly. I'll lend a hand. It will take a while. I know you've nothing to wear."

I'm amazed by their sisterhood. God must be amused seeing this pair in action.

Cosy in Dad's armchair with the Sunday papers, Mr Barrett heads for the sports page, while Anita and I make for the tiny stream that bubbles past our property. It's ideal for private talks and vivid imaginations. Anita listens intently as I relate tales of my adventures at camp. We debate whether the bleached bones I'd found in the sand dunes are animal or human and settle for shipwrecked pirates.

Privacy's sabotaged by a shout from the conservatory. Scampering back to the house, we find the adults in the drawing room and Mother ready to strut her stuff. She is wearing a lemon-coloured, tailored suit with matching accessories, from a chic, pillbox hat with wispy veil to two-inch Cuban heels. The full-pleated skirt stops mid-calf. Mother shuns the immodest new fashion of shorter skirts. I'm not sure whether she has knees. I've never seen them.

Cheryl, incidentally, has nice knees.

Hands on hips, Mother executes a pirouette. "What do you think?"

Anita's mouth drops open. "You look fabulous, Auntie Dolly."

I couldn't agree more and quietly state, "Very fetching, Mother."

"Exactly my thoughts," Mr Barrett says.

"You look pretty, too, Mummy, and you're always spiffy Daddy," Anita adds.

This winsome young charmer could go far. All the adult cats are smiling and looking smug. I'm about to un-smug them.

"It's time to hit the road. We're going to be late!" I shout.

I've corralled the lot with one throw, and in seconds we're tucked in the Mercedes. Cheryl allows pride of place to Mother and clambers in the back with the kids.

We giggle when she whispers, "It's lots more fun than sitting next to the stuffy chauffeur and Her Ladyship."

She jests, of course. It's impossible to be unhappy on such a beautiful day. As Charlie often tells me, *God's in Heaven, and everything's right with the world.*

Chapter Three

Reverend Bryan Marshall doesn't preach Hell and damnation. He has silver hair and a pleasant smile. The ladies idolise him and declare he's a matinee idol. Hovering on the steps, he politely greets us. Mother offers a lemon-gloved hand.

Our stately procession down the aisle has the congregation gazing in awe: men in admiration, women with envy. Mother loves an audience, though I suspect some of the drooling is for the pretty blondes who trail in her wake. Mother's fortunate to have such lovely ladies-in-waiting.

Mr Bellamy, the choir leader, is having fits. He's a nice guy but a worry-guts.

"You're late again. Thought you'd been lost at sea."

I don't mention Mother's fashion parade. He's unwed and wouldn't understand. He's still whining, "You'll probably miss your own funeral, too."

"Don't worry, sir. I won't be singing that day."

He gives a wry smile. "You're singing today—two verses of 'Abide with Me.'"

Studying the hymn sheet, I frown, seeing it contains all the old favourites.

"The rev's idea. Trying to boost people's morale," Mr Bellamy explains.

"A stick of dynamite under their backsides might be better," somebody mutters. "Half the blighters are asleep during the sermon."

"There's a full house today," I say. "Should have sold tickets."

"Everyone's a comic," Mr Bellamy moans. "Let's get this show on the road."

They're a great bunch, and they treat me well. We're a close-knit group. God forbid, if war comes, these men will march off, and I'll never see them again. Yet, today is our day. We sing from our hearts, bringing blessings, hope, and comfort to everybody. Prayers are fervent, hymns sung with passion, and the congregation throbs with ole time religion. Surely no one's dozed off.

The reverend mounts the pulpit. Rarely at a loss for words, he pauses to gaze at his flock. The notices he clutches are presently unimportant. "Sorrowfully, my dear brethren, I bring sad tidings. I've just received news that Germany has refused to withdraw its troops from Poland by 1100 hours. Therefore, Great Britain has declared war. May God, in His infinite wisdom, guide and protect us in the dark days ahead."

A hallowed silence follows. Praying for a miracle has failed. The Good Book states that man will destroy himself. Perhaps it's already come to pass. Many folks leave, and fired-up believers fizzle out like damp squibs. Why is everyone shocked? It's not God's fault.

My fans are waiting. "You sang beautifully," Anita says.

"And looked beautiful, too," Cheryl adds, giving me a hug.

"How about your talented boy now, Dolly?" Mr Barrett asks.

Mother shrugs. "I've heard worse."

"Nonsense. You were on the edge with every note," Mr Barrett retorts.

"Yes, but say nothing. That small body will never support his big head." She's not mean and does have a lovely smile.

Then we're told that we're lunching at the Barretts', and there will be a cricket match later with family and friends. We do it every year. Anita frowns at this news. I'm not sure why, but she's my friend. When she's upset, I feel it, too. Squeezing her hand, I offer her a brave smile.

Anita says, "Actually, Auntie Dolly, we're going to the cinema this afternoon."

We are? I'm surprised by the news but nod my head.

Mother's momentarily dumbstruck. "You children aren't roaming around alone. Who knows what mischief you'd create?" she protests.

Opportunity would be a fine thing, I muse, but hold my peace.

Cheryl's flexing her muscles. "Hold your horses, Dolly. Don't tell me how to raise my daughter. And they're not babies. We trust them. Right, Jack?"

Mr Barrett's selectively deaf. He's not getting involved when these two felines start hissing.

Dolly's shaken but not subdued. "Tell me, dear lady, how will they get to the match? They've no transport, and Albert wouldn't approve."

Holy moley! When does she ever seek Dad's opinion?

Injecting humour may help. "We're not asking Dad to come with us."

Anita pipes up. "No problem, Auntie Dolly, the bus comes past our house and stops by the cricket grounds. It's a fifteen-minute ride. We'd be there in time for tea." Patting Mother's knee, she adds, "I'll see that Eddie doesn't get into trouble."

Gracious, though defeated, Mother's smiling, and Mr Barrett comes to her rescue, saying, "We're lucky having smart children. They need some sense to handle life now."

The Barretts' property is on a deep corner lot, once blessed with a small cottage and forge. Tom Bennett, a crusty old bachelor, crafted a living here as a blacksmith. One day, with more wishful thinking than wise thought, he switched from horseshoes to brake shoes and opened a garage. At twelve years old, Mr Barrett left school and became Tom's mechanic. Miracles do happen, and with the blind leading the blind, they survived. Returning from World War I, the young man was given his job back. Tom died two years later, leaving his protégé the property, garage, and debts, too.

Already married by then, Mr Barrett had a wife and baby to support, little money, but fine friends. My maternal grandmother and my dad stymied the bank's greedy attempts at foreclosure and financially kept the Barretts afloat during the Great Depression. Owner of the finest dealership, garage and repair business within miles, Mr Barrett is now highly respected and also a gentleman.

I'm hardly in the door when a monster pins me against the wall with great paws on my chest and a sandpaper tongue licking my face.

Everyone's in fits. "I think he's missed you," Cheryl says.

He is a three-year-old purebred Alsatian. Bought as a guard dog but now the family pet, he adopted me immediately. The vicious snarl could set the stoutest hearts thumping, and while the postman is fair game, Silver only chases rabbits for fun. There's not a bad bone in his body. Wrestling his big feet off me, I set him down, telling him to stay. He squats, awaiting orders, though his tail is busy polishing the tiles. I'm happy chatting with my four-legged friend while the ladies prepare lunch.

After we sit and say grace, we dig in. Silver's big head is resting on my thigh, and his solemn, brown eyes watch me closely. He's forbidden to eat at the table but knows I'll not forget him. The Mercedes has been washed and is back in the showroom. Mr Barrett tells us he'll be driving his Rover this afternoon.

"Wish you'd said earlier," Mother complains. "I'd have worn my magenta outfit. It matches the car perfectly."

Everyone chuckles, except Mother. She's serious.

Teasingly, Cheryl enquires, "A cat can look at the Queen, then?"

"And who would know better than you?" Mother answers, sticking out her tongue.

I'm shocked by their behaviour. They should be smacked and sent to bed. Slipping the leash on Silver and taking Anita's hand, I head for the door. Mr Barrett's already gone. It's said that misery loves company, so we leave the feuding females to butt heads. By the time we return, they'll be bosom buddies again. Granddad reckons anybody writing a book explaining a woman's thoughts could make a fortune. I believe him. This bundle of energy alongside me often baffles me. I've promised myself a perfect day. With the sun shining and true-blue friends in tow, why let family spats bother me? Parents are always fussing, but as Shakespeare wrote, it's much ado about nothing. Adulthood isn't that special, and the day's too nice to be sad.

"Cheer up. The world's our oyster," I tell my buddies.

Anita's eyes twinkle. She has a lovely smile, and Silver shows me his teeth. Really, I swear it—he grins.

Despite everything, I must admit being a small boy is sometimes awesome.

Chapter Four

Waving the grown-ups goodbye, I can feel the chains dropping off my ankles.

Mother isn't keen on leaving us, but she's persuaded by Cheryl explaining how peaceful it will be without screaming kids around. Mother would be less happy if she was aware Anita's been working on a Plan B, and we aren't really going to the cinema. We are really going to the park. I'm amazed by her cleverness, but watching the US Army fighting the Indians on-screen pales in comparison to an afternoon in the park.

"It's our Christian duty to use God's gift on this glorious day," she avows.

We're fancy-free, without interference, to enjoy our rainbow world. There's a line-up on the jetty; the Brits take their fun seriously. Strangers shake hands and smile. The sun (or the Son) has brought out the fun. It's refreshing seeing such love and laughter amidst the horrors of war. We're only allowed one hour on the lake, due to demand, and Anita takes a turn rowing; Mr Barrett has taught her well.

The ice cream wagon's doing a roaring trade. Armed with giant cornets, we lick and drip our way around the park. Top of Anita's wish list is the petting zoo, and she hands me her cone while embracing the tiny Shetland pony. One hand's around his neck as the other feeds him sugar cubes. It's touching to see the love, though the attention that pony's receiving makes me feel rejected.

Yet, trusting me not to lick her ice cream suggests she *might* be fond of me. She has more goodies in her bag, and I know her plans. The walkway ends at a rickety bridge. Beyond it, a gravel path meanders to an oval-shaped pool. Folklore insists that for centuries the ducks have called this place home. They've seen us, and their quacking is deafening as hundreds of frenzied fledglings slosh up the muddy bank. Anita skips to greet them and waits patiently for stragglers, before scattering breadcrumbs to her faithful followers.

I'm wondering what excuse she'll give her parents tomorrow: *We've no toast for breakfast, Mummy and Daddy. I had to feed 5,000 ducks yesterday.*

Shaking crumbs from her string bag, Anita gives a brief curtsy to the crowd, who've witnessed such selfless devotion. Squelching back to civilisation while our shoes and socks are drying, we then lie in the grass, wiggle bare toes, and talk nonsense. Serious stuff is for adults.

Reality returns. "Wake up, Eddie. The chow will be all gone," I hear Anita say.

Fortunately, the bus stops outside the park gate, and twenty minutes later we're enjoying a salad supper. Full to the brim, I settle into a canvas chair to watch the end of the tight cricket match. Our team needs four more runs to win, and our last man strapping on pads is Dad, who seldom plays nowadays. The situation must be desperate!

Little Len, our groundskeeper, has propped up one end, and with more luck than judgement, scored three runs. Dad's unperturbed, although the opposition is agitated as he takes ages whispering to his partner. The natives are getting restless and umpires angry. Dad's surrounded. He loosens up with a practice swing. Fielders quickly retreat. Calmly, he tweaks his cap, adjusts gloves, and straightens pads. He is a man built for comfort, not speed.

Ben Bowyer, the visitor's fast bowler, is raring to go; his ferocity and pace have destroyed us today. One player has a broken arm, two more have bruised ribs. Cricket's no stroll in the park; it's a blood sport. Big Ben isn't having this clown stealing his glory. A sharp lesson is required, and here comes the first ball, which if not for nimble footwork, would have poleaxed Dad. The wicketkeeper fields it brilliantly with his head and collapses. The umpire wags a finger at the bowler, while Dad wags his bat, giving Ben notice to quit this nonsense. Umpires and captains confer while the keeper recovers, and it's obvious that any more tantrums will see the bowler tossed from the game.

Following the rush of blood, Ben's calmed down, and his next two efforts are on a perfect length. Dad survives thanks to defensive juggling and bravery. The old warhorse has the will but not the way; he's tired and his great smile's missing. The fans are mute. One could hear a pin drop, and there's a brick in my throat.

Starting his run, Ben gathers steam with each stride. Dad's bat is patting the ground in perfect time. He's counting, and his great smile's back. Overcomes the bowler's arm, down stamps his foot, and mightily, he hurls the ball.

Loud and clear, a high-pitched voice shatters the sultry air. "Knock the big ape for six, Uncle Albert!"

Dad dances down the pitch, swings his big shoulders, and hammers the ball high over my head for a fantastic winning hit and a fitting climax to a great game.

Applauded all the way to the pavilion, Dad and Len have clocked up more than a century in age, but you'd never know by their grinning, sweaty faces.

Miss Mighty Mouth reappears once Ben's ceased looking for the "little brat" who'd bad-mouthed him. She says to me, "It's your fault. You tell me if I pray, God will find the answer. I'm not bothered. The bigger they are, the harder they fall."

"Wrong! The bigger they are, the harder they hit you," I reply.

Anita smiles. I'm her white knight, although my armour's a tad rusty.

After the teams have showered and changed, everybody heads to the pub for food and renewing old friendships. Except we can't! There's a war on, which means a total blackout. Our guests face a two-hour road trip and will be fortunate if they're home before dusk. There are fond embraces, brave faces, and some tears as they leave. Having this extended family reunion every year is fantastic. Now it's over, and I wonder how many will be back to celebrate with the war on.

"You owe me three pence," Anita says. "Three times I've asked a penny for your thoughts. Why so sad, Eddie?" We've no secrets. She listens quietly while sucking her thumb. "It's not your fault. Let the adults sort it," she concludes.

Knowing she would find a solution, I feel brighter. Holding hands, we race over to the vehicles where our dads are revving the engines.

"Come along, you scruffy pair," Cheryl says. "We're going before it's dark."

Mother's giving me the evil eye. "Been swimming in the canal? Your shoes and socks are disgusting."

It's been a perfect day with fun, laughter, heroes, and villains. Why spoil things?

"Love you, too, Mother," I say, climbing into the car.

Despite the Madman from Munich, blackouts, bomb shelters, and air raids, some things never change.

Chapter Five

The main hall at school, though half-empty, sounds like a chicken farm. I take a quick look around for my friends. I'm too late!

Billy is bellowing, "Silence, you noisy cretins!"

All clucking ceases. I smile. Billy's bark is worse than his bite.

Dr Gregory sweeps in, nodding to his staff waiting patiently. Placing papers on his lectern, he adjusts his half-rims and gazes benevolently around at his scholars. Don't be fooled. He runs a tight ship and is respected by professors and students alike. Beneath the velvet glove dwells an iron fist. Clearing his throat, he begins with the usual pleasantries. He's charming but doesn't suffer from verbal diarrhoea and knows when to move on. There are urgent issues at hand.

"I'll be brief. During the summer, with the threat of war, the government drew up plans for the evacuation of schoolchildren." He waves a large envelope. "Following Assembly, your teachers will discuss this material with you, and you'll receive a copy to take home that your parents must sign and return tomorrow morning." Waiting for the muttering to subside, he continues, "It's not compulsory, but solely for your safety."

Discovering that Billy is our form master suits me. He's a no-nonsense man and a good egg, which makes sense because he is bald as one. Dropping the package on my desk, he says, "You won't dodge the bullet this time, lad." I look up, amazed. "Never knew I had a crystal ball, did you?" Billy asks, grinning.

How the heck? Then I remember him talking to Dad last Saturday when camp ended. *Dear God, is nothing sacred amongst adults?*

During summer recess, many kids have been shipped off to the countryside. It seems I'm not out of the woods yet, and this letter in my satchel isn't going to save my ass this time. I'll just have to grin and bear it—my soul, not my butt.

SITTING AT THE SINGER, surrounded by black curtain material, Mother's peddling away like an Irish clog dancer. "Policeman came reading the Riot Act. We've to cover every window. He's coming back tonight to check."

"Nice having admirers. He might bring flowers."

Her look is not endearing.

Dropping the envelope on the table, I say, "You've some stuff from school to read and send back tomorrow."

"Start preparing dinner. Peel the spuds and put them on to boil. The roast's already in the oven."

"What killed your last slave?" I mutter.

Charlie's bike is outside, but it's only 4:30. He's usually not home until 6:00 and seldom takes time off. He loves work and is a whizz-kid with electrical stuff. He builds wireless sets from scratch. All chores done, I go looking for Charlie and find him in Dad's armchair wrapped in a woollen blanket.

"I'm slaving over a hot stove while you're sitting with your feet up," I say.

"Doctor's orders. Felt poorly this morning and Mother summoned him."

"When are they cremating you?"

Charlie grins. He always likes my jokes. "The doc's suggested a few days' rest."

"That's what I need. I've dishpan hands with all this housework."

"Don't worry, Cinders. You shall go to the ball."

"That's the sickest joke I've heard today."

Mother breezes in. "Stop pestering your brother. Go and lay the table."

"No problem, Mother. Eddie's made me feel better already."

"Adieu, sweet prince. I can tarry no longer. Her Ladyship has spoken."

Halfway to the kitchen, I still hear him laughing and Mother's weary voice saying, "I swear that boy gets stranger every day."

Dad and Fred arrive home, hungry and peeved at having to hang curtains before supper, especially discovering I've been excused. Admiration of Mother's sense of fair play vanishes with news of a family talk after supper. The envelope next to her elbow does little to raise my hopes.

She wastes no time. "Eddie brought a letter from school, and we've a problem. They're evacuating pupils to the countryside for full-time education and safety. All students remaining here would receive part-time studies with possible danger from air raids. Do we send our youngest son and brother away or all stay together?"

It's quieter than a cemetery, although I feel my heart thumping madly.

Charlie breaks the silence. "I presume Eddie has a say in this matter?"

Dad and Mother lock eyes; neither cares to upset their favourite son.

Wicked Witch changes to Fairy Godmother. "It's a free country, isn't it?" She's sly. Rarely does anybody disagree with Mother, though she quickly adds, "I want him safe. I've lost one child and don't wish to lose another."

Playing on the heartstrings is clever, and she has a fish on the line. "He'll be out of danger, and I'll have the bedroom to myself," Fred says.

Cruel pig! Every hair on his head should turn into hammers and smash his skull.

Glaring at Mother and Fred, Charlie asks, "Why not get Eddie's opinion? He has my vote. We're family and should stick together."

Bless him, but I can fight my own battles. "I'm happy here and don't want to live with strangers. I don't even mind your snoring," I say, nodding at Fred.

"You need a good thrashing."

"I'm shaking in my shoes."

"Settle down, you bantamweights," Dad says.

"The ball's in your court, Albert, and don't take all night," Mother butts in. She might be overplaying her hand.

Dad hates being rushed and makes us wait. "I've not Solomon's wisdom and can't cut the baby in half, but we all love you dearly," he eventually says. "Life's about wants and needs. We want you to stay but need to know you're safe. Don't fret. We'll soon be one big, happy family again."

I'm crushed, yet not mortally wounded. Everyone else looks distraught. Maybe calamity brings out the best in people? I mean me, not my clan. Small boy feels humble.

The encounter's taken its toll, and I'm bushed. This little man's had a busy day and much to discuss with the Man upstairs.

My prayers tonight for everybody will be more fervent than usual.

Chapter Six

The past three weeks have been hectic. The air raid shelter's been erected, including the concrete floor and bunks. Fred's work rate shocked us, and Charlie at a slower pace has completed the carpentry. Buckets and stirrup pumps are standard issue. We all have to carry gas masks and identity cards while wardens and police keep telling us, "Put that bloody light out."

Germany's overrun Poland aided by Russia, which invaded from the east. The aircraft carrier *HMS Courageous* has been sunk in the Atlantic, and U-boats are creating havoc amongst Allied shipping. School's a disaster with few lessons but tons of homework. I'm grateful to see the train chugging into the station. Kids are packed solid on the platform screaming and yelling. I'm bored stiff, having done it all before, though sadly I've no pals here. Amidst deafening cheers, the train grinds to a halt. The teachers round up their darlings, stuffing them like sardines into carriages. All aboard, doors are slammed and locked, the guard blows his whistle, and away we go for pastures new. Squeezing into a corner, I close my eyes. It's tough to concentrate surrounded by this rabble. Surely Mother jests thinking such madness will make me a man.

Reaching Lydney Grammar School, we're greeted by a gaggle of tutors to show us our new home. Compared to Yardley, it's light years ahead, with bright, airy classrooms and big windows overlooking acres of green space. Sports facilities are top-notch, too, with dressing rooms and hot showers. We change in school and face a five-minute walk to the field. Trooping back to the hall, I'm anxious to know where we eat and sleep.

Miss Ramsey, our commander-in-chief, enlightens us. "Welcome, students. You must be tired, so I'll be brief. Once your name is called, step forward and your sponsor will collect you. These kind people are opening their homes and hearts to you. Please show them the respect they deserve and always remember if you've any problems, my door is never closed."

I adore this lady. She'd make someone a lovely grandmother. My reverie is shattered by a dig in the ribs. It's Jacob (Brick-head) Wall. He's rail-thin and has batwing ears.

"We've been calling you for ages. You daft or deaf?" He's well-mannered, too.

Standing next to him is a petite, red-haired woman with a pleasant smile. "Let's be getting along, shall we? It's only a short walk," she says. We're met at the gates by an older version of her with a small boy bawling his head off in a pushchair. "And here's Benjamin, my little hero. He's almost two," she says.

He'll be lucky to see his second birthday if he keeps up that racket.

During the twenty-minute short walk, we learn Mrs Potts's husband has been conscripted, and I'll be sharing a bedroom and bed with Brick-head.

Dear Jesus, have mercy on this miserable sinner.

However, it might work. Jacob's only as fat as a tent pole. We'll put a bookmark between the sheets to find him. My dad reckons a small bed is fine if you're good friends. It's puzzling though it must be funny; Mother always scolds him. Our room is small but spotless. The food's not fancy, just bangers and mash. We have seconds, followed by bread pudding and custard. Mother would be disgusted. I could have eaten a horse but don't mention it to the landlady. She might get ideas.

Jacob's asleep before I've finished prayers. He was shocked seeing me on my knees but kept quiet. Introducing myself as the angel with a dirty face, Mother's favourite phrase when I'm extra naughty, so God knows it's me, I ask forgiveness for improper thoughts and indiscretions. He hears that frequently, plus prayers for my family, friends, and Anita, not forgetting Silver the wonder dog.

Switching off the light, I clamber into the soft bed and snuggle under the warm blankets. The silence is deafening—even Brick-head has stopped grunting. It's so peaceful and difficult to imagine that some madman in Europe is trying to destroy us.

Chapter Seven

The day starts badly and goes downhill fast. We have to get our own breakfast as Mrs Potts is battling with Benjamin. Bread and jam hardly constitute a meal. I'd seen Mother giving the neighbours' children bread and jam during the Depression. We race to school with heavy satchels and arrive late. Miss Talbot, our form teacher, isn't happy, and passionately dislikes me. The feeling's mutual. Jacob, her star pupil, swears that our tardiness is my fault, and he is rewarded with a glowing smile. I receive a hundred lines.

Our morning's spent discussing the disciplinary code and the behaviour of students. No fraternising is allowed. I ask if that includes talking and touching, which amuses classmates and gets a drop-dead glare from the teacher. Obviously, the good folk of Lydney don't wish to have their maidens corrupted by city slickers. They should be so lucky!

During the week we're told normal social activities are cancelled. It's anarchy! Many of our real tutors have stayed home with loved ones; their stand-ins don't care. There are few blackboard lessons, mainly tests, and homework's boring too.

Worse still, we've no organised sports. Only senior students are allowed onto the playing fields and tennis courts, though I'm luckier than most. Trevor Palmer, the PT instructor, reckons I've great potential. We train at night after school, which excuses me from walking home with teacher's pet.

I'm packing my bag when Miss Ramsey's secretary, Jenny, trots in. "Eddie, glad I've caught you. The headmistress wants to see you right after assembly tomorrow morning."

"At your pleasure, milady. Am I being expelled?"

"We couldn't be that lucky."

"Now who's being cheeky?" I ask, grabbing my satchel and whistling merrily as I head out of the room.

"Cease that atrocious noise," a voice screeches. It's my nemesis barrelling down the corridor.

"After the beauty comes the beast," I mutter and quicken my pace, knowing she's no greyhound.

I'm halfway to the gates and still hear her calling, "I'll see you in the morning, Roberts!"

"Not if I see you first," I chuckle.

Charles Dickens wrote, *"It was the best of times, it was the worst of times,"* which sums up my day. Will tomorrow bring forth feast or famine?

HANDING MY LINES TO "TATTY" Talbot, I tell her I've an appointment with Miss Ramsey. She shrugs her shoulders, glad to see me go. Reaching the office, I'm nervous of what fate awaits me as Jenny leads the way.

"Here you are, Roberts," the Head declares, her pink, plump hand outstretched, indicating that I should take a seat next to my fellow students. "Let's get cracking. There's loads to do. We've heard the rules aren't popular. It's not our fault. Blame the Education Committee. However, we've jurisdiction over extracurricular endeavours, and ambitious plans are being hatched. We're going to launch a joint musical programme, and enquiries indicate that there's ample talent among staff and students to form a choir and an orchestra. You people here today can make this dream a reality by spreading the word. Auditions start tomorrow after school in the gym. Now buzz off. I'm busy."

Christmas has come early, I figure, as we file out. I've really missed my singing on Sunday mornings. Pausing at Jenny's desk, I say, "The Head's a lovely lady."

"Believe it, kid. Saved your sorry ass when Tatty came whining about you. Sent her away with a flea in her ear."

I've only a double period of geography to handle after lunch. No sweat! All I need now is to tie Brick-head onto a raft, set it alight, float it out to sea and my world would be perfect.

Chapter Eight

The seed planted by Rosemary Ramsey has blossomed, grown, and spurred us to dizzying heights, with everybody keen to be involved. Both schools are mixing more freely, and absenteeism's almost zero. Tutors are smiling too. Even Tatty Talbot's taken her flock to the woods, picking flowers. It's difficult to imagine her smelling the roses.

Feeling sad when first arriving, I'd never noticed the town's beauty. Lydney is a small market town, a mixture of old and new with a few thatched cottages among the modern, red-bricked ones, plus numerous cobbled alleyways. I'm aware that their peaceful existence has been ruined by our arrival. They're content and don't wish to be dragged into the twentieth century. I'd learned this lesson when asking Mrs Potts which church I might visit.

"Try the Baptist Chapel. It's the one we attend."

The wizened old man studies me. "I don't know you. To which denomination do you belong, boy?"

"That's because I've just arrived, but I'm a club member," I reply, thinking that humour might help.

His jaw muscle twitches. "You're not one of us. Anyhow, this church does not admit unaccompanied children."

"How long has the Lord's house been off limits? Jesus was only twelve when he sat with the priests," I respond.

We've a small crowd gathering. Surely common sense will prevail.

"Cheeky bugger, they're all the same, these city kids," someone shouts.

I beat a retreat before the noose and hangmen appear. Twice more I try my luck, but infamy has preceded me. A deputation from three churches invades Miss Ramsey's study, demanding my head on a platter; she sends them on their way, rejoicing. It's no surprise John the Baptist took off for the desert. Bigotry apart, Trevor's pleased with my progress in the gym, and the choir's fantastic. Our leader's brutal, the singing coach superb. They play good cop, bad cop, and it works. I sing solos and duets with Barbara Lewis, who has jet-black hair and deep-violet eyes, and she's heart-thumping beautiful. I've scarcely noticed her.

She's a pleasant voice, though on high notes a tad flat. Everything else though is in great shape. Every warm-blooded male vies for her attention, but the Ice Maiden displays a strong message: "You can look, but don't touch."

I'm the envy of all, being allowed to stand close and hold hands when singing a romantic duet. After choir practice, I escort Barbara home. She thaws out nicely on the way. Recently, I've been popping in for a quick cup of tea and chatting with her mummy and daddy. They like me too.

Clever Jenny, with Trevor's help, has arranged a dance to which all students and adults are invited. The gym's been converted into a ballroom, with coloured streamers crisscrossing- the room and balloons bobbing from the ceiling.

Host and hostess are working the room nicely, but parents seem more nervous than their offspring. The fruit punch is popular, yet the buffet table's regarded suspiciously. They'd fancy a big basin of stew, not triangles of salmon, ham, or things on sticks. Brian Phelps and the band are warming up while Barbara and I sit like trained seals, only reacting when the baton's waved. Our confrères return to the stage hand in hand. That's neat. They should be running the country.

Picking up the mike, Trevor says, "Good evening, everybody. And a very warm welcome to our social evening, thanks to the sterling work of staff, students, and my comely colleague, Jenny."

She gives him a dazzling smile. My heart flips.

Waiting for the applause to end, he continues, "Tonight is party night. Anyone not smiling will be sentenced to one hundred lines while wearing a hat stating 'I'm an old sourpuss.' I'd thought up a better word, but the Head censored it."

Seizing the mike, Jenny says, "After that, there's only one thing left to say. Take it away, Maestro."

The first haunting chords of "Charlemagne" fill the room, and... nothing! Not a single thing has stirred, not even a mouse. Jenny recovers first, taking Trevor's hand and waltzing him round the room. There are a few adults trailing out, but not a single student moves.

Barbara pulls me up, "Come on, Eddie, let's shimmy."

"Lead on, Ginger, I'm stepping out tonight."

Eureka! Kids, all shapes and sizes, flood onto the dance floor. It's hardly the Arthur Murray School of Dancing, but who cares?

Ted Newton, the school heartthrob cruises by. "May I have the next dance?"

"I hardly know you," I say.

"Not with you, stupid!"

"Flattery will get you nowhere,"

He's beautiful but not bright. "Seriously, can I have the next dance, Barbara?"

"Certainly Ted, who with?"

He looks confused.

"It's not a trick question," I say.

He ignores me and ploughs on, "You of course, Barbara."

"I'd sooner slit my throat."

"Consider that a no," I tell him.

"Keep quiet, Roberts, before I flatten your face."

His threats don't bother me. Trevor's been teaching me ju-jitsu, although I'd not take advantage of a dummy like Newton. Not hardly!

Switching his attention to Barbara, he asks, "What's he got that I haven't?"

"Good manners, good humour, and he's a good friend. Now goodbye."

"You did a very good job," I say.

"Don't worry about Ted, he's too ignorant to insult."

Brian and his boys are getting the joint jumping, while the patrons are dancing up a storm and the buffet table looks as though locusts have visited. Barbara and I render an upbeat version of "My Blue Heaven," during which she squeezes my hand, and I squeeze hers. One must be polite after the nice things she's said. Appreciation is shown for our vocal efforts, including my singing, "Try a Little Tenderness," which raises screams from young girls and complaints from parents. Barbara says I sound like Sinatra—I have blue eyes too, but look better nourished. Maybe the fruit punch was spiked and is taking effect?

Many friendships have been made tonight, and the volunteers deserve medals. Wishing friends goodnight, I stagger home and find Mrs Potts waiting up for me. We're closer lately. It's hard caring for two teenage boys and Ben, so after supper, I clear the table and do the chores to give her a break. I also take the toddler down to the park. We get along fine, and he seldom cries anymore. I guess he was lonely. I know the feeling. Anyway, it's nice to have a little brother.

Pouring two cups of tea, Mrs Potts says, "Come and sit down. We need to talk."

It's no surprise. We have cosy chats when Jacob's not here.

"I've had a letter from your mother telling me she wants to take you home. Aren't you happy here?"

"Not at first, but I love it now," I answer truthfully.

"I love having you here too. You're good company and a nice boy. Off to bed now, you must be dead whacked."

Climbing the stairs, I creep quietly into my room as not to disturb Brickhead, slip into my pyjamas, and, though tired, kneel down to give thanks for the day, ask forgiveness and understanding for my enemies, and then pose a serious question. "Dear God, why do adults always change their minds to suit their own needs? I know, Lord, you will give me the answer in your own good time."

Chapter Nine

I'm dozing through a French lesson when Jenny pops her head through the door. "You're wanted in the Head's study, Roberts." Hiding my joy, I follow her down the corridor. "You've a visitor," she says.

"I didn't do it, whatever they said I did."

"Why are you such an idiot?"

"I've had lots of practice."

Jenny pushes me into the office. "Go right in, Einstein."

Miss Ramsey, forthright as usual, says, "There you are, Roberts." Using my surname spells bad news.

Mother, tight-lipped and stiff, is sitting in an armchair.

"Hello, Mother. Lovely to see you. Did you have a pleasant journey?"

She wastes not a second. "I've had a letter from Mrs Potts. It appears that you fancy the rural life after all."

"You said to be a brave little soldier, and I like it here now."

"You've also more to say, though your manners haven't improved."

Miss Ramsey interjects. "Normally, Mrs Roberts, I do not interfere in family matters, but you're being unfair and casting aspersions on this school. Eddie's popular with staff and students. He's also polite and studious, only occasionally a pain in the rear end. Just a normal boy. Soon he'll be a man. Treasure him. Enjoy!"

Red-cheeked, Mother says, "Thank you, it's years since I've been up before the Head to receive a lecture. Please, may we speak in private for a moment?"

Women puzzle me. One minute they're scratching each other's eyes out, then chinwagging over tea and cake. No wonder Dad needs his whiskey. Methinks Mother's on a mission. It's not the letter that's lit her fuse. Something more grievous has brought her galumphing to Gloucestershire.

Returning to class, I spend a vexing afternoon ticking off the possibilities and refuting the obvious. Arriving home, the ticking stops. Sitting at the table, drinking tea and gabbing away are Mother and Mrs Potts. They clam up fast.

"Don't stop on my account. Thought you'd be arm-wrestling by now."

"Sit down, Eddie," Mrs Potts orders. "We have to talk."

"Why? I wish to stay. She's come to haul me off."

"It's Charles who wants you home. I've been told not to return without you."

"I'm sorry, I'll miss you, but your ma's right. Your brother needs you."

Mother's pit-bull style is tough, and with this wiry terrier as backup, I'm dog meat.

They're both waiting for me to erupt, yet I feel relieved knowing the truth.

Putting them out of their misery, I ask, "When are we leaving, Mother?"

"Mrs Potts has invited me to stay overnight. We'll start back after lunch tomorrow, which will allow you time to say your farewells."

Expressing my thanks, I turn to Mrs Potts. "May I take Ben down to the park before supper? I'll call on Barbara too."

Mother's head snaps up. "You've a girlfriend? Starting young, aren't you?"

"Not exactly. I know a girl who's a good friend."

She can't resist. "How does her father earn his living?"

"He's a farmer."

Intervening smartly, Mrs Potts says, "He breeds and trains racehorses. Owns the biggest string in the county, so I'm told."

I've never imagined Mother as a Samurai warrior. If I'm not mistaken, she's just fallen on her own sword. This tiny terrier certainly has a big bite.

Ben knows the word *park* and already has his boots on the wrong feet. Ten minutes later he's rewrapped and ready for the North Pole. I collect Barbara, then, armed with a bagful of stale bread, we head for the pond. It's Ben's favourite spot. We find a bench close to the water, and the ducks find us. I'm busy breaking up bread into bite-sized chunks for my buddy to throw. Barbara's not fooled.

"Cat got your tongue? I know something's wrong."

"I've bad news and more bad news."

"What's the first bad news?"

"Mother's taking me home."

"That's unfair. Why, when you're so happy?"

"She's no choice, and neither do I."

"Everyone has choices. What's worse than you going away?"

"My brother's very ill. I think he's dying."

Barbara's eyes fill with tears. "Oh Eddie, I'm so sorry. Of course you must go. I'm being a selfish pig."

Picking up the bread, she starts hurling lumps at the ducks, as if blaming them. Ben, thinking this fun, grabs the bag and hurls the lot into the pond. We collapse, laughing, while the whole covey scatters every which way.

We strap Trouble back into his pushchair and start for home.

"I'm going to miss you. You're the nicest boy I've ever known."

"You should get out more often."

"Will you miss me a teeny-weeny bit?" she asks.

"For sure. Where else will I find a pretty girl who says she's two inches taller and a year older than me?"

"You know I'm only teasing."

"No problem. I've always had a thing about older women."

"Can I ask a serious question?"

"Yes, and I'll promise you a serious answer."

"Will you write me, please? I'd hate to lose our friendship."

"Not only will I write, I'll say a prayer for you every night too."

Stopping by her front gate, Barbara grasps my hand. "I'll be praying for you and your brother too. Miracles do happen, you know."

She kisses me softly on the cheek, then runs up the drive. Halfway to the front door, she turns and waves. "Goodbye, Eddie Roberts. Be good and have fun."

Kicking the gatepost savagely, I mutter, "Make up your bloody mind."

It's the mantra of the clown. Always leave them laughing, right?

Chapter Ten

Brick-head sounds as though he's driving cattle to market. He's a lazy sod and never stirs until the last minute. Good! I can use the bathroom in peace and enjoy a quiet breakfast before leaving for school. However, this morning is a double-whammy. The full English is surpassed only by Mother and Mrs Potts gossiping like old friends. It takes bloody warfare to unite such people from opposite ends of the food chain.

The train doesn't leave Gloucester until two, which affords time to clear out my locker and say goodbye to friends. Miss Smart, our pianist, suggests I lead the morning hymn. I could strangle her yet accept graciously. The Head adds further embarrassment by saying nice things about me, while Tatty appears to have trodden into something nasty. It's no big deal. Most people love me.

During recess, Trevor tracks me down. "Not thinking of sneaking off without saying goodbye, were you?"

"Certainly not, sir, and thanks for everything. Though we've no PT classes at Yardley any more, I can join the YMCA next year."

"Glad to hear it. I've some advice. Keep training, you've rare talent, which one day will bring you fame and fortune or save your life. We'll make a man of you yet, Eddie. Oops! Have to run. There goes the bell. See you around."

Next stop is sweet Jenny. She and Trevor make a nice twosome, similar to a pair of Toby jugs, though much prettier.

"Hello, Loverboy. The Head and I are discussing your romance with the delectable Barbara Lewis. You're the school's Romeo and Juliet."

"Don't you two have any work to do? And what romance? We're just good friends and members of the same choir."

"Pull the other one, Sonny. It's got bells on."

"And Mr Muscles is teaching you to lift weights?"

She's the good grace to blush. "I don't know what you mean, and you're a cheeky young monkey."

"Stop your gibbering and throw me a banana."

Jenny holds up her hands. "You win. Miss Ramsey's waiting to see you."

"Glad you could tear yourself away. Sit down and rest your brains. I talked to your mother yesterday. Very impressive lady. She's a lot on her plate and sorely needs your support. Those last words are mine, not hers. She's too proud to ask. Nevertheless, our loss is your family's gain. You're a smart lad, but now it's time to become a good man. All our sympathy and prayers go with you on this sad occasion."

Her gentle words have me mumbling a hasty goodbye as I stumble into a grey day, feeling my world changing and the carefree days of childhood slipping away.

The train journey's never-ending, and not helped by long periods of silence. Mother and I aren't big on small talk, each content with our own miseries. Fred is home preparing supper; things have changed at the ranch during my absence. He greets me with a hug—that's another first!

Mother asks, "How's Charles today?"

"Jessie said he'd slept most of the day. I read to him a little, but he's dozed off again. You've just missed her. Done shopping, plus laundry, and taken a stack home to iron."

"She's golden. We couldn't cope without her," Mother says. "You can see him later, Edward. Take off your coat and shoes and sit by the fire. You must be perished."

I'm anxious to see Charlie, yet too tired to argue.

"Make a lovely wife, but she's only eyes for my big brother," says Fred.

It's impossible to resist. "Jessie's very smart too, Fred," I say.

A deep voice cuts off his answer. "Who's been sitting in my chair?"

"Mother said I could sit here, Dad," I say, jumping up.

"Sit down," he says and gives Mother a brief kiss then asks, "How's my boy?"

"He's been sleeping most of the day," Mother said.

"Good! He can't be in pain. The pills must be working."

Mother and Fred glare angrily at Dad.

"I'm no child, and I know Charlie's sick. I'll take his supper up," I say.

"Seeing you will do him more use than pills," Fred replies, ruffling my hair. "I'll get it ready lickety-split."

Leading the way, Mother whispers, "We'll see if he's awake."

Opening the door, she turns and nods. I'm shocked. The scarecrow propped up against the pillows can't possibly be my brother. Echoes of being "a brave little soldier" spring to mind. Easy for her to say.

Charlie's hooded eyes recognise me, and he holds up matchstick arms. Pasting on a big grin, I pull him into a tender embrace, willing myself not to cry.

"Everything's going to be okay," I whisper. "I'm here to stay."

My brother's knuckles press fiercely into my neck. He understands.

"Put him down," Mother finally says. "His supper's getting cold."

He eats slowly and listens intently as I jabber about my adventures. He's enthusiastic about my singing career and insists that one day we'll be a dynamic duo on a concert tour.

"Glad we haven't a cat," Mother observes, gathering up the empty plates. "It would starve to death."

"Thank you, Mother, that was great."

"Frederick deserves the kudos. He did the honours tonight."

"He's changed since Irene came along," Charlie remarks.

"One more soul sentenced to hard labour for life and no reprieve," I jest.

"That's something you're not guilty of, young man. Let's go eat," Mother says.

"I'll be back later to read you a bedtime story. How about the tale of Snow White and the Seven Perverts?" I ask.

Mother nearly drops the tray.

Chapter Eleven

Fred's pessimistic about my scheme. "They'll not be pleased. Mother is bound to blow her top, while Dad will dither as usual, and the school board could sue our parents too."

"I've promised Charlie. Anyhow, you're supposed to be my partner."

"I am, Ed. Let's go down and battle."

They're at the breakfast table, sullen and silent. Mother leads off, "You pair are slowcoaches today. You'll both be late."

Fred says, "Don't worry, Mother, it only takes fifteen minutes on my bike."

"I'm staying home and keeping Charlie company," I say. I say. Mother says.

Both parents have lost their appetites, though Mother's shaking her head. The silence is deadly.

Father reacts first, saying, "I've to get ready."

"Don't you ever make decisions, Dad?" Fred demands. "Shut your eyes and the problem will vanish." Turning to Mother, he says, "You can forget any fancy ideas too. Eddie should stay with Charlie as long as possible."

"It's your call, Dolly," Dad declares, slipping off to the bathroom.

Mother isn't fazed. "I applaud your frankness, Frederick, but I'm not some dominating matriarch. I've no choice." Snatching the envelope off the sideboard, she tosses it onto the table. "Miss Ramsey gave me this letter for you to deliver to your headmaster today."

"No contest," Fred mutters as we make a quick exit.

"Don't worry, there's always plan B." I do have another idea that has been haunting me all night.

Mother tries to pacify me, but I remain cool and calm until it's time for school. "I've packed your lunch, and I'll have a nice hot meal ready when you come home."

All this sweetness is putting my teeth on edge.

"I'll have to tell Charlie," I say, dashing upstairs, leaving Mother looking flabbergasted.

THE INCESSANT CHATTER AND TOMFOOLERY cease promptly at Billy's appearance. Spotting me, he gazes skywards. "Why me, O Lord?" he pleads.

"It's nice to see you too, sir."

"Aye lad, glad you're back, this place needs livening up, just don't burn the school down."

He's an excellent teacher and might be a useful ally. "Please sir, I have to see the headmaster. Miss Ramsey has a letter for him, and I need to discuss a personal matter too."

Well versed in schoolboy pranks, he asks, "Don't you trust me?"

I've fallen at the first hurdle and upset him too. "I can't discuss it with anyone, except Dr Gregory."

The class is enjoying this joust. "Once a clown, always a clown. Sadly, the hiatus hasn't improved your behaviour, Roberts. Hand me the letter. Let's begin."

Whining won't help. Faint heart never won the maiden's heart, or in this case, ageing headmaster's. His secretary guards him well, but it's only a minor hitch. I've enough money for one long-distance call. During break I sneak out. It seems a lifetime before the phone's answered.

"Good morning, Lydney Grammar School, may I help you?"

"Jenny, it's me, Eddie. I need a big favour."

"Thought you might be missing me."

"Certainly do but haven't time for jokes."

"This is serious, if you're serious," Jenny replies.

I'm explaining madly when stalled in mid-flight. "How can I help, dear boy?"

"How well do you know Mrs Macpherson?"

"Liz! She's my sister-in-law, we're pretty close."

"It's urgent that I see Dr Gregory today."

"Consider it done, but only if you'll be a bridesmaid at my wedding."

Seldom does she have the last laugh. Today she deserves it.

Billy is waiting for me. "Written permission is required to leave the grounds during school hours, Roberts."

"I had to make a phone call, sir, a matter of life or death."

"Don't jest with me, boy. It's no laughing matter."

"I agree, and it was very personal, sir."

"All right, I'll overlook the indiscretion on this occasion. Off you trot before I change my mind."

Halfway through History period, Luscious Liz glides into the room. Mr Brown stops writing, chalk in hand. "Can I be of any assistance?" he enquires.

Several boys snigger, having similar thoughts.

She flashes a sunny smile. "I'm looking for Roberts; the headmaster needs to see him."

"Lucky lad," Alan Cook, chuckles. "She may have her wicked way with you."

"He'll likely get six of the best," Ken Page adds.

"She's got two of the best," Alan mutters.

Reluctantly returning from never-never land, Brown says, "Off you go, boy. Don't keep him waiting."

"For those of us who're about to die," murmurs Ken.

"It's the best way to go, man," Alan replies.

Ambling down the corridor, the secretary says, "Don't worry, he doesn't bite."

"He's a vegetarian?"

"Jenny warned me that you have a peculiar sense of humour."

"Yet, you still wish to assist me as I overcome the forces of evil?"

"Beneath the goofiness, Jenny says there's a nice boy who needs our help."

"She's hit that one on the nose."

Entering the plush office, Liz lowers her voice. "Take a seat. I'll tell the Head you're here."

Rehearsing my spiel, I fluff my lines. Last night was easy, now it's too late. Liz beckons from the study doorway and guides me to a wooden chair. Perched in a padded model, poised and waiting, is the headmaster.

"Before we get down to specifics, I've a few comments." He waits for my nod then continues, "Every student's welfare concerns us, and it's amazing how much we know. You've achieved a good standard, though your high spirits cause some concern. Still, your music maestro believes you're hitting the high notes, and the PT instructor insists you're coming along in leaps and bounds. Au contraire, the French teacher thinks you're a bête noir. Don't fret, you can't win them all. However, this term you create waves wherever you sail. You've even managed to upset the religious community, and that's no mean feat."

"Excuse me, sir, I can explain."

Grinning, Dr Gregory waves an envelope. "It's all in here." And laughing loudly, he does a three-sixty in his chair and says, "How does it feel having friends in high places, young man?"

Liz dashes into the study, "Is everything all right?"

"Couldn't be better. We'll have tea please, two sugars in mine. I've not had such fun since shouting 'bum' through the vicarage letterbox as a child."

My ribs are aching at his wit, but there's more important stuff at hand. Seeing my expression, he says, "I'm sorry, you came on personal business."

"My brother's dying, and I want to be with him until the end. I could do my studies at home and honour his request too. We've only a short time left, sir."

There's a lull in proceedings as Liz cruises in with the tea trolley.

"Set it on the table, dear. It's cosier in the armchairs. Eddie's our guest. Those wooden monstrosities are for the miscreants."

We wait while the secretary pours tea and leaves, closing the door quietly. Sipping slowly, I await the Wise One's verdict. He obliges immediately.

"Bluntly, the Board of Governors' aim is that you receive the best education possible. Do I follow orders or shout rude words at God's advocate once again? A little knowledge is a dangerous thing, Eddie, whereas love will follow us to the grave and beyond. Go home to your dear brother, where you belong, and be assured all our prayers, blessings, and hopes will follow."

Chapter Twelve

D r Gregory's given me enough homework for life, maybe an elephant's. I drop the bulging satchel onto the kitchen table.

Mother, up to her elbows in flour, isn't amused. "Brought the whole school library?"

Ignoring sarcasm, I see Jessie wrestling with a sink filled with pots and pans.

"Hello, Chubby-Chops."

"Hello Short-House," she replies.

"Charming," Mother says, though she's heard it all before.

Jessie's a major player in our extended family and Charlie's best friend since childhood. Despite countless admirers, this beautiful, green-eyed girl with a mop of strawberry-blonde hair, is Charlie's darling. She's given up her job, though, knowing his life is ebbing away and still maintains her unsinkable style.

"How's Mr Wonderful?"

"He's fine today. Something you've said is working."

"Wait until he hears the good news."

"What good news?" Mother enquires.

"There's a note in my bag. You'll be over the moon."

Yeah, right! I think, making a fast exit.

Charlie's sitting up in bed, looking brighter.

"I'm working from home and writing tests each day. Fred's my delivery boy."

"Have you told Mother?"

"The Head's given permission and sent a letter."

"She'll not be pleased," Charlie remarks.

"So what's new? Fred and I are revolting."

"I've always thought so," Charlie quips.

"Smart-ass. Everybody's a comedian," I say. "Better have some lunch before Mother seasons it with ground glass. Fancy a game of chess later?"

"Sure! I'll shut my eyes and give you a chance to win."

Mother and Jessie are drinking coffee. I smell trouble, and it's not apple tart.

"You've gone behind my back when I wasn't looking."

"I thought you had eyes in the back of your head, Mother."

Jessie stifles a laugh.

"Don't get saucy with me. You're back to school if the work's not good. It's here in black and white."

Gold star for Mother—she's studied the small print.

"The Head and I had a discussion over tea. Providing I fulfil requirements, this agreement will stay in force, and before you ask, Fred's my courier."

There's a round of applause from Jessie.

Mother never knows when to quit. "He won't be your messenger boy."

"Wrong! We're a team now. United we stand, divided we bust."

"I'll drink to that," Jessie says, raising her coffee cup.

Mother's radiant when she smiles. "Don't encourage him, Jessica, his cap will never fit."

"I'll keep Charlie company unless you need anything."

"No dear. Charles enjoys talking to you, and you can wash those grubby hands before eating," Mother instructs me.

Today's a huge leap towards freedom, and I decide not to push my luck. The old fox could still trap this eager young chick.

It's a moment to treasure. Mother's actually talking to me, not criticising. I'm surprised by her knowledge outside her domestic world too. She says food will soon be rationed, unmarried men nineteen to twenty-seven are being conscripted, and the war's going to last longer than we thought. Her pessimism's dragging me down. I want to help, but she's in denial, and Dad can't function without a glass in his hand, convinced he's going to lose another son. The first-born, Arthur, died at seven and a half, just two days after my birth. Now they're on the brink again. I know they're anxious to protect me, and that Charlie's dying, but I'm not losing him. He'll always be here in my heart.

Meeting Jessie on the stairs, I say, "Be a doll, go and cheer up Mother. She needs some tender loving care."

"My pleasure. Charlie's got the board set up. Reckons he's going to whip your little pink ass."

"How do you know it's pink?"

"I used to powder it years ago."

"You're disgusting!"

"Yes, and lovely with it." Then she says, "Seriously though, Eddie, I'm glad you've come home. Charlie really needs you."

Taking her hand, I say, "He's not much time. You know this is his last hurrah."

"I thought you believed in divine intervention."

"He's already in God's hands. We're being granted more time by His grace."

"Yet he's content and eating better. How's it possible?"

"Charlie is at peace and ready to meet his maker."

"How does a small boy know so much?"

"It's what the Good Lord tells me," I reply.

"Do you think He spoke to our sweet boy?"

"Surely that's why Charlie told Mother to bring me home."

Chapter Thirteen

Jessie corners me in the study where I've gone to ground, trying to catch up with my homework. "You trying to avoid me?"

We're sharing Charlie's care, little lambs guarding the sheepdog. Conscious of Charlie's decline, we're trying to spare my parents' feelings. Mother, tortoise-like, has disappeared inside her own shell, and Dad looks older than Moses.

He goes to see Charlie every evening and sits with him awhile, then trudges downstairs to shake hands with his friend Glenfiddich. I never disrupt my father's thoughts, praying he's in some happier time.

"I'm swamped. It's back to school if I don't get this lot finished."

"Exactly why we have to talk," Jessie rants. "How much longer does Charlie have before God takes him home?"

"Only the Lord knows the answer."

"Pray it's soon. Your mother and Dr Mason are discussing morphine for his pain."

"It's an ideal way to commit murder," I comment.

"How can we stop them?"

"Charlie's got an idea. He heard their plans when they thought he was asleep."

"Aren't you going to tell me?"

"It's no miracle and might not work."

"Promise you'll tell me when it's over?" she begs.

The front doorbell chimes come to my rescue. It must be a visitor. Tradesmen have more sense and use the side entrance. The willing slave dashes to answer it, glory be! Faith can move mountains. The study door opens, revealing a giggling Jessie and a stocky, elderly gentleman with white hair and matching moustache.

He's a big voice for a small person. "Eddie! You've neglected me lately."

Mother blames him for my wicked ways; since Granny Robert's death, we've been extra close. There's a sixty-year age gap, but you'd never guess. He's a lovable old rogue, and extremely wise.

Granddad is adored by ladies of all ages.

"Thanks for the letter and birthday card, knew you'd remember."

"Happy birthday, Gramps," Jessie says, planting a kiss on his cheek. He hugs her longer than is decent.

Appearing in the doorway, Mother says, "Knew it was you with that ruckus. I've sent you a card. It should be in the afternoon mail." She gives him a warm embrace.

"Did you wrap it in a five-pound note?"

"Dream on." They're kindred spirits; it's the tonic she needs.

"Put the kettle on, Dolly, let's have a cuppa, then I'll go and see Charlie."

Eying my books, Granddad says, "Keep the cogs turning, Eddie, while Dolly and I have a chinwag."

Stifling a protest, I know he's right. We'll shoot the breeze later.

I'm not alone long. Jessie has remembered Charlie's plan.

"We didn't finish our conversation."

I adopt a vacant look. It's no stretch.

Switching gears, Jessie asks, "Why did you write your grandfather?"

"Charlie wishes to say goodbye to all his loved ones, and although I'm just a stupid kid, reckon that God talks to Granddad too."

"Stupid? You're smarter than all of us, my darling boy, and God knows it too. While we're all wallowing in self-pity, you're busy planning his trip to Eternity."

Looking into Jessie's shimmering green eyes, I say, "Don't cry and wet my shirt. Mother will kill me."

Dragging me into a fierce hug, she murmurs, "I'm not sure what the Lord intended when he made you, but don't ever change Eddie-Baby."

Paradise is lost with Granddad's return. "Put that young lady down. What the devil are you doing?"

"Nothing," I stutter.

"Move over then and give the old guy a chance."

Dissolving in laughter, Jessie wipes away her tears.

"Anyway, Miss, you're required in the kitchen. My daughter-in-law's baking me a cake but without candles as it could cause a fire hazard.

"Meanwhile, Eddie put away your crayons. We'll visit Bonnie Prince Charlie."

Showing no emotion at his grandson's condition, he quickly has Charlie smiling while chatting about better times and happy memories. Miracles come in many forms, and dreamily I muse at mission accomplished. Though only the messenger, my heart rejoices.

"He's dozed off," a distant voice says.

"Studying too hard has knocked him out," a louder one adds.

They're laughing at my expense, but I'm happy. The therapy's working.

"Why not beat each other's brains out at chess while I fix lunch?" I say.

We have to slow Charlie down and prevent him from getting too excited. I'm beginning to sound like Mother.

After a parley with Charlie and a cracking lunch, it's all systems go. I've only two more papers to write. Mind you, Fred will bring another stack tonight. He's brilliant, and we're a fine team. I grumble, he pushes. We've become tighter since Charlie's sickness. Revelling at being mentor and minder, Fred's a natural at running interference between parents and wild kid. Though not having Charlie's charisma, he's mellowed and rarely goes ape these days. According to Mother, the transformation's due to Irene, his latest heartthrob. She's a small girl, quiet too, unlike the dizzy blondes Fred often fancies. My parents are quite impressed by this demure damsel. Maybe their fears of a possible shotgun wedding are put to rest?

Jessie's coaxed Charlie into eating his lunch, and he's sleeping. She and Mother are in the kitchen preparing supper, and Granddad's relaxing in Dad's armchair. Whatever advice he's given Mother has completely changed her mindset and resulted in a birthday party with family and close friends invited. It's not by accident that my whole clan's here, but by God's grace, love, and mercy to witness my beautiful brother's passage to Heaven and Eternity.

Chapter Fourteen

The crafty curmudgeon's blindsided me. Though fidgety, I've concentrated on my work. Exclusion from his chat with Mother had puzzled me. Obviously, Granddad's set up the whole scheme. We've a full beef roast and all the trimmings. No one's hungry, except Anita and I, though the drink's hitting the spot with the adults. Fred gives me a sip of his wine. I've had better tasting stuff on my chips. Everything's cleared away, and we're socialising—those are Mother's words. Granddad says that's a posh word for nattering and boozing.

Jessie and young Jack return to shaking their heads. "Charlie's sleeping mostly. Wakes up, gives us a smile, and then dozes off again. He's not in pain, Mrs Roberts."

"Thank you, dear," Mother says.

Anita, sitting on the sofa next to me, asks, "Why is Charlie sleeping so much, Eddie? Do you think he's changed his mind or won't they let him in? Does he really have to go? I'm going to miss him playing the piano."

She's such a sweet child.

"He needs his rest. It's a long journey to the Pearly Gates, but don't worry, they will recognise him. God is probably looking for a new pianist."

"We haven't a choice then?"

"You've got that right. Listen to the Big Man, he'll never let you down."

"Is my daughter bothering you, Eddie? She's the curiosity of a cat."

I'd know those knees on the darkest night. "Not at all, Mrs Barrett, even a cat can look at a queen."

"You're too witty for your own good, and whatever happened to calling me Cheryl?"

"Mother tells me it's impolite to address adults by their first names."

"Phooey! You make me sound ancient." Dragging us to our feet, she says, "We'll see if Charlie's awake now."

Everyone's listening to the radio as we tiptoe from the drawing room.

Russia's invaded Finland, and the French are fighting Germany in Northern France, but the brighter news is that British troops have landed in France.

The bedroom's bathed in a soft glow. I move closer. Charlie's slim fingers are folded prayerfully on the gold-trimmed coverlet, his pallid cheeks standing out vividly against long, jet-black hair. He's breathing gently and almost run his race here on Earth.

Gripping my shoulder, Mrs Barrett says, "Be strong, Eddie. Take Anita downstairs and bring everyone back right away. Charlie hasn't long."

"He won't be gone before we're back will he, Mummy?"

"No, sweetie, he'd never disobey Auntie Cheryl."

They're both on the verge of tears.

I grab Anita's hand. "Stop yapping, child. I've told you a dozen times, Charlie's safe in the arms of Jesus. Let's go and fetch the others."

I'D NEVER IMAGINED IT WOULD be hard waiting for someone to die. We've talked it over for weeks and both know the score. Charlie's ready to go, eager for the trip. All his life, he's never been farther than Blackpool on a train. Watching people drink gallons of tea and talk of anything except my brother's departure is devastating. I know once he leaves tears will flow, but initially, grief will be for their own loss, not the joy and love he's given them. They're all God-fearing folk; it's a pity there aren't more God-believing ones. Talk has ceased now, and everybody's holding hands. Mother holds Charlie's right, Dad his left, and so forth around the bed. Jessie and Anita are crushing my fingers with their fierce grips.

There's no angel choir or trumpets, but I swear a soft, cool breeze brushes past my cheeks and is gone. My magnificent brother is finally on his way. Mindful of my ignorance, I send up a silent prayer. Sorrow has no boundaries. Tiny groups sob and console each other. Mother, of course, retaining her dignity, is phoning the doctor. Granddad follows behind while grumbling at her pretending to be "tough as old boots." This keening is getting me down. I'm a coward where sadness is concerned and must escape. The study's the ideal spot, though Anita's curled up in the armchair.

"What are you doing here?" I ask.

"I'm hiding. They make me sad. I bet Charlie isn't crying, especially if he's allowed to play the piano."

"That's the truth. Once he gets to Heaven, he'll have a great time. Charlie has God's gift. God will want His protégé to use it."

"When you reach Heaven, will you get to sing while he plays?" Anita asks.

"There's no guarantee. It's God's will. He decides who is good enough."

"You have my vote. I think you're a good person."

"You aren't getting rid of me yet, and I thought you were my best friend."

"You are. I didn't mean right now." Anita bites down on her thumb, pondering, then adds, "On second thought, you should stay here. There are thousands of angels with beautiful voices, and the choir needs you anyway."

How's a pretty lass so smart? The politicians should listen to this cute kid. There would be no more wars, cruelty or hunger.

Chapter Fifteen

My parents have done their son proud. The funeral's tasteful, and the horse-drawn coaches add a touch of class drawn by black Arab steeds, which Charlie would have cherished. People pause to remove their hats and bow their heads as our procession passes, while traffic offers common courtesy to this sad occasion. The interment's at a small cemetery with immaculate lawns, mature trees, and quiet serenity, if you like that sort of thing. Reverend Marshall conducts the service in the small, packed church. My brother was truly loved and will be sadly missed. There are both sad and happy stories, which make me more proud of him, especially Jack's eulogy, which has everybody in tears, relating precious boyhood days with his best friend. The lump in my throat's choking me, though I know Charlie's at peace. Once the "ashes to ashes, dust to dust" thing is done, the curtains will be opened, and the real hurting will start. Folks say, "You never miss what you've got until it's gone." Charlie was the glue that held this family together. His quiet, gentle manner kept everybody on an even keel. Now we're in the doldrums, with no rudder or star to steer by.

Mother's in her own world cooking, cleaning, and knitting scarves and gloves for the forces. Nothing pleases her. Fred and I try to help, but she insists on being a martyr. Dad rarely drinks at home, visiting the local for a few jars with friends. When he finally arrives home, his dinner is baked to a cinder. It's not a happy household. My parents are constantly butting heads; which came first, chicken or the egg?

Jessie's working at the car plant, which now makes tanks and armoured vehicles. Thousands of women have joined the workforce and are demanding equal pay. With young men being conscripted, we need every pair of available hands. Fred has to work longer hours too.

The Barretts hardly visit, possibly because of Mother and Dad's feuding. Weather is upsetting people too. The River Thames froze solid in January, the first time in fifty years. And Britain's had its worst storm this century. Russia has defeated Finland but lost nearly one million troops. Germany has invaded Denmark and Norway, while Dad's mad because the government has raised the price of cigarettes. The outlook's grim, the latest rumour being that Holland and Belgium will be Hitler's next targets, with the French fighting desperately to hold on. Britain might soon be battling alone.

I'm missing Charlie. There's no one to lean on. Fred's okay, yet rarely around since meeting Irene. Good luck to him.

Barbara's gone to Canada. Maybe she'll write; I won't hold my breath.

Mother's shopping, standing in line, ration book in hand, and preparing to give some poor soul a tongue lashing. I've no idea how long she'll be. One thing's for sure: I'm not staying here alone. There's blue sky between the scudding white clouds. Hopefully the rain's gone for the day. I can borrow Fred's bike now that he has Charlie's. I've a destination in mind where I'm assured of a warm welcome. Add a little razzle-dazzle along with boyish charm and I might even score a free lunch.

BREATHING EASIER ONCE CLEAR OF Solihull, I cruise the leafy lanes of Hall Green. The Barretts' place is a fifteen-minute ride. A gangling youth comes barrelling across the garage forecourt as I park my bike. He has ginger hair and a pale face and wears blue overalls three sizes too large, probably young Jack's cast-offs.

Skidding to a halt, he looks mean and menacing. I often have this strange effect on people. There's a strong hand on my shoulder. It's been that sort of day!

"Are you upsetting our staff, young Eddie?"

Eureka! The cavalry's arrived.

"I wouldn't dream of it, Mr Barrett."

"This is Richard, doesn't bite, but takes his job seriously. We've lots of urchins using this place as a skating rink."

Looking pleased, the boy displays a dentist's nightmare. I'm glad he doesn't bite. I'd need a rabies shot.

"Nice to meet you, Eddie," he says, offering a grubby palm. "My friends call me Dick for short."

Returning his handshake, I add a big smile. "It really suits you."

Uriah Heap trots back to his cubicle, ready to repel all boarders.

"Get whatever help we can, all our mechanics have been conscripted," Mr Barrett says and drapes his arm around my shoulder, squeezing hard. "We've missed you, kid. Let's go and meet the others. They'll be tickled pink."

Our timing's spot-on. Mrs Barrett, flushed and pretty as ever, looks up from the skillet, where onions are sizzling away. "What took you so long?"

I'm dealing with the attentions of Silver and Anita and not certain who has the wettest kisses, when Mrs Barrett joins the fray, wrapping her arms tightly around me. It's hard being so adorable.

Coming up for air, I say, "It's been all work and no play. None of you come to visit me these days."

"I want to come, but my parents say they're too busy." Anita pouts.

Mr Barrett's surrounded by paperwork. "Look at this stuff: government forms, bills, accounts to figure out, and no staff. There's scarcely time to breathe."

Mrs Barrett joins in. "Strangely, we're not making money. Nobody's bought a car in two months. Petrol's rationed, the store's hardly doing any business, and our shop manager's earning twice the wages we can pay. My boys are working twelve-hour days keeping us afloat."

"Stop grumbling and let's eat," Jack decides. "Make up a plate for young Dick too. He could use a good square meal."

Anita's parents aren't always in church, but Jesus is forever in their hearts. I'm too busy to talk while eating, but the cogs are turning, and an idea's taking shape.

"I've had a brainwave. There's a simple solution to your problems." Pausing, I wait for their attention. "Mother needs shaking out of her misery. She could do the books, run the shop, and have to be nice to customers, freeing the men to handle the dealership and garage."

"How do we persuade Dolly to work for us?" Cheryl asks.

"Tell the truth. Mother thinks she's indispensable. It's only stubborn pride that's keeping you apart."

"Sounds like a great idea. I'll phone Al and tell him we'll visit tonight. Knowing my pal, he'll do anything to get Dolly back on track."

"Can Anita and I come too?" Jack asks. "I like Mrs Roberts, and my sister can wrap Uncle Albert around her little finger."

"They won't know what's hit them, both barrels right between the eyes."

This angelic child has been watching too many Westerns.

Mrs Barrett pats her daughter's cheek. "Stow your pistols, Calamity Jane. We aim to take these two gringos alive not dead."

I'm astounded! Dearest Mrs Barrett's a John Wayne fan too!

Chapter Sixteen

My seed's blossomed, and with careful cultivation by the Barretts, the bonds of friendship are stronger than ever. Young Jack's been the leader, with backup from Jessie and Anita. Mother has a surrogate son, and I've a big brother again. The two girls help around the house now that Mother's working, while Miss Chief torments Dad, who enjoys every minute.

We've closed ranks just in time. The past weeks have been horrific. Sending our troops into Norway untrained for the poor conditions ends Chamberlain's reign as prime minister, and he's swiftly replaced by Winston Churchill. He's promising us blood, sweat, and tears, yet proclaiming we'll be victorious. Moans and groans have been replaced by dogged determination to kick Hitler and his goons up the Khyber Pass, one of Dad's choice remarks, which irritates Mother.

I'm no longer treated as a child. Good manners are still the norm, but everything's discussed and opinions sorted. I don't act smart, remembering Granddad's sage advice: "Be thought a fool than open your mouth and remove all doubt."

Thanking God every night for His grace, I wonder if He does watch from a distance as men try to destroy themselves. How can the meek inherit the Earth when so many innocent people are being massacred? Half of Europe has been trampled underfoot by the Third Reich, and the British are being slaughtered at Dunkirk as ships and boats strive desperately to evacuate them. Britain now stands alone before the might of the Nazis. We seem doomed yet are praying for a miracle. Surely such faith deserves God's deliverance.

Dad's joined the Local Defence Volunteers. More than a million World War I veterans do likewise, parading with ancient rifles and broomsticks, plus knives attached to use as pikes. They're mocked and called "Dad's Army." Things changed fast when Winnie took over. Issued with uniforms, boots, bayonets, and better equipment, they were renamed the Home Guard. Within weeks, Dad has been promoted to sergeant. Mother sews his medal ribbons on his tunic, and he's the proudest man in town. Once again, he's ready to fight for king and country.

Fred volunteers for service but fails his medical each time. He'd had meningitis as a child and is partially deaf. Fortunately, the local police force saves the day, appointing him special constable/courier. My brother's like a dog with two tails. I see Dad's sly hand—he and Chief Wilson are old friends.

It's a giant leap from child to teenager, and I've been making plans for months. A newsagent has given me a paper route. I'm old enough to enrol at the YMCA and eligible to join the Sea Cadet Corps. Most Sundays I'm at the Barretts' helping in the garage, doing small repairs and keeping the place tidy. Young Jack's teaching me about engines and reckons it might be useful one day. Anita and I go to the cinema after lunch. It's Mrs Barrett's treat; she knows the local Romeos are eying her pretty daughter, and I'm the cheapest babysitter around.

I'm guaranteed a welcome here on the Sabbath, and Mother has a day of rest too. However, today there are glum faces. "Look as though you've lost a pound note and found a penny."

"Right first time, the government's banned the sale of new cars. It will cripple the dealership, and I'll be patching up old bangers," Mr Barrett moans.

"We'll have to tighten our belts. I can get a job," Mrs Barrett says.

"The Navy will be keeping me soon," Jack adds. "I'll send some money home."

"I can lend a hand after school," I offer.

"And I'll make your lunch, Daddy," Anita chips in.

"Why am I worrying? I'll teach Silver to strip down an engine then I'll retire."

Crisis over, we close the garage and take an early lunch, but something's not kosher, and like a kick in the head, I realise Jack's going to leave.

Pushing away my half-eaten meal, I excuse myself from the table, escaping into the garden. Silver trails behind and snuggles beside me in the swing seat.

"You're going to miss him too, aren't you, boy?"

"Never knew you talked to Silver too," Anita whispers, looking over the trellis.

"All the time, and I would have told you later."

"Don't bother, bossy-boots. I know why you lost your appetite."

This twelve-year-old sprite going on thirty never ceases to amaze me. We're like peas in a pod. It's uncanny how she reads my mind.

"My brother is about to risk his life for our freedom. We have to be strong and pray for his safe return."

"That's true, sweet girl, but it's hard work being a brave little soldier."

Anita pulls me off the seat. "God put the wrong label on you, Eddie Roberts. You've lots more sugar and spice than slugs and snails. Let's go to the movies."

Chapter Seventeen

It's a crutch we sorely need. Twenty-three miles of water is all that stands between freedom and the sound of jackboots marching down the Mall. Goering's boasting that the Luftwaffe's going to blast our air force from the skies. Yet, he's having a wake-up call and suffering heavy losses.

This blow prompts another morale-boosting speech from Winnie in the House of Commons and is loudly applauded by the honourable members. "Never in the field of human conflict has so much been owed by so many to so few," being the main theme to our brave Boys in Blue.

Fat Herman, frustrated, aims his anger on London and the civilian population. Three hundred German bombers escorted by twice as many fighters launch a deadly attack on London's East End late on a Saturday afternoon in September. They bomb Woolwich Arsenal, a power station, a gas works, the docks, and the city. Two hours later, another two hundred and fifty planes appear, and further raids continue throughout the night, with the final strike at 0400 hours. The death toll is over four hundred, and the Air Ministry claims ninety-nine German planes were destroyed, against twenty-two British losses. Hitler, incensed by bombing raids on Berlin, Munich, and Hamburg, orders a wholesale blitz on London. September fatalities are seven thousand with nine thousand injured. We're bloody but not bowed, and the enemy's paying dearly. According to the BBC, the Luftwaffe's lost one hundred and eighty-five planes in one day. We're lucky. Birmingham is industrial Britain's heartland, and it's surprising that Goering's ignored us, which could change instantly. Here on the home front, everything's chaotic. Dad's out scouring the darkness for enemy planes. Fred's patrolling the streets, putting out fires. Mother's cooking the books at the garage, and between school, paper route, Sea Cadets, and the Y, I'm not sure whether I'm on foot or horseback.

Today's Sunday and Fred's snoozing. He deserves a rest. Besides, if I don't disturb him, the extra rasher of bacon will be mine. Mother doesn't chaperone me to church now I'm a teenager; only Anita and I go. She'll be here soon. Mrs Barrett will drop her off in the MG Midget.

Dad's in his armchair with pipe and newspaper. It's great to see him back from misery land. Mother's happiness is good medicine for him. It's nice to know your parents are maturing.

"I wouldn't cook Fred's breakfast. He needs his sleep."

"You're right. It puzzles me how he keeps going."

"Getting soft in your old age talking nice about your son," Mother says.

"Maybe so, but he's changed since Irene came along. He's a good girl there."

"So speaks the voice of experience," I remark.

"Cheeky young bug—" Dad's cut off mid-speech by the Barretts' arrival.

We eat in the kitchen, although Sleeping Beauty hasn't surfaced yet. Mother and Mrs Barrett are chatting, while Dad and Anita tease each other.

Opportunity is a fine thing. "When's Jack coming home?" I ask.

"He's still training, but expects a few days' leave soon."

"He's not going to sea for another six months, so he'll be safe," Anita adds.

Fortune favours the brave. "I've been nominated by my commanding officer for the entrance examination to the Royal Naval College next year."

"You're much too young," Mother declares.

I've rehearsed well. "One takes the exam before one is fifteen. If one passes and is physically fit, one enrols for five years' study at Dartmouth." Pausing briefly, I add, "After graduation, I'm appointed midshipman for six months and then promoted to sub-lieutenants in His Majesty's Royal Navy."

"Well, this one disagrees."

"You're being negative, Dolly," Dad replies. "Eddie's talking about a career. Let's give him the chance to see if he's wasting his time."

"Albert is right," Mrs Barrett chips in. "It's fabulous that Eddie knows what he'd like to do. He has my vote."

"Mine too, Auntie Dolly. Once he has his own ship, we'll be able to cruise around the world for nothing."

Mother doesn't appear disturbed by the democratic outcome, fully aware that without extra tutoring, there's faint hope I'll be ready. Leaving the ladies to clear up, I wander off to the study for a little solitude.

Fat chance! Anita shadows me. "Why so glum, chum? You've put one over on Mum." She grins. "I'm a poet and don't know it."

"There's no way I could do the work in time."

"Wish I knew how to knit."

Ignoring Granddad's advice, I ask, "Why is that?"

"To make warm socks for your cold feet."

"Very funny. You don't understand. It's impossible to learn all this stuff."

"That's a load of bull. You say anything's possible, just believe in the Lord. And you never tell lies."

"No way for a young lady to speak. Anyhow, I've no time or the money, so forget it."

Anita's eyes are awash with tears. "I'm not a young lady, just a little girl trying to help her best friend. If you don't know the answer, let's ask God."

"Don't cry," I say, handing her my hankie. "I think He's enough to handle without my troubles."

"I'll pray for you. I've not asked God for anything lately, only to make me a better person, but I think He forgets because I still do silly things."

I smile at her innocence. She sees nothing in black and white, only rainbow hues. "God never forgets any of His children, nor forsakes them. He doesn't expect us to be perfect, only to love Him and each other. Most important is that we've enough patience to let Him work miracles in His own wonderful way."

Anita's smiling again, though her nose is red. "I knew you were teasing, but I'm still going to pray for you. How could the Almighty possibly ignore two beautiful little lambs like us?"

Chapter Eighteen

Riding my bike to school is quicker than waiting for a bus. Many streets have deep craters from ruptured gas and water mains and are impassable to traffic. The back-doubles I take are strewn with bricks, rubble, broken glass, and broken hearts, as survivors of all ages search for memories of shattered lives. Police, firefighters, and rescue squads sift the wreckage like soldier ants. Ambulance crews, plus Red Cross workers, tend the injured and suffering. Neighbours provide sandwiches, soup, and tea, all laced with compassion, and complete a tragic cameo. Wheeling past, I feel totally useless. The past six weeks have been pure hell.

A strange thing happens one November night. The sky above London is silent. After two months of nonstop bombing, it ceases. Perhaps mad Adolf has finally got the message? Dream on! Twenty-four hours later, Coventry's ravaged from dusk until dawn. Vast areas are razed to the ground including the majestic cathedral. It's reported that more than a thousand civilians have perished from six hundred tons of high explosives and thousands of incendiaries dropped. It's said to be the deadliest air raid to date, and it's only the beginning. Sirens sound at 1700 hours every night over major cities and ports, with London still coming under attack but not so savagely. The all-clear greets us at 0800 hours each morning. Battalions of tired, unwashed people report for work straight from bomb shelters.

German U-boats are creating massive destruction amongst our shipping. Hitler won't need to invade Britain. He'll starve us into submission unless something alters rapidly. The Ministry of Food has informed us there'll be no more bananas until after the war, and housewives are hopping mad.

Finally, I'm allowed past the barricade after having my satchel searched. They probably think I'm a spy dressed as a schoolboy. My blue eyes and fair hair have fooled them. Three flattened houses explain the cop's worry about an unexploded bomb. Really, I should go back and shake his hand, but I'm late. No problem, everyone's outside staring at the school—or its remains. The left wing's a twisted mess of wood, glass, and shattered desks. The small church on the opposite corner is gone, suffering a direct hit. There's not been such excitement since Mr Jones blew up the chemistry lab during a gunpowder experiment, losing most of his shoulder-length white hair.

Visions of a day off are dashed as Billy hounds us into the main hall. We've lost six classrooms. The plan to double up is not popular. Even classmates we do not like are preferable to foreigners, though I'd willingly swap Brick-head, who's returned from the wilds, for the perky little redhead in Form 3B. My day is a disaster. With twice as many kids, how are teachers going to cope? I require more help, not less. It's easy for Miss Congeniality to say she'll pray for me, but who's coming to explain how I pass for college?

The blackboard rubber whistles past my ear and clangs off the radiator. "Stir your stumps, boy. You're required in the headmaster's study!" Billy barks.

Recovering from my trance, I see lovely Liz in the doorway. The girls are studying her outfit, the boys everything else. Only the teacher is unmoved; he must have ice water in his veins. Slowly, I put away my books, basking in my friends' envy. Small victories have to be savoured.

"Move yourself, Roberts. It will be dark before you get there," Billy says.

Walking down the corridor, it is useless quizzing the secretary what fate awaits me. She'd make a nun sound like a blabbermouth. Whatever sin I've committed needs careful consideration. I hear voices from Dr Gregory's study. He has backup, which isn't good news. Liz points to a chair. I obey without question as she enters the Head's study, returning with him obediently plodding behind; truly, a sign of the hand that rocks the cradle.

"Eddie, dear boy, it's good to see you."

First-name terms sound promising.

"Three teas please, Elizabeth, two sugars in mine," Doc says, taking my arm. "You have a visitor."

Miss Ramsey hasn't changed. She's still the cuddly white-haired teddy bear I fondly remember. Beating her to the punch, I ask, "Did you miss me as much as I missed you?"

She doesn't answer as she wraps her arms around me. Dr Gregory waits quietly, amused by this strange behaviour.

Coming up for air, I say, "I'll take that as a yes."

We migrate to the cosy alcove and comfortable armchairs, where Liz has set up the table. The china tea set's on show too. What have I done to deserve such largesse? Sipping my tea, with pinkie extended, I await their pleasure.

Miss Ramsey kicks off. "The Board has decided to boot this old gal into touch. I should have retired years ago, but they twisted my arm. I've had forty years of teaching. Seen the good, bad, and indifferent. We're not allowed favourites, but once in a blue moon, someone attracts your attention. They're not necessarily the brightest star in the sky, just different. You're so different Eddie, it hurts."

"Thanks for that vote of confidence."

"You're welcome, though I'm not here to boost your ego. We've heard you're keen to join the Royal Navy."

"I haven't told a soul at school."

"Nevertheless, someone's asked if we could prep you for the entrance exam."

"I can't afford private tuition, and Mother would never accept charity."

"Ah! There's the rub," Dr Gregory says. "We're under contract and not permitted to freelance. However, Miss Ramsey will soon be a free agent, so we've devised a plan. She will explain the details."

"Don't worry about Mummy. We've butted heads before. I'm not a big spender so my fee won't bankrupt your benefactor, who, by the way, insists on anonymity."

"Do you believe I can make it, miss?"

"We've had a meeting and are convinced you've the ability to succeed and have tutors willing to sacrifice their leisure time. Meanwhile, you'll have to work your little socks off."

The Head puts down his cup. "You're sound in most subjects but do need work on weaker ones. One of your strengths is neatness, Mr Williamson informed us."

"I should have known he'd have his finger in the pie."

"He's the main shaker and mover, even persuaded Miss Talbot to lend a hand. That's definitely a coup de maître," Miss Ramsey says.

"Sounds like Montezuma's revenge to me," I murmur.

"Au contraire, Mademoiselle is your finest champion, and convinced that beneath your clown's cape dwells a talented youth."

They sit enjoying their tea and await my response. Smart-ass remarks are not appropriate. I'm tongue-tied, experiencing a new emotion called humility.

Chapter Nineteen

Life's never going to be the same. My learned counsellors have assured me one hundred per cent support and watching my back. There'll be sound advice and moral courage too, but when push comes to shove, it's my call. The first training session is brutal. No punches are pulled and everything changes to make room for the extra work. Air raids have already slashed my social activities. The army's taken over the YMCA, and we can only use the gym and football pitch once a week. Choir's been disbanded through lack of members, and the Sea Cadets meet on Saturdays or a Sunday parade.

Anita and I aren't allowed to attend church, despite protests that God will not forgive us. Mother and Mrs Barrett are adamant after learning the city's received heavy damage. St. Martin's escapes unharmed, but the Market Hall's lost its roof, and there are rumours of an unexploded bomb inside. Adults can be so childish.

It's chilly on the domestic front too. Mother hates being outsmarted, though she's relieved when learning that my tutoring won't cost a dime. Dad remains neutral for the sake of harmony. He's reached a plateau in life, being down in the valley so often whatever's over the next hill doesn't concern him.

My industry surprises everyone, including me. Miss Ramsey encourages and bullies, while Dr Gregory marks my projects with a savage pencil, and Billy supplies the necessary backbone to get it done, especially the truce with Tatty Talbot.

"All you have to do, lad, is eat humble pie."

Sadly, my expression betrays me.

He delivers his verdict. "It's a command, not a suggestion."

Gritting my teeth, I mutter, "Put that way, sir, why not?"

The overture's frosty. We circle each other, as hungry lions round dead prey, though her two cats like me. She thaws a tad. I've cracked it; outside of school, she's quite a sweetheart.

War's taking a heavy toll. For every step we take forward, we go back two. Victory over the Italians is brief when the Germans arrive under the command of General Rommel. Within weeks, our army's defeated at Tobruk, and the Afrika Korps advance to the Egyptian border. Another barbaric attack is launched on London by five hundred and fifty bombers. Westminster Abbey and St Paul's Cathedral are damaged, and one thousand four hundred people are killed.

There's also disaster at sea when *HMS Hood* is attacked by the *Bismarck*. The ammunition magazine is struck, and the ship's destroyed with the loss of thirteen hundred men. Every available British ship gives pursuit, including our newest battleship the *Prince of Wales*, with dockworkers still aboard, as the killer heads south from Greenland, plotting a course for Brest and a safe haven. Spotted five hundred miles off Lands' End, she's crippled by torpedo bombers from the aircraft carrier *Ark Royal*, and one thousand German sailors perish as *the Rodney* and *King George V* finish her off, aided by a final torpedo strike from *HMS Victorious*. It's a great boost to the country's morale, though personally we're subdued knowing that Jack joined the *Prince of Wales* recently. Celebrating is all well and good yet has a hollow ring to families waiting for news of their kinfolk. Dead is dead, but not knowing is soul destroying.

"Why doesn't he call or send a letter?" Anita asks.

"Not allowed."

"That's baloney. I'd walk off the ship and come home."

"You have to wait your turn. There're two watches, port and starboard. Half the crew go on leave. When they return, the rest go. He'll soon be home."

Someone has to keep this bunch happy. Mr and Mrs Barrett are fretting too. Apart from Mr Barrett, the garage is going belly up. Yet why me? I've enough to do, without wet-nursing my friends. I could have stayed home and listened to Mother nagging for having my head buried in books.

Unable to suffer their sad faces any longer, I pick up Silver's leash and say, "Come on boy, let's go for a walk."

My actions stir the wounded. Grabbing her coat, Anita shouts, "Wait for me!"

"Don't be long, I'm making lunch," says Mrs Barrett.

"I'll close up," Mr Barrett says, following us out of the door.

We're halfway across the yard when a taxi pulls onto the forecourt and out climbs Jack. He's almost trampled underfoot in the mad rush. Silver, damping down a lilac bush, quickly joins in the action.

"I caught the milk train from Glasgow. It stopped at every bloody station," Jack explains when we've finished mobbing him. "Never thought I'd get here."

I'm so happy, I could cry.

We hustle him into the kitchen, where Mrs Barrett waits with mascara running down her cheeks. She looks like Coco the Clown.

"I told you not to worry," Mr Barrett scoffs as the enthusiasm ebbs.

We stare in amazement. He's been off his trolley for the past ten days.

Mrs Barrett is smiling serenely. Her boy's home. "Would you care for a nice cup of tea, Jack?" she asks.

"Fancy something stronger, Mum."

"Oh! When did you start drinking?"

"Ten seconds after the first shell hit the ship and dumped me on my ass."

"Were many boys killed?" asks Anita.

"I don't know, sweetie. They never tell us anything," Jack replies.

"Don't be nosey, Miss," her father scolds. "Remember the poster. Loose lips sink ships."

"Oops! Sorry, Daddy."

"We're in dry dock for a few weeks, so you've no need to worry. And before our next voyage, I'll get seven days' leave."

"I'll drink to that. Care to join me, son?"

"I thought you'd never ask, Dad."

Home is the sailor, home from the sea.

Chapter Twenty

We're into the third year of war between delight and desperation. One minute our heads are in the clouds, next we're plummeting to earth. Optimists, who'd insisted it was only a minor squabble, have been silenced, their confidence replaced by stubborn grit to see it through to the bitter end.

The summer of '41 has been fantastic, helped by Jack's company. It's great to enjoy the luxury of a big brother, if only briefly. Life returns to ordinary once he leaves. The sirens sound at suppertime and the all-clear wakes us for breakfast. People go about their business, ignoring the drone of engines and crump of anti-aircraft guns. Occasionally, a mother with kids in tow might watch a Spitfire harassing a German plane, though she's more concerned about using margarine coupons for clothing while waiting for real ones to be printed. Kids think it's better than playing cowboys and Indians, and wondering, who is the bloke with big boots and uniform that sometimes sleeps at their house? Praise God, one day they'll get to know and not be left fatherless, thanks to those mindless morons.

Impressed with my progress, tutors say I'm right on target and in less than a year could be at Dartmouth. Mother's face, when Miss Ramsey shares this good news, suggests there's something wrong with the drains, which lifts my spirits higher. There's little love lost between these two.

Meanwhile, Tatty and I have formed an entente cordiale. I'd never imagined conjugating French verbs could be such fun. It's possible that the cream cakes she keeps forcing on me are the reason.

Also, Fred's a local hero. During a recent air raid, he discovered a house on fire with an incendiary bomb stuck in the guttering, which he dislodged with a clothes prop. Hitting the ground, the bomb exploded and burned his ankle. Despite the pain, his quick reaction with a stirrup pump and sand saved the building from destruction. Bob Wilson's recommending my brother for a medal, who will need a beret three sizes larger. He's acting modest but failing, God bless him.

Germany's broken its pact with Russia and invaded their country, aided by Finland and Romania. The hopes that seven million Soviet soldiers would prove too much for the Nazis are dashed when barely two months later the Germans are knocking on the doors of Leningrad and closing in on Moscow. The Russians are defending bravely, but casualties are horrendous throughout both armies in this brutal campaign.

Dad's got one thing right: Germany attacking Russia has saved Britain from invasion. It's nice to have the pendulum swing our way sometimes. The loss of Greece and Crete in quick order hasn't helped, and in Egypt, the Eighth Army is up to its axles in sand. I'd hoped a name change might have raised their sagging spirits. The navy is enjoying a measure of success in the Med, though we're getting hammered by U-boats in the Atlantic. The Battle-in-the-Air is taking centre stage over Europe and Britain, with the Royal Air Force and the Luftwaffe trying to crush the heart and soul out of each other's populations.

Does God know the good guys from the bad ones?

Arriving home for his sea leave, Jack looks fit and relaxed, though quiet. He's something on his mind, but I don't bug him. He'll tell me when he's ready. After lunch, we troop into the yard. Anita stays behind with Mrs Barrett, who's teaching her cooking. It'll be nice when she can manage more than scrambled eggs on toast.

Putting our cups on the table, we settle into the swing hammock. The silence stretches. Jack's stuck for words and needs a nudge.

"I'm going to miss you. It's been great having you as my pal."

"My pleasure. I used to envy Charlie because he had brothers. He offered to share you, so when he died, I still had you, Eddie. It's eased my loss too."

"Amen to that. I'm being selfish. Charlie will always be with us, won't he?" Waiting for his nod, I ask the big question. "How long will you be gone?"

Noticing his eyes flicker, I know I've pushed the right button. He trusts me, and I feel ten feet tall.

"The *Prince* is ready to sail. We've finished sea trials and leave next week," Jack says, draining his cup.

I wait him out. I'm famous for my ice-cold, blue-eyed stare.

"We've been issued with tropical kit."

"Where are you going, the Isle of Wight?

It's harder than pulling teeth. I tighten my grip. "Let me guess. You're going somewhere warm, which means, the Med or Far East. Tell me!"

"We're off to the Pacific for two years. The Admiralty's decided our naval force needs strengthening due to the Japanese flexing their muscles in Indo-China."

"When are you telling the family?"

"I'm not," Jack says, glancing at the kitchen window. "Mum panics because I'm in Scotland. She thinks that's a foreign country. Her letters will be sent care of GPO London, and letters home are censored. She doesn't need my problems."

"The less they know, the sounder they sleep," I say, patting Silver's head. "Your secret's safe with us, Jack."

I clam up as Anita arrives with small, round objects on a plate, which she calls scones. We coat them with butter and jam. They're warm and delicious, much like the pretty cook who's baked them. Whoa! Daren't say that, she'll think I'm raving mad. She stands, hands on hips, waiting for our opinions.

Jack saves me from drowning. "They're fabulous, sis."

"Excellent," I say, treading water gently. "You'll make someone a lovely wife."

"Don't go overboard, sailor, it's not cordon bleu," she says with a knowing smile. I could swear this petite cherub has a crystal ball.

I'm saved by Mrs Barrett's voice. "Come on, you lazy pair, there's a party at the Roberts' shack tonight, and we're invited. Albert's phoning old pals right now."

This is akin to Lazarus rising from the dead. Dad has his mojo back.

Pre-war, shindigs were always popular and house rules simple. Admission and food are free. If you can sing, dance, or play a musical instrument, that's a bonus. All frowns are banned and smiles mandatory, but tops, you can forget about life for a while. The Depression left thousands without work and destitute. My dad, one of the few with a regular job and with Mother's strong support, gave people hope.

They made sure no kid on our street went hungry, and every adult received a welcome at the Roberts' open house. My parents never shout their faith from mountaintops but perform it right here on Earth.

Maybe it's their last kick at the can. How much longer can this dear couple tilt at windmills before the world comes crashing down around their ears? Every day we hear of friends and relatives being killed or maimed. The slaughter could go on for years, so why not have one more blowout before it's too late?

Chapter Twenty-One

Walking down memory lane's bittersweet, though many familiar faces are absent. I'm amazed how much booze and grub we have. No fee is asked, but no one arrives empty-handed. Even the police chief walks in with a suspect on each arm, but doubtless, the evidence will swiftly vanish, and justice will be served. Also, if neighbours complain about the noise, we'll refer them to Bob.

Bill Brown's seated at the piano, tickling the ivories. He's a virtuoso. After a few beers, even more so. He's the quietest Scot I know, only speaking when he's anything to say. He'd hit the bottle hard when his flaming red-haired wife, Annie walked out, taking the baby too. He survived thanks to the unselfish love of his two teenage daughters, Margaret and Billie, and his dear friends. I'll have to find the girls once I catch my breath. We'd great fun as kids.

Dad and Mother are wonderful hosts and their parties the talk of the town, but guess who's doing the graft? Mother's conned us into being busboys, waitresses, and unpaid slaves while she and Dad are all teeth and charm with the guests. Serving drinks isn't the worst job. I'm meeting people who are strangers but remember me as a toddler. The tales about my parents fill me with pride and also guilt. The reason I never received the electric train set from Santa or the two-tone coloured bike on my birthday makes sense now.

Mother and Great-Aunt Elsie, aka Eleanor, once a concert pianist, are sitting in a quiet corner sipping their wine and conversing. Should they fancy blackmail, they have enough skinny on tonight's revellers to make a fortune. Queen Eleanor's never officially retired. She's forever on stage. Arriving here in ermine and pearls, glittering with jewellery and her silver hair freshly marcelled for the occasion, she poses in the drawing-room doorway.

Bill, taking his left hand off the keys, salutes her. "How are ye doing Elsie me darling? Still wowing the auld guys down at yon Legion with your 'Moonlight Sonata'?" And he returns to "The White Cliffs of Dover" without missing a note.

He's the only male here who'd dare to speak this way. She despises men, never found one worthy of her respect. The worst-kept secret is that she has a deep appreciation for Bill's musical ability.

Goaded by good-natured friends on possible romance, the dour Scot says, "I'd sooner be hit in the face with a wet kipper."

Nevertheless, the beat goes on. After a couple of drinks, Eleanor turns into Elsie and mixes with the peasants. She believes money's made round to go around. Local orphanages and homes for young pregnant girls benefit from her generosity.

I'm curious to know what they're planning. Elsie is convinced I could become a professional singer. The requirements are a voice coach, dedication, and pots of money. Mother's keen, but sidestepped the issue so far, saying the family purse strings are tight.

Stopping Anita on her way to the kitchen, I say, "Need your help, honey."

"That's the only time you're nice."

"Stop whining, girl. Go and listen to what Mother and Great-Aunt Elsie are cooking up."

"You expect me to eavesdrop on their conversation?"

"Not really, just do a little snooping. You're brilliant at that."

She looks thoughtful. "I might, for a small consideration."

"I think your mum's teaching you more than cooking, miss."

Anita flashes a Mona Lisa smile worth a thousand words. I don't ask. Her logic would baffle Einstein.

Blissful in my ignorance, I leave to help move furniture. A drum kit's arrived, musicians are warming up, and the carpet's rolled up for dancing. The cabaret's impromptu. Anything goes, providing you don't strip naked. Another few minutes and the joint will be jumping. I hope Mata Hari has been successful because shortly you'll not hear yourself speak.

She's back but waits patiently while I listen to the Old Brigade crooning "Keep the Home Fires Burning." There's hardly a dry eye, though Fred does add comic relief, staggering in with an armful of logs.

"Don't worry, fair prince, they're not discussing you."

"You're an angel. I'd plight you my troth, but it's not cooked yet," I reply.

"Don't be daft! They're talking about the scoutmasters having it away with the Cub mistress. What do they mean?"

"Is that all they said?" I ask.

"According to the postmaster, who heard it from the vicar's wife, whose brother works for the Forestry Commission, these two persons have been seen together in Arden Forest, and it's not even public property."

I'm tempted to laugh but hate to hurt her feelings. Yet how can I lie? Easy! "It's gossip. He's only giving her tuition for her woodcraft badge," I say. Please forgive me, God.

My pixie pal accepts the explanation, though mutters that those witches should be burned at the stake. We've much in common.

Finally, I track down Margaret, who is surrounded by a pack of wolves, all with tongues hanging out. Small wonder, wee Maggie was pretty, but now grown up, she's ravishing. Elbowing my way to the front, I'm the envy of the big boys as she crushes me to her ample bosom. Locked in each other's arms, we're lost in a potpourri of memories.

The Browns arrived from Scotland, tired, hungry, and wearing the only clothes they possessed. Dad brought them home for supper, and they stayed for three months. Margaret, ten years old, became my minder, insisting on repaying my parents' kindness. Gaining a big sister and good fairy, I was the happiest four-year-old kid in Christendom and prepared to die for her. Nothing has changed.

She breaks the spell. "You still the dreamer. Care to share?" Maggie asks.

I settle for simple. "Remember our first meeting? You looked like something the cat had dragged in."

"Charming. How would you know? You were a wee bairn."

"Dad found you outside the railway station drenched to the skin. You all stood in front of our fire. There was so much steam the place looked like a Chinese laundry."

"And you were bright as a new penny ready for bed. I ken the blond curls and big, blue eyes. All angelic, which proves never believe first impressions."

"I recall offering you my cocoa though I couldn't understand a word you spoke."

"True, but you knew how to sweet talk the lassies."

"You've got me. I've always been a fool for a pretty face."

I enquire about Billie and discover she's Fred's problem. Though only a year older than me, she's been bitten by the love bug.

Maggie says, "He's a nice boy, and Dad likes him. My sister never got over Mum leaving until Steve arrived. He works on the bikes with dad, who reckons the lad's a genius with two-stroke engines."

"So, the business is fine. Your dad looks well, Billie's happy, and is sweet Maggie still fighting off the Romeos?"

"I'm busy and too picky. Dad still needs us. I'm not sure he's mended yet. We mind the office, while he and Steve deal with the bikes. Concerning love, I've not found anyone who can hold a candle to my da."

"God's working on someone extra special for you."

"He'd better get His finger out. I'll be an old maid soon. All the men my age are in the forces."

"Eureka! That's the answer," I say, seizing her hand. "As Charlie used to say, you shall go to the ball, Cinders."

She's too shocked to protest as I drag her into the conservatory, where Jack and his dad are having a serious talk.

Discretion's never been my strong point. "This is a party, not a wake. You're hosts and looking after the guests, not fighting." Without pause, I sweep on. "This is Margaret, Bill Brown's little daughter, Jack, but time marches on."

I know Maggie's not about to run by her bright smile. "You were Charlie's friend. That was a beautiful eulogy you gave at his funeral."

There's a pregnant silence while my dear friends gaze into each other's eyes. Do you ever have the feeling that you aren't needed? Mr Barrett and I drift away, not noticed or missed.

"I could smack him around the head," Mr Barrett says.

"He's told you then?"

"Had to drag it out of him. How did you know?"

A white lie is needed. "His sad face, but he swore me to secrecy. He didn't wish to upset anyone."

I'm not sure Mr Barrett's heard me. He's closely studying Jack and Margaret. It might be a mixture of yesterday's memories and tomorrow's dreams, though I've not the slightest doubt. Good things happen to good people.

Chapter Twenty-Two

Dad's right on the ball. It's not the greatest bash ever but has provided a second wind for the hard road ahead. Summer's gone, and dark nights are here. Personal and national tragedies are commonplace. The battle in Russia's ground to a halt due to heavy snow and Hitler at the gates of Moscow is frantic. An Italian sub has sunk the aircraft carrier *HMS Ark Royal*. Though few lives were lost, it's a sad day for the Royal Navy. In the western desert, the battle wages to and fro, while at home we all miss Jack.

Every day, relatives and friends are killed or crippled. Trevor Palmer was reported missing over Germany during a bombing mission. He never returned to Brum, but stayed in Lydney and married Jenny. He left behind a widow and small child. Mrs Potts's husband has also perished out in North Africa. I wonder if little Ben still goes to the park to feed the ducks.

I thank God for watching over me, although my social life is blighted. My time's spent studying and doing household chores. Now that I'm a responsible adult—Mother's words—I've been made head cook and bottle washer, which involves preparing meals for the famished workers. I'm often stirring the pot and reading at the same time.

"Watch the gravy doesn't burn," is usually Mother's affectionate greeting.

I nod without looking up. "The plates are warming on the rack, and the table's set. Did you have a nice day too, Mother?"

A blistering look is her response. Such is the chef's power, she can't afford to fire me. My impertinence prompts her to serve supper. We eat in the dining room. Mother still keeps up appearances. Conversation's limited; it's also a throwback to pre-war days. Now without a "by your leave," or "kiss my aspidistra," they eat and run. Dad sinks into his armchair, and Fred's off to see Irene; Mother's ironing him a shirt. She prefers that to helping with the dishes. Sadness grips me as I load the dumbwaiter. We used to be a happy family. Where did the love go? I'm just a serf at everyone's beck and call. It's not bloody fair!

"Stop that damn racket, lad, I'm trying to listen to the news," Dad yells.

"Break any dishes, and you'll pay for new ones," Mother adds.

What do they want, blood? Losing my temper will solve nothing. I'm calmer now, yet still upset. Has the world gone mad? I stay home most nights and don't mind helping around the house, even burn the midnight oil to do my homework. So what's my problem? In a few months I'll be down in Dartmouth at the bottom of the ladder again, but one I'll be able to climb.

Trundling the cart into the kitchen, I shrug off the blues and tackle the mess with a vengeance. After plodding my way through a mountain of pots, pans, crockery, and cutlery, I'm back to normal (almost).

Weekend's ahead with no chance to relax. I've the study to myself and two papers to write. It is hard graft but worth the sweat and tears. My tutors are quietly confident. They've made me a believer too.

My bubble's burst by Mother's voice. "You're supposed to be working not dozing."

The tray she holds has a mug of hot cocoa and chocolate biscuits. Perhaps it's a peace offering? Did they notice my sulky mouth? Whatever! I accept and wait patiently.

"Don't you tire of this swotting?" Mother asks. She's on a fishing expedition.

I toss some bait. "It's not hard. These projects are dummy runs for the exams. My gurus say I'm a shoo-in."

Mother has an expressive face. This one expresses concern, but she battles on. "Never be too confident. Pride goes before a fall. Your father and I are worried that you'll be disappointed."

She must be desperate—quoting scripture and using Dad is a major mistake. He's been in my corner since day one, but as usual is keeping his own counsel.

I cast a sprat. "Why are you wasting money if you think I'm going to fail?"

"We aren't. Some half-baked fool has offered to sponsor you."

I know yet wonder about the mysterious benefactor. "You never thought I'd make it. Now that it's possible, you're trying to dissuade me. My pride's not at stake, Mother, it's yours. I'd hoped you'd be proud of me."

She doesn't rise to the bait. "Drink your cocoa and eat your biscuits. There's more in the tin." She pauses in the doorway. "Parents know their babies are growing up when told they're wrong. Don't stay up late, you need your sleep."

Sometimes, one has to be cruel to be kind, yet I could have chosen a better moment. Tomorrow's the second anniversary of Charlie's demise and Granddad's birthday too. A change of plan is needed. We'll visit the cemetery first then call on Gramps and be back in time for Cadets.

I'll never see my fifteenth birthday at this rate.

THE SABBATH'S STILL MY FAVOURITE DAY. Spreading my wings is a grand feeling. Mother enjoys the break too. Dad drops me off at the Barretts' after breakfast. Mr and Mrs Barrett have practically adopted me. I'm keeping their son's chair warm while he's away. I stay busy around the garage, doing odd jobs and minor repairs.

After lunch, Anita and I take Silver for a walk, then leave him to his siesta and toddle off to the cinema. It's a Western, and as usual, the Indians finish up on the reservation. Anita tucks her arm through mine as we set off down the parade. I'm surprised, and it must show.

She enlightens me. "I told my classmates I'm going steady."

I act dumb. It's not difficult.

"They kept bragging about their boyfriends, so I invented one. You're not angry are you, Eddie?"

I shouldn't do this but do. "Who's the steady?"

Her jaw drops open. "You of course, stupid!"

I want to throw my arms around this cute girl, hug, squeeze, and never mind. "Flattery will get you nowhere. I'm not that easy."

She grips my arm tightly. My fingers are going dead.

"My dear, young lady, we've been going steady since toddlerhood. I knew it was love at first sight when you let me play with your dolls."

Anita's eyes are bright and shining with tears of joy. I've never seen a sight so beautiful. And that's only the outside. Public displays of affection aren't part of British culture. We raise a few eyebrows standing locked in each other's arms as the world and his wife pass by. There're lots of dreamy smiles from middle-aged women, plus the odd frown from some frosty-faced old fossils.

We couldn't care less. Deep down inside we know it is God's will and we belong together. Our happiness is greater than many people find in a lifetime. The five-minute stroll takes a half hour. Telling the adults is the next hurdle. Anita's parents will be delighted, but mine? That's a whole new ballgame. If somebody has seen us embracing in the street, Mother will die of shame! At least Fred will be on my side. He started hacking his way through the jungle of love at an early age. Then he found Irene—or she found him. Perhaps we shouldn't mention it, though that idea bites the dust as we enter the kitchen holding hands. Mrs Barrett's slicing cucumber, and Mr Barrett's chopping lettuce. I love their salad teas.

"You lovebirds took your sweet time."

Anita's cheeks match the salmon, while I'm busily patting Silver.

Mr Barrett stops in mid-chop. "It's not going to be a shotgun wedding is it?"

"Behave, Jack," Mrs Barrett scolds. "We've known for years you two were joined at the hip."

"I'm not sure we will be regarded as suitable in-laws," Mr Barrett says.

"Don't worry about Dolly. She'll be tickled pink when I tell her what beautiful grandchildren she'll have," Mrs Barrett replies.

"Could I have tea before thinking about changing nappies?" I ask.

Saved any further embarrassment, Anita looks grateful as we sit down to eat. Mr Barrett switches on the radio for the evening news.

The cultured voice of Alvar Liddell silences us. "A report from Washington states that at 0700 hours, the Japanese Imperial Air Force bombed the US Naval Base at Pearl Harbor in Hawaii. They sank or damaged five battleships and fourteen smaller ships, and more than two hundred aircraft were destroyed. Three thousand people were killed. Luckily, two aircraft carriers were out on sea trials. Japanese planes also attacked the Philippines, Guam, and Wake Island."

The announcer drones on. We scarcely notice, too stunned to absorb the horror. Despite warning signs over the past six months, the Americans have been caught napping. Britain, already stretched to its limits, now has another war to fight in the Far East. Only this is more personal. Sitting here with our half-eaten meal in front of us, we're aware beloved Jack is somewhere out there in mortal danger. Bugger being a brave little soldier. I feel like screaming.

Chapter Twenty-Three

The Japanese can copy and improve anything. They've done so with their lightning attacks in the Pacific and Southeast Asia. My friends are distraught. They've not heard from Jack for weeks.

I explain, "No news is good news. He can't write home until reaching port and is safer at sea." I'm sickened but maintain a brave face for their benefit.

Silver sulks, waiting for his master's return. People think me nuts talking to a dog, but he never complains. Today I've bad news. The glum faces at dinner might have given him a clue. "Their grief's dragging me down. Maybe they blame me? I said he'd be safe, and the *Prince of Wales* and *Repulse* get torpedoed. Two-thirds of the crews have perished, and there are no names of survivors yet," I tell Silver.

The troops at Hong Kong surrender on Christmas Day against overwhelming odds after a three-week battle and getting down to one day's water supply. The Japanese have landed in Malaya at Kuantan, pushing the British Army towards Singapore. They're unstoppable, both in Southeast Asia and the Pacific.

German panzer divisions have been badly mauled in Russia, and on some fronts pushed back. Hitler, frustrated, has turned his attention to North Africa, with Rommel's tanks attacking the British again. The victories by commandos, at St. Nazaire and Vargo Island, are small comforts compared to failures in the Far East. However, in a lighter vein, our young women (twenty to thirty years old) are being conscripted. Jessie and Margaret are discussing uniforms before going into battle. When Adolf spots this pair, he'll surrender right away.

The misery reaches new heights with the fall of Malaya, the Philippines and Singapore, yet life goes on. Following the RAF's relentless bombing campaign, the Luftwaffe retaliates by attacking England's historic cities. I'm mad. These maniacs should be strung up by their thumbs—or more painful parts.

It's agony, but I've done it. My fingers are permanently bent from writer's cramp. I stagger up the driveway, feeling I've gone fifteen rounds with Joe Louis. Mrs Barrett's car's here; I hope she's brought Anita. Opening the kitchen door, I find the place full of females and sounding like a chimps' tea party.

Anita almost bowls me over. "Jack's alive and well!" she shrieks.

Tears of happiness fill Mrs Barrett's blue eyes, mascara's making railway tracks down her cheeks, but she still looks stunning.

"I told you worry-guts he'd be all right. Have you heard from him?"

Their smiles vanish. They exchange glances. Something's wrong.

"We've had a letter from the Admiralty. Jack was picked up by the Japanese. He's in a POW camp in Singapore but not injured. We have to contact the Red Cross."

"At least you'll know where he is at night."

"It's easy to see why my daughter adores you."

Mother comes to life. "How did your exams go?"

"French isn't my best subject, but I might scrape through,"

The winning post is in sight, but there are still hurdles to clear. I don't trust Mother and believe she's some evil plot in mind.

"We have to dash. Your dad will be baying for his supper," Mrs Barrett says.

Anita looks as disappointed as I feel.

"Yes! We've to move ourselves too," Mother responds. "You've wasted enough time with your head stuck in books. I need a hand."

I ignore the jibe and walk my friends to their car with Mother shouting orders.

We giggle as Mrs Barrett murmurs, "Away, you mutinous dog. Get you gone to the galley. The captain's back on the bridge."

I wave goodbye and saunter up the driveway. The sun's warm and pleasant on my shoulders. God's surely in His Heaven today, Charlie. Jack's alive and things are back to normal or somewhere close. He who speaks in haste repents at his leisure. The words cut the air like a knife.

"Coming Mother, don't get your knickers in a twist," I say, sotto voce.

PATIENCE IS ESSENTIAL WHEN ONE is the youngest. You're last in line for roast potatoes, licking the Christmas pudding ladle, or being picked for the football team, and definitely the final one to get kissed when playing spin-the-bottle. Among the exceptions are taking a bath and bedtime. Each morning, I wait nervously for Sam. Mother enjoys my misery. "They're having problems with your handwriting."

Dad's more sympathetic. "They've hundreds of papers to mark. I'm sure you'll pass with flying colours."

Suddenly, I've time to spare. I listen to the radio and read books, which does zero to inspire me. It's a topsy-turvy world. The weather's beautiful, the world stage ugly. Innocent people are still being killed. The RAF carry out a thousand-bomber raid on Cologne that is four times greater than the worst attack on London. Air Marshal Sir Arthur "Bomber" Harris admits there were no specific targets. He should sleep well and, flushed by his success, has promised that the RAF and US Air Corps will be the scourge of Germany from end to end. His confidence comes with the addition of the four-engine Lancaster bomber, and the Americans' newest long-range plane promised before year's end. He broadcasts in German and doesn't mince words, explaining that missions will be carried out day and night. His avowed intention is to destroy the morale and hearts of these folk. Something about this man makes me shudder.

In three weeks I'll be fifteen. I've to pass a medical and have my documents signed, sealed, and delivered to the Royal Naval College by then. Suppose the post office is blown up, or even Sam. If I question the postmistress, she'll tell me there's a war on. I have noticed. Lab rats going round on treadmills have it made compared to me. We've finished school for summer break. It's Saturday, and I'm waiting for the mail. Mr Barrett's snowed under with repairs and asked me to help. I'm learning lots, and the pay's good. Mrs Barrett puts the money I earn into a bank account for my college fund. It's our dirty little secret; being a minor, I can't open an account without my parents' consent. Skating around this, she put it in her name, which pays a better interest. How can anyone so dear be so devious?

It's turned twelve. Sam's late, likely stopped for liquid refreshment. Does about four miles to the pint on that bike he peddles around town. Dad vows the old boy drove the first stagecoach through here. Here he comes. I contain my excitement, though feeling murderous. He's never in a hurry.

Grinding to a halt in a cloud of dust, he asks, "Expecting a letter are you, lad?"

Hearing all this chat before, I'm tempted to kick his spokes. Leaning over the handlebars, he scrabbles in the canvas bag, making a drama out of a simple task and hands me an advert for window cleaning, relishing my torment. Next time I see his bike outside the pub, I'll let the tires down.

"Hang on, I've something else," Sam says, plunging his fat hand into the sack and pulling out a huge brown envelope. "I trust it's good news."

I'm positive it's the best news. If I'd failed, the message would have been brief. This bundle contains my results and all the info for my entrance into His Majesty's Royal Navy. Look out world, here I come!

Chapter Twenty-Four

Mother accepts the news with customary good grace and tells everyone what a bright, talented son she's raised, hinting I couldn't have done it without her. Dad's ecstatic, though Mother's not amused by him and Jessie dancing an Irish jig around the kitchen. We're under siege, with friends dropping in to congratulate me.

Dr Mason declares I'm fit while pacifying Mother I'm capable enough to handle the stress and as safe in Dartmouth as at Yardley. All forms are now completed, and I wait impatiently for confirmation. This final document gives me the chance to withdraw my application. Fat chance!

Ignoring Mother's protests, Mrs Barrett's throwing a party for me. "It might be the last one until the war is over."

"I won't be her little bot anymore?"

"Don't be silly. You'll always be Peter Pan trying to fly. Now's the time to test your wings," Mrs Barrett says.

"Try telling my mother. She wants to keep me chained up."

"She loves you dearly but is worried. She's lost two sons, and Fred will be off soon. You're all she has left," Mrs Barrett retorts, wagging a finger sternly.

I idolise this lady, and Jack's absence must hurt without me grumbling, but does Mother still have a card to play?

She's quiet lately, which I mention to Fred, who says, "Let sleeping dogs lie."

Dad's more forthright and states, "When a woman isn't speaking to you, she's trying to tell you something."

She's good at spinning my wheels, and I'm a sucker for a sob story. Everybody teases me for my softness, but is the Iron Lady suffering in silence?

"Dad needs you right away, if not sooner," Anita says. "Someone's exhaust has fallen off his van."

"Well, blow me! No rest for the wicked," I say, ambling back to the garage.

SAM ARRIVES WITH ANOTHER PACKAGE, and I spend the morning reading. There's more to joining the navy than I imagined. Uniforms are provided, also food, although there's a system for purchasing extras. Living outside college means paying for that privilege. Obviously, if you're a rich kid you can have your cake and eat it too. Money's the main stumbling block, which Mother will be on like a whippet after a hare, but there's something Mother doesn't know, which I'll keep under wraps until I've blown out the candles on my cake. Advice from the Barretts will help me decide when to break the news.

They've kept the occasion low key, with only family and friends invited, one notable absentee being Great-Aunt Eleanor who, though not close friends, might have proved a valuable ally to Mother. What's not to love about my fellow conspirators?

My gurus arrive in Dr Gregory's Rolls-Bentley. It's dark grey, matching his suit and tie. "If you've got it, flaunt it," as the saying goes.

Granny Ramsey's cool and cuddly in cashmere. Billy, rotund and rosy-cheeked, looks comfortable in a Harris tweed jacket and cord pants, while Miss Talbot stops the traffic clad in a full-length scarlet evening dress. She's shed a bit of cargo and scrubs up well too. Politely, I escort and introduce them to my family, where Fred's besotted by "Trim-line" (my new tag for Tatty) despite the daggers being thrown by Irene. You shouldn't fall in love if you can't take a joke.

Mr Barrett calls for order. "It's our pleasure and privilege to host this party for Eddie for his birthday and for qualifying for the Royal Naval College. Both he and his teachers have experienced a hard year's work, especially his tutors, who've had to put up with his tantrums, too."

There's loud applause and much laughter. It's nice to have friends!

Mr Barrett continues, "However, there's lots of red tape and form filling required prior to him setting sail. Eddie feels he owes us the courtesy of discussing these matters and seeking our opinions before signing on the dotted line."

Good man! Couldn't have said it better myself.

"It's difficult to discuss something of which we've no knowledge," Mother argues. "We need to study the details first, and that could take all night."

"Thank you, Dolly, exactly what I told Eddie when he called. So I've had a dozen copies printed. We'll study them while we socialise."

My friends have a plan. Mr Barrett can always charm Mother, and she'll use this time to recruit help. I admire her tenacity. She works the room like a pro: sorting wheat from the chaff, heckling Dr Gregory for ten minutes before he flees for the bathroom. Billy, regarded by Mother as a peasant, is ignored, and my two female teachers become her prey. There's lots of pleasantry, but this pair is naturally polite and not fooled by good manners. Eventually, Mother traps Mr Barrett in a corner and switches to her seductive mode. He plays his part to perfection, and though Mrs Barrett and I are amused, Anita can't fathom what's so funny.

Having run out of partners, Mother's conspicuous by her absence. Everybody's into their third drink and patiently waiting. Anita tells us that Mother's on the front porch studying her printout. She's had time to read War and Peace by now.

Eventually returning, Mother asks, "Waiting for me?"

"Not really," Billy replies. "We've been enjoying the serenity."

Her glare would make a brass monkey shiver. His grin is reassuring. It's nice to have this grizzled old warhorse watching my back.

I've rehearsed my lines and begin by thanking everyone for gifts, especially the cash. This last remark brings polite smiles and a twitch to Mother's lips. Naturally, I extend my gratitude to everyone who's gone that extra mile for me, particularly my parents, whose electricity bill must be horrendous, and finishing on a serious note, plead that these official documents are confusing and welcome any advice. Sitting down to warm applause, I keep a wary eye on the wily old fox, though my mother seems relaxed, sipping her margarita. She's probably testing the water before dipping in her toe.

Dr Gregory thanks the hosts and helpers for their hospitality, excellent fare and due diligence, before launching into his official mode. "It's been a privilege both for my colleagues and I to have assisted in Eddie's success, which is a fine achievement. The examination's similar to the entrance course for university, and though no genius, this young man does possess a unique gift and something we rarely witness." The Head pauses, waiting for everybody's attention.

Mother's ecstatic. The doc's words have tweaked her radar. She opens her mouth, but the wise old owl recovers smartly.

"Eddie has the ability to read, retain, and recall vast amounts of information. He has a remarkable memory. Initially, we were cautious, then amazed and excited. Selfishly, we'd love to help him reach his full potential, but I digress. Our friend seeks advice and has a difficult decision to make. Whichever path he chooses, there'll be financial boulders. My colleagues and I were not born with silver spoons in our mouths and struggled to realise our dreams. Believe me, it's well worth the effort, whatever the cost," the headmaster concludes.

Word games are Mother's forte. She's a hardened trouper and gallops into the fray boldly. "Albert and I are proud of our son. He's worked hard and deserves this chance. I concur with Dr Gregory's statement that Edward could achieve his goal, financially and emotionally, by staying at school and thus to university."

Avoiding the doc's final sentence, Mother hasn't finished. "One salient point which hasn't arisen amid the excitement is his age. He's still an adolescent and could change his mind more often than his socks. I've read the small print. He has to enrol for five years and take seven exams. One failure and he's finished. No reward for all that hard work, and good money down the drain."

Mrs Barrett enters the ring. "Eddie's a smart young man, not a child, and has been saving hard for the past year. Jack and I would be willing to help out too."

"I don't need your therapy or charity," Mother snaps. "No doubt, it was your son who first put this stupid idea into my boy's head."

Fred's ahead of me. "That's a wicked thing to say. Eddie's always wanted to join the navy." He turns to Dad. "You going to sit there dumb as usual, while *she* wrecks his life?"

She glares at dad, who smilingly says, "Not this time, lad, but it's difficult to be heard when you two start arguing. *Eddie's* got my backing on this one."

There's wholesale approval around the room and anxious glances at Mother.

Her reaction's puzzling. We're not sure if it's shock or pride. The deadpan face and silence reveal nothing. She retires to a corner seat, a drink in one hand, forms in the other, still searching for a loophole.

All the guests have left by the time we've finished the paperwork, except the last page, which requires signatures.

"Dolly, we need your presence please," Mr Barrett calls.

"Thought you didn't require any help," Mother sneers, trolling across the carpet.

"It was a struggle, but we managed," Mrs Barrett says, returning the sarcasm. "Now we require your signature."

Picking up the paper, Mother studies it closely. Teetering on the brink, she's still putting on the style.

"Everything's correct, Dolly. Dr Gregory and Miss Ramsey kindly agreed to act as witnesses, authenticating its accuracy," Mr Barrett says.

"My boy should be honoured having such notable people vouch for his integrity. However, you've overlooked one small item. I'm his mother and legal guardian. He deserves a university education, which would be money well spent, not wasted in tying knots and paddling about in boats."

"I don't give a damn about wealth but do care about my boy. He can't stay tied to your apron strings forever, Dolly. Let Eddie go before you suffocate him. You'll not lose your son. He'll be back, I'll guarantee it," Dad responds.

They profess to care for me yet are fighting like alley cats. It's sickening, and I feel like a blind man on a galloping horse. How can mutual love bring such pain?

Mrs Barrett breaks the deadlock. "Will you two stop snarling at each other? We have to settle this for everyone's sake. Please be sensible and sign, Dolly."

I know exactly what Mother's going to say.

"Not until Hell freezes over."

I hope the good Lord can forgive her. I'm not sure about me.

Chapter Twenty-Five

Everyone's waiting for the aftershock following the earthquake, expecting me to have a screaming fit. Instead, I leave as my parents argue. Anita and Silver are at my heels. Rocking in the hammock, we gaze into God's starlit Heaven. I shush Anita when she calls Mother mean, saying grown-ups act strange in the name of love. She apologises, kissing my cheek, as Silver licks my hand.

I spend the next week alone. There's no sense getting mad, though getting even may help. Mother has won the battle, but not the war. I'm polite yet quiet, speaking only when addressed. She treats me like a baby. So be it. I'm no longer asked to do chores. Maybe because I dropped a few plates and let the toast burn? You can't trust a child with such tasks. It's a nice life, but bloody frustrating. Plans to punish Mother have failed. She doesn't give a damn.

God is good, along comes Kenny. He's a wild one and spent time in a few remand homes. His mom has a nice smile, lots of grey hair, and says she's a widow though Kenny reckons Daddy did a runner when he was little.

Kenny's mom tells me, "You're what Kenny needs. He doesn't have any pals. The kids tease him because he hasn't a father. He respects you like a big brother."

He's younger than me but six inches taller. God has a strange sense of humour.

Mother's succumbed to Kenny's natural charm and invites him to dinner often, maybe to please me, or just sorry for this fatherless boy. We hook up at Cadets. He hates taking orders. I straighten him out. We're buddies now. My fun-filled life comes to a screeching halt when arriving at the Barretts' house and finding sour faces. There's evidence of excessive brutality being used at POW camps in Southeast Asia. The Japanese do not acknowledge the Geneva Conventions, and all prisoners have to work. Harsh beatings and torture are a daily ritual, with many soldiers and civilians dying. Malnutrition, malaria and disease are rampant. Medical treatment's inadequate, and food parcels are looted. No wonder my friends are brooding. Levity is needed.

"A funny thing happened today on the bus. A woman had her eye on a seat, but a man sat on it," I say. Not a titter. "Little boy brings his report home, his ma asks, 'What are these zeroes?' Boy says, 'They're not zeroes. Teacher ran out of stars, so she gave me moons instead.'" Not a snigger. "How do you make a Maltese Cross? Give up? You stick a lighted match down his shirt." Don't worry, I'll wear them down. "This is harder than rearranging deck chairs on the *Titanic*. You three are a miserable pair, if there ever was one," I say.

Mrs Barrett and Anita snigger, while Mr Barrett shakes his head. "Go and put the kettle on, idiot. Let's have a cup of tea."

"Jack's a strong lad. He's more muscles than I've had hot dinners. Anyhow, we're pushing the Japs back in Burma, and if he's not home by Christmas, I'll fetch him myself," I brag.

"You're too young to go without Dolly's permission," Mr Barrett says.

"Captain Todd's told me if I sign on for twelve years, I can join up now."

"True, but you can't go to sea before you're eighteen. They changed the rules after the *Prince of Wales* and *Repulse* were sunk with those boys aboard."

"I think Eddie's very brave, wanting to go and find my brother."

"So he is, precious, and when Eddie's old enough, we'll send him to bring Jack home. How does that sound?" Mrs Barrett responds.

I often wonder if life will ever be normal again. The wound between Mrs Barrett and Mother hasn't healed, though Dad and Mr Barrett are still friends; the ladies are stubborn and prideful. I've learnt much from Kenny during the past year. There are no penny candles in this boy's house. He has a smile to light up Wembley Stadium. Although not book-smart, he's streetwise. I've been cosseted and protected, while he's been battered and peed on most of his life. Leaving school at fourteen, he works five and a half days in a factory and three nights serving fish and chips so that his mum can stay home. He gives her most of his wages, and they idolise each other.

Strangely, he's never short of cash. I know Kenny's no altar boy but don't ask questions. True friendship has no borders.

My lifestyle's changed dramatically, which doesn't bother me, though it concerns teachers. I'm not surprised when summoned to the Great One's study.

"There you are, Roberts," sets a grim note. A dozen files sit by his elbow. "The GCEs are here, and we've to determine which pupils are competent to take the exams. Your marks are atrocious, and you've no interest. Many adjudicators think you're unworthy of this opportunity. What say you?"

My heart sinks into my boots. The key to success is the General Certificate of Education, and thanks to Anita's sharp ears, we know Mother's plans. I'd gone running scared to Dad, who, still in the doghouse from the last quarrel, comes up with a solution, which he insists is foolproof.

It's grovel time. Without the Head's blessing, I'm dead. Let's hope the humble pie I'm about to eat doesn't choke me. "I apologise, sir, for my lack of enthusiasm. After my mother's treachery, when I'd worked so hard, I thought, what's the point? Let's live a little as most boys my age do. Come GCE time, with a little revision, I'll be home and dry. Never imagined with my track record I'd be banned."

Not the wisest words. The doc pounces before I've time to extract foot from mouth. "For a smart youth, you're incredibly dim. There are no free lunches. Life isn't fair, and you're not entitled to anything. Just give me one good reason why I should plead your case."

I feel bad upsetting him. He's still willing to support me and champions winners not whiners, plus it provides a perfect opening. "Actually, I've a job offer. The prerequisite being a good result in the GCE, and I know I can succeed if given the chance."

"Why didn't you say without pussyfooting around? Miss Ramsey will be overjoyed. Such enterprise shall bring forth just rewards," the headmaster trumpets. Then frowning, asks, "Might one enquire what your mother thinks of this scheme?"

"We haven't mentioned it. She's abandoned the university idea for a more elaborate plan, which we accidentally overheard. Dad decided to strike first, saying once I've passed the exams and have a job, there's nothing Mother can do."

"Just so, but your mother thwarted would be an awesome sight."

"Then again, it will stop my parents bickering over my future."

"You're not so green as cabbage-looking are you, lad? Be gone, I've work to do and so have you," Dr Gregory snorts.

Slogging back to class, I listen to Pete and Jimmy brag about enlisting for the navy. They've altered their birth certificates by one year and reckon by the time school's out will be on their way to training camp.

I pay strict attention during an intensive French lesson with Trim-line, who is both puzzled and pleased. My momma didn't raise a fool!

I arrive home to see Elsie's Morris Minor sitting on the drive. The Grand Diva's here, and I'll bet my boots it isn't a social call.

"Look who's come to see you, Edward," Mother greets me.

Whoopee! I think, forcing a polite smile.

Great-Aunt swoops, arms outstretched, still thinking I'm a child. I put up a hasty hand, not wishing to be engulfed by chubby arms and drowning in jasmine perfume. We touch fingers gently as Mother steps in to avoid any further embarrassment.

"Let's have a cup of tea and your favourite scones, darling. Great-Aunt Eleanor has some exciting news."

She's taking a world cruise by canoe? I should be so lucky. Slowly buttering my scone, I wait for the first shot across my bow.

Dabbing crumbs from her pillbox red lips, Auntie says, "I was talking about you yesterday to Antonio Fattorini."

Acting dim, which comes easy, I ask, "Is that the greasy wop who owns the ice cream parlour at the bottom of the Bull Ring?"

"Silly boy, he was a famous operatic tenor and is now a singing coach. We often performed together on the concert circuit."

I'm way ahead of you, dear, I think and settle back, awaiting the next salvo.

Mother can't resist running her colours up the mast. "You've the potential to be a great singer, and Mr Fattorini's agreed to coach you. You'd become rich and famous, plus doing what you love most."

It's true, singing is my great pleasure, but I've no wish to stand before a bunch of starched shirts and glittering tiaras, sounding like Figaro in a fit. While these viragos have been plotting, Dad's scheme has taken shape. This is the moment for which he's patiently coached me.

Bringing the big guns into action, I say, "Sorry, but I must decline your generous offer. I've booked another engagement."

My broadside has scuttled them, but Mother's great failing is not knowing when to abandon ship.

"Don't be stupid boy, you're still at school and too young to work."

"Just so, the Employment Bureau collaborates with school for applicants once the exams are completed."

Fuming, Mother demands, "Why wasn't I consulted?"

"It's called initiative. The student takes full responsibility for their actions."

"You don't know your own mind," Mother scoffs. "Do parents have any say?"

"If you think it necessary, Mother, I suppose it could be arranged."

"Good! Believe me, someone's going to get the rough edge of my tongue."

Keeping a straight face is difficult. It's easier than taking candy from a baby. My work is done. Leaving the witches stirring the cauldron and concocting evil spells, I hop on my bike and peddle to the George, where dad's enjoying a tipple after a tough day.

Chuckling at my news, he says, "They can stew awhile longer," and orders another glass of Dutch courage.

We stroll home in the evening sunshine. The Green Machine's still here. I tug dad's sleeve. "Don't panic. Your mother's desperate and needing Elsie's support. Just stay quiet, and I'll do the talking."

Auntie and nephew-in-law exchange brief nods. They're not close.

Stiff-backed, Mother's poised for battle. "Glad you're home early. Some idiot's filled Edward's head with stupidity."

"That's me," Dad says. "I heard you were hatching another plot. He doesn't trust you and asked my advice. I told him there was a vacancy on the sports desk, but he did all the groundwork. I'm content to watch his back to see he's not blindsided. Journalism's a good calling, though the salary's poor until you've learned the business. To supplement his pay, we've a contingency plan in place." Dad's final touch is exquisite. Pick the bones out of that, Mother!

Elsie's hammering her chubby fist on the table. "Back up, Albert, I've missed something. You're saying Dolly never told anyone?"

"Not a dicky bird. We found out by accident."

Mother finds her tongue. "Your reward for eavesdropping."

Great-Aunt's on her in a flash. "That doesn't excuse your behaviour, and using me in your cunning scheme is unforgivable. I'm here in a professional capacity to advise my great-nephew on his chosen career path, which I now know is untrue. I'm ashamed of you, Dolly."

I listen, dumbfounded. I've always figured Elsie as a pompous old windbag, whereas she's a heart as big as her bosom. I've not been paying attention.

She's not through yet. "You needn't smirk, Albert, you're no hero. Why don't you pair stop kicking lumps out of each other and realise your son isn't a wind-up toy but needs love and happiness? It might put your own selfish whims to rest."

Sincere words spoken from the heart are to the listener food for thought, and Elsie's offering a feast for my parents to sample, with no extra garnishing required. They sit quietly, digesting every syllable and smiling across the table.

The silence stretches, and the room's filled with rare serenity. It's lovely to watch them swallow their pride, but I wish they'd hurry it along. I'm bloody starving!

Chapter Twenty-Six

It's taken three weeks for the dust to settle. I'm beginning to think Mother's taken a vow of silence. She's subdued, and Dad's polite. The thaw sets in when presenting her with my school report. I'm amused, seeing the drama queen back in action. She's seated in a Windsor chair with Queen Anne legs—the chair's, not Mother's—as she scans the pages. Time spent watching her isn't wasted. Every raised eyebrow, frown, and smile are giveaways. She keeps me waiting while playing cat and mouse. The voice is cold, her eyes warmer. "You've managed to scrape through, then."

"I've had lots of practice."

"Don't be grouchy, I'm only teasing. You have excellent marks. The Head's suggesting you stay at school, confident you could pass for university."

Masking a smile, I shake my head. The doc's a born diplomat, and you have to admire Mother's determination. Nevertheless, in two years I expect to be in Asia, hacking my way through the jungle looking for Jack. Life will be more peaceful, now Mother has her bragging rights back, and it's nice to see Dad off the hook, although he's not fazed by the silent treatment.

"It was like being on a sabbatical. A man has to do what a man has to do," he says, settling into his chair with a single-malt whiskey and stoking up his pipe. He's managed to calm Mother's fear of me being ravished by lonely women who frequent the dance halls while their menfolk are fighting for their country. Having me sing with a local band to boost my income was a master stroke. Bob Hayworth, the band leader and family friend, acts as chaperone. I'm not allowed to fraternise. Yet Kenny has freedom to roam the dance hall; being friendly with the resident vocalist pays dividends. Kenny's big, handsome, and popular with the ladies, especially married middle-aged women. He'll be dead in ten years at the rate he's going, much sooner if a husband arrives home unexpectedly.

Despite Bob's eagle eye, occasionally some lonely local lass will offer to take me outside. I refuse politely, never sure if she fancies me or wishes to punch out my lights because she hates the voice. Refusing to continue education, I take the job at Dad's office working for the sports editor. Initially, Mother's displeased but simmers down as I hand her my wages to assist with the housekeeping.

Dad books another gig for Fridays. I now entertain three nights a week. We'd only meant to outsmart Mother, now I'm committed to my calling and Dad's keen to see me succeed.

Living in the fast lane has affected Mother too, who now manages a wine bar and restaurant in Birmingham. The arrival of American GIs with money to burn and lonesome females eager to help creates a hectic nightlife. Mother leaves home at noon and returns around midnight. Her world has completely changed. She dresses and acts ten years younger. The Yanks adore their blueblood hostess. The lady has found her niche and a thousand sons. Be patient and God will supply your needs.

Mother's happy. So is Dad, who's away most weekends on Home Guard exercises, the main one raising his elbow. If enemy paratroopers land, they'll be overwhelmed by alcoholic fumes. Kenny and I meet up at Cadets on Saturday afternoon and then the dance hall. Later, he goes into Birmingham to boogie with one of his squeezes then calls at the bodega to escort Mother home.

God wraps His presents in strange packages.

Dad says it will take two years to conquer the Germans and the Japanese. The longer it lasts, the more Jack's in danger. I'm determined to find him, and even if unable to affect a rescue singlehanded, must do something to shorten this nightmare.

I've searched everywhere for my birth certificate. Perhaps they're right. I'm a kid. Anita's dad says I look too young for a library card, and instantly there's a ticking inside my skull. Something's nudged the brain into gear. I'm in the study, which I've searched thoroughly: the huge roll-top desk, magazine racks, and table drawers, even checked out Mother's huge collection of romance novels. We've more books than the Central Library, and that's the key word! It's where you go for information to find stuff. There's a full set of *Encyclopedia Britannica* from *A* to *Z* lining the top shelf. It's a classic filing system. I adore Mother's tidy mind. Inside Volume C is a large envelope containing every certificate from birth to death, including my GCE. Bless her little cotton socks!

Yet, as Granddad says, "When one door closes, another one hits you in the head." My certificate is here, all shiny and new. Too new! The original went off to Dartmouth, with Mother buying a copy in longhand and impossible to fake. My language is ungodly as I shuffle papers back into the envelope. A tattered, creased paper catches my eye. Unfolding it gingerly, I spot my brother's name. Studying both certificates, I figure Frederick and Edward not too big a stretch, except his name's on record and mine could come back to haunt me. Cunning is required, also a new Christian name, and right away up pops Billy to help me. Changing Frederick to Edrick is simple, even better, Edrich. The old boy's always raving about Edrich the cricketer. Turn *F* into *E*, blend it into the *R*, thicken the *D*, and the rest is easy.

I always reckon it's better to speak a half-truth than tell a complete lie and spend the next hour forging my masterpiece and ageing it by rubbing it in the gravel. Despite the sun's warmth, a shiver runs down my spine while stuffing the altered document inside my sock.

Jimmy and Pete have put me wise about enlisting. "Answer all questions, fill in the forms correctly, don't shave for three days, and you might fool them."

They're halfway through training, and in three months' time will be sailing the ocean, up to their ears in U-boats. Meanwhile, I'll be in deep water if I dally. The workers will soon be home howling for their chow.

Peeling spuds, I begin singing "All the nice girls love a sailor," and stop, waiting for Kenny's line, "And some naughty ones too."

Stupid! He's not here. I'll miss him and his lovely mum. It's no coincidence that they came into my life. God doesn't make mistakes. He allows everybody to smell the roses, and you've permission to pick them too. Pay close attention and the thorns can be avoided. His beautiful garden is full of wonderful flowers, though the ugliest weeds are encouraged to flourish too.

Chapter Twenty-Seven

My journalistic career so far has consisted of fetching tea and doughnuts for the sports editor, plus delivering messages; once more I'm a bonded slave. Despite my lowly rank, there's never a moment to relax. I've scarcely time to nip into the washroom to check out my comic. I'm one lamb in a field full of Border collies.

Dad's assistance is required, but can I trust him? We're halfway to town before I open up. "Need a favour, Dad."

He folds his newspaper. "Fire away, thought you'd never ask."

"You knew I'd something on my mind?"

"You've been like a cat on hot bricks for days."

"We can't tell anybody."

"Especially she who must be obeyed. How can I help?"

"Time off work. Could you square it with Crawford?"

"Gladly, and I'm pleased. My lips are sealed, and the best of luck, which you will need with Her Ladyship."

Two days later, with a dental appointment engineered by Dad and the forgery burning a hole in my pocket, I'm sitting in a café opposite the YMCA murdering a bacon-and-egg sandwich, waiting for the doors to open. Acting casual, though my heart's banging like a drum, I stroll across the cobblestones and, once inside, follow the arrows on the wall.

"May I help you?" a big man asks. He's a friendly, ruddy face and glitters with gold badges. A prime example of Royal Navy discipline and every recruit's nightmare; the Devil's Disciple aka chief gunner's mate. But don't be fooled by the bonhomie. He'll chew you up and spit you out as nails. Much one learns at Mother's knee. In this case the Cadets.

"I'm here to enlist, Chief."

His smile turns to laughter. "Thought you'd brought your dad's lunch.

They get younger every day," he says, looking at the wren sitting next to him.

They've done this patter many times. It relieves the boredom I suppose. I await the next question.

"Why choose the Royal Navy, lad?

"Because it's the senior service, and I want to see the world."

His grin spreads. "You certainly will. Fill in these forms, we'll process them, get the doc to check if you're warm, and before you can say 'Up Spirits,' we'll have you in the crow's nest looking for Krauts."

Everything's straightforward, and sticking mainly to the truth, I state that I left school at sixteen and have four years' experience as a mechanic. I'm sure Mr Barrett won't fail me if push comes to shove.

There's no gold star, though the wren rewards me with a dazzling smile, and I spend the next hour waiting for a medical, which I pass, and a lengthy interview with the assessment officer, who's impressed with my knowledge of engines and hobbies. Guns and his pretty stooge congratulate me, and I've wings on my heels cruising back to work.

Dad's on his regular stool in the Windsor, laying the dust. "Crafty sod, they must be blind thinking you're almost twenty but just keep quiet until the papers arrive, and too late for interference."

"Do you imagine Mother will try to stop me?"

"She'll not be happy. Let her think you're lying, not a forger. That's our ace."

Behind Dad's calm, grey eyes lurks a cunning mind. He and Kenny make an ideal couple of henchmen. I spend the next three weeks in What-if Land. Sam is struck by lightning? The post office burns down? Mother kills herself? And the coup de grâce, peace is declared, and my application's cancelled! The only tunic I'll be wearing will have buckles up the back. Meanwhile, Dad looks prepared to walk on water. I'm surprised Mother hasn't noticed, though she's happy also. Perhaps they're late bloomers and intend to enjoy some sunshine before the storm clouds gather.

We accost Sam on our way to the bus. "Stand and deliver," Dad orders.

Never bonny before lunch, he grinds to a halt. "You're interfering with His Majesty's Mail. My sworn duty is to see all letters and packages reach their prescribed addresses."

Wrong answer, Dad's not smiling. "All you'll see is grapes from your wife at the hospital, where you will be in traction if I don't get my mail."

I've never thought our postman religious, but he's a devout coward. "Help yourself, Albert, no problem. It's probably the Admiralty one you want."

Plucking the official envelope from the bundle, Dad hands it to me, shoving the rest into Sam's fat fist. "On your way, Cowboy," he says, slapping the postman's backside and gives him a push-start.

The letter keeps us occupied all the way into town. Every scrap of information is here. I've to report at the Y at 0900 hours, Friday, 3 September 1943. There's a railway warrant to Skegness, then to *HMS Royal Arthur* for initial training.

"We haven't much time, but tomorrow's ideal. It's your mother's day off. I'll invite the Barretts—Fred and Irene too."

"Who are you kidding, Dad? You've been working on this for ages. It's a crafty move, all singing from the same hymn sheet."

"No one knows, except you and I. There's safety in numbers. Look surprised when the Barretts arrive."

"Thanks, I'm proud you're my dad."

"Me too. Who else would tolerate you without going insane?"

Dropping off the bus, Dad troops into his office, and I head to the canteen for tea and doughnuts. Two more days and Crawford will have to find another skivvy.

Tuesday is family day, and Mother takes over. There's always a sumptuous meal ready and waiting. Tonight's no exception, and we're clearing up when the bell tolls. Fred, who hates drying dishes, answers the call and returns with our friends.

"Haven't seen you for a while. Thought Dolly might have been kidnapped by a rich Yank."

"I should be so lucky," my parents say in harmony and burst out laughing.

Good one, Mr Barrett. He always knows which buttons to push.

Dad's happily dispensing drinks while Mother prepares hors-d'oeuvres. The log fire's crackling brightly, old buddies are chatting again, and the room's cosy. I've a nervous eye on Dad, waiting for a signal. Excusing myself, I stop at the hall closet, take the envelope from the jacket, and slip it inside my shirt. I'm tired of pretending and eager to get it sorted. Edrich Roberts isn't a sixteen-year-old kid anymore, he's a mature young man. I'm motionless in front of the fire ages before being noticed. Bob Hayworth has taught me well: "Make your presence felt. Capture your audience. The first impression counts."

Taking a deep breath, I leap off the precipice. "Glad we're together tonight, as I've some important news. My papers have come to join the navy, with orders to report next Thursday."

Everyone expresses surprise except Mother, who's frozen in time and space, hands clenched tightly in her lap. Their merry mood fades, with their attention focused on Mother. They know she'll not quit quietly, and my gut tells me it's too early for a victory lap.

She returns to Earth ready to play ball, not with my head, I hope. Her smile tells me there's a game plan. My cards are on the table. Is she going to scoop the pot? The dream's becoming a nightmare, and she hasn't opened her mouth yet. We're on the edge of our seats, while Mother's playing mind games and keeping us on tenterhooks.

Breaking the deadlock, she says, "Frederick, dear boy, I need your advice. Would you inspect that document and verify its validity? Or is my son playing a cruel joke?"

Mother knows her progeny well. Fred is the last Boy Scout and couldn't lie to save his life. He also adores the limelight and scans the form as though it's the Holy Grail. If he notices the name change, my cover's blown, and Mother will be heartbroken knowing there's a felon in the family. Dad's already at the drinks cabinet pouring himself a stiff one.

Fred is about to deliver his verdict. "I'm positive it's genuine. Sadly, I've never made the grade, but Eddie's going to make us all proud of him."

Talk of fifteen minutes of fame. My brother's answered the question superbly. He's told the absolute truth and pronounced the document official, though he studied the railway warrant minutely.

Mother's not ready to surrender. "Isn't there a law to prevent a young boy from volunteering?"

"I'm afraid not, Mother. Once a youth is sixteen he can sign for eight or twelve years, classified boy seaman, but not allowed to go to sea before he's eighteen. The war will be long finished."

Every word Fred has spoken is gospel. I'm sure he spotted the name change and the status: H/O (hostilities only), but that wasn't the question.

I've bent the rules, and Mother knows, but I'll bet the farm she'll not disgrace the family name by challenging me in front of guests. Nevertheless, she gives me notice. "He won't be put in irons then?"

"No, princess, he won't be in trouble, though he might bring a couple of medals back," Fred says, kissing her forehead.

He's played his part nobly, and Mother revels in the attention. It's a smart move, switching the focus away from my impending departure. Mother's mistress of all she surveys and everyone's smiling. It's doubtful if I've her blessing, but she's called a truce. Maybe rubbing shoulders with those doughboys thousands of miles from home has influenced her outlook.

Thankfully, the household is back to normal, but let's not go overboard!

Chapter Twenty-Eight

Running away with the circus would have been easier. Everybody's wishing me well and pressing money into my palm. I know how Judas felt walking away with a handful of silver and nary a backward glance.

My joy fades in dawn's early light. I'm a raw recruit in His Majesty's Royal Navy, en route to England's east coast. We've assembled at 0900 hours, and an ancient medalled officer checks our names. He hands a package to the eldest looking victim and instructs us to catch the 1015 train to Lincoln, where we'll be met and chaperoned for the rest of the journey. Anyone changing their mind will be classified a deserter and could be shot, which is a novel start to the day. We all make it without mishap. Looking for a friendly face, I spot one. He's a few months older than me but too young for service. We shared the same desk at junior school before going our separate ways. Les Carter took the poor kid's route to senior elementary, while I travelled the yellow brick road and grammar school system.

We spend the trip in the corridor reminiscing. There's a card school going in a carriage filled with smoke. I'll need oxygen before making base. We've a two-hour wait for the local train in arctic conditions before staggering into the arms of a petty officer at Skegness station.

"Come on, my lucky lads. Form up in two ranks." He says, taking the papers from the old guy. "Don't salute me and get in line with the rest. A brisk walk is the order of the day. By the left, quick march! Left, right, left, right, swing those arms, let's see some swank. You're in the senior service now."

HMS Royal Arthur's a shore base, known as a stone frigate. Pre-war, it was a holiday camp. A brief stay here could break the bravest heart, with the fierce Siberian winds blowing in from the North Sea. The Officer of the

Day looks us over. He's underwhelmed. Half the squad are turned thirty and wheezing away like pensioners after walking from the station.

"Chief, get this rabble to the mess hall, they look ready to keel over. We must really be scraping the bottom of the barrel."

"Stir your stumps, you dozy bunch! Let's get some victuals inside your bellies. Pick them up. Your feet, not your bellies."

The mess is the size of a carrier's flight deck and full of scrubbed wooden tables and matching benches to seat thirty bums each. Supplied with cutlery and plates, we march down the hall to be served by the wannabe cooks. The food's not special but it's hot, tasty, and there's plenty. We've designated seating, but still subject to rude remarks from the old salts who've been in uniform a couple of weeks. Ignoring them, I concentrate on eating. Tomorrow's another day, except this one's not finished.

The chief's back shouting the odds. "Chop chop! Get the lead out. Your nursemaid's waiting."

We hustle out. It's starting to rain again. There are two dozen unhappy young men standing in line, waiting. Pacing back and forth is a sinewy, hatchet-faced man with a sour expression and a chest covered in medal ribbons.

"About time," he greets us. "Fall in and follow me. We've miles to go before we sleep."

Despite his lack of charisma, I like him. Anyone who loves poetry can't be all bad, and we're certainly on the road less travelled.

He's not kidding. "You'll be glad to get your heads down tonight after the doctor, dentist, and barber have done you over, plus being stabbed in the arm three times. You'll rise at oh-five-thirty hours. Breakfast is from oh-six-hundreed hours. Make sure you're washed, shaved, bright as new pennies, and assembled on the parade ground by oh-seven-fifty-five, where I will meet and greet you and attempt to turn you into sailors."

Due to the Sea Cadets, I'm familiar with the Kings Rules and Regulations. Nevertheless, the wooden shack with two double-deck iron bunks is a culture shock. Nor do the one-inch mattress and two harsh grey blankets inspire me to rest. A rolled-up towel will have to pass for a pillow.

THERE'S A BUGLE IN THE DISTANCE. The Apaches are attacking. I sit up and crash my skull against the top bunk. A voice from above questions my heritage, and the quartermaster's beating a tattoo on the door, imploring us to "Rise and shine, the morning's fine!"

How the hell does he know? It's still dark. There are words to make a stevedore blush as we tumble from bunks into Arctic surroundings. Standing here in navy-issue long johns, with crotches closer to our knees than scrotums does not make a pretty sight. Under the muted lighting from the single sixty-watt bulb hanging from the ceiling, we'd terrify children. You have to laugh, or you'd smash your head against the wall. The wash station is fifty yards away. We need coats, socks, and boots for the trip. The place is packed solid. A Moroccan kasbah is calmer in comparison. It's a long wait for basin and mirror. The name of the game is ruthlessness. We make the breakfast queue by 0630 hours. We sit down at 0700 hours, then hustle to get dressed. I've a head start, having done it before. I show my roommates how to tie bows and position lanyards. Already, they owe me. The morning parade's nothing new, though there are more officers with scrambled egg on their caps. The rest is the usual bull.

The trainees are formed into squads, and instructors appointed to each one.

Les and I are in B squad and draw Hatchet Face.

He's all business. "My name's Brian Nevett. I'm your drillmaster. The anchor on my arm stands for Leading Seaman. That's how you'll address me. Not Sir, Mr Nevett, nor Brian, or I'll have your guts for garters. You'll not salute me, and there's no talking in the ranks. You speak at my discretion or if addressed by a superior officer, which includes the wardroom cat." His mouth creases into a grin. "Discipline's the name of the game. I'm a hard man, but fair. Be warned! I've no time for comics. Play ball with me, I'll play ball with you. Cross me, and you'll rue the day you joined the Andrew. Understand?"

"Yes, Leading Seaman Nevett," we mumble.

"I said do you understand?" he shouts.

"Yes, Leading Seaman!" we chorus, our voices echoing across the square.

For the next two and a half hours, he puts us through the wringer. Short breaks from the physical are spent watching other squads. LS Nevett leads by example and makes it look easy, though he's probably a grandfather.

There is lots of grumbling, which LS Nevett takes in stride. "You shouldn't have joined if you can't take a joke."

After dinner, we're afforded make and mend time, which involves the issue of dog tags, pay books, cigarettes, and tobacco, plus beer tickets.

Priority is marking every item of kit. Anything lost, stolen, or strayed has to be replaced out of our own pocket. I was surrounded by thousands, yet alone. Survival's the key word. Jack Barrett was more than a friend. He taught me the ropes. I've always been a good listener. Coupled with Kenny teaching me how to make a fast buck, how can I fail? For six months, I've to exist on six shillings and sixpence a day, the same as all recruits. Wrong! The majority smoke and drink. I do neither. Some might call my scheme illegal, but we're dealt in beads and trinkets since time immortal. It's a fair trade. God knows.

After three weeks, B squad are brilliant. LS Nevett has bullied and blessed us nonstop. It's worked. We're ranked the best drill squad, and our glorious leader comes up with a bundle of beer tickets. Les and I jump for joy as the train leaves lovely Lincolnshire and heads for the Malvern Hills. We'll be only forty miles from Birmingham, and surely there's time to get home for a few hours. Gazing around, I realise I'm lucky. The majority won't see their families for another couple of months. Silently, I thank the Lord for His mercy and pray to Him for the well-being of my companions. So much for looking out for number one.

Chapter Twenty-Nine

W e've been wined and dined on the journey. The feast comprises a double sandwich of corned beef and cheese and is washed down with a bottle of water. New Street station hasn't changed much. However, this time I'm in company with four hundred rowdy sailors and a gang of naval police. More annoying, I'm a stone's throw from Dad, who'll be enjoying his lunchtime tipple at the Windsor.

There's lots of shouting and whistle-blowing as we tramp up the stone steps to the main bridge that spans all fourteen platforms. Civilians are swept aside by the wave of navy blue cutting through their midst, while the glass-domed roof echoes to the sound of a thousand marching boots. Outside waiting to whisk us away are a fleet of battleship-grey single-decker buses and a dozen trucks. Naval tradition dictates a head count, performed alphabetically. Once your name's called, you sling your kit onto a truck and climb aboard a bus. We're underway in less than thirty minutes. I'm one of the last to leave, and Les is long gone.

Turning to my companion, who's occupying two-thirds of the seat, I extend a hand. "My name's Eddie. Pleased to make your acquaintance."

He looks up, stares at my hand and back to the novel in his lap. Perhaps I should have made an appointment? A decision reached, he closes the book, *The Grapes of Wrath*, and places it on his knees. Obviously, he's well read and not half as dumb as he looks.

"Please forgive me," he says elegantly. "I was engrossed in reading." He extends a huge hand and shakes mine. "My name's Maurice."

"Are your parents fond of automobiles?"

He frowns. "I don't quite follow, old chap."

Surely this kid's yanking my chain. I go for broke. "Calling you Maurice."

Browsing, until the penny drops, his face broadens into a pleasant grin.

"That's extremely droll. Wish I had such swift repartee."

"You're mixing with the wrong people, Maurice."

"So true. I've never mixed with anyone. The original spoiled brat on whom my parents lavish all their love and care. The best schools, clothes, tennis lessons, and vacations. You name it, I've done it. They've my life planned from cradle to grave, even to marrying a wealthy neighbour's daughter."

He needs a sympathetic ear.

"It's hardly cricket, old boy. The final indignity occurred when Father appointed me manager in one of his companies. I sat behind a huge desk for a year slowly going mad. So, I've taken a quantum leap to discover the real world. And here I am."

"Poor little rich kid, but you couldn't have chosen a better place. We're all in the same boat."

"I've definitely jumped in the deep end. I might finish up the creek without a paddle." Maurice says, beaming at his comedic wit.

"There you go! You're already doing funnies. Remember what the Bard of Avon said: 'Never regard life with a jaundiced eye, for you'll not conquer immortality.'"

Maurice looks puzzled. "Did Shakespeare really write that? I don't recall it."

"I'm not sure, but it's possible. Maybe his quill was bent at the time."

My newfound friend's tittering like a schoolgirl. "You're a complete idiot. How do your parents tolerate you?"

"I'm not complete, just a work in progress. Anyway, they ran away when I was a child."

His hysterical laughter brings a sharp rebuke from the petty officer. "Stow it, you pair. You'll not find this navy funny much longer."

Lowering our voices, I discover beneath this young man's chest beats the heart of a small boy seeking freedom. I know the feeling well. By the time the bus reaches *HMS Duke*, we're practically blood brothers. Two hours later, drafting-in completed, we totter down a dim corridor to our dorms. Each room has four double bunks and lockers for each rating. It's not the Ritz but an improvement on Alcatraz. Everyone's whacked and after supper we collapse onto our bunks. Though from different backgrounds, we've one thing in common: we're bottom of the heap. The bilge rats command more respect than new recruits.

We're inspected and dissected, by the Officer of the Day, who looks bored to tears and our leader doesn't inspire confidence. It's said that beauty's only skin-deep. This brute's ugly to the bone. He nitpicks his way among us, staring into faces for future reference. He's a schoolyard bully who's never kicked the habit.

He wastes no time on pleasantries. "My name's Stone. I'm hard by name and nature. It's my job to turn you into sailors. Since you're the biggest shower I've ever seen, it's going to take a miracle."

Up yours too, trips lightly through my mind.

We learn he'll be our worst nightmare. Maybe we've broken our mothers' hearts but won't break his. I'm doubtful he had a mom, more likely hatched off a barn wall on a hot day. Stone is unperturbed, he's our undivided attention.

"Right, my lucky lads, playtime's over. Let's cast off. We've been swinging on this buoy way too long."

His manner and methods are predatory; fear and intimidation being his weapons of choice. The Seamanship course is tough enough without his medieval meddling. Limbs ache from marching, hands blistered from rowing a bloody thirty-two-foot boat across this huge lake, and shoulders bruised due to ancient Lee-Enfield rifles, plus the flag waving, Morse code, tying knots, and fire drills. Shore leave's banned. Even so, the nearest pub's three miles away, and we're too shagged to reach the front gate. Occasionally, we drop into the canteen, but mostly we write letters or do laundry.

We're a mixed bunch. Along with Les and me, there's another six in our dorm. Apart from Maurice, Jimmy from Rochdale has joined our elite group. Despite Maurice's high IQ and posh voice, the big lad has two left feet, and Stone torments him constantly. Jimmy, educated in the school of hard knocks, suggests ambushing Stone and giving him a good kicking.

Maurice shrugs it off. "Don't be vexed. With that face, he's enough problems."

Les and I land a weekend pass, but we're almost broke. The other six rally round to raise our fares. I recall Jack's words: "You'll meet great mates in the navy. Treasure them."

Job one is to get into a uniform that fits. Although I'm a raw recruit, the world doesn't have to know.

All the Barretts, including Silver, are waiting at the bus depot. The ladies almost suffocate me, and my ribs ache from Mr Barrett's fierce hug. My cap flies off my head. Silver retrieves it and sits down to wait his turn.

The car's filled with chatter on the journey. Anita, who grows lovelier by the day, clings to my arm, while Silver nuzzles against my leg, not to be forgotten.

Cheryl fills me in. "Your mother has to work, but she'll be home at nine. Fred and Irene are cooking supper with Jessie's help. She's home on leave. Tomorrow you're having tea at our house, then you cherubs are free as the birds. Just don't do anything I wouldn't, which gives you plenty of scope."

Fred thinks it's hilarious that they've chopped off my curls, but he's concerned about the abscess on my gums, the result of having had a tooth pulled. A broken leg wouldn't have stopped me coming home, brother!

Courting has made him soft. He hugs a lot. Perhaps he's realised what a brilliant kid I am. Dad's and Jessie's greetings are lump-in-the-throat events. They really wear their hearts on their sleeves.

Mother, assured and elegant, isn't overwhelmed by my new hairstyle but admits having missed me. "It's been quiet," she adds with an impish grin.

The evening's outstanding, and being with people I love priceless. Time slips away unnoticed as sand through the fingers. I wish there were forty-eight hours in a day and we could store memories in a bottle. Already coats are being buttoned, goodbyes exchanged, and I'm exhausted. I can't remember my head hitting the pillow, yet I'm bright-eyed and bushy tailed at 0630 hours.

Mother's to blame for this rush of blood. Having determined that family comes first, she suggests I spend my morning at home and the afternoon with the Barretts. Absence does make the heart grow fonder. In a few weeks, I've experienced a few twinges. My kin, who freely admitted being glad to see the back of me, have relented and sprayed the black sheep a different colour. Though I don't own it, I'm pleased to possess Solomon's wisdom. Fred's on duty after lunch. Dad has a church parade and is anointing his head later, while Mother will be heading into town at noon. Helping her prepare our pre-war Sunday breakfast pleases her, but what really plucks her heartstrings is watching me lay up the dining room table. I'm favoured with a gorgeous smile, and during the meal, I'm allowed to speak, which is reward indeed!

As each leaves, there's a deep sense of loss, which vanishes the minute Cheryl arrives. There's no room for sadness; the Barrett clan forbids it. It's been a wonderful weekend, but time flies when you're having fun. All too soon, we're holding hands tightly on the trip back into town. There's no need for words. A warm, brief kiss; a brave smile; and it's true: *"Parting is such sweet sorrow."* Les and I climb aboard the last bus for Malvern. We've to be back by midnight. One minute adrift, and, unlike Cinderella, it will be the glass house not a glass slipper. It is three miles to base. We wait an hour for a taxi and arrive with ten minutes to spare. Our mates are worried. Stone has been stalking the corridors counting heads.

Speak of the devil. "Time you lot turned in, you've a busy day ahead," Stone says, eying the goodies we're munching. "Midnight feasts aren't allowed."

Maurice unfolds himself from his bunk, and the room suddenly seems smaller. "Try one of these custard pies, they're yummy. Carter's mother slaved all day baking them for his friends," he says, pushing the plate under Stone's fat nose. "We won't tell anyone."

He backs away, perplexed. Join the club. If our mate decides to rip this cretin's head off, running interference might be difficult.

Stone probably thinks the big ox has popped his cork and intends to beat the crap out of him. The humiliation would linger long after bruises have faded. His best bet is to swallow his pride and the custard pie. I'm sure the PO's no coward, as his medal ribbons prove. Yet, despite his unblemished navy record, he's been fooled by a mere youth, which would make him the laughingstock of the base.

We think Stone is smiling, though it's hard to tell. Taking the pie from Maurice, he says, "Thank you, lad. All comrades together, eh?"

We'll keep quiet. Two more weeks and this dump will be history, and Stone will be just another pebble on the beach. He'd promised us nothing but blood, sweat, and tears. He's kept his word and turned us into men. We've given him our best, didn't break his heart, but certainly made it skip a beat or two. Should we ever never meet again, it will be much too soon.

Chapter Thirty

I'd done some trading last night, securing beer tickets for the farewell party. Sadly, our close-knit pack's been blown away. Jimmy, Maurice, and I are going back to Lowestoft on the east coast. The Gold Braid has decided that we're best suited for patrol service. It sounds like a Boy Scout troop, but we discover the gruesome truth. It's the Royal Fleet Reserve, comprising fishermen with their trawlers converted to minesweepers at the outbreak of the war. I'd joined up with visions of becoming a diesel-electric mechanical engineer, not heaving a bloody great shovel aboard these old coal-burning tubs.

We're sitting on our gear waiting for the train. Jimmy lights a cigarette. "Do you feel you've been here before?" he asks.

"The common terminology's déjà vu, dear fellow," Maurice responds.

"Piss elegant twit! What does that mean in English, Eddie?"

"You've been here before."

"You're worse than Tiny Tim," Jimmy grumbles while grinning.

There's no class barrier, though we're from diverse backgrounds. Jimmy swears he'd never worn shoes until starting work. Once the cotton mills shut down during the Depression, his family suffered. Maurice looks choked by these grim tales. Often, feeling like Piggy in the Middle, I thank God for finding me this odd couple.

My love of trains has faded since childhood, and I'm relieved to finally reach *HMS Europa*. The one-hour wait at Norwich for the local hasn't improved my spirits, and the blustery rain lashing my cheeks doesn't help. The grey three-storey stone building a hundred yards from the seafront offers a faint glimmer of hope, except during supper we discover that, pre-war, this place was a lunatic asylum. A quick glance suggests there're still some lunatics here. Calling the Home Guard "Dad's Army" makes these hooligans Harry

Tate's Navy. The phrase "slinging hash" takes on new meaning entering the mess hall. There's a mob of matelots throwing plates of grub at each other.

Standing clear, we watch the furore. "This is the real world, Maurice, what do you think now?" I ask.

He gravely studies the scene. "I suspect the chefs have seasoned the gravy too liberally."

We've anxiously watched his first faltering steps, and suddenly he's up and running. Escaping the shackles of a privileged childhood, he's plunged headfirst into the whirlpool of life. "Welcome to the club."

Jimmy nods his agreement. "What took you so long?"

Maurice shrugs. "It's not half the fun I'd expected."

Dead tired from our hectic day, we finish supper in silence. There's no shore leave, the rain's still coming down, and we've little cash. Without taking a vote, we turn up greatcoat collars and head for the canteen. Smoke-filled and packed to the gunwales, the bar's awash with singing. Booze and ballads make good buddies. A rickety piano's hammering out golden oldies, and it sounds like old home week. Maurice is dispatched for beer, while Jimmy drags me over to the pianist and says I'm a professional artist who'll sing requests for a small fee—one token, no less. Jimmy's only pint-sized but has a big mouth.

He could sell fridges to Eskimos and seals the deal with a handshake, plus my bottle of beer. Touting me as the choirboy pays off, and I'm amazed at the songs requested. Many are for hymns or serious ballads. My Lancashire impresario's cheeky chatter keeps the pot boiling, and by the time the bar closes my pockets are loaded. So are my mates'.

They look dreadful at morning parade and the Officer of the Day even worse. Maybe he's been sampling the local jungle juice too?

My derision turns to panic when told to fall in with the common herd. I've been selected for a course, but that doesn't excuse me from some basic training. Feeble protests fall on deaf ears. It's not funny, especially when introduced to my initial task. In a corner of the square stands the mock-up of a boiler-room, with a hinged door. Also, there's a heap of rocks, a giant shovel and big rake. The exercise is to heave the 'coal' into the oven and bank the fire using the rake. Once the instructor's satisfied, you drag the bloody lot out for the next poor sod. Royal Navy rules are simple: if it moves, salute it, if it doesn't, paint it. And never, ever argue. I spend the next three days taking turns at stoking this boiler, firmly convinced that lunatics are running this nuthouse.

Hallelujah! Arising on the fourth morning, prayers are answered. I report to the Drafting Office to discover I'm off to Oulton Broad on a diesel/electric course. I've accommodation in a private house, my own bedroom and all meals found. There are no parades or bull. Sadly, nothing comes without cost. By the time I'm done here, my mates will be long gone. Mrs Dawson's a widow and reminds me of Miss Ramsey. She has a boy in the navy and two teenage daughters in school. Her cooking's wonderful, and I eat with the family. The only restriction is I have to be home by 2300 hours, which suits me fine. I'm bushed after eight hours graft every day. They're working us hard, but we're not inside every day. Sailing on the Norfolk Broads is great fun on a motor torpedo boat.

Yet time flies, as the monkey said when the clock fell on his head, and after teary goodbyes from the Dawsons, I'm back at the funny farm. I go walk about, seeking familiar faces but find Sweet Fanny Adams. Back on my bunk, I write some letters, do a little laundry, and crash my head. The day's been far too hectic.

The navy's big on tradition. Everyone belongs to a watch and must be doing something, even if there's nothing to do. Since returning, I've been assigned to perimeter clean-up, picking up cigarette packets and chewing gum wrappers. It's exhilarating and tiring too, keeping an eye peeled for the petty officer in charge. I'm lookout while the smokers take a crafty drag behind the hut. I learn to add "Up with the Jolly Roger, boys" to my repertoire, when I spot danger on the horizon. Great-Aunt Eleanor would be proud of me. She probably took tea with both Gilbert and Sullivan. I break into song now with the enemy approaching at a fast rate of knots.

"Looking for Roberts!" he yells, still twenty yards away.

"That's me, Petty Officer," I say, snapping smartly to attention.

He looks doubtful, then rattles off my service number. "You sure?" he asks.

It's tempting to reply, "Only a wise child knows his own father," but I remain silent. Men wearing gold buttons have no sense of humour.

My nod sets him yapping again. "There's a draft ticket with your name on it. Be packed and ready and outside the office by fifteen hundred hours. You're going by truck to Yarmouth Docks."

I'm uncertain whether to laugh or cry. I've been in the Andrew only three months and I'm off to sea. There's no long journey, but no mention of leave either. I'll have to check later. At least this dump will be history.

THE TRUCK SCREECHES TO A halt, and a well-scrubbed chief petty officer hops out. "You must be Roberts," he says and starts slinging my gear into the back. "Glad you made it in time. You've saved my bacon."

It's unusual to find someone who's polite and helpful. Keeping quiet seems smart; I've had my quota of queer folk. I settle back as the barrier clangs down behind us and we begin our fifteen-minute trip into Yarmouth. This one-on-one touch is great, and I tell my driver so.

"Enjoy it, son. It will be your last smooth ride for months. Crossing the Pond in a corvette isn't for the faint-hearted. It's like going to sea in a barrel."

"Thanks for boosting my morale."

"Your virgin voyage, don't worry. They're a good bunch aboard the *Daisy*. Served on her myself for three years before becoming a barrack stanchion. I volunteered for this run. You're relieving my mate. We're painting the town red tonight."

Confession's good for the soul. "I've always wanted to sail round the world. Now that it's happening, I'm terrified."

"No sweat, Choirboy. All matelots are sentimental sods. They'll love your warbling."

Noting my surprise, he adds, "Nothing's sacred on my watch, Jack." He wheels onto the quay and skids to a halt.

Off-loading my kit, we stagger up the gangplank, drop the gear, and both salute the quarterdeck. I turn to thank him, and he's gone! The quartermaster studies my papers and blows down a windpipe. Within minutes a wiry, weather-beaten figure appears. He's black hair, eyes to match, and frowns at me.

"Thought Williams was blowing smoke. It's worse. Not your fault kid, but we need experience, not someone wet behind the ears."

It's tempting to smack his head, but sensibly I ask, "Who's Williams?"

"He's the scumbag who brought you aboard. He had more fiddles than the London Symphony Orchestra. The skipper could have hung him out to dry but instead shipped Taffy ashore for his final years. Still, that's ancient news. Welcome to the *Daisy*. Like my granny, she's old and reliable. I'm your watch commander, Leading Stoker James Spencer. Off-duty I'm known as Jim, which is a privilege you'll have to earn. Bet you're starving after that trip. Let's get some victuals in you before you keel over. Follow me." He picks up my hammock and trots off.

"Aye aye, Leading Stoker," I respond. I'm pleased to know that beneath his hard crust there's a soft centre.

Making our way below, we weave along dark alleyways and through narrow hatches. I'm wondering if I'll ever see sky again when LS Spencer stops abruptly and points. "The hatch to hell, where you'll eat, sleep, and dream of home." He pats my shoulder. "They don't bite. You're lucky most of the boys are ashore, enjoying their last night of freedom. We sail at first light tomorrow."

I've imagined this a thousand times. Now I'm panic-stricken, but my new boss is disappearing into the lengthening shadows. It's tempting to run after him or just keep running. Yet, there's a delicious smell wafting through the hatchway, and my stomach's sending out distress signals. Some things never change.

Feeling like Daniel entering the lion's den, I step boldly over the transom and into a brand-new world. Except two ratings eating supper and a lanky red-haired dude waving a soup ladle, the mess is deserted.

Seeing their blank faces, I remove my smile. They've lost a pal and gained a stranger. "Leading Stoker Spencer told me to report for supper."

The spoon-waver recovers first. "You must be Jessop's relief. We thought you had done a runner," he replies in a cockney accent. "My name's Gus, also known as Knocker. Park your body. I'll grab you a plate and some tools."

Typical of his breed, he's a talker and curious too, whereas I never let chatter interfere with eating. Besides, living with a false name and identity has made me cautious. Already I've figured Knocker as a player. It takes one to know one. My wheeler-dealer skills have been honed razor-sharp by Kenny and polished by Jimmy. This cockney doesn't realise our friendship will be strictly quid pro quo.

Feeling shattered, I decide to crash my head. Knocker offers to help me sling my hammock, which I politely decline. I sling the hammock myself while delivering a prayer. God obliges, and I settle into my cocoon without mishap. It's amazing how cosy it is, though my pillow's a rolled-up towel. Swaying in the semi-dark, I'm bone-tired, yet brain-alert. My life's balanced between hopes and dreams. Tonight, moored at Yarmouth Quay and tomorrow, free and sailing the high seas. Finally, Charlie, the world will be my oyster.

Chapter Thirty-One

L et go for'ard!" Jimmy the One, our first officer, bawls through the bullhorn. The fo'c'sle crew springs into action, hauling in the thick rope hawser released from the bollard by two dockyard workers. Deck plates throb beneath my feet. The starboard engine slowly pulses ahead, port one to the rear. Seamen heave the rope fenders aboard, and the bows swing slowly from the quayside. Fifty yards away, the pilot boat bobs gently on the tide waiting to escort us through the boom to open water.

"Let go astern," the first lieutenant calls, and the drill's repeated with clockwork precision.

We move slowly ahead on both engines, following in the wake of our mother hen. The white ensign proudly flutters on the quarterdeck, and the masthead's alive with bunting. I haven't a clue what it means but puff out my chest with pride. The bo'sun's whistle brings the whole ship's company to attention as we pass ships of the line. Every Royal Navy ship follows this grand old tradition. Today's a brand-new experience; it's my maiden sea voyage, first watch, and initial tot of rum. Not to worry—I'd managed not to tumble out of my hammock last night, much to Knocker's surprise and mine.

A blast from the pilot boat's siren returns me from space as we leave harbour and enter choppy water. On the eastern horizon, a putty-sliver of light bisects the slate-grey sky from the green-blackness of the North Sea, welcoming another blustery, ice-capped day. It's awesome feeling the ship pick up speed and slosh through six-foot troughs.

A mile out, she makes a wide sweep to starboard, heading for the English Channel. My pretty balloon's quickly burst by a bearded petty officer ordering me below and into the rig of the day.

This morning I'll be meeting my messmates, and the new kid's always good for a giggle. My patience and pride will be truly tested. All conversation ceases. I switch on a nice-to-see-you smile, and who'd guess my knees are knocking? There are a dozen ratings sitting at the scrubbed, wooden table, most in uniform, a few in boiler suits. They cease attacking the breakfast trays and acknowledge my presence. I'm bombarded by many strange tongues, though all claim to be British. Responding to their remarks briefly, I receive strange looks. My speech reflects the wardroom rather than lower deck.

One acne-spotted youth comments, "He sounds a right ginger beer to me. I'll bet he's a funny walk too."

There are some frowns, but no protests. All eyes are glued on me, waiting for my response. Closely eying the tray of sausages, I stab the fattest one with my fork. "There you go, dear heart. The lads wouldn't deny you the biggest one first." I plop it onto the joker's plate.

The mess erupts with laughter. Gracious in defeat, the boy squeezes out a grin. I've broken my vow and allowed wit to conquer wisdom, but I do feel better for it.

"You're not so dumb after all," LS Spencer whispers in my ear. "Williams told me about your caper at Europa. Created a stir didn't you, Choirboy?"

"It was a little entertainment for lonely sailors."

"Pull the other one, son. I've got one Artful Dodger and don't need another. Understand?" LS Spencer murmurs.

"Perfectly, Leading Stoker. I'm no troublemaker," I answer quietly.

"All hands on deck!" Further talk is deterred, and a scramble ensues for the hatch.

"The skipper loves his morning prayer and hymn," LS Spencer says while we're making our way up top. "He's also a tough bugger."

A bracing wind whips the bell-bottoms about my legs, and spray from the bow-wave stings my cheeks. Away to starboard, the limestone cliffs of Dover stand rampant under a pale morning sun. Keeping my knees slightly bent, I go with the flow. The rise and fall of the deck is the stuff I've imagined since childhood. I'm so happy, there's no time to be sick. Looking at the horizon and knowing the whole world is mine is mind-bending!

The skipper's arrival breaks the spell. He's revered, respected, and runs a tight ship, no bull, yet bags of bustle. The inspection's short, hymn and prayer brief plus a few words from the first officer.

"Well men, there's good news and bad news. We're off to Londonderry to link up with a force of destroyers and corvettes. Thence, Canada to support a large convoy back home."

"So! What's the good news?" a voice asks from the rear.

Jimmy the One beams. "I thought you loved Canada, though they're not fond of Jack smashing up half their bars last visit."

"It wasn't our fault, sir," Knocker says. "The local guys started it, but what's the worst news?"

"We're short-handed. Three ratings are adrift; two are sick. Outward bound shouldn't be a worry, but things could be rough on the return trip."

This snippet isn't well received. We're dismissed and return glum-faced to our mess, where watch commanders issue work quotas. I understand the grumbles. There'll be extra duties and less relaxation, particularly on the home run.

Eventually, LS Spencer notices me. It's not difficult. I'm the only one left. "You're with me, Roberts. There's lots to learn. Keep pace and ears pinned."

He dives through a hatchway and down a steep iron ladder into the bowels of the corvette. Throbbing fans, turbines, and oil-soaked air attack my ears and nose. A rivulet of sweat courses down my back and answers the nagging question of why stokers wear little beneath their coveralls. Our watch commander is all business. A name or nod suffice with no time for gossip. Half the ship's company appear to be named Jock, Geordie, or Skouse.

My head's spinning as Spencer climbs three steel steps to a six-foot platform, which runs the width of the engine room. The area's thick with men studying dials and gauges.

"Chief Engineer wants a word with you, Roberts," LS Spencer says.

"I've done nothing," I protest.

"Don't panic. Mr Campbell likes to meet all new boys. He's too soft for an officer, but a genius with engines."

The chief's plump cheeks dimple. "Welcome to Hades," he says. He tells LS Spencer to stand fast and motions me to follow him. Retreating to the end of the engine room, he pulls aside a curtain and enters a tiny cubicle furnished with a camp bed and fold-up chair. "Not exactly the Savoy, but it serves my purpose," he says and points to the seat. "Take a pew." He squats on the bed, puffing on his pipe and collecting his thoughts. "I like to meet all new men," he begins. "Once we're underway, there's no chance. Nevertheless, there's another reason for this chat. A signal came aboard concerning you an hour ago. The contents are privy to the skipper, Sparks—the wireless operator—and myself. They'll stay that way, for your peace of mind and harmony on the mess deck."

I'm scuttled. Mother's written to the navy and dropped me in the deep end.

Campbell isn't simpatico; he's chuckling. "The navy's made a royal cock up. You passed the Diesel/Electric exam with top marks, and the Commodore had recommended you for an engine room artificer course. The papers were being processed when we applied for Jessop's relief. In reality, you should be enjoying a spell of leave before going to Havant for training and possible promotion to petty officer/engine room artificer."

I've read about pregnant silences; never thought I'd experience one. "Thanks for telling me, sir, though I'd have been better off not knowing."

"Life's not always fair, lad, but the Royal Navy's never wrong."

"Couldn't you drop me off at Londonderry?"

"Impossible! We're not making landfall. The *Daisy* has to meet the rest of the escort. This convoy is priority for the invasion."

"I suppose I'll be doing something useful, sir."

"That's the Nelson spirit, Roberts. Chin up. Pleasure to have you aboard and I'm sure you'll be a valuable asset."

Returning to LS Spencer's care, my feelings are mixed. I've not only dodged a bullet but experienced a friendly officer. Fears of doing a stretch in Kingston rattle are fading fast. I'm ready to face the future, and the grouchy matelot galumphing ahead of me could be the ideal role model.

Chapter Thirty-Two

Jim doesn't lie. For three hours my feet scarcely touch the deck. The *Daisy's* one hundred and forty feet long with a thirty-foot beam. After climbing up and down four levels, plus the wheelhouse and bridge, I'm wilting. The tannoy's calls of "Up Spirits" and "afternoon watchmen to dinner," are music to my ears. The tour's a revelation. LS Spencer knows everyone's first name and each rivet that holds this sturdy tub together. He's well regarded, and I suspect beneath his crusty exterior there's a compassionate human being.

He grills me with pointed questions. With months of lying, answers are easy. "I'm not a nosy parker, but I have to know if you can do the job."

I admire his honesty, and it's time to establish that I'm not a nodding dog. "You aren't the hard case you pretend, Leading Stoker Spencer."

"Don't push your luck, Choirboy. Those innocent blue eyes don't fool me."

Acting sad, I scuttle after him into the noisy mess deck. It's a baptism of fire today. Officially, I'm twenty years old and entitled to draw my tot. I'll be the main attraction and watched closely while collecting my mug from the locker.

A petty officer's keenly supervising the rating, doling out the grog, and, recognising Knocker's face, can appreciate the non-commissioned officer's concern. I also notice each man's name's ticked once he's drawn his ration. There's no double-dipping here. Yet contrary to regulations, each man takes one sip before sitting down to eat.

Offering me a friendly grin, the buffer tells White to maintain a steady hand. It's an old trick to stick a thumb inside the measure and displace some liquid.

"It's strange how Knocker's hand trembles when there's a fresh face," the

PO says, handing me my cup. "Welcome aboard, sailor. Don't spill any now."

"I'll lick it off the table if I do."

"A man after me own heart. May ye be in heaven a half hour before the devil knows you're dead."

"Thanks, Paddy," I say, raising my mug. Fumes savage my nose. The aroma's overpowering and seductive. I'm aware of an awesome silence and realise this is a test. Drink too fast, I'm a lush, while sipping gently might confirm the spotty one's words. Smiling, I drink slowly, smack my lips and find myself a seat.

LS Spencer watches me stack my plate with roast beef, mashed spuds, and greens. "On a diet?" he enquires, then nods at my rum. "Managed that well, but it's nicer out of a glass. I'll get the officer's steward to rustle one up."

"Will he want sippers or gulpers?"

"Neither, the boy's temperance. It's my treat."

"You'll have the sausage queen sounding off about you."

"He's only on board under duress."

"How is that?" I ask.

"His name's Francis Warner. He's the chief stoker's nephew."

"No wonder our beloved Weary looks sad."

"Frannie's a little snout. Stay clear of him. Do you hear?"

I nod and carry on eating while LS Spencer takes off on his mission. I've another three hours until reporting for first dogwatch. It will take ten days to reach Nova Scotia, providing the weather's kind, and twice as long getting back with the snail-like convoy. I'll be a seasoned sailor before seeing England again. There's barely time to think about home and loved ones, but I continually pray for their safety, especially Jack stranded in the jungle.

My master's voice brings me back to reality. "Shake a leg. We've work to do. Stow this in your locker," he says and hands me a tumbler.

Spending the afternoon studying the whistles and bells that keep the engines running smoothly makes my head spin. I'll never remember half of it. LS Spencer tells me not to fret, as he and a young Scot will be with me.

At 1530 hours we take supper, after which I strip to my underwear and slip into a navy-issue boiler suit, one size fits all. I create great amusement, and Frannie leads the attack, but I suffer the laughter graciously, much to his dismay.

"You handled Frannie well," LS Spencer says on our way to the generator room.

"I canna stand the wee cretin," Hughie Gallagher, my new watch partner, says.

"Which proves you've good sense," I tell him.

"I like my new mate already, Hooky," Hughie replies, directing his comment to our leading stoker.

"There's no accounting for taste," LS Spencer grunts, unlatching the hatch door.

Padding around in my clown suit like Chaplin for the next two hours, I'm introduced to the wonderful world of watch-keeping. It's not rocket science but requires concentration. I'm not happy being here but committed to playing my part. God's at the helm and watching my back. Despite the detour, the experience is useful. Jim Spencer's no slouch when it comes to mind games. Pairing me with the Scot is smart. He's from the Isle of Skye. Quiet by nature, he has an impish humour and a beautiful brogue. He claims there are ten times more sheep than people on the island. We've an instant rapport, and I see Hooky's plan. Hughie and I are viewed as oddball characters by our shipmates. Why not make us bookends?

"I'll get Auntie Betty to alter those overalls. You look like the back end of a pantomime horse."

"Who's Auntie Betty?"

"By day, he's Leading Cook Arthur Betts, by night, a genius with needle and thread. Not expensive either."

"He sounds my kind of tailor. Is he temperance too?"

"You should be so lucky. He drinks like a fish and smokes like a chimney," Hughie says. "Don't pay him up front or you'll never see your finished goods."

We spend ages shooting the breeze and drinking hot cocoa until Hooky says, "You two should crash. The next weeks are going to be tough."

It's only 2030, but following Hughie's lead, I unroll my hammock and sling my hooks, both of them. The pitch of the corvette's heavier as we approach Land's End and we're exposed to the contrary currents of the Atlantic. A good deal of strength and skill are needed to swing one's body into a canvas shroud that sways over five feet above the deck plates, particularly when witnessed by a bunch of jeering sailors. It's amazing how small things amuse small minds. Succeeding at my fifth attempt, the jeers turn to cheers. Acknowledging the applause, I almost fall out, which creates louder laughter. Subsiding into the soft blankets, I'm tired yet pleased, knowing I've cleared another hurdle. No one gets a free pass. You have to earn respect. The warm and fuzzy comes later.

Doubting LS Spencer's pessimism of slumber amid this chaos, I find the chaos reassuring. Without noise there would be time to reflect or even regret. The fact that one is never alone aboard a ship must be a blessing from above. My first day has been tough, but nobody promised a rose garden. Mother's often said that making my own bed means I have to lie in it. Dearest Dolly always knows best.

Despite the background buzz of voices and engines, I am comfy. One could hum along with the motion. I snuggle further under the blankets and begin. It's soft and soothing, and with eyes shut sounds sweeter. Singing yourself to sleep is a stupid, childish notion. Then again, isn't it the truth that inside every grown man there's a small boy hiding?

Chapter Thirty-Three

Up Spirits is my day's highlight, but wakey wakey is the pits. Yet I react fast when the quartermaster pokes my hammock with his baton. "Shift your ass, son," he encourages. "It's oh-three-fifty."

I'm tempted to question his ancestry but refrain. Man with big stick hit hard. Slipping into overalls and boots, I'm wide awake. Three years on a paper route have paid off. Early mornings are no hardship. However, I'm the great pretender: sixteen years old going on twenty-one. It's easy being a smart kid, but I'm a foreigner in the adult world; the language is lewd, and the jokes range from doubtful to disgusting. Some tales are downright embarrassing. I've not been the butt of their humour, except weak efforts from Frannie and his buddies.

Privacy's hard to find, though my alliance with Hughie's kept the wolves at bay and the Choirboy tag haunts me because I rarely laugh at their vulgarity. I'm convinced one can be witty without a foul mouth.

Hughie tells me the jury's still out. "They're old washerwomen with nothing better to do. Be yourself and ignore them."

It's sound advice from a wise young man. My wide-eyed enthusiasm annoys those who perform their duties by rote. I'll have to change tactics and put on a sad face because misery always loves company.

LS Spencer interrupts my meditation. "Still enjoying the trip?"

"Certainly, Hooky, wish I'd joined up sooner." I'm instantly regretting my motor mouth.

"Why didn't you? How did you dodge the column so long?" There's been a parley, and Big Jim's chosen to discover whether the newbie is being honest. He might be winding me up, or Campbell's blown my cover. It's hardly a crime, but the crew would torment me.

"Are you calling me a coward, Leading Stoker?"

He's lost for words.

Prodding harder, I ask, "Is this your opinion, or the clowns below?"

LS Spencer shakes his head. "They think you're strange."

Smoke and mirrors are needed. "Fair enough, Jim. I know you've to sort the bad apples from good ones, but I'm not from another planet. Leaving school, I had to work in a munitions factory and was not available for call-up. Finally, I got fired and volunteered the next day." I pray God and Fred will forgive my transgressions. "It was a dream come true when my papers arrived."

I've given Big Jim food for thought. He's having trouble swallowing. My smidgen of truth's a brilliant touch.

"It's almost twenty years since I escaped poverty and the Depression. At sixteen I was king of the world. Some things you never forget."

I know he'd love to chat, but Gramps always says, "Quit while you're ahead."

Confident the doubters will be told I've no evil powers, I return to my duties. Hughie cruises by, eager for news. I give him a brief rundown. He responds with a told-you-so look and imparts many pearls of wisdom from his own experience. He's four years' service under his belt; I listen well and absorb.

"They're your family, warts and all. Learn to live with it," he concludes.

There's no answer to that, and I've the feeling this canny Scot's just spanked my bum. It's not my style to be humble, but the old navy adage, *"If you can't beat them, join them,"* seems a better solution than slashing my wrists.

Knocker's my relief, and we haggle for a brief spell. He needs cigarettes, and I'm keen to start my distillery. By the time we reach port, I'll have enough cash stashed away for Auntie Betty to run me up a smarter uniform.

Thoughts of a stuffy mess deck with sweaty, unshaven sailors clamouring for breakfast offers little cheer. I opt for top deck and am rewarded tenfold, as the Good Book promises. Groping for the rail, I grimly hang on while the howling wind mercilessly buffets me. The sea dogs below would be laughing their socks off.

Gathering wounded pride, I retreat from the shards of spray. The initial terror subsides, and I'm beginning to enjoy the experience. Maybe it's the calm before the storm. After all, we're barely a couple of miles off the Irish coast. I've been entertained with tales of thirty-foot troughs and gale force winds once we're into the North Atlantic. I sense sympathy beneath their banter. They've all had to conquer this fear of the unknown. I pry my fingers off the rail and hustle to the hatchway. I'm not built for bravery or foolishness. Anyhow, I'm famished.

"We thought you'd jumped ship," Frannie greets me.

"What and miss breakfast?"

"You're not as daft as I thought."

"Thank you, Francis. I'll take that as a compliment."

He conjures up a genuine grin; the natives have been talking. Does absence really make the heart grow fonder? The men watch me stack the tin plate with a full English; I stab a sausage.

"Still watching your weight?" LS Spencer asks.

"No, Hooky. That spell up top has made me hungry."

"Good for you, lad. Keep that lot down, and you'll have this miserable lot thinking you're a real sailor," LS Spencer says, regarding them with savage eyes.

Chapter Thirty-Four

There's a bone-chilling wind and persistent rain heralding our late arrival at Londonderry. The flag officer aboard the lead destroyer isn't happy; his signal lamp is working overtime.

"Captain 'Bulldog' Drummond's keen on having his ass blown off," our chief engineer says, puffing at his pipe.

It reminds me of Lowestoft at low tide.

"Maybe he's after Mountbatten's job and wants to be top dog."

There are a few polite smiles, but no applause at LS Spencer's jest.

Being second banana, I should know better, but add, "Who can blame him? He must be straining at the leash."

LS Spencer grins. "Thought you were a crooner, not a comic. Never mind, I've the last laugh—the water boat and oiler are coming alongside."

I'd wondered why we'd been ordered on deck at the double. Clambering into boots and greatcoats, we assemble amidships. LS Spencer heaves black oilskin coats at us. I scramble into mine, although it's too late. I'm already drenched. Hooky throws me a pair of canvas gloves and points to a bunch of stokers standing by the rail. A one-inch rope whistles over my head, whacks the deck, and starts snaking back to the ship's side. I stamp on the line, grasping it with both hands and curse my stupidity. My arms are being torn from their sockets. I brace my feet and lean back. Pain rips through every tissue down to my toes. I survive three seconds of agony before others take the strain. Everything's gone dark. I must have shut my eyes. Opening them, I see LS Spencer's anxious face.

Realising I haven't snuffed it, he says, "On your feet, lad. Don't just lie there."

Scrambling up, I grab the rope, which is attached to a canvas-mesh, oil pipe. We huff and puff across the slippery surface to the engine room housing and couple it to the fuel line. I lean on the bulkhead, absolutely whacked, choking on fumes.

"Good work, lads," Campbell says. "Smart thinking, Roberts. Saved us from a bloody rocket from Bulldog. He hates corvette lads, even on a good day."

My mates nod. I've another gold star, but not everyone's happy.

"Proper little hero," Knocker jeers, appearing from behind the smokestack where he's been enjoying a smoke while we've been grafting.

His absence hasn't gone unnoticed. "Jim, get your team a hot drink. They've earned it. Leave me one rating to supervise the fuelling. Stoker White knows the routine well," Campbell says.

We peel off our oilskins and scatter for the mess deck and a fanny filled with throat-scalding cocoa. I ease the shredded gloves from my palms, which are laced with cuts, some already congealed, others still weeping.

Frannie's face is pallid. "Can't stand the sight of blood, even my own."

Hughie has the first aid box open, a cotton swab in one hand, and he's shaking a bottle of iodine in the other. If he says this is going to hurt him more than me, I'll kick him in the head! He doesn't and gently tends to one hand while I bravely sip my cocoa.

Alf Biddle, the sickbay rating, arrives with his case of goodies. "You're doing a grand job, Hughie."

"I'm useless at tying bandages but think the patient will survive."

The tiffy takes a seat opposite. I put down my cup and extend my hands. He examines them closely. "The cuts are superficial but look at the state of your nails, Princess. Never fear, we've a new tape which sutures the flesh beautifully. In a few weeks, you'll be belle of the ball again."

There are huge grins around the mess, and I'm sure there's empathy among these hard men. The tannoy cuts short any further bonding. It's Drummond's vow to have his flotilla steaming westward before dusk. In less than an hour, we're closed up for sea, weighed anchor, and heading northwest for Iceland. It's a majestic sight, with the powerful, faster destroyers on the outside V and the smaller corvettes on the inner. The bridge lookouts are posted, though doubtful any U-boat captain will be *dummkopf* enough to attack us. There're a dozen or more crew members standing on the quarterdeck, each lost in his own thoughts. The Irish coast is cloaked in a grey shroud, and each turn of the screws takes us farther away from our loved ones and home.

I wonder what the Barretts are having for supper. How's my sweet girl? And whose knee has Silver got his big head resting on, waiting for leftovers? I bet Mother's buzzing around the Bodega like a blue-ass fly, separating the Yanks from their greenbacks, while Dad's sitting in his Home Guard hut studying the world through the bottom of his glass. Fred's smooching on the chesterfield with Irene, and Kenny's holding some fair young maiden's hand. If the gal's sensible, she'll be holding both of his tightly.

Breaking the spell, Hughie says, "I thought you'd be greeting, not grinning like an idiot. I'm not surprised they think you're queer."

There's no time to explain as LS Spencer shows up. "Get along to the sickbay. Alf has found you a bunk away from these rough sailors. You're on light duties."

"Lucky sod!" my mate scoffs.

"Don't be miffed, Hughie, he still has to stand his watch. There's nothing wrong with his eyes."

"Thanks, Hooky, you're all heart."

"We're pulling a double tonight, better get below and grab some chow. It's only an hour till watch," he says and strides off without waiting for a response.

"There's more to Big Jim than folks realise. 'Heart of Oak' could have been written for him. He's a great human being."

Such praise from the quiet Scot is unusual.

"So why hasn't he achieved a higher rank?"

"Listen and I'll tell you. Jim was once a chief stoker. A drunken officer slaps his face for disobeying a stupid order. He doesn't retaliate, but tells the captain, who advises him to forget it. Later, the officer's found dead at the foot of the engine room ladder. Jim's clapped in irons, and the provost marshal arrives to investigate. Seeking to protect the navy's reputation, the captain and his fellow officers close ranks, leaving Jim to carry the can. He's popular on the lower deck. Everybody rallies round to support him."

I'm fascinated, and never heard Hughie talk so freely. "How long he rotted in that cell, I'm not sure. A lesser man would have cracked. He finally has his day in court, but as usual, the Royal Navy's never wrong. A verdict of misadventure is entered, though many witnesses swear the engineer was legless. Nevertheless, Jim's found guilty of disobeying a direct order and reduced to stoker, first class. He's been selected for promotion often but insists on serving with men he can trust and who trust him."

I sail into uncharted territory. "He must have great faith to rise above that kind of experience."

Hughie takes ages to reply. "Sometimes I think God isn't listening and along comes a man like Spencer. Do you know the feeling, Eddie?"

"Yes, it's amazing how one can see other people's problems yet struggle with their own."

We return quickly to the secular world, though I've a tinge of conscience. Since coming aboard, I've been trying to fit in and be a team player. The Lord's help wasn't needed. Yet this isn't the first time I've discovered that He will take care of the consequences. This time my back's being monitored by two willing disciples. I pour lashings of gravy over fried chicken and roast potatoes while silently counting my blessings.

Chapter Thirty-Five

Hughie and I are leaning on the fo'c'sle rail. The stiff breeze is freezing our nose hairs, but it's ambrosia after the sweaty socks and tobacco-laden air of the mess deck. The human spirit can tolerate only so much. All sailors grumble, but the bickering and bad weather's making the crew nervous. It was clever of Spencer finding me a berth in the sickbay. Officially, I'm on light duties under Alf's supervision. Nevertheless, I stand watch, eat with the lads, and run. Recent events have opened my eyes. I'm the wheels, not the engine. God will keep me on track. I've been so busy that important issues are ignored. Most things are beyond my control, so why fret?

The blaspheming and cursing will not calm the wild ocean nor stop the Arctic winds sweeping down from Greenland and skinning our cheeks at both ends. The destroyer, dead in the water for twelve hours with electrical problems, wasn't helped by complaining. Though my bland optimism assures my shipmates that I'm a prime candidate for the loony bin, we're approaching the Grand Banks and less than a day from a safe anchorage.

If pride wasn't considered a sin, I'd say, "I told you so."

"There are two American frigates overtaking us and lots of small craft ahead," Hughie says.

There's a huge Stars and Stripes ensign on the stern of the closest ship. "Even with flags, the Yanks must have one bigger than anyone else."

"You're jealous. Remember, they're our comrades-in-arms."

"The only thing they want in their arms are our bonnie English lassies."

"I'm not bothered," says the guy from Skye. "My Jeannie's champion hammer thrower in the islands." He could be joking, but I wouldn't bet on it.

The US vessels are weaving a course through our column. They've bunting fluttering from their main masts, bugles are blowing, and the decks crowded with marines and sailors, all in full-dress uniform. Aboard the *Daisy*, we lean on the rails and watch the show. There'll be harsh words from Bulldog. We don't care; we're on a business trip, not a day on the lake. The corvette bounces erratically in the frigate's bow wave. Our cooks will be spitting blood. Altering course to avoid the trawlers and their fishing grounds, I realise that the US Navy's riding shotgun on these fishermen. It's hardly a stroll in the park.

The mood aboard the ship has improved. Men who've threatened to punch each other's lights out are now planning to set Halifax alight together. I'd settle for two days' bed rest. A run ashore in a foreign port will be a first for me. Venturing out alone is precarious, and with most of this hard-bitten mob, it's a death wish!

My watch draws the short straw. We're on duty. I've dodged a bullet. At least for twenty-four hours, I escape the excitement in the mess for the sanity of the upper deck.

Our opposite numbers are kids on their first carousel, all bright-eyed and bushy-tailed, preparing for the invasion of Nova Scotia.

Any parent with girls between the ages of thirteen and thirty would be wise to lock them away until Jolly Jack's back at sea.

We watch the liberty men shuffling into line for inspection by the Officer of the Day.

"A fine body of men. Butter wouldn't melt in their mouths."

"Aye and a brick wouldna' choke them either," Hughie mutters.

"I've been searching for you two. Engines don't maintain themselves. I want them as bright and shiny as new pennies. Understand?"

"Yes, Hooky."

"Once you've finished, report to me. You're not done yet."

The High Priest has spoken. We take off fast. "Someone's rattled Jim's chain," Hughie remarks, always the diplomat.

My hands are almost healed, and for three hours we work hard. Every surface glistens. Each bit of brass and glass sparkles. We've done LS Spencer proud. Though we'd never admit it, our leading stoker holds a special place in our hearts.

"Don't get excited. We're not out of the woods yet. Let's hope when we reach Grandma's house, the Big Bad Wolf's gone and gentle Jim's back," I say.

LS Spencer looks up from his book. "What do you jokers want?"

"You told us to report after we'd finished in the engine room."

"I trust you've done a good job and are wondering what else I've in store?"

My face betrays my fears. Something's not right. LS Spencer's shaking with mirth. I look at Hughie, who's also grinning. They've cooked up some scheme.

Hooky pulls out a silver flask and tells Hughie to find glasses. "The wee Scot and I have something to discuss with you."

Settled comfortably, the rum already tickling our tonsils, Jim begins. "Your private life's your own, but we know you've a lovely girl back home. Hughie says you never stop talking about her."

I tell my mate he's a blabbermouth. He flutters his eyelids.

"He's a bloody good mate too and worries about you. Some of the lads are keen to take you into town and show you a swell time. After a few beers, the girls look prettier. By midnight, their grannies are ravishing too. You could hit the jackpot. A ten-day vacation spent in Rose Cottage with all meals found and daily injections for only fifteen minutes of horizontal recreation. How's that sound for a wonderful memory of your first trip overseas?"

Slowly draining my glass, I'm astonished how much detail LS Spencer's put into his sermon. Every recruit entering the Royal Navy is warned of the moral issues that abound in foreign lands, often preached by some dried-up old stick of a medical officer. Coming from the horse's mouth makes it more realistic.

"Jim's not trying to frighten you," I hear Hughie say.

"You could have fooled me," I mutter, reaching for another drink. I take a hefty slug and feel no pain.

The leading stoker picks up the pace again. "Hughie has a solution to your predicament. We're not interfering, only offering help. You're not the first to have this dilemma and won't be the last. Before you start sewing your wild oats, listen to what this canny bugger has to say."

"You've heard the expression 'Up Homers,' right?" Without waiting for an answer, Hughie plunges on. "Tomorrow we'll be met at the dock gates by Ian and Maggie McClaren, Scottish as single malt whiskey, haggis, and heather. They're our hosts. We'll be wined and dined to the manor born. There's also a big, soft bed and a feather pillow for your head."

My upbringing seizes me by the throat. "I can't waltz into someone's house without an invitation," I protest. "It's not good manners."

"Stuff your etiquette up your nose, lad. It's been sorted. You don't think I've been sitting with my feet up while you two were working. I paid the Macs a visit. They're over the moon. I bet Maggie's up to her elbows in flour, and Ian is down in the wine cellar taking stock as we speak."

"You pair had this planned days ago and let me stew in my own juice."

"It's great to out-kid a kidder," Hughie says as they toast their success.

"Suppose I refuse your offer?"

The main shaker doesn't blink. "You're too smart to be that stupid."

His fellow mover adds, "I'll take your place. We can always off-load you onto Frannie and the Artful Dodger."

"Who's taking my name in vain?" Knocker says, stepping through the hatchway, his arms loaded with supper trays, closely dogged by Francis Warner, who's hefting two huge pots filled with soup.

There's a warm glow deep inside my chest. The rum was pretty smooth too.

Chapter Thirty-Six

As the *Daisy* takes up position heading for the Grand Banks and rendezvous with the convoy, the overcast, slate-grey sky brooding above Halifax harbour matches the crew's mood. The buzz is, when the group's fully assembled, it will contain over a hundred merchant ships and two dozen naval support vessels. It's a daring venture, which must have the U-boat crews licking their chops.

It's taken over three hours to jockey our charges into line, but we're finally underway and sloshing along at a moderate seven knots an hour, covering twenty-five square miles of ocean. One guard dog for every five sheep is barely enough when the wolf pack starts prowling.

Spirits hit zero when the skipper tells us we've lost three more crew due to "drinking and debauchery." It's a wonderful turn of phrase. We've heard varied accounts from returning revellers but paid small heed. Jack tends to romanticise his exploits once his feet hit dry land. Now we hear the unabridged version.

The Stooges, full of derring-do and booze, decide to visit a house of ill-repute. Unfortunately, they're spotted by a naval patrol. To evade capture, they elect to jump out of a window. It seemed a good idea. Wrong! It was on the third floor. One suffered a broken arm, his buddies a broken leg each, and all with badly dented pride. Curly, Larry, and Moe are now in traction at a Halifax hospital. There's no sympathy expressed. Their absence means more duties for us. I hide a smile when Knocker asks why the police didn't wait for a while instead of spoiling the lads' fun. There're also many faces reflecting, "But for the grace of God, go I."

Thanks to Hughie, my Up Homer was a blessing; the McClarens were magnificent. I'd returned back aboard happy and contented though not legless like most of my shipmates.

Now, with duffel coat collar shielding my ears, and Nova Scotia's coastline a distant memory over the horizon, I scan foam-flecked waves for German U-boats through powerful binoculars.

Vigilance is essential. Even in daylight, we've lost ships to a lone raider and long-range torpedo, this close to land, while herding our charges into formation.

A brace of Royal Canadian Navy Tribal Class destroyers sweep down our left flank, heading for home with their lamps flashing "bon voyage." We've air cover from Greenland for the next twenty-four hours, courtesy of the Yanks. Then it's fingers crossed until reaching Western Approaches, and backup from our own navy and air force.

The Germans are waiting patiently at the Killing Ground, running silent and deep, then shrouded in darkness the U-boats will attack en masse. Surface in the middle of the flotilla, fire their torpedoes, crash dive, and escape in the confusion. I've heard these tales endlessly, watched wan faces describing death, destruction, and loss of good friends. They're not trying to frighten, only to prepare me for the worst.

A hand grips my shoulder. Startled, I almost fall off my perch. It's my relief, Knocker. He looks ghoulish. I'm tempted to ask who's dug him up but resist the temptation. He's in pain. Instead I cluck my sympathy, climb down, and hand him the glasses. Making my way below, I strip off, wolf down some hot grub, swallow my tot, and crash my head. Sleep's a luxury once the enemy subs have our scent. Even when you're off duty, action stations may signal all hands on deck.

For seventy-two hours we're lucky; the Germans haven't launched a single foray. "Maybe they've gone home for Christmas," one optimist suggests.

No one believes him. This cat and mouse game is nerve-racking. Surveillance systems are on full alert. Every radar blip and ASDIC ping's analysed and recorded. Our job is to guard the convoy. We're not a search and destroy force. The Germans know this but try to entice us by riding a thousand yards off our flanks, appearing and disappearing at regular intervals. The weather's been our friend since leaving Nova Scotia five days ago with calm seas; moderate swells; starry, moonlit nights; and cloudless days. Still, we're not kidding ourselves. The real battle's still ahead.

The crunch comes at 0345 hours, shortly before watch change. All hell breaks loose, as the heart of the convoy erupts. Alarm bells ring, klaxons wail, and within three minutes we're closed up, watching the carnage take place, helpless to intervene. It seems the whole ocean's ablaze with a dozen burning or sinking cargo ships from the initial bloodthirsty strike, including a massive oil tanker carrying high-octane fuel, which explodes in a monster ball of orange flame. We maintain position, frustrated and angry. Clusters of star shells rain down but fail to reveal any subs. The frigates and destroyers are weaving patterns among stricken vessels attempting to rescue survivors. Many have already drowned in the frigid ocean. Dozens more are burnt to a crisp in the oil-inflamed waters. Predators have vanished as quickly as they appeared, already fifty fathoms down and geared for silent running.

We're receiving plenty of signals but afraid to strike back for fear of killing our own seamen, who are clinging onto life rafts and odd bits of debris. I grimly grasp the bridge rail as the *Daisy* comes about in a tight arc. There's a freighter dead in the water three miles astern. She's no steerage, listing but still afloat. We're to ride shotgun while an ocean-going tug attempts to take her in tow.

The corvette's buzzing. Coxswain is at the helm, telegraphs are clanging. Bridge lookouts have been doubled, and gun crews are already in place. Tin helmets have replaced normal caps. The chaos and inferno fade in the distance as my mates below battle to wring every last rev from this game old gal. It's hard to focus my glasses with the vibration that threatens to shake loose every last rivet.

At fifteen hundred yards, I spot the crippled vessel. She still rides high in the sea, though her port rear quarter is down. Probably holed below the waterline. There are a bunch of seamen milling around on the prow. In the shadow of the ship is a fat-bellied tug preparing to take the big brute in tow.

"Freighter and tug sighted, Skipper. Ten degrees off port bow!" I call, not sure he hears me. Twin flashes and explosions numb my senses, shaking my addled head. I do a double take and yell, "U-boat, dead ahead! Surfaced and stationary!"

Silhouetted against the blazing merchant ship I see antlike figures on the sub's sleek hull, ripping the canvas cover off their deck gun. Having torpedoed the cargo ship, they're going to blow away the defenceless tug. More Germans appear and start firing at the ship's crew with rifles as they're attempting to launch lifeboats from their doomed vessel. We're less than five hundred yards away when the Germans realise they have company. It's too late. Our guns are deafening. From this range we can hardly miss. The killers are plucked from the U-boat's deck like rag dolls by the rapid onslaught of twin Oerlikons, and a direct hit from the four-inch gun shatters the sub's stern.

Fewer than fifty yards separate us when the skipper orders, "Cease fire!"

There's no time for evasive action. I doubt the thought crosses his mind. The conning tower hatch slams shut, leaving a dozen Germans condemned to watery graves. The quarry vanishes from sight under the *Daisy's* bow. I brace myself for the collision, hearing the skipper tell the coxswain to hold steady on his course. He's picking his spot. There's a terrible tearing of metal—the corvette seems to have hit a brick wall.

The stern's clear of the water and the props are screaming for purchase. She staggers drunkenly then plants her back end down and grinds slowly forward. We've not escaped scot-free but are still afloat. Damage control's summoned to the bow as depth-charge crews go into action, trundling drums over the stern and launching more from port and starboard quarters, completing a diamond pattern of destruction with another batch down aft. I gaze over the stern, watching mammoth water spouts and listening to the muffled explosions.

"May the Lord grant them grace and mercy."

"Amen to that, son," the skipper echoes. "Whatever creed or colour, we're all someone's bairn."

Pulling out his pipe, he lights up and orders the coxswain to come about. We meander back, eyes searching the waves. I can smell and almost taste the stench of diesel fuel before spotting it. The flotsam, human and otherwise, is evidence that this is for real. I hear someone retching. We've all been there. I'd lost my supper long since when a faceless, mangled corpse had bumped against then careened its way down the port side of the *Daisy*. It's amazing how quickly the macabre becomes mundane. All emotions are buried in the mind hopefully never again to see daylight.

The doomed freighter's keeling over, ablaze from end to end and rapidly shedding deck cargo. Most of the survivors are safely away in lifeboats, and the remainder are being collected from the freezing sea by the sturdy tug. I stare down at haggard, hapless faces, many clad in their underwear, some with no more than a blanket about their shivering bodies. These are the unsung heroes risking life and limb for ten pounds a month. Our crew is passing down food, cigarettes, and flasks of cocoa and bottles of something more potent. I'd seen the officer's steward with some vintage scotch inside his coat, and I'm well aware Captain MacIntyre's applying the Nelson touch. The tug hitches the rafts and whalers to her starboard quarters, then alongside f the corvette, stands off a hundred yards to catch the dying ship's death rattle of groans and sighs as she gently sinks beneath the surface.

It's tough seeing this wholesale grief, as these brave souls watch their home and personal effects vanish. Within weeks, they'll be back to battling this cruel ocean and the men who seek to destroy them. Upon the misty dawn, a frigate arrives to pick up the orphans. We're the guardian angels while the transfer takes place. Our nightmare's over. The U-boats are sniffing at the convoy's heels and waiting to pounce. The frigate and tug, with more powerful engines, are ordered to make haste.

Flag Officer Drummond tells our skipper, "Extract your finger out and try to catch up before we reach Liverpool."

We're expecting the skipper to explode; instead, he's beaming. Turning to Vince, he says, "Just affirm, Sparks, and add we're maintaining silence for security reasons."

"No daily report, sir?"

"Not a smidgen. I'll have the pleasure of presenting my daily log for Bulldog when we get back."

He's weathered but wily. Every incident has to be verified by witnesses and evidenced. Sinking a U-boat is a great achievement, especially by a corvette.

He has statements from survivors, tugboat crew, members of the ship's company, and numerous bits recovered at the scene. He's no glory seeker but will relish seeing Drummond eating humble pie—or as Kenny says, "A bully getting his ass kicked."

Morale's high. We're proud of our success and having come this far unscathed. The frigate and tug have long since disappeared and so has my cigarette stash and rum stock. It's not a fair trade on God's part but has put smiles on a few faces, which should make the Big Man happy.

It takes two days to catch up, and things look different. The huge convoy has been split into smaller groups and enclosed by a formidable force of naval support vessels. The U-boats have made little impact and suffered losses at each attempted attack. The defence of the convoy has improved with the arrival of two cruisers and an aircraft carrier from the south. The Germans, who love to bask on the surface during daylight hours, now find it impossible, as the Fleet Air Arm patrol the skies and have claimed a half-dozen victims.

Another strong buzz is that there's a VIP aboard the aircraft carrier. Maybe it's Winnie himself, returning from a conference in the Bahamas with Joe Stalin and FDR. It could be a public relations stunt, but it's working wonders. If the old dog has a bark, then his young pups certainly have a bite!

Working four hours on watch and four off most of the trip is tiring. I've spent more time on this bridge than in the engine room. I'm exhausted, but the skipper's still here. Doesn't he ever sleep?

Staggering below, I grab my bottle. There's one good swallow left. Kicking off my boots, I swing into my hammock. Ten minutes later, I stop shaking. Hughie had warned me this might happen.

I'd boasted, "When I'm tired I can sleep on a clothesline." Now, with my body running on empty and my brain racing like mad, his words come back to taunt me.

"Don't worry, you'll get used to it. The first ten trips are the worst."

Within two days we'll be in sight of Ireland and comparative safety. I'm hoping the rumours are true. A few weeks in Greenock to repair the sharp end wouldn't hurt. We're due at least seven days' leave.

Be nice to make it for Valentine's Day and surprise Anita, although the biggest shock might be seeing me sampling Dad's single-malt whiskey. I hope the trauma will not be too much for Mother.

My happy, relaxed mood's abruptly shattered by the blaring klaxon sounding the call to action stations. Boots on, my feet hit the deck running. There's some unfinished business up top that requires attention first.

Chapter Thirty-Seven

There's a cloudless sky and not the slightest sign of the enemy anywhere. The skipper smirks at our puzzled faces. "I've got your attention, though it's ruined your beauty sleep. Despite lack of action, the worst is yet to come."

Playtime's over. The captain's back on the bridge. "We've a change of plans. Intelligence says we're being shadowed by more than twenty U-boats. They've thrown a net around us but can't afford to surface during daylight, thanks to the Fleet Air Arm." The Old Man really has us listening. "By this time tomorrow they'll be submerged and waiting. So we're changing tactics, altering course every hour to keep Jerry guessing. He'll be using more power, and his air getting fouler every minute. If he gets too close, we'll put a few depth charges up his backside. The longer he's down deep, the madder he'll become. It will be a busy night. We'll lose some ships and brave men, but it will shorten this bloody war," the captain concludes.

Jimmy the One steps into the breach, trusty clipboard under his arm. "The armed and faster merchant cruisers supported by a strong naval escort are making a run for it at dusk. We believe the Krauts will deploy some subs in pursuit, which will shorten the odds against us." He pauses briefly, waiting for comments. Embarrassed by the silence, he shuffles his feet. "We've received a message from the commodore too. Until further notice, every ship under his command will be closed up around the clock, and he prays for God's grace and mercy for every man under his wing in the difficult times ahead."

Looking at their hard, battle-scarred faces, I know half of these men are old enough to be my dad, and many of the younger ones come from the wrong side of the tracks. Mother would be ashamed of the company I keep. Yet I wouldn't swap one of these misfits for a pot of gold.

A sharp elbow nudges me back to life. "Head in the clouds again?" Hughie asks. He must have mystical powers. "I was saying, we should get breakfast before these gannets scoff the lot." Food always has this effect, and we scurry below.

I'm surprised: the mess deck's deserted. "Where is everyone?"

"On deck," Hughie answers. "Many sailors have died trapped below. Even those who sleep in their hammocks do so fully clothed. The couple of minutes getting dressed can be the difference between life and death." He falls silent.

We've all demons. Perhaps he'll tell me one day.

Refilling our mugs, we return up top. The air's balmy for midwinter, and the ocean's dotted with ships. It reminds me of the annual regatta except for the sea hawks buzzing like angry gnats over the calm sea. This weather will hardly please the Germans. It must be hotter than hell in their sardine cans.

Wandering down to our duty station, we see all the stokers are here. Some are playing cards, though most are leaning on the rails, staring at the ocean. A few, including LS Spencer, have binoculars to their eyes. We're an ill-assorted yet tight group of brothers, and I know it's where I belong; it must show.

"If you keep grinning that way, they'll be putting you in a rubber suit," Hughie hisses in my ear; he doesn't miss a trick.

Hooky joins us. "You two snatch a break before your watch, then report here for Fire Party. You'll just be in time for the fireworks."

There're only Knocker and Frannie, the duty mess-men, busy with mops. They are not friends on a good day. Hughie and I adjourn to a distant corner, leaving them to their chores. LS Spencer has a weird streak, putting these two dolts together. Maybe he thinks they deserve each other. Any moment, I'll see a fight breaking out and feather dusters at five paces. Hughie's shaking his head. I must be smiling again and hastily explain. He smiles as though he's becoming used to my acerbic wit, which is a nice way of saying *childish*. Knocker pulls rank on Frannie and sends him for the dinner trays while he trolls off to collect the rum issue.

The mess is filling up. We're ready to eat. The sea air has definitely spiked our appetites. The tots are being downed eagerly too, and I'm no exception. There's not much chatter and little bawdiness or bad language. We've closed ranks and are being considerate for the common good.

Hughie and I trek to the engine room and the four-hour stint drags by with only the telegraphs announcing changes in direction and the odd shudder when the corvette's bows dig into a swell. It's a shame there're no portholes. We'd know what's happening or not! This ignorance can frazzle the strongest nerves. I study Hughie's pale face and pray for him. I'm unsure what beliefs this quiet Scot holds. I've never asked. Some topics are strictly off-limits.

My Choirboy tag has stuck but is never used nastily. The fact that I don't swear or follow the brothel run doesn't faze them. A few admire my monklike abstinence. Most of this status has been achieved due to Hughie and his lessons when I first arrived. His sheltered upbringing on the Isle of Skye must have been a hard row to plough. He's standing next to me. Our vigil must be over.

"I dinna ken what you're aboot, but I'm awa up top."

"Excellent idea, though you speak in tongues my bonnie boy."

We're greeted with a fanny full of hot, steaming cocoa and a grinning Jim Spencer. "Dig in, lads. It's been as quiet as a tomb all afternoon." Bad choice of words, but he means well. "Sea's like a millpond, and there's a full moon tonight. If Jerry comes out to play, he'll get his ass shredded."

"It could be a decisive Battle of the Atlantic. The Admiralty claim Germany lost more U-boats last month than we had ships sunk," Hughie says.

Following orders to close all scuttles, darken ship, and out pipes, most chatter dribbles away; each man is mute and vulnerable in his own world, yet all are strengthened by the unspoken bond of his shipmates.

The sun's almost gone, and the moon's rising to greet us. God has crafted a perfect evening for man to kill himself. We're told to pray for friends and enemies; the problem is knowing the difference. I concentrate on my nearest and dearest ones first. Who knows how long we've got. Nowhere near long enough.

Calmness dissolves into a maelstrom of destruction. Within minutes, three merchant ships are ablaze and sinking. The whole scene resembles a Mardi Gras parade with explosions, gunfire, and bells ringing against a backdrop of myriad star shells illuminating the wholesale devastation.

We stay on station, helpless to intervene. Taking a sweep with the binoculars fewer than a thousand yards away, I spot six U-boats tracing their torpedo runs into the belly of the convoy. They're mocking us knowing we can't give chase. I'm not sure whether the Germans are brave or deranged. Their usual plan is to surface, fire half a dozen missiles, then dive deep and escape in the confusion. This is suicide. Once our destroyers and modern frigates arrive, there'll be many *fraus* back in the fatherland mourning the losses of their sons. I can't stomach any more and hand the binoculars to LS Spencer and turn away.

"You all right, lad?" he asks.

"Sure, Hooky," I say, forcing a smile. Have I been praying aloud? "Out there are men like you and I, all prepared to die. May God help every one of us."

I never hear his answer. There's a huge *whoosh* and deafening *bang*. The *Daisy's* port side rears violently, and I'm airborne. I crash into the smokestack abaft the wheelhouse. I slide down the casing onto the deck-housing, thrashing about, trying to find a handhold. The corvette's almost on its beam ends, the starboard rail already under water. Old sea dogs claim these old tubs are unsinkable. I've picked a fine moment to find out if they're lying! It's no big deal. I'm too weary to worry. My head's wet and sticky. They'll have to manage without me. I'm in God's hands now. Blow out the candle, Mother.

Chapter Thirty-Eight

The inky blackness is great. I'm floating, free falling. My eyes tightly shut and enjoying the ride. I've never had such fun doing nothing. Though I've a feeling I should be elsewhere. It hurts my head to think, so I keep on drifting, finding things not to do. God never issued earflaps. It's easy to shut out light, but noise invades the brain. There's a constant drumming getting louder every second. I risk a peep but close my eyes fast under the dazzling lights. Trying to move, I discover I'm strapped down. The pleasure trip has turned into a nightmare. Am I being transported to another planet? Maybe the gates of Hell to become a sacrificial lamb to some cruel, three-headed monster. Keeping still, I listen to the background drivel. Whirring fans and drumming engines are simple, not so the gibberish.

However, one nasally voice sounds familiar. "I swear he opened his eyes."

"He's opened his eyes a few times, only to drift off again. It's not a simple concussion, but a coma brought on by shock. Don't worry, he's tough."

Recognising Alf's bedside manner, I know it's safe to open my eyes.

Frannie's first to react. "Choirboy's back," he says, dropping to his knees and planting a wet kiss in my left ear. It's the only place without bandages.

"You had us worried, but we will soon have you fit and well."

I've a thousand questions, which Alf shrugs off, insisting that we've to concentrate on my health. Visits from the rest of the crew are limited, and their sadness speaks volumes.

We've suffered double jeopardy, being simultaneously hit by gunfire and struck by a torpedo. All the Fire Party blown to bits with the exception of Jim, who was unidentified and presumably killed by the blast.

My survival's hailed as a miracle. I've suffered head trauma, broken ribs, and a dislocated shoulder. I'd spent hours on the deck-housing bleeding out until Frannie came along, wrapped a mile of bandages around me, pushed my collarbone back into place and carried me down to the sickbay.

Who knows who God puts to work?

We're limping home on one engine with the tug for company. They reckon it's our due. We're a day behind the convoy but fairly safe. Despite our losses and damage, we're still afloat. We've lost 10% of our charges, yet were victorious.

I'm still in the sickbay under Alf's watchful eyes, and it's not solely for my benefit. Sailors are superstitious sods and might regard me a Jonah. Standing next to me could get them killed. Suppose I crack under pressure? I'm not sure of that answer myself.

Once strong enough to travel, I'm going on leave, then have a medical to determine my fitness. I'd been nervous stepping aboard, now I'll hate leaving her. Perhaps this is God's plan. I could apply for a Far East posting.

The skipper steps through the hatchway as I'm busy writing to Anita. "You look brighter than last time I saw you, Roberts."

"I'll take that as a compliment, sir."

I shuffle my writing pad. Twiddle my fountain pen. Will he take the hint?

"I'll not take up much of your time, but we need a chat."

"Fire away, sir."

The captain looks around anxiously. "Whist lad, we canna speak here. Alf's a nice boy but has radar ears. Let's take a turn on deck. The fresh air will bring a bloom to your cheeks."

Ten minutes later, we're on deck, surveying the damage. I'm shrouded in a big duffel coat with the hood shielding my bandaged head. The skipper kicks off. "There's to be a board of inquiry, Roberts, and we've to report what happened."

"We were torpedoed, sir. So I'm told."

"Did you hear more than one explosion? What were your last words to Jim?"

I stare at the mangled wireless cabin and buckled smokestack. A shudder runs through me as I search my brain for some deep-seated memory. The skipper's working on his pipe, giving me time and space.

"Handing LS Spencer the glasses, I said, 'There're men out there like us, waiting to die and seeking God's mercy.'"

"Did he say anything?"

I ponder a moment then shake my head. "The last thing I remember is this whooshing sound and a terrific explosion."

"There was only one explosion. Which came first?"

"I remember one loud bang, sir. It almost deafened me, which means that the whoosh came first."

"Good thinking, lad. That could be important."

Seeing my dumb expression, he explains. "All the info states there were two explosions. The first came from a torpedo. It struck some wreckage and detonated close to our port quarter, and all the Fire Party were killed except young Francis. He was saved by Jim pushing him out of harm's way. The sub surfaced within five hundred yards of the ship, and we were a sitting duck. A frigate spots her, comes barrelling down our port side, all guns blazing. Their gunners were too eager and put a shell through our wheelhouse. That was the whoosh you heard. We lost a dozen good men, but the frigate boys redeemed themselves. They hounded that U-boat down and blew it to rat shit."

Re-stoking his briar, the skipper takes his time. He's not finished. "You've to put your statement in writing. It could be months before it's settled. You could be on the other side of the world."

Optimistically, I ask, "Please sir, couldn't I stay aboard the *Daisy*?"

"No son, we'll be in dry dock and only need a C&M party, who will be older ratings. The navy needs all its young men at sea. Besides, you're too smart to be a grease monkey. Apply for the course that you missed. We owe you that much."

"I'm not interested anymore, sir."

He's not pleased. "You disappoint me, Roberts. You're clever, good service record. Ideal officer material, so I've heard. We're not playing cowboys and Indians. It's the real McCoy. A few of your mates die, and you lose interest. Tell me, lad, why did you join the navy?"

I hate telling lies. "To find my friend and bring him home."

Puffing on his pipe, the skipper digests this tidbit. At least he doesn't burst out laughing or call me daft. "Knew it wouldn't be simple, but I'm a sailor, not Harry Houdini. Still, "a trouble shared is a trouble halved.""

I state my case. It's as simple as falling off a log. You can read this stuff in comic books.

He's deep in thought and listens without interruption. "You didn't think this through. Wingate's mob in Burma is where you should be. Your young lady would be even more proud of you."

"Couldn't I apply for a transfer, sir?"

"It's too late. By the time the pen-pushers sort out the red tape you'd be lawn bowling in a nursing home."

"How about volunteering for a Far East posting, Skipper?"

"God forbid, man! Your shipmates will be washing out your mouth with soap and the quacks locking you away."

We're standing on the fo'c'sle. The skipper pokes out a spidery finger. "Look away over there. That's Galway Bay. This time tomorrow we'll be sailing up the Clyde, but I'd better get you below before Alf comes gunning for me."

We pause at the sickbay door. "Thank you, sir, for your time and patience. I needed that wake-up call."

"The privilege and pleasure's mine, Roberts. Anyone who has room in his heart to pray for his enemies must possess great faith. I'm not a man of the cloth, just a hard-drinking old sea-dog, but I do believe in miracles and witnessed quite a few. I'm positive, with God's grace and favour, you'll find your friend."

Sometimes words get in the way. I nod and watch him stump off to his cabin. I know he's not trying to humour me. Has one door closed, or did another one open? I'm busy juggling these balls in the air when I notice Alf leaning against the bulkhead and frowning. "If your boyfriend can't bring you home earlier, you'll have to stop seeing each other."

I collapse against the door weak with laughter. I've not felt this good in days.

Chapter Thirty-Nine

D on't argue with me. It's Skipper's orders. You're not fit to travel."

"I'll put in an official request."

"He's gone ashore. Won't be back until after lunch and is bringing you something to brighten your day."

"Doubt it. The *Daisy's* a ghost ship, most of the crew on leave. Think she will ever be the same, Alf?"

"Certainly you can take sailors off a ship, but she retains the soul of everyone who's sailed on her. You'll remember this lady till your dying day."

I'm tempted to laugh yet know he's serious. I've found a sense of belonging and security. This old tub has a heart. It's no coincidence that ships are referred as "she." Perhaps the knock on the Head has drained my brain. Though on the sick list, I'm allowed up top. I drag on an oilskin. My arm's still sore, but usable. We've been in dry dock a week but not seen the sun once. It's small wonder Scots leave home to seek fame and fortune elsewhere; who wouldn't with this weather? The deck's deserted except for John Byrne, the quartermaster, who's sheltering under a canvas awning, taking a crafty drag.

Creeping up quietly, I demand, "That man there, what the devil you doing?"

Byrne chokes on his smoke, whips round sharply, and nearly drops his rifle.

"You daft wee bugger, I almost had a heart attack."

My day's improving. "I should report you for smoking. Instead, you can do me a favour."

Not sure if I'm joking, QM Byrne hesitates. Shrugging my shoulders, I turn to go.

"Okay, I'll do it. What do you want?"

"Tell me the minute Skipper comes aboard"

"I might be gone off watch," QM Byrne wheedles.

"You'll have to pray the skipper doesn't get lucky."

I'm regretting my true-blue honesty. Something's caught the captain's notice.

Billy used to say, "Forewarned is forearmed, boy."

Where's a smart-ass when you need one? I'm missing LS Spencer's cool logic and Hughie's infinite patience. The wind's stiffened again, rattling the halyards against the main mast. Startled, I look round. The corvette's decks are empty.

Yet I'm sure someone said, "Climb back on the horse before you get trampled."

Have I become unhinged? Talks with God are on a different level. This voice sounded familiar.

Alf told me, "Skull injuries can create short-term memory loss, headaches, and hallucinations. However, in your case, no one will notice the difference."

He's such a comfort.

Roll on tot time, I'm shaking, and not because of the climate. Any mention of voices could find me holed up in a padded room. Whatever the skipper's cooking up has to be more appetising. I'll be happy if he brings me back a yo-yo.

Propped up by giant timbers, with hundreds of steel-booted workers swarming over her, the *Daisy's* enjoying a well-earned sabbatical. The janitors are doing a fine job, decks are swabbed, brass work polished, and weapons overhauled each day. There are only a few ratings aboard, so discipline isn't too rigid. We muster for duty at 0800 hours, finish at 1130 hours for dinner. All lower-deck ratings eat in one mess, and there's ample room for everyone. Afternoon is set aside for make and mend. Many men are local, only a bus ride from home. I'm pleased, if slightly envious. It's torture waiting for my number. I'm as nervous as a virgin at a bacchanalian orgy.

It's hard to be sad with great grub and a generous tot of rum too. Just one week ago, we were burying dead comrades at sea, though deep in dreamland I missed that honour and privilege. A stranger might think we don't care. They'd be wrong. The hurting is deep inside. The clowning and laughter help to hold down grief.

I see QM Byrne framed in the doorway, trying to attract my attention.

He's as subtle as the king without his clothes. "You dozy twit. I said tell me, not the crew."

He looks like a pup that's peed on the rug. Feeling guilty, I give him the dregs from my mug. If he had a tail, I'm sure he'd wag it.

Alf greets me, "The skipper wants to see you right away."

His ears are twitching. "Would you like a full report?" I ask.

"Thank you, dear boy."

"Dream on, Alice, and get down your rabbit hole." Such a nice lad. Shame he has the nose of a ferret.

"Come along in," sounds cheerful, as I enter the captain's cabin. His cheeks wear a rosy hue; obviously, he's enjoyed a liquid lunch.

"Sit down, Roberts, take the weight off. You'll need that strength during the next two weeks."

That's encouraging. A fortnight's leave right off the bat. He's been pulling some strings, but what's the old adage? Beware of strangers bearing gifts. I show my simple face. It's second nature.

"We've X-rays from base. You've no cracked ribs, just extensive bruising. Alf says your shoulder's doing fine, and your fitness is excellent. I've managed to fiddle you a few more days. Sadly, once it's done, you've to report to Lowestoft."

"Thank you, sir. I've been happy here but losing my mates has disturbed me. A fresh start may be for the best."

"What's the rush, lad? Your railway warrant, ration book, and pay won't arrive for a few days. Sit down, and we'll have a wee dram to deaden the pain."

"Is that allowed, officers drinking with ratings?"

"It's my ship. I'll do what I bloody well please. And you'll not tell a soul if you dinna, and that's an order." The skipper frowns. "I canna give you rum, you've had your quota."

Diving under his desk, he produces a bottle of fifteen-year-old Glenlivet and two Waterford crystal glasses. He pours two hefty measures, then slides me one and raises the other. "Here's hoping 1944 will be a happier year than the last five. *Slangevar!*"

Déjà vu grips me as I respond. Behind Captain MacIntyre's smile, I recognise the pain I'd seen in my father's eyes after Charlie's death. The captain carries the burden of each lost soul but makes room for the wounded too. Sackcloth and ashes are not his bailiwick.

"Take a gander at this dross," he says, shoving a stack of forms at me.

There's a common thread here. Everyone is from the Admiralty, advising all ranks of courses. Contrary to the skipper's comments about volunteers, it's the carrot he's dangling. I do not wish to be a hero, but a draft to the Far East might be handy. I'd be closer when Jack's set free. Stupid as it sounds, I know we will be together one day.

Finishing his drink, the skipper pours another and lights his pipe. "Cat got your tongue? Need a push? I've been snooping and discovered you've hidden talents."

There's more than one ferret on the fo'c'sle.

"You're a fitness fanatic, got diplomas and certificates too. No wonder Jerry couldn't blow you away."

I stay dumb; he's an agenda.

"The navy's short of skilled personnel. Among those forms is the ideal job. You're already half-trained and passing the course should be easy. It's worth a hook on your arm and better pay. No more watches or brass monkey weather, and you'll be home every weekend."

"Making me a barrack stanchion won't save Jack."

"Use your noodle, son. You'll be a physical training instructor and showing our boys the ropes. The Germans and Japanese kicked our backsides because they had fitter men. Next time will be different. What better incentive can you have for revenge?"

He's stirring the pot, and I'm slowly simmering. Object to the taste and he'll add more seasoning. He's got me by the short hairs.

I make a weak effort. "So my trip to the tropics is a formality?"

"I canna promise that, but the sooner you apply, the better. Imagine how proud your sweet lassie will be."

Lost for words, I search the stack and unearth a form with the distinctive Admiralty stamp. The return address reads: Loughborough College of Physical Education, Leicestershire. Busy at his desk, the skipper refuses to meet my eye. The place is only one hour from Solihull. Has this canny Scot done a number on me?

He's certainly gone farther than an extra mile, and it would be impolite not to study the material. There's no obligation, and the decision will be mine alone. Gathering up the paperwork, I bid the skipper a fond farewell. Closing his door quietly, I'd swear there was a smile on the face of the tiger.

Chapter Forty

Compared to me, Bedouin Arabs have it made. They pack their chattels, bed included, load it onto a ship of the desert, and off they trek. Staggering up the drive after an eleven-hour journey, I'm tattered! I tip the driver a half-crown. It's worth every penny. He presses the doorbell and nearly suffers cardiac arrest at the Houses of Parliament chimes.

Some things never change.

Mother appears in the doorway, elegant and unruffled. "Oh! It's you." Who's she expecting, the Pope?

She turns and trolls back to the drawing room, leaving us to drag the kit into the hall. I'd not expected a brass band, but even for Mother this is over the top. Dad's relaxing in front of a blazing log fire, puffing away at his pipe while listening to the news. There's a single-malt whiskey at his elbow.

"See what the cat's dragged in, Albert," Mother says with underwhelming enthusiasm.

Dad's on his feet, across the carpet fast, and wrapping me in a bone-crunching hug. Behind him, Mother's smiling. It's a rare, beautiful sight.

Her maternal instinct quickly returns. "I expect you're hungry. I'll get something to eat and make you a cup of tea."

"Sounds great, but I'll pass on the char. Need something stronger."

Mother absorbs the shock well. "Your father can take care of that while I start the meal."

I say, "You're the best cook in the world." She responds by raising her glass and toasting my safe return.

Draining my second rum, I glance around for a refill. Mother passes the bottle without comment. They've eaten, but being gracious hosts, they keep me company. It is nice having parents who are well brought up. We avoid bad news and catch up on the welfare of friends and neighbours. The Barretts are healthy though Mr Barrett's business is ailing, and there's no recent news of young Jack. My brother's working his socks off and pounding the beat, but as for Irene, who knows? She seldom speaks, according to Mother, though Dad vows that will change once she's a wedding ring on her finger. Jessie's home on leave, but Maggie's gone to India.

It's midnight. I excuse myself and drag my weary body up the stairs. It stirs memories of a tiring trip from Lydney to see my dying brother. There are no ghosts lurking on the landing, though a shiver runs down my spine. Death is ever-present.

The room's exquisite, straight from the glossy pages of *Country Living*. Large, fluffy pillows peep from beneath pristine-white sheets. A rose petal duvet drapes the bed. Has Mother gone to all this trouble for me? Maybe His Holiness declined at the last moment? There're pyjamas folded neatly. Mother must live in the Dark Ages. I'm a vest and briefs man these days, sometimes less. It's amazing, the sights one sees climbing out of a hammock. Stripping down to my underwear, I pull back the covers and sink into the feathery softness, all ready for bye-byes.

Except, I don't! The room's a tomb full of nothing, a black void. I'm used to throbbing engines, whirring fans and sailors' curses when awakened by the quartermaster's baton, plus the lilting sway of the corvette's keel riding the waves. This silence is driving me up the bulkhead. I throw off the quilt and stagger to my feet, stumbling over a chair as I try to escape this insanity. I must get help before it's too late. I find a door, wrench it open, and run into black space. Why are my mates avoiding me? Where have they gone? "Where are you all hiding?" I scream.

There're soothing voices, and a firm hand on my shoulder prevents me rising from the cosy armchair. The room's basked in soft light. I'm wrapped in Dad's paisley dressing robe. A tartan blanket covers my legs and feet. A turkey couldn't be trussed tighter.

"Be still a minute," Dad says. "Gave us a nasty shock, seeing you dashing about screaming like a banshee."

I'm glad to be on the green side of the grass. Apart from pain in the brain, I feel good. Whatever genie popped my cork last night has vanished with the dawn. Between reality and oblivion, I sense having walked a narrow line.

"Charles had that problem too," Mother says.

"What problem?" I ask.

"He walked in his sleep. I'd find him downstairs reading. His eyes were open, yet he was asleep. I'd tuck him back in bed, and he'd remember nothing."

"Eddie wasn't sleeping," Dad says patiently. "He was shouting for help, then fainted. It was a nightmare."

Mother shrugs her shoulders. "Edward has always been weird. I called Dr Mason to check him out."

Thanks a bunch, Mother. The last thing I need is having the Shaman from Solihull shaking his beads at me. Still, for family harmony, and Dad's best Scotch (the quack's halfway down his second glass) I must play nice.

Mason steps forward, stethoscope already around his neck. I suspect he's been doing exploratory work while I've been napping. I've no time for fancy dancing. "What's up, doc?"

He's too shaken to lie and launches into his spiel. "All your vital signs seem to be fine. It's the mental status that concerns me."

"Are you suggesting that I'm a nutcase?"

"No, dear boy, but you've been under enormous strain. It's bound to affect you and requires careful observation."

My dove of peace flies the coop. All the emotions bubbling inside my head come to the boil. "Dear boy my ass!" I say, pushing my hair back. "I'm a man, and I've got the scars to prove it. The only strain you have is trying to button your vest over that belly. Take a hike, Dr Dolittle. Go peddle your potions and pills elsewhere."

Peeling off the blanket, I shove away Dad's hand and struggle to my feet. The doc backpedals smartly, stepping on Mother's toes. He's rewarded with a resounding smack to his well-groomed head; he'll not remember this as one of his better consultations. Gathering the robe about my knees, I hobble from the room and head for the study. It's my favourite bolthole, the ideal spot in which to dream or fly to the moon. I draw back the curtains. It's nearly daybreak. A pearly frost covers the lawn clear down to the shallow stream. The twin willow trees wave. I wave back. Witness this scene and the quack will have me sectioned pronto. Perhaps Mother's right. She's always said I'm quaint.

Solitude's shattered by a tap on the door. "May I enter?" a soft voice asks, and in trots Mother bearing the remedy for all ills: the good old English cuppa.

She's come to bury the hatchet—hopefully not in my back. Placing the tray on the desk, she pours tea while searching for the right words.

I give her a nudge. "Sorry about the commotion. It was rude of me speaking to the doctor that way."

Mother's smile is tepid. "I've apologised on your behalf, though he thought it amusing. I didn't know my teddy bear had such sharp claws."

Taking the lid off the biscuit barrel, I see chocolate digestives. "I hope these aren't leftovers from my schooldays."

"That bang on the head hasn't improved your manners. Care to tell me what happened?"

"Not a syllable. Let's just say I had an argument with a funnel and lost."

Mother's smile is warmer. "You may claim to be a man, but that cheeky child is still inside. Drink your tea before it gets cold."

Dad arrives for breakfast, cheerful though he's had little sleep following my rampage. Mother and I have fixed a breakfast fit for a king and without quarrelling. There's an unspoken truce being forged here.

Mother's allowing her youngest son to run on a longer leash. Yet whether seventeen or seventy, I will always be her little boy.

Chapter Forty-One

Dad, rosy-cheeked and thoroughly sated, leaves for work. Fred arrives home exhausted after a twelve-hour shift. There are dark smudges under his eyes. He's twenty but looks middle-aged. Still, his face is radiant as Mother slides a plate in front of him loaded with a full English breakfast.

"Dig in, our kid. Fill your boots," I say in thick Brummie dialect.

Dolly shoots me a vicious glance, which Fred misses. He's busy decorating his meal with ketchup. There will probably be sparks off the knife and fork. We spend the next hour catching up on news of friends, good and bad, those who have been home recently and many who'll never return.

Mother notices our eyes drooping. "You both need sleep before falling off your chairs."

She's not pleased when I refuse my beautiful bed, but suggests I use the huge chesterfield in the study, sugar-coating the deal with, "It's cosy and quiet."

"Not to mention being out of sight, out of mind."

"I sometimes forget what a clever boy—oops—man you are," Mother replies.

I'm too tired to argue. Anyhow, she usually has the last word.

The couch is loaded with enough pillows and blankets to open a stall in the Rag Market. Throwing off Dad's robe, I dive in headfirst. It seems only minutes before some idiot starts banging the dinner gong. I'm still seeking an answer when the door crashes open, and Fred appears. "Rise and shine, it's suppertime," he hollers, looking brighter than a full moon.

Whatever happened to the ghoul from the lagoon at breakfast? It must be payback for the stunts I'd pulled on him. I smile gracefully. It's his due. He ruffles my hair, a habit he's adopted since Charlie died.

Supper's on the table when Dad walks in at 1800 hours. He's eaten, has changed into his Home Guard gear, and is hustling down the drive by 1900 hours. Fred's already off to the station. They look good in uniform. My brother in black with silver buttons, and Dad dressed in khaki, sporting sergeant's stripes on his battle-dress tunic and campaign ribbons from World War I.

I feel like little Orphan Annie all alone in this big house. Mother won't be home before midnight. Hordes of American GIs will invade the city searching for booze, broads, and beefsteaks, not necessarily in that order. Naturally, there're thousands of winsome young girls (some not as winsome or young) keen to aid these endeavours. And so the world turns.

It's not how I'd imagined my welcome home. I remember a poem, which kicked off "Home is the sailor, home from the sea," celebrating the return of a hero.

The poet must have been drunk or daft when he wrote it. Looking around me, all I see is a sink filled with pots and pans.

They're not intentionally cruel, but I'm the monkey, not the organ grinder. It's a dirty job, but someone has to do it. Send for Eddie. I could leave the dishes and go to Anita's. After all, I'm on leave. No! That won't work. Mother would change the locks.

Maybe they'd notice if I did something brave. Being shot out of a cannon might make them realise I'm the right calibre. A drink might ease my sorrow. I bung the plug in the sink and run hot water. Dad hasn't stashed the rum away. Knew I'd need the hair of the dog. The bottle's half empty. Someone's given this a thrashing. I pour a generous measure and enjoy. Topping up the glass, I return to the kitchen and roll up my sleeves. God's victorious again.

Up to my elbows in suds, I plan my next move but remember I've no wheels.

Mother had rained on my parade earlier. "Don't call Anita. She's in school all day, and Cheryl has a full-time job. There's plenty of time to kiss and cuddle."

She's right as usual. I've snoozed most of the day, but with this lot draining in the sink, it would be an ideal time to give my friends a bell.

Cheryl's squeal almost fractures my eardrum. Switching the phone to the other side, it receives a similar bashing as she screams for Anita. Pandemonium breaks loose. They sound delighted. Silver's barking. He's happy too. There're dozens of questions and no space for answers. I'm intoxicated listening to their lovely voices. It can't be the rum. A little order's restored, and I receive orders to stay put—they're on their way. I finish my drink and rinse out the glass. What the eye does not see, the heart will not grieve.

I've shaved, showered, and fastening the last button on my clean shirt when the gang arrives, minus Silver. He'd have destroyed the drawing room in his excitement. Never mind, he'll have his turn tomorrow.

Hugs and kisses are endless, smiles and tears ebb and flow. The house rings with laughter. The war's in someone else's backyard tonight; this is what I've dreamed for months. The ancient scribe wasn't so dumb after all. We sit around the fire chatting, eating, and raising our glasses to welcome each happy wanderer. The noise level revs up fifty decibels, and that wise old sage must be turning in his grave, wishing he'd penned more verses.

How selfish can one be? Unfortunately, young love isn't big on patience. Anita and I slip away unnoticed. Who am I kidding?

She traces a finger down the scar on my forehead. "Will it heal, darling?"

"If it doesn't I'll have to grow my eyebrows longer and brush them back."

"My parents say you've changed, that you're quieter and more mature. I think you're just as charming and silly."

"The first comes with the territory, the second takes practice."

"Don't you ever take life seriously, Eddie Roberts?"

My heart flips at her dimpled smile. "According to my granddad, you never get out alive. However, precious one, our love is very serious. You're the keeper of the secrets in my heart."

Anita moves closer. Putting soft, warm arms around my neck, her clear, blue eyes gaze into mine. I feel I've stepped off a cliff and am free-falling. I hope she sets me down lightly. The answer's in her kiss. It's luscious and lasts a lifetime. She breathes gently in my ear. "Mummy says be careful what I wish for, but I'm sure this isn't on her list."

Oh ye of little faith. God must often shake His head at me.

Bravely, I release the stranglehold and return to normal, or somewhere close. Now would be the time to reveal the plan to this gorgeous girl. Listening intently as the plot unfolds, she gives a squeak of pleasure, learning I'll be home every weekend. I've no need to swear Anita to secrecy. We adore our parents but know they're natural gossips and would want to put in their two cents' worth. They've enough problems.

We return to the family hand in hand. The giant leap from friends to forever is frightening; losing sight or touch could be disastrous. The ladies are busy in the kitchen while Dad and Mr Barrett are polishing glasses, ready for the next shindig.

"Here come the young lovers. We thought you'd eloped," Cheryl chuckles. Mother's frowning.

"Or at least got yourselves a room," Mr Barrett adds.

"Don't be crude in front of the children," Mother retorts.

Drunk or daring, Dad says, "Get with it, Dolly. They're not kids. Eddie's in the navy, and if Anita's not a gorgeous girl, then I need a guide dog."

Mr Barrett and Cheryl nod their approval. She, feisty as ever, says, "Remember when you were young and had all the boys gagging for your attention?"

Without flinching, Mother replies, "We respected our parents, were polite, well behaved, and did as we were told."

It's a once-in-a-lifetime chance. "Only when they were watching," I respond.

The tension's broken and everyone's laughing, especially Mother.

"I'm surrounded by a bunch of adolescent lunatics, but thank the Lord for His grace and mercy," she says.

Chapter Forty-Two

Mother nearly drops the teapot. "Is the chesterfield on fire? It's not daylight."

"Serve the tea, Mother darling, and listen."

She pours two cups, too shocked to question my rudeness. I stir sugar into mine while getting my ducks in a row.

"Will this take long? I've heaps to do. Cooking, cleaning, shopping, and breakfast for you hungry lot."

Brilliant! She couldn't have supplied a better lead. "This family reminds me of the navy. We're ships that pass in the night. I've hardly seen anyone but have an answer to your problems."

I pause, waiting for a smart remark.

Nothing. Mother's puzzled.

Shifting into second gear, I add, "Monday to Friday, I'll do some of the chores. You take care of shopping, plan the menus, and leave the cooking to me. This will give us more quality time."

Mother's speechless and smiley-faced. My moment of triumph's dashed. "You're home on leave, not to work."

"I'm alone until school's out. So hush up and relax while I start on breakfast."

The onslaught doesn't happen. Mother perches on a chair, sipping her tea and looking serious, but without much success. We sort the details while eating. Fred's delighted, though his joy's short-lived when reminded my duties start Monday. Mother also wipes the smirk from Dad's face, saying he's no cripple and can lend a hand too.

Lying on the couch last night, still on cloud nine after my declaration of love, I think about how I'd felt compassion for these brave people on the home front. They're the real victims of this bloody, stupid conflict.

Beneath the thin veneer of laughter, there's weariness. They've endured over four years of hardship with the rationing of food, clothing, and household goods. Thousands have lost homes and loved ones due to wholesale bombing by the Luftwaffe. Shaking off the dust, they report for a ten-hour work shift each day. Nearly everybody wears a uniform. The older, less physically capable ones are armed with knitting needles, making sure the lads and lassies in the Services have gloves, sweaters and scarves. Compared to these stubborn Brits, I'm lucky. All it took was a cute, blonde-haired angel to make me see sense, although it may have been the Big Man jogging my elbow.

The men eat and run while mother scoots into Solihull on a shopping spree. Waltzing around the house with the vacuum cleaner, I'm as happy as Larry.

Mother's back and laden down with goodies. Strictly speaking, it's the delivery boy's basket that's overflowing with groceries. He's directed to the tradesmen's entrance and eyeballed by Mother as he struggles into the kitchen with his load. I give the poor little sod a helping hand. Satisfied everything's correct, Mother gives him a silver sixpence and sends him on his way rejoicing.

She's famous for her frugality, and this almost supersedes the second coming, but she's not finished. "The sun's almost over the yardarm. It's time we had a tipple to celebrate a fine morning's work."

"You're a bonnie lass, Mother. I'll drink to that."

Without batting an eyelid, she appoints me barman while she makes lunch. The clinking of glasses is an unspoken truce between mother and son, followed by a meal sprinkled with polite conversation. I feel jaded when she leaves yet pleased we'd talked together and not at each other.

I hustle once she's gone, clear away the debris, take a bath, clean my teeth, and check the weather. It's stopped raining, which is good news. Thanks to Fred, I can use my bike. He's the eternal Boy Scout, and in return for my slap-up meal, he's inspected and repaired my transport. The Barretts know I'm coming, so their greetings are more subdued than yesterday, except Silver's, whose energy is endless and tail unstoppable.

Passing on hard liquor, I settle for a cup of tea and a slice of Cheryl's homemade cake. We sit at the table exchanging small talk, avoiding the serious stuff. Sensing tension in the air, I keep quiet. I know the devil but not the details.

Last night I'd been too engrossed to see anyone apart from my sweet love. Today I note the worry lines in her dad's face. In tandem with his business, he's going downhill. Crossing the garage forecourt earlier, the almost empty showroom shocked me. Once filled with new cars, whose gleaming chrome bedazzled one's eyes, the sole occupants now are a couple of pre-war Morris Minors, scarcely visible behind the dusty windows. The Barretts, after twenty-five years of hard work, are in danger of losing everything. They're in my prayers nightly, and Anita's too. I recall her saying she was all prayed out. Is it possible to take your bucket to the well too often? God knows. I seek His assistance continually. He never lets me down.

"I pray today, Lord, the bucket isn't leaking, and more important that the well hasn't run dry."

Silver's licking my hand and regarding me with sad brown eyes. Can he read my thoughts, or is it thumbs up from above for message received?

Cheryl brings me back to Earth. "Come in, Peter Pan. Your time's up. Jack's asking if you'd care for a tour of the workshop."

This might be time for a man-to-man talk.

Anita moves to follow, only to be stopped by Cheryl. "You can help me with the cooking and show your handsome prince how smart you are. After all, you can't live on love alone."

Silver pads beside me. Whatever's said between Mr Barrett and me, you'll never get a whimper from this canine.

Mr Barrett shuffles his feet, not sure how to begin. I go on a walkabout. There's one car on a hoist. The other two bays are empty. In the far corner, under a tarp, is the MG. I peer into every nook and cranny, even ratchet up the roller door to look down the yard. I let go of the chain. The shutter drops with a loud clang.

I'm being cruel but have to know. "Where's the Mercedes, Mr Barrett?"

His short laugh sounds like a sob. "Sold her to pay my way. I'm on the rocks. Nobody's buying, even old bangers. Can't get spare parts, and petrol sales barely keep the lights on. For the past year, we've been using savings to stay afloat."

"Won't the bank give you a loan?"

"They're only interested in a remortgage on the property, including the house. If the war ends tomorrow, it'll take five years for the dust to settle. Default on one payment and the bank takes everything, pays the taxes, and sells to the highest bidder."

"That's not fair. You've lots of friends. Couldn't they support you? My parents would help, and Auntie Elsie's not short of cash. Cheryl has money in my account, which might buy a few candles."

"You're a good man, Eddie, but it's not that simple. Albert and Dolly have grafted for their money and will be retiring soon. What would that make me?"

"The best person they've ever known, Mr Barrett. Someone who knows that friendship counts more than money."

"I've considered selling, but who's going to buy a run-down garage?"

He's not slipping off the hook that easily. "Can I ask a serious question, sir?"

Mr Barrett shrugs but manages a nod.

"What do you think Jack would say?" Without waiting for a reply, I plunge ahead. "Every son and daughter dreams of coming home. He loves this place. Told me a thousand times how he's going to help you run this business. It's probably the one thing that's keeping him sane and alive."

"You make it sound easy, but I'm bleeding money."

He can't see the wood for the trees. "Follow the bank's lead. Close the doors until the war's over. Bury your pride. Go out and get a job." I hold up a hand as he's about to protest. "Drive a tram or a bus. Clean a few windows. Do anything to cover your taxes. If you're lucky, you'll get a refund for the defunct business. My offer's still on the table, and your loving daughter intends to leave school this summer to help financially too."

He's not sure whether to kiss or curse me. Instead, he asks, "Is Cheryl aware of this scheme between you and Anita?"

"I forgot to mention, there is one small snag."

Mr Barrett sighs. "I thought it too good to be true. Tell me the worst."

"You've to convince the others that it's your idea. They love a hero."

Clapping a hand on my shoulder, he says, "Let's give it a whirl, cowboy. John Wayne's got nothing on me."

Emotional blackmail's a powerful weapon, and the thought of having young Jack home for keeps seals the deal with the ladies.

Imagining Mr Barrett as a tram driver brings out the worst in Cheryl. "I've always loved a man in uniform. It's lucky I do, sweetie, or you might not have had a big brother."

Anita's pressing Daddy to explain. He's red-faced and tongue-tied, much to his wife's delight. The past half hour has put roses back in her husband's cheeks, and the fun's infectious. They're presently discussing the merits of him being a short order cook, and Cheryl says that he's too tall.

They are worse than a couple of kids and completely out of control. Meanwhile, I'm squashed on a two-seat settee between Anita and Silver, and both of them frantic for attention.

Ain't life grand?

Chapter Forty-Three

It's been a fantastic leave, except the initial bumpy ride. I've until midnight to reach Lowestoft and business. My duties as head cook and bottle washer are done. I hand Mother the apron. There's a mountain of gear lying in the hallway awaiting the chauffeur's arrival.

Fred shocks everyone by appearing an hour before usual. "I wanted to spend some time with our kid before he sods off again."

Mother's eyes roll. Despite her best efforts, he clings to his dialect. "My mates would think me barmy if I spoke toffee-nosed."

One can't help loving him for his honesty.

Mother's pleased I'm going to Lowestoft instead of Greenock. Being one hundred per cent English, she's convinced the Scots still eat their young. More to the point, she's aware I'll be safer on land and one day nearer to coming home. God must take extra care when selecting mothers. The car's horn, followed by chimes, announces Mr Barrett. Mother brews the tea while we load my kit.

Fred's hug is tight, Dad's energetic, and Mother's warm and unexpected.

We drop Dad at the bus stop and cruise over to Mr Barrett's place. I'm surprised to see Cheryl. She should be working. "Told the supervisor I had to take care of a sick person. It's true—you've never been right in the head."

It's nice to know who one's friends are. "Are you playing truant?" I ask Anita.

"No, Your Highness, teacher gave me the morning off. I told her my boyfriend is going out east. She was sympathetic; her husband's stationed in India."

"You didn't mention I'm off to the east coast of England not the Far East?"

"She never asked."

"That's known as ignorance by omission."

Anita throws me a gorgeous smile. "If you say so, sweetheart."

Mr Barrett excuses himself. He has a client at 1000 hours. "Paying cash, too."

A plague on pessimists who claim prayers are not answered. My train doesn't leave until 1400 hours. We settle comfortably for tea and trivia. I read Jack's letter. The news is two months old yet gives his parents comfort knowing he's still alive. This gives me a chance to mention plans, especially the overseas caper. Expecting complaints, I'm showered with smiles from mother and child.

Anita breaks first. "I told you so, Mum!" she shrieks, startling Silver, who's snoozing at my feet. "Eddie's going to find Jack and bring him home."

Cheryl's happy but calmer. "Not so fast, honey. Eddie can't drop everything and take off. These things take time. Nevertheless, I'm proud of him too."

I'm stuck for words. It's strange to be regarded as a hero without firing a shot, but it makes a fitting end to my leave. My family and friends are back on track.

I do know the mantra, Charlie. God's in His Heaven, et cetera, et cetera.

MY TRAIN'S PUNCTUAL. That's a rarity. Stowing the baggage, I grab a seat. There's no time for tears: a blast of the guard's whistle, up goes his green flag, and we're off. Hanging from the window, I wave like a one-armed paper hanger until my cherished ones are lost in plumes of smoke. The compartment's loaded with khaki uniforms and not a single sailor in sight. I shut my mouth, ears and eyes. Thank God it's only one hour to Northampton and the first change.

My romance with railways is over since I've enlisted. It's no fun humping kit on and off trains. Avoiding London's the answer. It's too much hassle crossing the city to catch your connection. Most service folk returning from leave are broke. Even so, finding a cab's difficult. They're as rare as sausage rolls in a synagogue.

Local trains bring less heartache. You only have to change platforms and may snag a porter. Often the old boy will refuse a tip because you're fighting a war. I've an hour to wait for my Norwich train, but the bar's open. I've been too busy to think about drinking. Now I'm thinking. The barman's old and grizzled, and his name's Dan. True to his calling, he loves to natter.

"Served in the Big One, and afore that was a bugle boy at Mafeking. We were under siege for seven months before being relieved. Then some Canadian boys turned up. Couldn't understand a bloody word they spoke, but sure glad to see them. These army blokes today don't know they're born."

I look at the big clock. There's ample time for another rum and black. Dan sets the drink down and reaches for the money from my change on the bar counter. I stay his hand and slip him another half-crown.

His rheumy eyes glitter. He's an ancient, proud old man.

I raise my glass. "Cheers, Dan. It's been a privilege meeting you. I've a train to catch and Germans to fight."

Leaving the bar, I glance back through the glass doors; the old boy is counting the coins in his hand. I'm not sure if his wrinkled face is smiling or sad.

This Puffing Billy takes longer to reach Norwich than the Pope's New Year's Day message, and it stops for stray cows crossing the line. The last leg of the journey's no improvement either. It's taken five and a half hours to reach here. It would have been quicker by camel.

Returning to base isn't for the faint-hearted. To gain access, you have to report to the Drafting Office and obtain a station card. Chief Petty Officer William's face does nothing to improve my temper.

"Didn't expect you, Choirboy. The *Daisy's* crew not fancy your singing?"

Bullies love an audience. Chief Petty Officer Williams gazes around, seeking his staff's approval. Their response is underwhelming, with just the odd smirk. The smart move is to ignore his taunts.

Sadly, as Mother often tells me, "Eddie, you let your heart rule your head."

"We were too busy during the voyage, and when we reached Greenock, it was too late. Fifteen men were dead. You see what happens when you send a boy on a man's errand, Chief?"

Falling silent, the whole room's now closer to tears than jeers.

CPO Williams is red-faced, but he's no dummy. "I apologise for my bad manners, Roberts. We heard of the *Daisy's* misfortune and can assure you we're sickened by the loss of those brave men."

The office is full of nodding heads. When the navy loses some of its own, everyone feels the pain. Noting the chief's guilty expression, I recall

LS Spencer's suspicions about him. Had my draft been a naval cock-up or stage managed?

Spitting into the wind isn't smart. "Great mates too. In a few months, the *Daisy* will be back at sea looking for revenge," I say and then hand over my notes. My words seem to please the staff. Perhaps they know more than me.

"You've no hard feelings then, Roberts?" CPO Williams enquires.

"According to my superior officers, who are numerous, you shouldn't join up if you can't take a joke."

Speculating until the cows come home will not unearth the truth. My only clue is the CPO's curiosity and obvious discomfort. His best bet would be to draft me. The Far East might prove a good option.

He's way ahead of me. Handing back the papers, he says, "I see you're fit for sea duty. Better deal with it smartly. Once the quack gives the word, I've the ideal number for you."

He's got his mojo back and is practically drooling. "We can save on red tape too. Draft you in and out in the same breath."

Cunning old codger has broadsided me. While I've been baiting the hook, this sneaky shark has bit my ass. Granddad would be disappointed. He's constantly preached, "The Golden Rule is, he who has the gold makes the rules."

Chapter Forty-Four

I've just digested my reconstituted dried egg when the tannoy requests my appearance at the Drafting Office. CPO Williams has been burning the midnight oil figuring out a hellhole for me. I'd risen at dawn, praised the Lord for a good night's sleep, and welcomed a brand-new day. I ran three circuits around the base, shaved, showered, and put away a king-sized meal.

Opening the door, I see CPO Williams's grinning, chubby chops, which alert me that he's back in the saddle. "Pull up a chair and relax."

Shaking my head, I remain standing. I'm wary.

The ball's in his court. He's itching to serve. "You're going south."

"Am I off to South Africa or the South Pole?"

"Neither. It's to Dover in Kent."

"Know where it is, but they've only white cliffs."

"No problem, you're joining a motorized torpedo boat cruising the English Channel, and I've better news: there's a refresher course at Oulton Broad. You're with the Dawson clan again."

"You're better informed than the Mafia."

"We like to keep tabs on our inmates." He hasn't finished and hands me a chit. "Take this to Lucy, that cute redhead. She'll give you all the info."

"Thanks Chief. I'll not forget this."

"Wish you would, Choirboy. Every time you're here, there's trouble."

There's nothing wrong with his vision. Lucy's combination of curly auburn hair and deep green eyes would make a monk regret his vows. Her friendly smile is appreciated too. Being on a diet doesn't mean you can't study the menu.

She makes the process bearable, nay enjoyable, despite the leering CPO Williams. "You must be good friends. The chief's given me strict instructions about your draft."

"Not hardly. If walking the plank was still legal, your boss would have one made to measure for me."

She's awfully pretty, though frowning. "That's strange. Thought you'd be happy to be billeted with the Dawsons."

"You arranged this package?" I ask. One has to give CPO Williams his due; he's a conniving old creep.

The young lady's eyes are solemn and searching my face. Did I mention they are a fascinating green? "I'm sorry. I thought you'd be pleased."

It's hard to concentrate. "No. I mean, yes! I'm tickled pink. I'd have to be twins to be happier," I stammer, finally getting my act together. "You're an absolute darling," I say, trailing off into gibberish, noticing the crossed anchors on her jacket. She's a petty officer. Obviously my attention's been elsewhere. She's no mere slip of a girl but a mature, full-fledged young woman—and I mean fully—and at least five years my senior. Then again, who's counting?

Displaying her maturity, Lucy regards me and quietly says, "When you've finished the routine, report here for your station card. Anything else you need, do not hesitate to ask."

I'm tempted yet settle for safety. "There's no answer to that is there?"

We exchange enigmatic smiles. She's stunning and a very nice lady. She must be to be so caring for a complete stranger.

Returning my hammock to the store, I recall the chief's dire warning: "Get a signature. If you don't, those thieving Jack Dustys will spirit it away to Yarmouth market by the weekend."

There are long lines of trainees milling about, but my light-blue collar affords me access. I feel like Moses parting the Red Sea, carving through their ranks. I get the signature from the storeman, as the chief recommended, and within the hour I'm back and chatting with luscious Lucy.

She's booked transport and called ahead. "They're expecting you for supper. You seem to be popular. Are you always so charming with the ladies?"

"I'm not sure, ma'am. Guess a man's got to do what a man's got to do." We're having fun and receiving strange looks, particularly from CPO Williams. "The chief's getting restless."

"Ignore him, cowboy. He's not happy unless he's miserable," she says, handing over the cards. "Drop by when you're in town."

Not sure whether she's teasing or testing, I go chicken. "I may be back sooner than you think."

Lucy doesn't look dismayed. "I'll be here. Don't be a stranger."

I let her have the last word. She outranks me anyway.

It's a ten-minute drive to the training base. I report at 1400 hours, and by 1500 hours I'm engulfed in the warm, chubby arms of Mrs Dawson. Her daughters inflict more punishment on their return from school. It's a hard life being irresistible.

There are no watches to keep or enemy to fight, but it's no fun. We work a ten-hour day, with a short break for a Spam sandwich and a cup of cocoa. Most of the time is spent on the Norfolk Broads performing drills and dummy torpedo runs. Each crew member also has to be proficient with firearms.

Thank goodness for a hot, cooked supper and a soft feather bed. I'm bushed yet content to sit and chat with the Dawson clan or write letters home. My classmates urge me to join them on pub crawls, but swigging pints of beer isn't my idea of fun. On the other hand, a couple of tots of rum and blackcurrant might touch the spot. With that thought in mind, I grab my greatcoat and shoot out the door.

The Navigation Inn is owned by Pat McCoy, a chunk of Galway granite who discourages hookers, good lookers, and servicemen in general. The fact that I'm one of Mrs Dawson's boys and possess a "sweet brogue" allows me entrance. I get polite nods from the locals and a cheery welcome from the landlord. Though I'm not a regular, he knows my preferred poison, and it's sitting on the counter the moment I've hung up my coat.

The publican raises his glass of whiskey, Irish of course, which I've bought him. "Your very good health, sir. May the road rise up to meet you, may the—"

I stop him in mid-verse. I've heard this mantra a thousand times.

"Thank you, Patrick," I say, clinking glasses. "It probably will if I drink many of these."

My host shakes with laughter, and the yokels like it too. It's not the funniest remark I've ever made, but when in Rome, etc.

"Trying to seduce the gents now, sailor?" a husky voice breathes in my ear.

Uniforms, especially women's, are not glamorous, but this lady would look sexy in a flour sack. I'm still forming words when Pat comes to the rescue. He's poised and ready with a small tumbler in his big mitt. "Your usual, miss?"

I assume indifference. Maybe Lucy's a lush as well as lovely? Shame on me; who am I to judge?

Pat pours a vodka and tonic, adding a slice of lime. That's Jessie's favourite, but I don't believe in coincidence. Well maybe once in a while.

"Shall we sit in the inglenook? You're disturbing the gents with their game. You're much prettier to watch than spots before their eyes."

Lucy's smile almost stops my heart. "I'm glad you've got your funny bone back. You looked shocked to see me."

One on one, I'm more comfortable. "It's a pleasant surprise. Were you passing by or have you a crystal ball?"

"Neither. I came looking for you. You're different from the usual mob. They're only interested in one thing. You're polite, talk nice, and make me laugh. Isn't that enough for a friendship?"

"I do have a girlfriend back home."

"I'd be amazed if you didn't. I'm not expecting happily ever after, just someone I can trust and who can keep away the wolves who regard me as a groundsheet."

"Maybe we should take another drink?"

My comely companion's contrite. "Have I upset you, being so pushy?"

"Never, sweet lady—I adore your frankness. These drinks are to celebrate our newly formed union and all who sail in her."

"The hens at Europa will have something to cackle over now."

"It couldn't happen to a nicer couple. I recall Williams boasting he was going to paint Yarmouth red. He hasn't seen nothing yet, babe!"

"I took the liberty of jotting down a couple of dates on the off-chance that you might succumb to my feminine charms," Lucy remarks.

"Is the Pope Catholic?" I ask.

We both fall about laughing.

Chapter Forty-Five

I'm not sobbing but do feel melancholy. Rattling across the rain-sodden Kent countryside pales in contrast to the frenzied whirl of the past week. Our instincts are right on. We're compatible. The bonding is cemented by the mutual trust we have in each other. Lucy's not only beautiful but bright. Ground rules are simple. We live in the moment, yesterday's gone, and tomorrow's out of sight. We spend our evenings wining, dining, dancing, and at the movies. There's a war being waged and no time to waste. God understands. It's His way of preparing me for the next steps on life's rocky road.

Dover's not an awe-inspiring sight, and I've not left the station yard yet. This is the end of the line. Travel farther and there'll be a big splash. The place looks as though a bomb's hit it, and I curse my foolishness. German cannons shell it daily from Calais twenty-two miles away. I need to put lovely Lucy on my wish list for a spell.

The man has the face of a constipated cow and manners to match. "Get your dirty, great boots off my gunwale, sailor."

There's a fine start to a relationship. I try charm. "A good day to you too. I'm looking for *MTB 198*."

The man looks mortally wounded. "Oh! My God! You must be Geordie's relief. We're getting them straight from the nursery now."

I remain unruffled. If he wants to play silly buggers, he's found the right man.

"Jolly good show. Just made it for tea and crumpets."

Picking up my gear, I prepare to board, only to be confronted by a rail-thin figure who reminds me of the Ancient Mariner. He's an able seaman with three good conduct stripes, and on his shoulder is a rifle that's possibly not been fired since the Crimean War.

A gnarled hand grips mine. "I'm Tom, the coxswain." His battered face is smiling. "Take no heed of Harry. Under that bluster, he's a pussycat. Do your job, you'll be fine." Taking my papers, he briefly eyes them. "Patrol Service and used to roughing it. Good! This isn't your daddy's yacht, lad, but we're family, first names only, including Dally, the skipper. There are no bugles or bullshit. Rig of the day is usually what you crawled out of last night. We work hard, play harder."

He picks up my kitbag. "Let's get below and introduce you to the other heathens. They'll be curious to see who's come to dinner."

The aroma of the corvette's mess deck comes flooding back as we descend the wooden steps into the bowels of my new abode. The smell of cabbage, sweaty socks, and drying laundry mingles freely in a space hardly big enough to swing a cat around. A pall of smoke drifts aimlessly despite the extractor fan's plucky efforts. I count heads while Tom adds names. It's impossible to know their jobs. They're all dressed in vests and shorts.

I meet the rest of the engine room branch. "Petty Officer Tracey, christened Neville, but everyone calls me Dick." We exchange nods, he eyes me shrewdly. "Been on a corvette I hear."

My new boss takes two tots of rum from the table. Hands me one and raises the other. "You have my respect and deepest sympathy, Eddie. Bottoms up."

It's great to be back on neat rum. "You're the nicest Dick I've met today." I remember Gramps's lore: if you're going to play the game, play it right.

Dreaming of pirates is one thing. Living the dream is *incredible*!

Williams must have friends in high places and cast a lot of nets to land this fish. No wonder Harry was discombobulated when I'd rolled up on the quayside baby-faced and cheerful. And explains why the men are ten years older than me.

I'll win them over with boyish charm and make the skipper my ally. Hearing my speech, he declares, "At last, there's someone who speaks real English."

There are fourteen crew including two officers and two NCOs. Everyone mixes and mingles. It's called democracy but has drawbacks. Patrolling the English Strait is boring. The enemy avoids our firepower, content to seek easier prey. German E-boats flex their muscles yet offer no threat. Dover Patrol does a magnificent job keeping the sea lanes clear, but when push comes to shove our boat can be closed up and under way while the big ship boys are shaking the spit from their bugles. We're mavericks and proud of it! Our conditions wouldn't be tolerated by a pig. Seventy-five per cent of the vessel is fitted with machinery and equipment. Eight men live in an area of twenty-five feet by fifteen. Here we cook meals, eat, sleep, and spend our leisure. Officers double up in a tiny cabin. Sparks and the bunting tosser crash in the wheelhouse. It's hardly high living, even for a hobo.

Fair dues though. The Admiralty, in a gesture of goodwill, grant one shilling a day to all ratings subjected to these primitive conditions. This bounty's called hard layers and includes a tot of neat rum each day. We're the envy of all General Service matelots who have to survive on watered-down stuff. The living is not palatial, but the grog and grub are fine.

From day one, I've marvelled at the closeness fostered amongst the crew. Whether pauper or prince, bonds are forged and relinquished only in death. Reality hits home one grey dawn as one of our flotilla returning from patrol hits a mine a mile from the harbour entrance and is blown to smithereens. There are no remains to provide a naval burial. We honour comrades with a quayside service, then adjourn to our regular watering hole to get hammered—the least we could do.

We're pulling extra duty with one boat gone; the crew's tired and edgy. Bruce decides to splice the main brace, and in the midst of our delight imparts good news. "Captain Ian 'Bonnie' Brookes is pulling us out of line. We're going into Dymchurch for a paint job. He's also fiddled us ten days' leave."

I suspect Dally has done his share of wheedling on our behalf but hold my noise. He's setting up the chessboard, yet I sense he's worried.

"Had a letter from my sister. Wants me to visit. I haven't been home for a year."

I'm no agony aunt, but he needs help. I keep mum waiting for his confession.

"We had a bust-up, and I walked out, swore I'd never come back. Now she needs me. How can I apologise?"

He needs logic, not laughter. "Just fold your tent and go. Tell her how much you love her."

"Do you think she'll forgive me?"

"She's already done so by inviting you. Where does she live?"

"Jeannie's from Scotland, in the Western Isles. It's a two-day journey from here. My excuse for not going, I suppose."

His words stir a distant memory in the back roads of my mind. I'm struggling to connect the dots.

He's not done. "Her husband was killed a few months ago. Last week she received a DSM for his bravery. The villagers are erecting a statue in his honour, and she's asked me to attend."

His words paint a perfect picture, and I'm speechless. I reach out a shaky hand for the bottle. Bruce would think me crazy if I screamed my thoughts.

I know the place well. There're ten sheep for every human. Hughie's a five-year-old bairn, and his wife's a hammer thrower, which I don't believe for one second.

Instead, I raise my glass and swiftly toss back the rum. "Excuse me, Dally, I need some air. It's stuffy down here. I'll talk to you later."

Chapter Forty-Six

We catch the London train with minutes to spare, fragile from last night's farewell party for Harry and Tom. Following leave, they're off to Devonport, and with thirty years combined service, we can't imagine them as barrack stanchions. The one absentee is Sub-Lieutenant Ken "General" Montgomery, still in the loving arms of his merry widow. Who can blame him?

Bruce steers us into the Hope and Anchor, next to Victoria Station, where we down a few jars before breaking ranks. Three of the lads have a short tube trip; the remainder set sail for Euston Station. Dame Fortune smiles on us as we collar an empty compartment. We've a card school going, the sun's over the yardarm, and drinks are flowing. My mates are a motley crew, but to me, likeable rogues. I'd dreamed of pirates. God provides.

"Got your mind focussed on that gorgeous girl again?" Bruce asks.

Nobody would believe me if I told them. The skipper's comment sparks rude remarks, which I ignore. My skin's thicker these days.

All too soon I'm on the platform, watching the train depart. Nice to be home, sad to see my mates leave. I pick up my gear and head for the bus depot.

The house is empty. Stripping off the uniform, I climb into civvies, then grab the bike and scoot.

The garage forecourt is a fairground with balloons and coloured ribbons everywhere. The razzle-dazzle's working, though the pretty girl is possibly the main reason. Patrons are content to wait; there's nothing wrong with the view, and that dog is not here for show.

Neither Anita nor Silver having seen me, I look for Mr Barrett. I see his boots poking out from under a van, and I kick one of the soles. He comes barrelling out, his face and overalls coated in thick black sludge. He'd picked the wrong time to remove an oil plug. I stagger about in hysterical laughter. Mr Barrett's savage and wipes his face with a cotton swab. I go into fits again. All I can see are the whites of his eyes.

"Sing me three choruses of 'Mammy,'" I beg.

He's looking round for something to throw. Quickly, I pass him a hand mirror. Flashing a whiter-than-white smile, Mr Barrett starts to chuckle. Within seconds, we're rolling on the floor roaring with laughter. Anita dashes in expecting to find Daddy crushed under a car but instead crushes me into her arms. I'm too weak to resist.

Mr Barrett recovers first. "You'd better get up front before that Hunt gang strip the place."

"They wouldn't dare with Silver standing guard. He'd rip them to shreds."

"More likely lick them to death."

"True! But they don't know that."

It's great to see them happy. They're going through a rough patch, but Anita is the glue that holds this family together. Persuading her to take a break, I man the pumps, which allows Jack to concentrate on repairs. He's not making a fortune, but getting by with his wife working full-time and his daughter's help.

Cheryl arrives as we're shutting up shop. I surrender to her warm caress and marvel how fresh she looks, following a ten-hour shift.

Anita finds the energy to cook supper. It's déjà vu once more. Silver's head seems bigger than ever, but I'm not complaining. The banter's lively. There's a war on, but tonight we've booted it into touch. Nothing can harm us. Says who?

I've avoided the tragic news. My friends are fragile enough without knowing a POW ship was torpedoed on its way to Japan. One thousand eight hundred men were left to die beneath battened-down hatches. Instead, I boost their spirits, saying paratroopers have dropped behind Japanese lines in Burma and are making progress.

By 1000 hours, I'm nodding. Mr Barrett runs me home. Only Dad is here. He looks how I feel. "They're disbanding the Home Guard," he says.

"You'll have to go back to the George."

"It won't taste as good."

"I'll drink anywhere when I'm thirsty."

"Help yourself. It will be nice to have a drinking buddy."

I pour myself a generous one. We raise our glasses.

"It's great you're home, son." He hesitates, searching for words. "Do you regret not going to Dartmouth?"

"No, I wouldn't have made a good officer. It's tough taking orders without giving them. I'm happy on the lower deck."

Dad's not convinced. "You've some good mates?"

Nodding, I describe the gang aboard *MTB 198*.

He's chuckling long before I've finished. "They sound like my platoon in World War I," he says, reaching for his glass, hand unsteady. "Most of them bought it at Verdun and Mons. The biggest load of rogues that ever breathed. Bless them all."

This is a first. He never mentions his war. Maybe the liquor or our chat has triggered a dusty memory from his youth. Then again, he might be warning me of the road ahead.

No matter the reason, this less than perfect man but wonderful Dad shouldn't be sitting alone in the firelight, and I say so.

"Throw another log on the fire, Ed, and let's raise a glass or two for auld lang syne."

"That's the best idea you've had in a coon's age, Dad."

For the next two hours, we drink steadily and talk nonstop. Evidently, my law-abiding father was a young scallywag, but I'm not bothered. Granddad's schooled him well. Mother arrives, tired but happy. By the tight hug and full-frontal kiss I get, I suspect we're not alone at tipping the elbow. Mother's passion usually amounts to a swift peck on the cheek. It's turned midnight, which to the drinking class is early. We top up our glasses. I'm enjoying intelligent conversation without smart remarks or smug answers. With the clarity that only a drunk can muster, I realise I'm being treated as an adult.

DAD, WELL GROOMED, HIS SILVER hair neatly brushed, and tucking into bacon and eggs, cheerfully greets me as I totter to the table. Plainly, the old bull has much to teach the younger. I suffer his jibes silently while Mother clucks her sympathy. She too is radiant. They must be on some magic potion.

Resolution is easy in the cold light of day when you're hurting because little men in hob-nailed boots are beating your skull with claw hammers. There're no protests when I volunteer to help with household chores. Afternoons, I'll assist Mr Barrett, and evenings will be reserved for Anita. My altruism does have an ulterior motive: it will keep me off the booze.

Presently, it's no contest, because I've more love than one could shake a stick at, but back aboard literally, all in the same boat, judgment or destiny may take command.

Leave is over too quickly, and it's back to reality. The invasion of Europe will begin shortly, and another bloodbath will unfold. Apart from casualties on the battlefield, thousands more innocent women and children will perish because of the aspirations of a madman. Question: who's going to pick up the pieces? Stretching out my legs, I close my baby blues and bask in the solitude. I've walked the length of the train to find this haven next to the engine posted with no-smoking signs. There's not a soul to prevent Peter Pan spreading his wings in flights of fancy.

The door crashes open, and it's Bruce. "Searched everywhere. Knew you'd be hiding someplace. Had a fantastic reunion with Jeannie and all the clan," he says and rambles on for five minutes. He stops suddenly and pulls out a flask. "Forgive my manners. You must be dying for a snifter. We have to be in shape for the welcome home party."

I deliberate but then take a hefty swig. My wings are more than singed; like Icarus, I've crashed in flames.

No good intention goes unpunished.

Chapter Forty-Seven

The homecoming's under way. I've seen wakes with more action. Bruce is at HQ consulting with Bonnie Brookes about our future. Harry and Tom's departure has left a dent in the crew's life; we're down to a dirty dozen, and there is worse to come.

Downing my drink, I wave to Rosie. Another round might liven up my mates. They're as much fun as shoving lighted matches up one's nose. Seeing the skipper, I show the barmaid two fingers. It's not rude, but for a double scotch.

He's two-thirds down the glass in one swallow. "They've scuttled us, lads, and are sending us to Harwich. Most of you are being recalled to depots. Worse news, the party's over. We sail on the morning tide."

"Let's hope the general knows it's a long haul up the A2 in a four-poster bed."

"How can you stay so cheerful, Eddie?"

"Easy, Skipper. If you didn't laugh, you'd cry."

There're many a true word spoken in jest.

We leave at dawn before the seagulls dump on our new paint. We turn left at the boom and head north. Though it's only a two-hour cruise, we're closed up for action and keeping a sharp lookout. Contrary to my gloom, I see a chink of light. It could take weeks for a relief to arrive, and our new base is a one-hour drive up the coast road to Lowestoft. Hitching a lift will be easy.

Dally doesn't question my motives. "Be here by 0800 hours, Monday."

We're restricted to harbour duties and to running top brass between ships and shore. The bars are teeming with sailors, and there's not a decent pub for miles. Rosie and the Lord Nelson are distant, fond memories.

Purely by magic and a tot of rum, "Tommy" Gunn, our Sparks, patches me through to Europa and Lucy. Her squeal probably wakes Williams from his nap. It's been two weeks since my last letter; she's been fretting. I reassure her that only the good die young, and I'll see her Saturday.

We're still yapping as Tommy rips the phone away. "You'll get me shot," he moans, though smiling. He's married, got three kids, and he's a romantic at heart.

Hopping a ride is easy. I'm in Oulton Broad and Lucy's embrace by noon. The three-day wait has seemed a month. However, on the plus side, I'm the Dawsons' guest for the weekend thanks to my lissom lass. Momma Dawson thinks we're an ideal couple and hears wedding bells in the distance. Dream on! Our adoration's mutual but maybe in a different life or time.

We've drawn a line in the sand, knowing there's a boundary not to be crossed. I know Lucy's been hurt. She doesn't trust men in general. I'm lucky and treasure her respect. I've learned through the experiences of wayward shipmates and the Dear John letters they've received how much grief can be caused by stupid actions.

It's too late for the movies or the dance hall, so we amble down to the pub. Pat's quick with the drinks, and we settle into our usual seats by the fire. Away from radar ears and wagging tongues, I tell Lucy about my impending return and ask her to chase up my application. This liaison's more than kisses and cuddles. Passing this course will help me secure an overseas draft.

"It may be a long wait. Combined Ops are trying to recruit everyone for landing craft and minesweepers. They're keen to go ahead with the invasion this summer. There's said to be thousands of Allied troops along the south coast, just waiting."

"No wonder we got booted out. There're hardly any civilians left in Dover," I say.

"Cheer up. Think how pleased Williams will be to see your smiling face."

Her words light another candle. If I work hard on Williams, he'll gladly pack me off abroad. Waving goodnight to Pat and the domino demons, I walk Lucy home. She pouts when I refuse a late-night coffee, saying my fairy godmother will banish me if I'm not home by midnight. I remind her I'm not due back until 0800 hours Monday, so she rewards me with a huge smile and warm hug. Women baffle me. I'm not sure what game Lucy's playing, but it beats Monopoly.

The Sabbath's still special, and the Dawson clan devout. Following a hearty breakfast, we stroll up the hill to the Seaman's Chapel. God's a full house today. It's amazing how siege can bring forth Christians. There's no choir, no sixteen-bar solos, and it's miles from St Martins Church, yet it's heart-warming for a small boy far from home.

Mrs Dawson, with Lucy's blessing, has organised the rest of my day, including a scrumptious Sunday dinner surrounded by a bevy of beautiful females. My welfare is their concern, and between cups of tea, friendly chitchat, and a stroll along the beach, the afternoon flitters by. Lucy and I slip away after supper for a couple of drinks at Pat's place. It's a pleasant end to a perfect day.

My surrogate mum wakes me at 0500 hours. I'm on the road by 0600 hours, hitch a lift, and I'm back aboard by 0730 hours. The lads tease me. I'm the only one in uniform. Even Bruce has a dig: "Today we're honoured by a real sailor. Ignore him, he may go away."

Time flies and the crew too. By Friday, we're down to five. I'm helping Dally to pack his gear and consuming the remains of the rum before Jack Dusty pulls the plug. Once the keg's empty, we'll blame the mice.

Dally's been promoted but whining. "I'm to be first lieutenant on a destroyer and act like an officer and a gentleman."

"Impossible! If you were, I'd never speak to you again."

"Just imagine never hearing you calling me Bruce Baby anymore or being known as Jimmy the One."

"Nonsense, you're not one. I've never seen you carrying a handbag."

"How would you know? You're as bent as a corkscrew."

"Charming. This is the last time I help pack your underwear, honey."

Dally falls off the bunk laughing. "You're the silliest bastard I've ever met."

"You've been reading my mail again."

"My granddad used to say, 'It's a great life if you don't weaken.'"

"We'll drink to that if I can find the bloody bottle," I say.

I'd love to tell you more, but the next twenty-four hours are a pothole in the back roads of my mind. The Samaritans, who carried us back aboard, swear we had a fantastic blowout. I'll take their word.

Lucy's sympathetic, though I'm a day late and suffering. She knows it's more than booze. We take the bus to Gorleston and stroll along the cliffs. She tucks her arm cosily through mine. During sombre moments, I think about our friendship. I'd been grieving the loss of mates when this green-eyed goddess crossed my path. It can't be happenstance that we met. This beauty, I'll never forget. One day my grandkids will learn about the luscious lady from Leeds.

A wise soothsayer once said, "It takes but a moment to find that special person, an hour to appreciate them, a day to love them, yet a lifetime to forget."

We drop into the Regent Restaurant on High Street. It's pricey yet elegant. They cater for a high-class clientele. My gal has a naughty streak, which I adore. The place is full of navy officers with their wives and ladies.

One would have to be blind or in a coma not to notice Lucy's entrance. She's stunning, even in uniform. Gliding to a small alcove and table for two, she awaits my arrival, unfastens the buttons of her topcoat, and wriggles it seductively off her shoulders in a move that Gypsy Rose Lee would applaud. Pulling out her chair, I adjust it until she's comfy. Lucy rewards me with a bewitching smile, placing a hand lightly on mine, which rests on her shoulder. We maintain the pose for the audience's edification of true love. It's brilliant! Neither Mickey and Minnie nor Tracey and Hepburn are in our league.

"You're enjoying this," I say, watching Lucy working the room.

Her exotic green eyes speak louder than words. There're looks of distaste for the females and contemptuous glances at their partners, who seem ill at ease. I've no sympathy for these silver-haired lechers. They're probably sweating blood, afraid this glamorous gal might dish the dirt to their companions.

Plucking a scone off the plate twixt thumb and forefinger, Lucy takes a tiny bite. It makes the task of eating look sinful. "I certainly am, darling. There'll be some awkward questions around dinner tables tonight."

"You've already bruised their egos, consorting with a common matelot."

"Not as much as the bruises they've left on my bum," Lucy replies. Her words are sheer poetry.

I'm wondering if we'll get out alive. There's no problem. The café is emptying faster than rats from a sinking ship.

Lucy surveys the room, wide-eyed. "Was it something I said?"

Chapter Forty-Eight

The journey's bittersweet, buoyed by thoughts of being with Lucy but saddened by the loss of friends. What lies ahead? If my application's in the pipeline, I'll enlist Williams's aid. He'd love to see me gone. Maybe he fancies Lucy. I've seen tortoises with more speed. I arrive mid-afternoon and report to the office. She's not here. That's a shame. Neither is Williams. That's a relief.

His Majesty's Royal Navy prides itself on efficiency and discipline. There are rules, regulations, and instructions for everything and a dim view is taken for anybody circumventing their use. This is nothing to do with being Jewish; however, if there's a fiddle to be found, Jack's the lad. In this case, a string section, Tommy, Dick, and myself. Officially at 1000 hours, our boat's paid off. The chief Jack Dusty comes aboard and checks that everything's kosher, that no rum, stores, or equipment have gone adrift. He's suspicious but satisfied, signs the docket, and leaves. We have a lavish lunch and dispose of the rum extracted from the keg before it was sealed. The draft chits say we're on our way to base and will miss Up Spirits, but the navy has that one covered. On arrival, my station card is stamped *In transit*.

Roll on 1700 hours. It's not a patch on neat rum, but it's welcome after a hard day. They say, *Tiny things amuse tiny minds*. Still, it's nice to bamboozle the brass. I've soon finished the routine and am back at the office.

The chief's squatting in his usual chair, obnoxious as ever. "I heard you were back."

"Hope you baked me a cake."

"Fat chance. You'll be away by Friday, and no time to sweet-talk Lucy."

"She's not here?"

"She's on compassionate leave. Her father's sick. It's not your day, lad."

It's tempting to rearrange his face. Instead I say, "I'll call her later."

He seems surprised I've her number. I don't, but he doesn't know that. One of Lucy's colleagues might help once I off-load this bozo.

I'll have to be polite, though it hurts. "Where's my next posting, Chief?"

"To Combined Ops on the Sussex coast. There's a tough, one-month commando course. I should wish you well, but I'd be lying. Hopefully, I'll not see you again."

Picking up my station card and beer tickets, I afford him a pleasant smile while quietly saying, "If wishes were sausages, pigs would be an endangered species."

Williams is faced with a decision. Does he charge me with insubordination or pack me off on the next train? Leaving him frowning, I trot off to the stores for my well-earned tot.

I'm saddened by Lucy's absence. Selfish motives apart, I pray for her father's survival. He's silicosis of the lungs due to working down a colliery, and he's not much older than my dad.

I feel useless. If I could talk to her, it might help. Maybe Mrs Dawson has an address or phone number. Sitting on the bus to Oulton Broad, I start shaking. Guess I'm not such a hard case after all.

Everyone's pleased to see me, though concerned hearing my news. Sadly, Mrs Dawson is not allowed information. Following a restless night, I try plan B, which bites the dust. Wily Williams is ahead of me. I'm met by a wall of silence from his staff. He's won this battle but not the war.

Feeling sorry for myself is no use. My goal is to rescue Jack. The chief knows I'm still breathing. I've planted my spear firmly in the ground and will be back.

Chapter Forty-Nine

The person issuing travel arrangements must be sadistic. Who else on a rainy, ball-shrivelling night orders a train to carry a hundred sailors on a four-hour jaunt into barren land? We've been herded aboard trucks belching diesel fumes and whisked off into the hills. The lads in khaki tolerate this, but we're the Senior Service and worth better treatment. I've done character-building as a boy. This isn't it!

The huts are a hundred feet long with double bunks. Two pot-bellied stoves are separated by wooden bench tables down the centre. The floor's concrete. Storage lockers are steel. Lighting's dim and so is the outlook. These huts were designed by a man named Nissen. I think he had something missing.

It's difficult being sociable at 0300 hours, but finding one's temper once it's lost is hard too. Sometimes, turning the other cheek saves bloodshed. I've already silenced one yobbo by selecting a top bunk with a gracious smile; he's spent ten minutes apologising for his rudeness.

He's probably a nice kid on a good day, but it's not his fault that snakes like Williams exist. The chief was practically drooling as he called my name. I'm brain-dead and physically shattered. Stripping off my tunic, but retaining my thick blue jersey, long johns, and socks, I slide under the rough grey blankets. The stoves are beginning to glow, yet the place is frigid. It's almost 0700 hours when the QM urges us to rise and shine. We're told there's an information meeting at 0900 hours, which is treated with derision. Rarely does the navy depart from tradition, especially morning parade, and confiding in the ranks is absurd. There're many suggestions what their Lordships can do with their info. None are polite.

The auditorium's vast, packed to the gunwales and the stage loaded with top brass. There are more medals on view than at the Olympics. Many faces are familiar, especially the ferret-faced RAF type. Love to take one of them up a dark alley; I'd change his outlook on life.

A tall, husky guy steps up to the podium. "Good morning, I'm Barry Stewart, your liaison officer. I'll get straight to the point. Combined Operations is the name of the game, but it's serious stuff." He pauses, looking ready to plunge a dagger into our hearts. "We have to put men on the beach. It's not for wimps. The RAF will provide air support, and our big ships attack from long range, but we've to get the ball rolling. Our assault craft have one thing in common: they're all flat-bottomed, difficult to handle, little steerage way, and slow. Any questions?"

LO Stewart's beaming now. He's done this gig before but needs a second banana.

Sticking up my hand, I ask, "Can I change my mind, sir?"

A few titters run around the room. Good! I don't wish to steal his thunder.

"I haven't come to the fun bit yet," he answers.

Stop one maverick running and you'll prevent a stampede. He delves into my service record and in minutes convinces the audience I could navigate an aircraft carrier up the Manchester Ship Canal without scratching the paintwork. Like all good hustlers, he saves the best till last: the fact that we qualify for hard layers and neat rum carries the day. There are a few stupid queries, which LO Stewart easily fields or sidesteps, and the reluctant heroes file out, believing they've found a soft number. I'm thinking Greeks and Trojan horses.

Outside, a horde of vultures waits disguised as petty officers. They'll be our daily shadows and nightmares for a month. We're herded into squads and doubled back to our huts. Anyone thinking it's a picnic should have brought a packed lunch.

Running doesn't figure highly on a sailor's wish list, which explains why shipmates regard me as weird. The PO waits until the wheezing stops then he lashes out. His language is brutal, but his meaning is clear. We're a menace to ourselves and comrades. I find myself in agreement. He's challenging our manhood. He's twice my age, but I'll give the old boy a run for his money. It's macabre in a funny way. If you're going to die, at least be healthy.

Petty Officer "Flash" Gordon explains the house rules. "First week are field exercises to toughen you up. Sea drills come next, followed by two weeks of simulated landings. There's no escape clause, but we're selective. Only about thirty per cent will qualify. The rest return to base and normal duties."

We break for lunch and are told to muster for kit issue at 1300 hours. There's little talk during dinner. This boot camp's getting worse every minute. Bad news is faster than the speed of light. There's no leave Monday through Friday, and all villages are out of bounds. Weekend passes are from noon until midnight. The seven-foot-high fencing's topped by razor wire, and it's electrified. Communal traffic is nil, except the Liberty bus to Brighton. Maybe breaking a leg is the only solution; some hearts seem to have already taken that route.

I've always known the PT course would be tough. This jaunt's a step in the right direction. Running a few miles a day has never bothered me, but five miles in battledress and army boots doesn't light my fire. Yet I keep pace with Flash, who's breathing heavier than I am at the finish.

Drawing me aside, he has words of wisdom. His manner's courteous and firm. "You've done this before, haven't you, son?" Without waiting for a response, he adds, "Don't be a smart-ass. Understand?"

"I wouldn't dream of it, Petty Officer. I thought it might help."

NCOs have a common flaw. Their brains run on narrow-gauge tracks. I hear the gears meshing as Flash struggles to switch points; the signals are against him. He applies the brakes. "Enlighten me," he says.

"Easy. Between us, we can shake up this bunch, and you'll have the best squad here. No way are they going to let a young kid kick their ass. I'll bet my tot on it. All you do, Petty Officer, is watch my back and see I'm not bushwhacked."

"You've done this before! You're a devious swine and a man after my own heart."

"Is there an echo in here?" I ask.

I'm speaking his language. Our scheme works like a charm. Everyone's keen to kick my rear end. Occasionally, I falter. It keeps the pot boiling. The sauce bottles are filling up nicely. The sea exercises are challenging, but my time on the *198* wasn't wasted, although landing craft tend to bounce over the waves, not ride them. Also, in an emergency, I have to double as coxswain. Fully loaded, with fifty men and equipment, they're obedient as Silver when he spots a rabbit.

We practice simulated landings, and everything's fair game, except live ammunition. Defending our homeland is the Home Guard, and we're the enemy. When you're hit by a bullet, it explodes and covers you in paint. You're dead and have to retire from the battle. Regardless of their age and poor eyesight, these old sweats are crafty. Kill the driver and engineer, and you've wiped out a boatload of invaders. I've learned how a rubber duck feels sitting on top of a fairground waterspout.

Loading troops into landing craft is fraught with danger too. Trying to get close to the ship's hull in a heavy swell is futile. Many men break limbs. Victims fall from sodden rope ladders. Tragically, half a dozen men die.

It's been an eye-opening, gut-wrenching month, but we've made it and tonight are celebrating our success. These unruly peasants in our hut are diamonds. More than half have qualified. They all love me. The fact that I've broken out the rum may account for it. Tonight's our last night together. We're tying one on. There will be many sore heads come the dawn.

It's long odds we'll see each other again. I've learned that lesson the hard way. God willing, some of these beautiful, drunken heathens will survive this crap and live long, happy lives. I'll never remember all their names, but one thing's certain: their faces will stay young and fresh in my mind for the rest of my days.

Chapter Fifty

It's a shame the navy hadn't issued buckets and spades. We could have played on the beach while spears were being sharpened for the invasion. This travelling back is driving me crazy. Watching troop trains going south with rowdy soldiers hanging from the windows makes the gates of Europa seem divine.

Suppose these brave warriors finish up in a camp similar to the one we've just left? That will dampen their enthusiasm. I feel brighter already.

My joy is brief. It will take ages getting this rabble sorted; Williams struggles valiantly to maintain order. We've spent a month with hard instructors and aren't intimidated by gold buttons. Should the chief have toes trodden on or an elbow in his ear, I won't cry.

There's no sign of Lucy. I quiz her friend, Angela, but she's not talking. I leave, promising to call back. She's not pleased. Join the club.

By the time I've made the rounds, the office is closed. I'll have to pick up my cards tomorrow, which means I can't leave base tonight. I'm dead in the water. Private lives are off-limits. Lucy may have a boyfriend or husband. We know our friendship's pure but try telling that to the marines.

Williams doesn't improve my day. "There's good news and good news: you've double beer tickets and a weekend pass."

"I'll take the leave. You can stick the beer tickets where the sun doesn't shine."

"It could be your last one. I might be marking your card for good."

"A man of your experience should know better, Chief. Never say never; it will come back and bite your ass."

Williams, like all bullies, is a coward at heart. He hops into his private burrow and slams the door. The scene hasn't gone unnoticed.

"Have a good war, folks. I'll be seeing you." I'm smouldering inside, but

John Wayne couldn't have made a better exit.

FRIDAY NOON I'M THROUGH EUROPA'S gates, and by 1700 hours, pushing open the door of the Bodega. Mother's delighted and pours me a drink. I'm starting how I mean to finish this weekend. Feeling no pain, I down another and take a leisurely stroll to Cannon Street. I snag dad as he's leaving work and steer him into The Windsor. I sample another dram, courtesy of Lou the Landlord, while Dad puts away two swift halves, explaining Fred will start nagging if we're late. These words come from a man who used to arrive home at 2030 hours, his supper cooked two hours previously, usually representing a sacrifice or a burnt offering. Stranger still, five years ago, tonight's cook would have exploded if asked to boil an egg.

The meal is excellent company. Dad takes a shot of whiskey; Fred opts for a glass of red wine. I pass. I'm off to Anita's and don't want the cops to arrest me for being drunk in charge of a bike.

I arrive as they're eating. Silver looks forlorn. Creeping into the kitchen, I steal some tasty bits off the meat dish for him. Cheryl pretends not to notice.

Anita and I slip on our coats, collect Silver and stroll along the Parade. We're not self-conscious anymore. Passers-by see two young lovers oblivious to the world. Who'd wish to disturb them, especially with that huge hound in tow?

Cheryl and Mr Barrett tackle the chores while I enjoy a beverage and read their son's latest letter. It's taken six weeks to arrive. It's bland and identical to his last one. The Japanese are touchy about content. They even black out "God," as young Jack blesses us, but it makes our day knowing he's alive and fit enough to write.

"He might be home by Christmas," Cheryl says. "What do you think, Jack?"

We exchange glances. He seems nonplussed. I pick up my drink.

There's a long pause. Maybe he's dozed off. "It all depends on Ike," he finally says. "He's the man with his finger on the trigger. The sooner the invasion gets under way, the better. What say you, Eddie?"

Thanks pal! I think, scratching the dog's ear. The message in Silver's eyes is clear: "Don't ask me."

The ladies believe I can walk on water. Nothing short of a miracle's going to please them. Divine intervention's a long shot, whereas a half-truth may suit.

"We've thousands of troops and equipment raring to go, but the weather is against us. I know from experience the English Channel can get rough. Many lives could be lost through drowning. You know how finicky the British summer can be. Make a pot of tea, and you miss it."

Start serious and finish on a light note. It usually works. I'm not giving away state secrets. Eisenhower's face is in every newspaper. It's common knowledge we're only days from a full-scale onslaught of France.

Everyone's waiting for the sun to shine, but the girls are happy. Mr Barrett's relieved, and I look forward to his next oil change.

They never question my activities. The subject's off limits. All leave's enjoyed within the comfort of your own home amongst loved ones. There's ample time for tears when you're leaving.

Anita and her parents are discussing her future. She finished school and passed all her exams. This young lady has brains to match her beauty. She's had a couple of job offers already. She's anxious to start work, but Cheryl wants her to go to university, where Anita's been awarded a scholarship. Mr Barrett, as usual, is sitting on the fence. Silver and I are lounging on the couch watching the contest. Neither camp's giving an inch. I reach for the bottle, which is a major mistake.

My move attracts Cheryl's attention. "What do you think she should do, Eddie?"

I can see where Anita gets her guile. Mummy's using blackmail. I'm damned if I do and damned if I don't. Folding my arms, I frown, as though contemplating. Truthfully, I haven't a clue. Yet, in the blink of an eye, I've the answer. Stand the problem on its head.

"Mother had the same aspirations for me, but I took my own path. It caused the family pain and time to mend broken bridges. Anita's an intelligent young lady and capable of making her own decisions. Whatever she does, I guarantee you will be proud. Even if I didn't love her, that would still be my answer."

"Well, shut my mouth," Cheryl says, her huge grin putting a lie to her words.

Anita takes the victory modestly. "Now I've to decide which job will be best. You two will help me, right?" she asks her parents.

I'm dumbfounded. How can an innocent heart conceal such an ingenious soul?

They hardly notice Silver and I slip away, busily debating Anita's plans. I owe my buddy some quality time. He listens patiently as I explain my plans to bring his master home. People may think me mad, but I know he understands every word.

"That dog's going to miss you." Engrossed in confidential matters, I hadn't heard Cheryl approach. "He'll sulk for weeks after you've gone back."

"I've told him it won't be for long."

"That's what I came to discuss. How do you know?" She's on a mission and needs her son home while we dither, failing to supply an honest answer.

As the walrus said, "The time has come to talk of many things."

"Truthfully, I don't. We've a war in Europe to finish. Once our troops are on French beaches, I'll be back and going out to fight the Japanese. The Fourteenth Army in Burma's doing fine. Jack's survived for two and a half years, and he'll soon be home for good. Silver believes me, don't you, boy?"

The dog barks on cue and Cheryl smiles. "You're a ray of sunshine on the dullest day. You make life sound simple. What's the secret, Eddie?"

"You put your life in the hands of the Lord and change your socks every day."

I'm rewarded with a warm kiss from Cheryl, not Silver, and we trot back inside.

My leave expires at 0800 hours Monday, which means catching a train Sunday evening. My vow to make this a great weekend is in danger of being sabotaged, as Mother's working Saturday. Fred saves the day by booking a table for seven at the Bodega. We've a fabulous party, without getting plastered, although Anita's a tad tipsy after two glasses of red wine. Mother's the perfect hostess, and the patrons adore her. She's found her calling.

Following a fierce hug from Fred and a sad smile from Irene, they leave. The rest of us wait for Mother to count the takings then take a taxi home, dropping off the Barretts on the way. It's barely midnight, but it's been a hectic day. A little bed rest and church tomorrow seem ideal.

Church's less appealing in morning's early light, but Mother's been up ages. We're off to St Martins for the morning service, which gives Mother the chance to explore her wardrobe, searching for the perfect outfit. This could take hours.

It's said that beauty is in the eye of the beholder. I'm doing lots of beholding today. Mother looks regal, Cheryl's bewitching, and Anita is definitely dazzling. I may be biased, though I'm not the only one. Our procession sparks admiring glances from the congregation.

I feel guilty. It's been months since I visited God's house. Shrugging it off, I know our association's closer than these one-day-a-week Christians. He knows that I'm a work in progress. I never promise to be good, but say I'll try. Sometimes the Holy Spirit becomes high spirits. I always apologise. He always forgives me. After all, He is the Father, and I am one of His children.

There's a tiny voice in my ear. Not the Lord's, but one of his closest admirers.

"Half the people here today never attend church. Why would God listen to their prayers when they don't believe?"

It's a great question and deserves a good answer. I hold Anita's hand tightly while working on it. "He doesn't reject anyone. Neither does He promise them salvation. The Kingdom's open to all who follow His commandments. Sadly, when loved ones die, through lack of belief, they blame God, failing to realise they could have easily been saved."

Anita's brow furrows then suddenly she blossoms. "So! The believers go to heaven and get to hear Charlie play the piano!"

I knew my beautiful cherub would find a simple solution to a complex problem.

Chapter Fifty-One

Waiting for the "Off" is creating havoc at Europa. All leave's been cancelled, and we're sitting on our bunks chewing our fingernails. It's the first week in June, and the weather's not cooperating. Heavy seas are running in the Channel, which will prevent minesweepers doing their jobs and swamp landing craft too.

Rewards come to those who wait, as do calluses on the bum. Friday blooms bright and clear, though farther south it's probably persisting down.

We muster for the morning parade and encouraging words from the base commodore. "Well chaps, we're ready to roll, and you'll be traveling light. There is no brass band to see you off. Jerry knows we're coming, but not when or where. Reaching your designated area, you'll be loaded aboard landing ship tanks. They'll be your mother ships from which you'll be assigned to landing craft and responsible for putting our troops onto the beaches. It's not an easy task, but I know you can do it. Godspeed and good luck to you all." He's a grand, old wavy-navy man. You have to admire his style. Just get it done!

The frenzy dies down though there's lots of nervous energy unwinding as the trucks cruise the coast road towards London. Each one carries twenty-four ratings, which allows room to stretch our legs. There is no ban on smoking or panic to reach the rendezvous. It's nice to know that beneath the bull beats a compassionate heart.

We've passed through the flatness of Suffolk and the rolling hills of Essex, heading for Deptford and the A2. We've a small pot running regarding our destination. Any town between Dover and Portsmouth is fair game. With equal parts of sentimentality and acuity, I've chosen Seaford. Dally and I got smashed there on our farewell bash. Milestones in life one never forgets.

The crowing of the men who've picked the Dover area turns to groans when the truck takes a right at the A23. We've passed through Lewes and are heading into Seaford. It's looking good, except we're not stopping, but making for Eastbourne. Ten minutes later, we're pulling into a parking lot filled with empty trucks.

A petty officer who's been riding shotgun pops his head over the tailboard. "Grab your gear and hop down. We're here," he informs us.

The undulating greenness of the South Downs surrounds us. I fear the worst. Are we bound for another prison built by that nut Nissen? Looking over my shoulder, I see a phoenix rising from the ashes. The natural stone tavern must be three hundred years old. It's a ringer for the Admiral Benbow and straight off the pages of *Treasure Island*. Sallying down the cobbled path to greet us is Black Dog himself. He's brawny and broad in the beam. The grin creasing his ruddy cheeks would brighten the dullest day.

"Ahoy, me lads, welcome to the Buccaneer. I'm Daniel Morgan, mine host of this inn. Step inside and savour a brew or two."

His rambunctious mood matches his robust build. It doesn't take a genius to recognise an old salt. Even without his rolling gait, the fruity language is a giveaway.

Petty Officer Meakin butts in. "Sorry, sir, these men are under orders to report for duty immediately."

I'm mortified! Morgan isn't pleased either. The PO must be suicidal. This genial giant could smash him into the ground like a tent peg.

My oasis is turning into a mirage. They can cope without me. I need a drink.

"Excuse me, landlord," I say. "We've had a wager and need to know if we're closer to Eastbourne or Seaford. Your answer will settle the dispute, and we'd be extremely grateful."

Meakin compounds his first mistake. "It's against rules and regulations for ratings to gamble while on duty or aboard ship."

"Glad you mentioned that," Morgan says. "I spent thirty years in the Andrew from cabin boy to warrant officer. I've seen more laws broken than you've had tots, son. Strictly speaking, these men are not on duty, and it will be hours before they're aboard. Why not have a drink and something to eat instead of standing on that jetty freezing your rear ends off?"

He drapes a huge arm around the PO's shoulder. "I'll make you an offer you can't refuse. The meal's on the house. First drink too."

It's no contest. We troop inside to a sumptuous feast and drink of our choice. Lady Luck smiles, and I collect my winnings after Morgan affirms my guess is closest. I immediately pass a large portion back for our second round. The day's going well and though Meakin waits patiently, duty calls. We bid farewell to Morgan and his buxom barmaids, appreciating the hospitality even more when reaching the jetty chock-a-block with sailors scattered around the bay waiting for transport to the LSTs.

Tempers are raw by the time we've bounced across the briny in a thirty-foot cutter and climbed the gangway to the quarterdeck of *LST-374*. We're received cordially, shown to our mess, and provided with a hot meal and a tot of neat rum. I'm puzzled at the generosity then realise the objective. We're all in this together.

Twelve hours ago, a truckload of strangers left Lowestoft, and now we are mates. The stern PO's still our chaperone; hell of a nice guy too. Soon we'll be split into pairs and ferrying troops ashore, but we're still a team. God willing, and by His mercy and grace, I pray each one is spared, unlike the young men we're transporting to their deaths.

Sleep doesn't come easy. Common logic dictates that goodness will prevail, and we'll win the war. The bigger question is, who will win the peace?

Chapter Fifty-Two

There's one thing worse than missing your tot, and that's swinging on a buoy. After the carefree road, we're back to naval discipline. PO Meakin sets the ball rolling with negatives issued by the captain. The first blow: there's no shore leave. We see sentries patrolling the upper deck with Lee-Enfield rifles and presume their presence is to safeguard the ship. Wrong! They're to stop us escaping while another brood guard the jetty; not dangerous, but like warts, unsightly. We've nothing to do and nowhere to go, except keep our mess deck clean, which is off limits apart from eating and sleeping. The only other area we have access to is the tank deck. We've relieved the boredom with games of tennis, cricket, and five-a-side football, though these often end in brawls.

Lazier ones sit cross-legged on the deck plates and engage in cards, dominoes and other dubious pastimes. The sun hasn't appeared since our arrival, yet the northwest winds and needle-sharp showers are preferred to the sweatbox below. I'm better conditioned than most, following my spell aboard the *Daisy* and the *198*, but I haven't my Fagin-like bargaining powers. Nevertheless, ignoring instructions to travel light, I've found room for cigarettes and leaf tobacco in my ditty bag. I'd received strange looks, with the drawstring wrapped tightly around my wrist. Most of the squad are nearly out of smokes and will soon be desperate.

Sunday blooms, not bright and less than bonny. I'm positive, if the world were to explode, the navy would fit in a church parade. Somehow, they cram us all onto the tank deck. More surprising are the services of a full-blown naval padre. He's in for a hallelujah day. Smuggler's Cove is burgeoning with ships; like dandelions, they've sprung up overnight.

Luckily, God's in our midst. Today, even the sincerest disbeliever thinks he qualifies and will be fighting the good fight against the devil he knows.

The British rarely show deep emotion, but there's raw sentiment on every face. We'd prefer to be elsewhere, yet this is our destiny. The sombre tone's lifted by the news that the American Army has taken Rome. It's a boost to morale and couldn't have happened at a better moment.

Sweepers are clearing mines off the French coastline, and the activity above has increased dramatically. The sky's swarming with planes heading for Europe, and ships are going every which way.

I'm confused and say so to Meakin. "Top brass are playing silly sods," he assures me. "It's a ploy so Jerry won't know where we're going to attack."

It makes sense, but I've more urgent business. Someone has to put a smile on the smoke addicts' faces. They're gasping for a drag. Yet I can never understand, if God intended us to smoke, why didn't He put a chimney on our heads?

We're busy doing nothing after lunch when Meakin spoils the fun. "You men should be filling your lungs with fresh air, not skiving down here." Something has crawled up his nose. He's about to tell us. "The clowns at Whitehall are pressuring Ike to push ahead with the invasion, and reports say the weather's diabolical. Launching an attack will be crazy. We'll lose half our craft and thousands of men before hitting the beach." He stops, his face full of pain. "Nevertheless, we set sail for our rendezvous at sundown. So! Get your fingers out, you dozy lot."

I'm way off course. This man's concerned. We're eager, young kids, and he's responsible for our survival. By suppertime, we're underway. In typical navy fashion, after kicking our heels for two days, it's full steam ahead. Don't those windbags know the Sabbath's a day of rest? The pace is slow, and away from the sheltering limestone cliffs, we experience the vulnerability of these flat-bottomed bastards. There's no sharp end to deflect the waves. Each time we hit a trough, a huge wall of water crashes over the ramp and floods the tank deck. How the helmsman maintains steerage is a miracle. These tin cans wallow side to side, crab fashion. I sigh with relief when all hands are excused, duties are piped below. We retire to our mess, soaked to the skin.

It's a hopeless situation. We can die from drowning or smoke inhalation. The mood's surly. Many men are too sick to care. This seesaw motion's getting them down. They've stripped to the buff and crashed on their bunks. Some of the more robust, myself included, have broken out the medication. We steadily sip and indulge in idle chatter.

Tomorrow's a million miles away, today's fading fast, but yesterday's tales are worth repeating and are a sailor's best friend.

Meakin steps over the transom. He's not here on business. We shuffle along the bench to make room. I slide him the bottle. Someone puts a glass in his hand. From here, he's on his own. He looks capable.

"To wives and sweethearts, may they never meet."

His words stir distant memories. The PO doesn't resemble Spencer yet has the same style. Could God be running interference again? It isn't the first time I've been down memory lane, initially with Hughie and Dally, and now Spencer courtesy of Meakin. Alf said you never forget your first ship. Does that apply to friends too? I'm tempted to ask the PO if he's served on the Bermuda Station but instead pour him a refill. Never knowing can't hurt me. Spencer will always be the hero I envisaged.

Searching for gold among life's muddy waters, I've sometimes seen a glimmer of goodness among the muck. Often it's fool's gold, but occasionally a real gem restores my faith in humanity. Referring to Petty Officer Meakin as a jewel would bring me blank stares, but he fits the mould perfectly.

I've possibly had too much to drink and should crash my head. There're only dregs left in the bottles, and most of the pigs are snorting in their troughs.

A heavy hand smacks my shoulder. "Thank you. You're a scholar and a gentleman," Meakin mumbles.

"Who came in?"

He's struggling to stand upright. Either the room's swaying or he is. "No one. You've been here all the time."

"Are you sure? Thought I left half an hour ago."

He collapses onto the bench. "It's definitely you. Your face is unforgettable."

"Thanks a bunch. What's your first name, anyway?"

"It's not Anyway. It's S-S-Samuel," Meakin stutters.

"I probably will do after this drunken orgy."

He's mystified.

"See you in Hell. God's going to take a dim view of our actions."

Meakin's still searching his brain when I say, "We had a postman called Sam. He was a pompous, fat old bastard."

Meakin goes into peals of laughter again. We'll need a mop and bucket soon. Clapping a hand over his mouth, he says, "You just used a bad word."

"Which one? Pompous, fat, or old?"

There are groans from the herd. Meakin tells them to stow it. The grumbles subside. It's awesome having friends in high places.

We've just finished the third hug and fourth handshake when we realise the ship's slowing down. Maybe the clanging telegraphs were a clue? All the mess deck's awake and alert. There's been no call to action stations or orders to close up."

Meakin grabs his cap and is up the ladder faster than one in a nylon stocking. The squad goes into mushroom mode: left in the dark and fed a load of crap. There are no starring roles. We're the supporting cast, and without us, there would be no drama. Once the curtain falls, we'll be forgotten. Politicians will receive the accolades while the be-medalled top echelon write their memoirs. With God's good grace, we'll return home and wait for the next tragedy to unfold.

Chapter Fifty-Three

As the landing is officially aborted, we run for cover, scuttling for the serenity of the shore. We've shortened our attack by thirty miles, though I've sympathy for the soldiers who are at the mercy of the turbulent ocean. Seriously, by the time they sample our landing craft and wade up the beach, there'll be little stomach left for the battle ahead.

I think Meakin's a fan of the Good Book. Following the morning muster, he puts the phrase *"the Devil finds work for idle hands"* into practice. Providing us with squeegees, deck scrubbers, and mops, he issues orders for the tank deck to be cleaned. He also believes in miracles, expecting these drunken bums he's inherited to perform this Herculean task. He must be reading my mind.

"You're a disgrace to His Majesty's Royal Navy," he says, as we shiver in the chill morning air. "Never fear, hard graft will do the trick. I want this place spotless. Do you understand?"

"Yes, Petty Officer," we mutter.

"I said do you understand?" he yells.

"Yes! Petty Officer!" we chorus loudly.

Strutting along the front rank, with hands clasped behind his back, he sniffs the air as if something's gone off. I wish he would, but his sermon's not finished. "I'll be inspecting your work, and if it's not up to snuff, you'll do it again. Also, you're now a working detail, and directly under captain's orders. No smoking's allowed on duty." He's gloating while hammering the final nail into the coffin.

This apostolic man is a Judas in disguise. He's taken his thirty pieces of silver, in my case half a bottle of rum, and bolted. He deserves a permanent hangover. Adding insult to injury, he's said we're worthless. Maybe we're not the best thing since the last shower of rain, but we've sweat blood to get here. No bag of wind is bad-mouthing us. We'll shove the words down his throat.

We tackle the job with vigour. Every slosh of the mop's a slap in Meakin's eye, and each dab of the deck scrubber dents his skull. It's a grand team effort. Even the carton-a-day smokers keep up to speed. There are a few minutes before Up Spirits, so we take our sweet time returning the gear to the stores.

Seeing no sign of Misery Guts on deck, we go below and are surprised to see him sitting at the table. "I thought you might jump ship after this morning's roasting. It's a great job, men."

It's too late to start toting the olive branch, and he can't put two dozen of us in the rattle. We're sailing into battle shortly. He couldn't replace us at such short notice. A wee chat might clear the air.

"We couldn't do that, Petty Officer. Without you, we wouldn't know which way to swim. Though some suggested throwing you overboard and sounded serious."

Expecting fireworks, we're disappointed. There's not even a damp sparkler.

Meakin's still grinning. "Got your attention didn't it?" He breaks off as the rum arrives. His words are for our ears only. He waits patiently until the duty PO has departed. We crowd round him again. He doesn't look intimidated.

"I'm not your enemy but do owe you an apology. Seeing you lot at Lowestoft made me think God had forsaken me. After twenty years' service, I'd finished up with Patrol Service, which according to legend, everyone's a pariah."

He stops, searching for the right words. I shove my glass across the table. Taking a sip, he nods his thanks. "And until last week, that included me. I'm put in charge of the biggest group of villains one could ever meet and enjoying every minute. Mind you, I'm taking some flak. Every man-jack aboard the 374 has run me ragged, telling me what rogues you are. Today I proved them wrong. Whatever you think of me, I'm proud of my deadbeats."

Picking up a canvas bag, Meakin places it on the table. "I told those General Service assholes to put their money where their mouths were." He produces bottles of booze and lines them up in rows. "They obliged. Why don't we celebrate for a task well done?"

It only takes a sniff of the barman's apron to soothe a sailor's ruffled feelings, but beneath Meakin's banter there are more than casual thoughts for his losers. Within a few hours, he'll be praying for our safe return and probably experiencing more pain than us.

I'M FAMOUS FOR MY PATIENCE. Mother would confirm that fact. Banished to my bedroom for misbehaving, she'd find me two hours later still engaged in flights of fancy to fairyland. I learned a valuable lesson at a tender age: You can make a prisoner of someone's body but never capture their spirit. My inner happiness has always confused her. She fobs it off by calling me weird.

We'd arrived three hours ago and spent half of it navigating past hundreds of vessels to nestle closer to the troop ships. The passage through this armada's awe-inspiring. I've seen photos of these huge battleships and cruisers, but it's scary to observe their bulk and firepower first-hand. Another three miles in, we're among destroyers and frigates. These will be bombarding the German defences and adding strength to our soldiers.

I've been too absorbed by the panorama to heed the weather. Now the eternal waiting brings it sharply back into focus. Below, a few hardy souls are attempting to catch up on missed sleep. It's nigh impossible with the buffeting sea. The only crumb of comfort is hearing the drone of Allied aircraft heading eastward and knowing they're preparing the way forward. There's a grey fringe on the horizon. It's almost dawn. How much longer can it be? Whoever has the starting pistol, please fire the bloody thing! Flights of fancy with Peter Pan or trips to Treasure Island are passé. Reality has kicked in. I'm standing on a mountaintop, and about to be given orders to jump. It's going to be one hell of a journey to the bottom. I pray fervently to God that my parachute will open.

Chapter Fifty-Four

It's nothing like the movies as Meakin, for the tenth time, takes us through the loading and landing instructions. We're dressed for the ball in full uniform, including tin helmets and lifebelts. Meakin ticks off names as we board the cutter and head for the troopships and landing craft moored alongside. We've practiced often, but today's for real. The rope ladders are wet and slimy. The soldiers, weighed down with forty pounds of equipment and a small boat bouncing around, aren't happy. Many suffer broken limbs and some die when they fall between ship and boat. There're fewer than a dozen craft loaded and heading for the beaches when the navy's big guns open fire, closely followed by the smaller ships' barrages. The cacophony rattles my teeth. Through the haze, I see palls of smoke and huge water spouts dotting the beach. Overhead, the skies are throbbing with planes strafing the German defences.

Loading our boat's a battle between a relentless sea and determined men, with the hard part yet to come. We put distance between us and the ship. Running with the tide means catching a wave at the right moment. No problem, when the breeze is pleasant, and the sea is calm. Nobody told us there would be days like today! The coxswain's in charge. I'm the grease monkey.

Presently, he's not capable of organising a piss-up in a brewery. I'm waiting for his okay and could wait in vain. Miller's frozen in time and space. Prayer's no use, but Chinese scripture might help: "When donkey fails to start, apply boot smartly to rear end."

My kneejerk reaction brings the swain crashing back to Earth. "Listen up! When I tell you, put your hands on the helm and wait for my signal. Swing it to full port rudder and hold her. I'll do the rest. Once the boat's clear, she's yours." He hesitates. I kick his ankle. "Do it! Or I'll toss you overboard!"

Miller surfaces and smiles gratefully. They say time and tide wait for no man, but I'm content to wait for the right wave. There's a pattern to the sea's action. I'll know exactly when to dig Miller's ribs.

The landing craft is in the bottom of a trough, and I wait a couple of seconds while the wave starts to build, then I give him a prod. He hauls the wheel hard over. I put the engine into reverse and crank up the revs. The boat holds steady as the water rises. I feel the front end dip, move into forward gear, and boost her again, the cresting wave and the engine thrust swings the bows in a wide arc from the ship's side.

Miller spins her to amidships, and we're heading for the shore. "What the hell did you do?"

"You should see me walk on water, brother."

Miller doesn't answer, now chatting to a British Army captain, who's waving his arms wildly in the air. Perhaps the fool's got us lost? The argument finally settled, the boat bounces crazily as Miller lays on thirty-five degrees of port wheel, and we're weaving around assault craft, all heading for the beach except us. Fishing a carton of smokes from my toolbox, I approach the army captain. "Excuse me, sir, could I give these cigarettes to your men as a gesture of our appreciation and goodwill?"

"Delighted, old chap," the captain replies in a cultured voice. "My lads would be grateful. It's jolly decent of you."

Pleased to hear "good English," I say, "Sir, when in Rome, do as the Romans do."

His smile's beauteous. "And when in Normandy, sailor."

"We're going to France, then? When we altered course, I had my doubts."

"No such luck, old boy. We're with General Crocker's lot at Sword Beach. I'm amazed by all this traffic. There are more than a dozen landings taking place over nearly a hundred miles of coastline. I'm sorry for you navy chaps having to run this gauntlet God knows how many times. My men only do it once."

It's fewer than two hundred yards now as we jockey for the final run in. Down in the well deck, the soldiers crouch, quiet and still while bullets ricochet off the boat. Keeping their heads low ensures some degree of safety. Their horror begins once the ramp drops, and they hit the sand running.

I'm not so lucky. The steel-plated deck across the stern gives little protection despite its barrier of armour plating. Miller's even less fortunate. At least I can put my head down while his hands are full keeping this capricious brute on course. The noise level's increasing as this massive force moves sluggishly towards the beach. The continuous rattle of machine guns and artillery from land and sea batters my eardrums and fragments brain cells. The constant drumming of heavy bombers far above, and the angry, whining fighters diving to attack the enemy's defences, brings neither comfort nor relief.

Through the smoke and murk, there are heaps of capsized boats with little sign of life. Lots of flotsam floats on the turning tide. It's impossible to know if it's human or not. I'm too heartsick to try.

I'm astonished by Miller's tenacity, wrestling with the helm. He's sturdy and has Popeye arms. His erratic course isn't due to the strong currents but to avoiding boats returning to pick up fresh troops. We've put men ashore, though there're more bodies lying dormant than making progress. We're not storming the beach but waddling towards it like geriatric turtles. It's fewer than fifty yards, and our LCI is barely making headway. We can't run her onto the sand. There has to be enough water under our keel to reverse after unloading. Get stuck and we'll be slaughtered. Under fire from the Germans and stray shells from our navy, aren't my idea of fun.

We've underestimated the ocean's strength. Our approach is too fast. Miller tries to control this wayward beast but hasn't noticed our predicament. It's not my call, but I'm not good at taking orders. I slam the knob back through neutral into reverse and boost the revs. Feeling the deck plates shudder as the prop changes direction, the captain looks at Miller, alarmed.

Wearing a benign smile, Miller says, "No problem, sir. It's only the mechanic testing the brakes."

Panic averted and almost stationary, I cut the engine speed to let the tide glide us the last few yards. The coxswain's back in charge. All I can do is watch and wait. He gives the nod to the captain, who has his men ready to go. Many look green around the gills. The wild ride has been no pleasure cruise, and their day has just begun. Miller presses the button and the ramp descends. The troops wait until it's fully lowered then evacuate the craft. They splash through four-feet-high water.

Whoever named this a landing must be stranger than me. It's tough to watch, harder to look away. Up close, this bloodshed's impossible to figure.

The noise of battle's rampant, and this vast stretch of sand is littered with bodies, some only inches from the lapping ocean. God willing, they never know what hit them. Dragging my eyes from the horror, I hear our ramp bang down and watch the sacrificial lambs, laden down with equipment, rifles held high, sloshing through foam-flecked waves just to be met by the unrelenting chatter of machine guns. They're going down like ninepins. Half the platoon is already dead and not a shot fired. Suddenly, it's a lot more personal!

We've no time to mourn. Shells are dropping all around our craft. The Germans are trying to take us out too. I hear Miller screaming for me to get my ass in gear. It's painfully slow-going astern, but we've no room to turn with so many incoming craft. Another fifty yards and we'll be clear and have room to manoeuvre.

Says who? A loud explosion off our port stern signals a near miss. The blast stands the boat on its beam ends before heavily smacking it back into the ocean. I'm thrown over the engine housing and slam into the winch then into the scuppers. Sitting up, I move my arms and legs, checking for damage. I'm still alive and struggle to my feet. We're going round in circles. There's no one at the helm. Where's Miller? He can't swan off and leave me here alone for God's sake! I stare out over the stern, searching the sea. He's little chance in this maelstrom. Even so, how could I haul him aboard? Shaking myself mentally, I say a prayer for Miller, thinking about my own destiny. I've no qualms handling this craft, thanks to Dally Duncan. He'd insisted that all the *198's* crew knew how to handle her in case of emergency.

The LCI sounds healthy. Its engine's running, and there're a thousand friendly ships waiting offshore too. I'm free of the muck and bullets for a while. What else does a clean-cut, good-living boy need to brighten his day? Mind you, a tot of rum would taste great right now. I've lost my tin hat in the explosion. There's Miller's hat lying by the wheel, but it's no use. His head's bigger than mine. Strange, I've always thought him indestructible. He's a dour, plain-speaking farmer from the Yorkshire Dales, strong as a bull but less handsome. We would never have been mates, but we made a good team. Despite the enemy's lack of attention, I should find my helmet; the navy will charge me for a new one. I see a bundle by the storage locker.

Taking a closer look, I realise it's Miller lying in a foetal position. Had I not known better, I'd have said the lazy bugger's taking a snooze.

Blood oozes through his balaclava and pools on the deck plates. He's breathing slowly and cursing. I don't know whether to laugh or cry. Carefully, I ease the knit cap off his head. There's a huge gash in his skull, pumping blood at a fair rate of knots. He has found the ideal spot to settle; inside the locker is a first aid kit. I need to staunch the flow before he bleeds out. Miller is alert and not going into shock. I'm hardly surprised; it would take an elephant gun to put this man down. There isn't time for finesse. Soaking a cotton swab with antiseptic, I mop the blood from his head, apply a thick gauze pad, and wrap yards of plaster round his skull. It's not Florence Nightingale standard, but he's not grumbling. I button up his duffel coat, pull the hood gently over his head and promise to tell him a story later if he's a good boy.

Heading for the wheel, I ask for God's guidance and glance back at my patient. His wistful smile is my reward.

Chapter Fifty-Five

Time's of the essence. The words haven't made sense until now. It's imperative to obtain medical attention for Miller before he goes to glory. To save his bacon, I need a rocket, not this heap of scrap. There are thousands of vessels, but is there a doctor in the house? The *734* can provide. All I've to do is find her. Landing craft are not ships. They're panels of steel welded together and easy to spot. I haul on the wheel. She's a stubborn bitch, and I tell her so in Anglo-Saxon. Miller is awake and listening. He cracks a weary smile, unused to my profanity. The devil's put evil words into my mouth, but God understands.

I'm surprised by the boat's response. Previously, she sloshed through waves with a heavy load, but now she's skipping across them in gay abandon. Lashing the helm amidships, I check on Miller; the dressing's seeping blood. Stripping off the dross, I wipe his forehead; I apply a dry pad and new plaster. His eyes flutter open. Thank the Lord, he's alive. He knows I'll never forgive him if he dies. Wrapping him up again, I return to the wheel just in time to avert disaster. Our incoming craft are having to take evasive action against my runaway girl, and they're not pleased. I give them all a two-fingered salute.

It's easy to spot empty LCIs heading back to the troopships, which soon lead me to the *734*, still swinging on the same buoy. A sailor points a rifle at me as I clang against the side. He looks prepared to shoot me if only to brighten his day.

My life's spared. "Throw that man a line, he's one of ours," a voice bellows. How could one forget the mellow tones of Petty Officer Meakin?

Miller is whisked away to the sickbay before I've even saluted the quarterdeck. Meakin's hovering. I'm not ready for mind games, and he's content to wait while I change into dry kit.

"The captain's not a happy man."

"Tell him to get a divorce."

"This is not a laughing matter."

"Who's laughing?"

"He's responsible for all the landing craft and men aboard this ship. Five craft plus crews have been lost. Three never reached the beach. Your LCI was seen floating aimlessly with no signs of life."

I'm angry but try humour. "A slight exaggeration on someone's part."

Meakin's not amused. "Nevertheless, there's to be an inquiry. The skipper requests your attendance, and my advice is don't keep him waiting."

It's standing room only in the captain's cabin, except for him. No one bothers with introductions. Does it matter if the judge and jury know the victim's name? I recall the PO's advice and remain silent, waiting for the skipper's spiel. He's a tall, burly man with a friendly smile, but I'm no patsy.

"Damned pleased to have you back, sailor. How do you feel?"

I'm having trouble staying on my feet, and the truth will always set you free.

"Honestly, sir, I feel well and truly shagged," and I feel better instantly.

There's a poignant, brief silence, though Miller sighs.

Within seconds, a beer-bellied bo'sun is in my face, his beady eyes inches from mine. The snarl almost bursts my eardrums; spittle splashes my cheeks. "You do not address an officer that way, boy! You're in the real navy now. And stand to attention when I speak to you."

Thoughts are cruising my mind of giving this baboon a Glasgow Kiss and spreading that bulbous nose further across his face.

My dream's shattered by the captain voice. "As you were, Chief Petty Officer Watson. You're not on Portsmouth parade ground now. Go and make yourself useful somewhere else. Try inspecting the sentry's rifle but be certain there's not one down the spout."

Watson slinks away, dismayed, while the skipper's face wears a satisfied smile. I'd swear he's just fulfilled a lifetime ambition.

I'm not expecting any get-well-soon messages from the chief.

"You don't seem too steady on your pins, lad," the captain remarks. "Take a seat. Hasn't anyone looked at this man?"

Blank stares supply the answer. Someone foolishly offers an excuse. "There hasn't been time, sir. We're up to our ears writing reports."

"Screw the reports! My men are more important than materials. You clowns are worse than Watson," the skipper rants. "This man and thousands like him are the real navy; they go in at the sharp end, no questions asked. I've lost a dozen brave souls today and don't give a rat's ass about a few dents or scratched paintwork. Whatever happens never affects the Whitehall gang or their pensions. The real losers are the loved ones left behind to mourn."

He's drained yet contented. The passionate outburst's removed a burden from his broad shoulders. He'll probably never make Admiral of the Fleet, or retain his command, but this is how I think a Royal Naval Officer should behave.

Meakin's the first to recover. "I'll take Roberts along to the sickbay, sir, with your permission."

"Good idea, Petty Officer. A brief statement in his own words, when he's able, will suffice. I can fill in the blanks later to satisfy the vultures."

Miller is sleeping like a baby. "We sedated him after the doc stitched him back together," the tiffy says. "Terrible deep wound in his forehead, and he's lost buckets of blood. He's topped up again and stable. Hell of a hard nut. Babies aren't born in Yorkshire, they're quarried."

These medics are more emotional than they'd have you believe.

I arrive on the mess deck with impeccable timing. The rum issue's here, but nearly half our squad aren't. It's a subdued meal. I wonder how many mates have perished and if any have survived.

We've to muster at 1400 hours. Meakin and I are arguing. He's saying I can't go, and I'm telling him to find a coxswain.

"Your mates won't think any less of you."

"Maybe not, but I will. We're a team, Meakin. I can't let them down. Anyway, I've a couple of tots owing, so it's important that they get back safely."

"I'll contact the other LSTs, check if there's anyone we might borrow, but do not hold your breath," Meakin concedes.

"You're a lovely man. I could marry you myself," I lisp.

Meakin laughs. "As well as being a daft bugger, you're weird too,"

"You must have met Mother," I tell him.

I'm whacked and ready to nod off; the remedy's ten minutes' shut-eye.

Benny Levin's trying to rip my arm off. "Wake up, you dozy sod, and get your gear on. Meakin wants us up top in five minutes and ready to roll."

God bless his cotton socks (Meakin's, not Benny's), he's found me a coxswain. By the time I reach the deck, every craft has gone except my

LCI. A duffel-coated figure is at the wheel and shaking his fist. It's not the ideal start to a brand-new partnership. Ignoring his tantrums, I descend the gangway carefully; breaking a leg will render little sympathy from this bundle of joy. He waves me to my station, and we're away.

Miller is no chatterbox; leastwise he's pleasant. This deadhead's sullen and mute. I'll chew the fat with anyone, but Attila the Hun had more personality than this dingbat. Any attempt to open a dialogue is rejected with a grunt.

A devilish idea attacks me. I wonder how he'll fare putting troops ashore. This time I'll do it by the book. He's the organ grinder.

The naval barrage has ceased, and the firing from the Germans less fierce. Nevertheless, the weather hasn't improved, and beaching could still be hazardous. I've ceased trying to communicate. I'm hunched over the engine, the coxswain's on the wheel, and never the twain shall meet. There're dozens of craft struggling to off-load their charges. It's bloody rough. I'm ready to assist, yet the call never comes. We jiggle, dance, and prance, but still settle gently on the shore.

Everywhere there are soldiers moving up the dunes and masses of equipment lining the beaches. We're back in Europe and on the road to victory. My dream's getting closer each day. *Hang on, Jack, I'm coming.*

"We ought to be shoving off, young man," a familiar voice says, pulling the balaclava from his face. "Who says you can't fool all the people all of the time?"

"You fooled me. Why the secrecy?" I ask, recovering from the shock.

"Pride I guess. Trying to prove I'm as good as I once was and curious to see if you can take orders, not a loose cannon."

"Are the rest of the squad aware of this skulduggery, Meakin?"

"They are, and the rest of the crew. The skipper calls it the acid test. I think he's trying to prove a point to the bo'sun and his ilk."

"You've certainly made me look small."

"You are small. It's only your mouth that's big. Everyone's delighted you haven't had the last word."

"Why didn't you speak? Afraid I might recognise your voice?" I ask.

Meakin makes a couple of false starts, then says, "I was too bloody terrified to open my mouth." Pulling off the thick woollen mitten, he extends his hand. "No sweat, though, Roberts. Today it was my privilege to meet a real sailor."

Chapter Fifty-Six

I'm enjoying a tasty breakfast of fried eggs, bacon, and sausage, when along comes Meakin to ruin my appetite. "Move your rear end, Roberts. The sickbay needs you immediately, if not sooner."

"No way those vampires are having my blood—I need every drop."

"That's an order. Not mine. Miller's. He's awake and demanding to see you. He's going bananas. They may have to tie him down."

The words stop me in mid-munch. This could be serious. That blow to Miller's skull and loss of blood may have caused brain damage. I can't imagine this gentle giant blowing his top. We're not bosom buddies, but he's my partner. I'm up and running, even as Meakin tells me to slow down.

Peace and quiet are priorities, but this morning's the exception. The sickbay's corridors are subject to one almighty rumpus. A gaggle of white coats are round the cot trying to steer clear of Miller's huge arms. Erasing foul words leaves little to say, though his face would shrivel a sergeant-major's scrotum.

Elbowing aside the drug pushers, I approach the bed. Miller's cheeks blossom. "I've come to tell you that story," I say. I turn to the medics. "Has he been good?"

They nod in unison. I'd make a fine dog trainer, or they're just relieved.

"Okay, old son, what's your problem?" I ask, sitting down on Miller's bunk.

"They're insisting I have bed rest, and I'm raring to go."

I've a problem: How does one give fatherly advice to a man twice his age? Apart from the two-inch plaster decorating his broad head, he looks in fine fettle. The pale-blue eyes are clear, and his manner's calm.

"It's no picnic out there," I say. "The guns may not be booming, but the seas are running high and wild. One slip, crack your head open again, and you'll be a goner. How do you think I'll feel having to tell your family after persuading you to come along? You're being selfish."

Sometimes one has to be cruel to be kind, and I see his pain as he's staring vacantly at the bed sheets. Maybe he's forgotten me. Wrong!

"I'm sorry, Roberts. It's horrible just laying here knowing you've saved my life, and I need to show you how grateful I am."

"So you will, by behaving yourself and getting well. That's the finest thing you can do."

Miller nods and offers a gentle smile. He's a big wounded teddy bear.

Our quiet time's ended by Meakin's appearance. "I thought they'd be washing the blood off the walls by now."

"It will be your blood," I tell him, "if you pull that stunt again."

"Don't shoot the messenger, that's what the doc said." Meakin gives me an evil grin. "Made you sit up though, didn't it?"

Meakin's enjoying this game of cat and mouse. Maybe the best fun he's had in years. Sadly, it will soon be over and back to routine.

My thought train's derailed by his voice. "Come on, lad! Let's get moving, we've work to do."

He's not kidding. The deafening thunder of guns, bombs, and brave men dead or dying on beaches less than twenty-four hours ago is relived as our boats forage to the shore. Yesterday, I'd been too terrified to feel fear and just lived in the moment. The shell that almost took us out was a gift from God. There hadn't been room for anything else. I'd lain awake in my bunk, shaking in every limb, trying to convince myself it was a nightmare.

This morning on the LST, surrounded by mates, I'd put on a happy face, assured that the worst was behind us. How wrong can one be? Hearing the ramp grinding down and seeing the latest batch of soldiers, eager for battle, scramble across the beach, brings it flooding back. It's hypnotic. In spite of my grief, I stand and stare. The sands and shallows are still strewn with corpses. There's no clean-up crew with bags to carry them off to a green-grassed, tree-lined cemetery, where the birds sing plaintively all day. You'll have to wait for the movie or for the politicians to finish patting each other's backs.

Yet who am I to criticise? I've been selected to drive one of the hearses. It's a necessary evil. The gallant soldiers who storm the beaches dearly need a hand. The more support we provide, the sooner this mayhem will be over. Please God, for good!

It's no nine-to-five task. Although there are fewer bullets to dodge or shells to soil our pants the demand and pressure's endless. By day's end, with the sea-mists rolling in, there's enough ordinance to fight two wars. Already, there are huge, floating docks waiting to be floated into position. Once they're in place, the supply ships can off-load troops and cargo directly onto the jetties. We'll not be needed and can go home. I'll drink to that!

These twelve-hour working days are taking their toll on the squad. We're now reduced to four seaworthy craft and eight able-bodied sailors.

Miller's sleeping a lot. He has a concussion from the head trauma. The rest of us are bone-tired, and not exactly full of piss and vinegar. Some are flat out on their bunks, others play cards or dominoes, anything to soak up time until 0500 hours then back on the treadmill to fetch and carry all day. We don't complain, and we rarely discuss it. Wish we could forget it and snatch a little dreamless sleep.

How's it possible to stay sane in a world filled with maniacs? Prayers are answered. I'd slept better last night and thank God for His blessings.

Hopefully I'll enjoy breakfast without disturbance by Meakin and immediately think of Miller. He's as strong as a bull, but not the sharpest pencil in the box. How cruel if he doesn't regain his mental faculties or motor skills? I off-load my concern on to Meakin, who promises to check on Miller and keep me posted. He does not inspire confidence, looking ready to keel over himself. Another day like the last two, I'll be alone ferrying soldiers ashore in a canoe.

The sun's barely out of bed when we chug towards the Normandy coast again. Compared to forty-eight hours ago, the area's quiet apart from the ceaseless drone of Allied bombers above and muffled gunfire reminiscent of jungle drums. Still, urgency's apparent. The sands are alive with beach masters pushing the soldiers to greater efforts. Their message is clear: we're here to stay.

It's infectious. We shrug off our aches, pains, and grouchiness. Seeing these poor buggers stripped to the waist and grafting hard makes us realise we've got it easy. We catch a lunch break following a busy morning, which puts us in a good mood. Somehow, Meakin juggles us an extra tot. One does not question the devil when he drives. Our afternoon proves hectic, with the arrival of more troopships. These boys are eager and too loud. They've come to win the war and know more about it than we do.

Obviously, government propaganda's doing a fine job. I hold my tongue. It's difficult to describe the true colour of blood. One has to see it leaking from a man's body to understand the plain truth. Once you're dead, you're dead.

Climbing three dozen steps from the LCI to the *374's* quarterdeck in the gloom is torture, and having a rifle thrust under my chin for not saluting the flag brings no great joy either. I'm about to inform the quartermaster what to do with his gun when the rotund figure of the bo'sun rolls up.

"You look absolutely shattered. Thompson, stop waving that gun, he's a friend."

That's not the sort of news I'd want spread around, but the chief with gold buttons wishes to converse. A wise child should listen well.

"I've been talking to Petty Officer Meakin about you."

"He's a good man," I reply.

"He's been saying nice things about you too."

"You shouldn't believe everything you hear, Chief."

"He also said you've a smart mouth," Watson says, raising a stubby forefinger as I purse my lips. "I'll tell you when it's your turn."

Whether it's going to be Proverbs, Revelations, or the bo'sun's going to read the Riot Act, it will not lift my spirits. "My first thought was to do you for dereliction of duty, dangerous use of a naval vessel and endangering lives."

I stay dumb. There's more to come.

He indicates the deserted tank deck. Maybe he's going to administer justice for the humiliation I've caused him. "Fortunately, there were cooler heads than mine. How you brought that boat and the coxswain back astounds us. I'm a pragmatic man, Roberts, and seen many strange things in thirty years' service. Yet despite your constant chatter, you're very quiet about the whole incident."

He's on a mission. Even in the dusk I note the inquisitive eyes of an atheist seeking a reason. I'm no holy roller, believing that a person should take time making crucial decisions, but I'll light a candle for him.

"I haven't an explanation, Chief. God knows, whoever enquires is the person who decides whether I'm posing a question or providing an answer."

Chapter Fifty-Seven

I leave the chief studying the universe and make my way below.

"Benny reckons you've been cozening up with the bo'sun."

"I've been giving him some religious instruction," I answer truthfully, which prompts laughter and rude comments.

It's strange how people rarely believe an honest tongue.

Meakin starts his chat again. "As I was saying, at noon tomorrow we're being withdrawn from the line and returning to base. All ratings fit to travel are under my orders until reaching Yarmouth or Lowestoft."

"What's happening to Miller, Petty Officer?"

"He's gone. The doctors said there's nothing else they could do."

My heart sinks. "You mean, h-he's dead?"

These hard-faced dumb-nuts are laughing.

Meakin's grinning too. "Don't get your knickers in a twist. He's aboard the *Royalist* en route to hospital, where he'll be comfortable and warm. Though he might die of ecstasy, surrounded by those pretty, young nurses."

There're no celebrations. We've played our part, but I'm saddened by losing so many friends. There'll be more battles and casualties. I'm becoming used to it. My brittle emotions are becoming bulletproof, but I'm relieved Miller's going to be okay.

The skipper's keeping us on our toes. We do a run at 0500 hours and muster for morning parade at 0800 hours. He's looking chipper today.

"We're being relieved at noon, and I thank everyone for a damned good job. Tragically, we lost many good men, but you can't make a cake without breaking eggs," he says then leads the *734's* officers in three rousing cheers.

The bo'sun bellows for silence. Captain's not finished. "The rest of the forenoon will be spent cleaning ship. Petty Officer Meakin no doubt will set us a good example."

For our reliefs, our leader has us cleaning out the landing craft and returning gear to the stores. We hasten slowly and finish minutes before Up Spirits. We've weighed anchor and are heading for Smugglers Cove by 1300 hours. It will be suppertime before reaching there. Still, another night aboard the *734* won't be bad. We'll snatch a well-earned rest and possibly a couple of hours ashore. Meakin says transport will not arrive until midday, leaving ample time to make base. He'll be glad if they fail to show. Ten days ago he'd adopted us, and two-thirds are now dead. Now the survivors are leaving. Life isn't fair.

The return trip's an anticlimax to the frenzy we've been exposed to for the past week. There's no gunfire nor blood and guts.

I walk the decks aimlessly; doing nothing is driving me crazy. I'm closer to screaming than to seeing my first headless corpse and console myself knowing that our mission qualifies us for leave. It's the therapy we need, and it couldn't happen to nicer guys.

Sussex's coastline hasn't changed, though the cove's almost empty. There's a half dozen LSTs anchored offshore, and LCIs resembling stranded whales litter the beach. My eyes settle on the twin red-brick chimneys of the Buccaneer, which stands atop the limestone cliffs, inviting weary sailors to tarry a while. Rest assured, if our luck holds, we will do our best to uphold the traditions of the past three hundred years. I'd stake my tot we're up to speed with any pirate or villain who's ever inhabited this inn. I'd not be surprised to see more than one swash that's buckled tonight.

The Royal Navy in a rare fit of altruism, or common sense, has cancelled shore leave for all naval ratings, except those aboard *LST-734*.

We listen to Meakin's wise words. "Leave is from 1800 until midnight. Defaulters will be dealt with severely. There will be naval police outside the Buccaneer at closing time, and no sailors are allowed to escort the ladies home."

There's muttering in the ranks as we consider our options. Personally, I'm neutral but enjoy watching their crafty minds at work. Meakin waits patiently. He's head honcho, not nursemaid. His intentions are similar to mine. We'll get blasted. Stupidity loves company. Draw up a chair.

The boys simmer down. Meakin speaks. "I do not invent the rules, just pass them along. I've been invited to the NCO's party and have graciously declined. I intend to spend the evening with my team, not only to celebrate our return but to pay homage to the boys who didn't make it. It's been a privilege to serve with you all." Rising swiftly, he snatches up his cap and is gone.

We're first in the bar and subjected to firm handshakes from Daniel, plus warm hugs from his bonny gals. Nothing's understated even the beer has a full top. Local lassies are arriving by the busload. Every half hour one pulls up outside to off-load its cargo of gorgeous girls. Many look young enough to be doing homework and a fair proportion, needlework. Whatever age, when Jack's ashore, every warm-blooded female has a chance to roll the dice. Later tonight, Daniel will produce the magic brew, and with each glass, the women become lovelier. Drink up, sailor!

We've blown the first kitty in two hours and are passing the hat around. I'm taking it easy despite our evil plan. Also, I notice that Tessa's giving Meakin the glad eye. She outweighs him by twenty pounds, and it's all nicely distributed. He's not resisting and guess who will be walking home alone tonight. Always the bridesmaid, but don't panic I'm neither cloistered nor closeted, though it might be safer.

Earlier, I'd been accosted by two middle-aged harridans eager for my attention. Only Satan knows what else. I'm unsure whether they're friends or if they came by separate broomsticks, but they share the same hobbies. Perhaps desperation has set in. The younger crowd nabbed the best produce on show earlier. Remember Granddad's sound advice? "If you snooze, you lose."

The way this duo's shaping up, it's going to be fight-night at the Buccaneer. Their scarlet claws are itching to tear each other's blonde hair out by its dark roots. I feel like a bonded slave up for auction in a Marrakesh market. Fortunately, cooler heads prevail, and Petty Officer Meakin steps in to smooth ruffled feathers. His explanation's quietly accepted with sad smiles in my direction. Words like *wounded* and *not functioning* easily trip off Meakin's lying tongue. He buys the ladies a gin and tonic each and points them in the direction of the NCO's party. This man has a cruel, wicked streak. You can't help but love him.

In the end, we've had a great evening, and none of us is drunk. More astonishing, all the squad's here except Meakin. He's in the tavern emptying ashtrays and helping to clean up the debris. I'm delighted. He deserves some compensation, dealing with this delinquent shower. I hope Tessa's gentle with him. He's in charge for another day. I don't fancy carrying him up the path and loading him into the truck. I'm thinking positive. If

Meakin's too sick to travel, Dan might give us shelter until our leader's fit.

My optimism's unnecessary. Meakin steps briskly from the Buccaneer, shaved, showered, and full of General Service bull. The party's over. There's no need to ask about his dalliance with Tessa. His sunny smile and pink cheeks say it all. These brief encounters happen often, especially in times of stress, but they rarely blossom.

Initially, this behaviour bothered me due to my sheltered upbringing. But then I realised it's an interlude between hope and despair. Is it possible that God and the devil conjoin to form some insane therapy for these people? Though not guilty of the ultimate sin, I'd been grateful for Lucy's compassion and affection following my experiences aboard the *Daisy*.

I'm accepted as a villain: a hard-drinking, soft-spoken man with a bad-ass attitude. I do not discourage this image. It's no stretch.

It's my second day aboard the Daisy. *Leading Seaman Benny Levin pulls rank and pulls a knife on me in that order. The first is silly, the second a grave mistake. I chop him across his nose, wrench the knife away and poke it in his belly button.*

He's quivering. Knowing I've everyone's attention, I say, "Try that again, and I'll cut your ears off." Satisfied he understands, I stab the shiv into the table.

Granddad told me many moons ago, "Being small does not mean you have to be insignificant. BS will baffle brains anytime." Ain't that the truth?

Levin and I are tight now. Strangely, he's not changed a bit, which makes me wonder, what's become of the smart-ass kid who was ready to conquer the world?

Whatever happened, I've grown up. And it's not what it's cracked up to be.

Millions more people are going to die before this slaughter ends. Let's hope to God it doesn't take long. The question is, what kind of life can we salvage from wholesale carnage? There are older, wiser heads than mine to find the solution. Why don't I close my eyes and my mind, the same as my dozy mates aboard this truck? We'll soon be back in cloud-cuckoo-land.

Chapter Fifty-Eight

Angela's pleased to see me. Women are fickle creatures. She'd avoided eye contact last time. A quick scan confirms that Williams is not in residence, hence the warm welcome.

Perhaps there are glad tidings. She cuts me off at the pass. "I haven't heard from Lucy, though Mrs Dawson has a letter for you."

"You're a sweetheart. I could kiss you."

"Promises. Scoot before Dracula's back. You'll put him in a foul mood. Just tell that lovely lady we miss her."

I'm feeling ten feet tall. A thousand questions batter my brain, but Lucy's alive and well! I'm still in Combined Ops and returning from combat, qualified for leave that starts at midnight, which gives me time to visit my second mum. The journey seems endless before I'm pushing open the front gate.

Mrs Dawson hugs me tightly without embarrassment. I return the favour. This house is a haven of love and trust. It's nice to be home. There's a cheerful coal fire and a large brown teapot on the hob. The homemade scones will soon be here. We exchange small talk, discussing everything and nothing. She's teasing me, saving the best till last.

"I almost forgot, a letter came for you," she says, sifting through the contents of her handbag as though panning for gold; she hands me an envelope. "Here we are. I'll leave you in peace while I look at my baking." She trots off to the kitchen.

There's no stamp or address, only my name. Obviously, it's been sent inside another letter and sealed with a single X across the flap. Mrs Dawson's aware I've not dropped in casually but granted me privacy to read my letter. She knows the devil but will be interested in the details.

I read Lucy's letter twice. It's a message from the heart. Her father was dying so she applied for a transfer to Harrogate, nearer home. He died within a few weeks, but Lucy's request for a posting back to Lowestoft was denied, as she's on a two-year contract. Chief Williams arranged the transfer but forgot to inform Lucy of the clause. No wonder he's boasted that I'll never see her again.

It's not jealousy that's driving him to distraction. He's terrified I might spill the beans to Lucy about his dirty deeds, and in his cesspool mind, the spectre of blackmail must loom large. Twenty years of his life would go up in smoke. Mrs Dawson is back with scones, butter, and jam to break my muse.

"More tea?" she asks and pours two cups without waiting for a reply. "Good news from your lovely girl, Eddie?"

She's not a nosey person, just forthright.

"It's probably like yours," I say, handing her the envelope. "Lucy's coping fine, everything considered."

Waving aside feeble protests, I tell her she's my surrogate mum and entitled to read it. I add that I'd never let Mother catch a glimpse, which seals the deal. I sip my tea and munch the delightful scones, while Mrs Dawson dissects every word. The frowns give way to gentle smiles as she reads. I know exactly where she is on the page by her expression.

"He's a wicked man, trying to keep you apart, but true love always finds a way."

She's a grand lady and superb optimist. Lucy and I are distanced by miles, and Williams can off-load me with a flick of his pen.

My pessimism's plain to see, but Mrs Dawson's undaunted. "Lucy loves you dearly, and I know you treasure her. Don't shake your head at me. The war will not last forever, and you can always write each other. You deserve to be happy."

She's right. Although our relationship's on a day-to-day basis, never seeing Lucy again is unthinkable. The tone of her letter mirrors my fears. We've never figured undying love, even less matrimony, but when does the heart ever listen to logic?

Mrs Dawson smiles; she's probably hearing wedding bells already. Pleading there're many chores to do before leaving tomorrow, I excuse myself. This isn't the truth. I'm curious to know what Williams is cooking up.

It's a sad day in East Anglia. There's a casualty list on the notice board.

Our combined losses for the Normandy invasion totals over four hundred. It's a heavy toll we've had to pay for our entry back into Europe.

Undoubtedly, my nemesis has run his grubby finger down the sheet and been disappointed at not finding my name. Pushing open the drafting office door, I see Williams standing straddle-legged in the centre of the room watching his peons work. It's a trait among NCOs. He's aware of my presence as a rabbit is when a fox is close at hand. We twitch eyebrows.

I take the initiative. "Hi Bert, thought you'd been put out to grass."

Every eye is on the chief's face. It's too late for flight. I've already clipped his wings, and he's not silly enough to hit me with some tale of misconduct. The staff hate his guts, and other ranks will swear they've not seen a thing.

Williams is a pro and good in the clinches. "Choirboy, glad to see you back," he says, striding towards me. He pumps my hand with his fat paw. "Come through, old buddy. We've been thinking about you."

His colleagues look on open-mouthed while Williams leads me into his lair. The draftees, mostly new entries, are starry-eyed at this old boys' reunion. A one-on-one arrangement suits me nicely. Contrary to the greeting, I'd noticed fear in his beady eyes. I'm an expert on this subject having seen it a lot recently. My prayers were sincere for those men. This bag of lard's past redemption. Sitting down, I make myself comfortable, waiting for the CPO's counsel. He's looking confident, and I'm expecting his usual bull at the gate approach. After all, he has the power and is playing on his own turf.

He's two goals down, and we've hardly kicked off. I've moved the goal posts, and Williams has taken his eye off the ball. You should never scorn a lady and always keep your enemies closer than friends. Lucy's message and Mrs D's remarks have sparked a couple of ideas.

"You're a persistent little swine aren't you, Roberts? I'll have to find somewhere farther away next time."

"You do know any posting has to be ratified by the chief of Combined Ops, and Patrol Service has no priority in the decision."

Some of the longer words may baffle him, but since his recommendations and name are on all the documents, he'll find it difficult to alter course now.

Deflated he's not and bounces back. "But that doesn't get you any closer to Lucy, does it, son?"

This is easier than I'd thought. "That's the reason I'm here. Just received a letter from her. She's not pleased with you."

I'm content to let him stew. His hand is shaking as he lights the cigarette.

"She knows you conned her and is looking for your head on a platter. Your villainy doesn't bother me, but Lucy's preparing to blow the whistle."

"That scheming bitch could ruin me."

"All's fair in love and war, and if you bad-mouth Lucy again, you'll regret it." Already on my feet and leaning across the desk, I add, "Stay off my back. I'll be seeing her while on leave. A little sweet talking might do the trick, but be advised, any more mad antics and you'll be mouse droppings."

Chief Williams is in a quandary. He's not sure if I'm lying, but he's a coward at heart and guilty as sin. I should be jumping for joy, yet the victory's hollow. I've been raised to be polite and considerate, not cruel and vindictive. Where's the small boy gone who once grieved over fallen sparrows?

Chapter Fifty-Nine

It's breaking dawn as I trot out of Europa's gates and take the cross-country route in hopes of reaching home before Mother leaves for work. The tale I've spun for Williams doesn't include seeing Lucy, though my letter explains the gory details and tells her not to fret. The chief's a toothless tiger, and the rest of the message is sacred. So there!

Hitching a ride to Norwich, I cop the milk train to Northampton then a quick connection to Birmingham. Mother's applying her war paint as her fledgling walks through the door. Her smile's genuine though the embrace is delicate. It's taken a while to achieve this flawless complexion.

Mother looks stunning. She accepts the compliment with a genteel nod. "It's nice to see you've good manners, in spite of your lowly station."

Mother's baiting me. A witty answer's easy, but I've changed since the last visit.

"It's your fault, Mother. You can take the boy out of the home, but you can't take the home out of the boy."

She makes no attempt at hiding her delight. The hard-fought battle to change her ugly duckling into a beautiful swan has finally succeeded. There's little time to gossip, and all too soon I'm bidding adieu to Mother as she leaves to attend her adoring public. I fling off my uniform, climb into civvies and cook a huge meal. I'm free to do anything or nothing. The problem is everyone's working, though Mr Barrett will be happy to shoot the breeze. The garage has lost its charm: balloons are gone and the forecourt's neglected. There's no sign of Mr Barrett. I prop my bike against the office window. The doors to the workshop are closed too. Maybe he's unwell? I turn towards the house.

A loud voice stops me in my tracks. "What do you want?"

Two large men step out of the shadows. They're wearing double-breasted

pinstriped suits, white shirts, and matching ties. There's a thirty-year gap
in age between the two, yet the pale complexions and fat bellies suggest a
lack of fresh air and exercise. Like father, like son. The apple hasn't fallen
far from the tree.

The younger version of the suits makes another effort. "I asked you a
question, boy! This is private property. You're trespassing."

This pompous little brat needs an attitude adjustment. "You are the ones
trespassing. The Barretts are friends, and I'm not your boy. Understand,
sonny?"

Realising strong-arm tactics aren't working, the older man steps up and
slips a hand into his pocket. I'm expecting a gun, but it's a business card
he pulls out. "Desmond Bingley, your local, friendly bank manager," he
says as I study the card. Like many people in high offices, he thinks anyone
not wearing a tie can't read. "We're here by invitation and engaged on our
initial survey."

"I've arrived in the nick of time. Apart from friends, we're business
partners too. You'll have to excuse me, I've been out of the country for a
while, and have lots of catching up to do."

Junior lays a hand on my arm as I turn to leave. Some kids never learn.

"Mr Bingley," I say, addressing the silver-haired one. "Tell this slob if he
doesn't remove his sweaty paw, I'll tear it off and shove it down his throat."

I glare into the pudgy face as Bingley relays my message. I hope the lad
sees sense or he's going to feel pain. He doesn't deliberate long, releases his
grip, and slowly walks down to the highway. Within twenty-four hours,
I've proved once again that the Royal Navy alters one's mindset.

Wandering around to the kitchen door, I know to expect to see Mr
Barrett drinking tea or swigging a beer. Things have to be grim if he's not
working.

Silver comes bounding across the tiles and leaps up to greet me. What
he lacks in manners, this dog makes up with enthusiasm. Mr Barrett's
concentrating on the tea leaves in his cup. Maybe trying to picture what the
future has in store? He's not pretty. I've seen vagrants living in cardboard
boxes look in better shape.

He turns haggard eyes towards me, alerted by Silver's excitement.
"Eddie! Glad you're back safe and sound. We've been worried. The girls
are driving me mad."

He's not getting off this easily. "Not to mention the vultures skulking around the grounds. Thought we had this sorted."

"They're my last hope. I've no money to buy parts. Even if I had work, I'm not credit-worthy, and who wants to buy a bankrupt business? What choice have I?"

"Beg, borrow, or steal, but don't sell your soul and family's future to the bank. You'll stay afloat as long as it suits them, then they'll foreclose on the loan. You'll be homeless and jobless too. They don't give a monkey's ass. You're grist to their money mill."

Leaving Mr Barrett cogitating, I collect Silver and head out the door. There's something screwy here. I'm not bothered about the cash I have in the garage but am concerned about young Jack's dream. My childish chatter's developed into a passion to bring the rightful heir home. Each passing day makes it more do-able. The Bingley Barons' greed for gold isn't going to destroy my friends' lives.

I'm beating my brains out while we saunter down the Parade in the sunshine.

Silver has food on his mind. There're surprised glances from people who see me talking to him, but they're reassured by shopkeepers that I pose no threat.

"The dog's smart enough to keep the kid out of trouble."

Sliding to a halt at the pedestrian light, Silver squats on his haunches and waits for someone to push the button.

Should anyone step off the curb before it flashes, he'll bark. Believe me, he's doggone smart. I've not told him where we're going, but I think he knows or perhaps he's following his nose.

Leslie Smith stands in the doorway of the butcher's shop, smiling and waiting to greet us.

"I see you've brought the big mutt."

"It's impossible to leave him behind," I remark.

"I was talking to the dog, not you."

Acknowledging the insult, I slip Silver's leash onto a hook and raise my forefinger. He sits and shows me his tongue. I swear he's smiling.

Three generations link the Smiths and the Roberts. Our granddads went to school together, and it's rumoured they sowed their wild oats together too.

Their sons marched off to war; some never returned.

Leslie, the third Leslie and present manager of the Hall Green shop, and

Charlie had been great pals. Next to Charlie, he's Mother's favourite.

It's a bittersweet moment when we meet. I'm the closest tie to his late chum. His handshake's firm, as if losing contact means I'll disappear in a puff of smoke too.

We exchange the usual pleasantries and the welfare of our families, especially Fred, for whom Leslie has empathy. Due to a childhood accident, and in spite of his enthusiasm, he can't enlist for military service either. He doesn't grumble and is always ready with advice. "You've got it made—the prettiest girl in town and a wonderful dog that loves you."

"Lucky me, but Silver isn't mine. I'm caring for him until Jack returns, and you keep those beady eyes on your own charming wife."

"I'm no nature lover, but one can still study the scenery. I'm usually opening the shop when she's passing. Anita's a real traffic stopper."

Men do look at beautiful women, and plain ones too. So why am I miffed? Maybe the recent hassle has left me a little fragile.

"Funny you mention that Silver's the same," I say and explain this morning's episode while Les prepares his dinner. Taking in the sun, we watch the dog make short work of his meal.

He says, "I've some nice steak for the Barretts' supper but do me a favour, tell them you bought it. They're going through a bad patch and after being kingpins on this Parade, find it hard to accept charity. I hear the Bingleys are moving in fast."

"Met them earlier, wasn't impressed. Junior looks a slimy character and ready to chop your hand off for a fistful of silver."

"They're bloodsuckers and already own a dozen properties. Once the war's over, Jack's place will be a goldmine. You're the only one who might persuade him to hang on. Nobody wants those parasites running the show."

"We've discussed it. He's desperate. Cheryl and Anita are grafting hard, and he feels guilty. Thanks for the meat. It'll put them in a good mood before I begin my heart-to-heart chat. I've an idea simmering."

"You've always been a crafty one. Get lost and take that hound off my step. My customers will think I'm selling dog meat."

Mr Barrett's in the kitchen preparing supper when we arrive. He's overjoyed as I unwrap the sirloin steak.

"Would sir appreciate a nice burgundy?"

His smile's worth a thousand apologies. "I don't think there's anything in the drinks cabinet."

"That's why God invented wine lodges. Put the kettle on while I go in search of succour."

Mr Barrett and I are sipping tea and exchanging small talk when the ladies walk in. Their voices are loud and unpleasant. Cheryl's moaning about the foreman while Anita's complaining what a beastly afternoon she's had. The foreman's fate is forgotten when Cheryl spots me. Her happy shriek alerts Silver, who dashes for cover as she smothers me with warm kisses, hot breath, and soft loving arms. I feel dampness on my cheek, aware it's not all for me. Her beloved son, who is nine thousand miles away, lives on through me.

Anita's bending her dad's ear while her mother's trying to devour me. He's smiling at the wild antics, although my love's face wears a cool look of appraisal. There are subtle changes to her appearance too. The wavy hair's cut and styled in a chic fashion, and the teenage prettiness is enhanced by make-up. From the red, tailored business suit to the matching high-heeled shoes, Anita's elegance is personified. Her girlish chatter's altered too and is more languid. Maybe it's bank speech?

Our reunion's less boisterous than Cheryl's and mine. Anita responds to my kiss with as much warmth as yesterday's rice pudding.

"I'm overwhelmed," I whisper in her ear, not wishing to ruin my friends' meal because their daughter's having a temper tantrum.

Cheryl scolds me for extravagance but laughs when I relate the incident about Silver seeing me safely across the road. Anita's quiet and broody, but bad manners are inexcusable and foreign to her nature.

One thing's certain. My high-spirited lass will waste no time speaking her mind. "I've never been so embarrassed in all my life." We cease our after-dinner chores, awaiting enlightenment. She obliges. "My employers came here today to discuss business with Daddy and were accosted by Eddie, who threatened them with bodily harm if they didn't leave the premises."

Mr Barrett and I smile. Anita's fuming, and Cheryl's perplexed.

"Are you quoting the King James version or Bingley's fairy tales?" I ask. "The only physical contact was when Tubby tried to stop me talking to your dad, and I told him to back off. I'd never do anything to hurt or embarrass you, but neither will I see this family destroyed through greed. Do you think I've a vested interest? Damned right. His name's Jack, and I'm going to bring him home. He's not given up hope, how can we?"

My suspicions are confirmed by Anita's outburst. The fat cats have been scheming for ages and believe they've a valuable ally. She's being brainwashed by these leeches, and her dad sees salvation on the horizon.

My arrival's thrown a spanner in the works, but this isn't the time to act. "Sorry to be a killjoy. It's been a hard day, and I'm exhausted. Things always look brighter after a good night's sleep."

"On your bike" was never more appropriate. I'm through the kitchen door and peddling madly for home, leaving the Barretts speechless. I ease off the power as my anger cools. Each passing day brings us closer to victory and Jack's return, yet barring a miracle or my robbing a bank, that could be light years away. My one slender hope lies in Cheryl's support and unshakable faith I'll bring her son home.

Chapter Sixty

Dad's dozing in his chair when I arrive home. "You back from the battle so soon?"

"Yes! Dropped a few boys on the beach at Normandy and left them to sort it."

"Care to share?"

"Not really, Dad. You want to discuss Vimy Ridge?"

"I've got you, son. Bet you could use a drink though."

"I thought you'd never ask."

Having established what's off limits, we chat about the health and well-being of family and friends, which brings up the Barretts. Dad says since Mr Barrett's refusal to accept help, they've had little contact, and it might be only weeks before the bank steps in to stop the bleeding.

I surprise Dad by refusing another drink. Instead I say, "I'm shattered, and sleep's the best cure."

SOMEONE'S BANGING ON THE DOOR fit to knock it down, and sunlight's flooding into the study. "Are you alive?" Mother calls.

"No! Get the mortician," I answer, watching her trot in with the tea tray and a big smile.

"How's sleepyhead today? It's nearly ten o'clock and my day off. Also I've had an idea. Let's go to Stratford after breakfast, take our lunch, and have a picnic by the river. Hire a boat too. What do you think?"

"Brilliant!" I say and mean it.

I'm sure women have a God-given gift that tells them what is best for their brood when often the child doesn't know.

Naturally, Mother Duck has to attend to the rest of her covey before we leave, including cooking their evening meal and leaving notes.

The amount of gear suggests a jaunt to Timbuktu, not a bus ride down the road. Stratford-upon-Avon's hardly changed. Some of the smaller, cobbled streets have been paved, but the black and white cottages still flourish. I'm a frequent visitor, and each time is a pilgrimage. I was five and a half and unhappy being uprooted from my cosy home in Birmingham to a huge mansion in Solihull. A family trip was organised to appease me and to inspect the new Shakespeare Memorial Theatre; the old one burned down six years ago. The grandeur of this market town took my breath away. There were acres of grass sweeping down to the river where the water was a burbling potpourri of fish, frogs, and insects. Not a sad face to be seen, except mine when it was time to leave. I'd have stayed, played, and been happy to die here. It was the perfect world for a child, especially one who wanted to fly.

Most kids have hobbies collecting marbles or cigarette cards, but mine was visiting Stratford. I'd save my pocket money for the bus fare and persuade Charlie to take me. Later, Anita and I would go on our bikes.

Mothers always know what's best. It's uncanny. I hide a smile and smooth out the rug while she prepares lunch. The luxury of eating without whistles, sirens, or distractions is heaven. We lean back and soak up the sun. War's a world away, perhaps in another universe. It's an ideal moment.

"Will the Barretts lose their livelihood?" I ask.

Mother's a pragmatist who thinks with her head, not heart. "Without secure financial assistance, the bank will foreclose, maybe retain Jack as manager, wait until the economy recovers, then sell to the highest bidder."

"There's no legal way we can stop the Bingleys?"

She looks pensive. "Les Smith and I have talked it through. We could assemble a consortium to extend his credit, guaranteeing payment. He doesn't have to know, and he'll have some wiggle room. Problem is, the bank will snap up all his credit notes then he'll be bankrupt and homeless too."

"Will your plan work?"

"Short-term it could, but he needs more business to survive."

"Fear not, Mother. I'll ask my friend upstairs. Let's go canoeing."

Two hours on the river has put a bloom on Mother's cheeks and a blister on her heel. Being a dedicated follower of fashion, she's worn high heels. Now she's feeling the pinch. Stopping at a market stall on the way to the tea shop, I buy her a pair of backless wooden sandals.

Mother's delighted they're so comfy. Possibly it's the first time she's done business with a street trader. It's taken me seventeen years to learn that beneath the skin of the lady of the manor dwells a charismatic child.

She also reads minds. "Thank you, Edward, I've had a wonderful time." She tucks her arm through mine. "We should do this more often."

"The pleasure's all mine. Where else could I find a more charming and elegant companion with whom to spend such a perfect day?"

Mother's cheeks are flushed, matching a bewitching smile.

Arriving home, we discover a rare scene: Dad and Fred are in the kitchen being supervised by Irene.

My parents adore her and believe she's the ideal partner for my brother. Rarely does she express an opinion, though I suspect Fred's given an earful later. Her weapon of choice is a grey-eyed stare, reminiscent of a tabby cat, which can be hypnotic. I smile brightly when she fixes her gaze on me. It's safe to assume we're not close. She'll make someone a wonderful wife.

I thank God for His grace and mercy.

Thunderous door chimes announce the Barretts. Perhaps my prayers didn't go unanswered last night. We deal with the niceties while mixing our drinks, then move onto the patio. Anita and I sit holding hands. Yesterday's silliness is gone. Love is to the bone.

Mr Barrett's fraught and definitely not the soul of the party. Maybe he needs a few drinks to loosen him up. Someone has to break the deadlock, or he'll be heading out of the door. Relief comes from an unlikely source.

"Can I ask your advice, Uncle Jack?" Fred enquires. He's not our uncle but my brother's circumspect, though not Jewish.

"Fire away, Fred."

"I'm buying a motorbike, and Bill Brown says you're the best one to ask."

"Bill's too modest. He's the finest mechanic for miles. I gave him a job when he first arrived from Scotland. Watched me for hours. Within a month, he could strip an engine and put it back together with his eyes shut. You'll find no one better."

Fred's frowning. "That's the problem. He's too busy and has no staff. Steve's been called up, Maggie's in India, his lease is done, and he's running out of space."

Everybody is deep in thought except Irene, who seems to be contemplating riding shotgun on a motorcycle.

Why doesn't someone state the obvious? The elephant tromping around the room is too big to ignore.

The voice is soft but firm. "You could do it, Daddy. You've time, space, and the know-how. It's better than moping about the garage all day."

It's not a query, it's a challenge. Mr Barrett would hate to disappoint his darling.

He's everyone's attention. Even Irene has returned to Planet Earth from a distant galaxy and is paying heed.

Cheryl adds weight to the argument. "Without Bill's graft for five years, we may never have made it. We owe him that much."

Outnumbered by the nodding heads, Mr Barrett tries to remain serious but fails. "Okay, I surrender! If I refuse, you'll probably nail me to one of your willow trees."

Fred looks smug. Irene's smiling too, which is rare and alerts my radar. I've missed something. Coincidence is a no-no. Divine intervention may have occurred, though probably human interference brought about this fait accompli.

Approaching my brother, I ask, "On your Scout's honour, was everything you said the whole truth and nothing but the truth?"

"Absolutely. I want a bike, Bill needs more space, and Jack could use the work. Leave the planning to us, kid. Your job is to bring his son home safe and sound."

How can I be so dumb? I've been fighting dragons while the others are building bridges against disaster. Borrowing my brother's identity was only one small step, but I've many miles to travel before attaining his knowledge of human behaviour.

Chapter Sixty-One

I'm astonished at the speed of Bill's legal eagles. The last days of my leave are spent at Jack's kitchen table, listening to their finagling over his renaissance. The contract's more watertight than a duck's bum. There are no loopholes when the Bingleys come calling. They depart dismayed. Their threats to call in Jack's markers falling on stony ground. Bill's paid a ten-year lease on half the garage, and with an account lodged in a different bank, Jack's cleared all outstanding bills.

The dealership will sell motorcycles, new and used, with room reserved for the occasional car. The workshop's shared, and Bill's using the Barretts' setup for subcontractors for maintenance and repairs. It's a win-win situation and nice to see smiling faces, but I need some sleep. I've another hour's journey ahead.

"Come on, Jack! The ship will be sailing without you." Opening leaden eyes, I see an ancient ticket collector grinning at me. He's possibly worked this route since Roman chariots passed by.

"Thanks, Pop," I say, flipping him a shilling. "Get a tankard of mead."

I jostle through the crowds. It's just after four, and I've ample time for a quiet stroll to Liverpool Street before I catch a connection to Norwich followed by a slow train to Lowestoft. Long before midnight, I'll be snoozing in the nuthouse. It's been a busy week, but I'm pleased the Barretts are back on course, and everyone now knows I'm committed to finding Jack. Nothing's impossible. Faith can move mountains, even one pebble at a time.

Freshly shaved, showered, and a big breakfast under my belt, I'm on top of the world. Chief Williams is sour, though Angela wears an impish grin. As usual, my appearance creates a stir, but today I've more urgent business. Williams retires to his office, slamming the door behind him.

"I've a letter for you, lover boy," Angela says.

"I didn't know you could write."

"Smart-ass, it's from lovely Lucy in Harrogate."

My heart misses a beat. The chief's staring through his window. "Does Taffy know it's here?"

"Didn't you see steam coming out of his ears?"

"You're a doll, Angie. There's another favour I need."

"Give me a good reason why I should help you."

"You can't help yourself."

"I asked for a good reason. Lucy's a lucky girl, though you're a headcase."

"Would you put that in writing?"

"What's this favour? You'll get me shot."

"I'll put flowers on your grave, but I need an application chasing up. Would you, pretty please?"

"Stop grovelling, it's no trouble. Now scoot, I've work to do and don't forget your billet-doux."

Sitting on my bunk, I read the letter again. It's sweet and poignant. There's no self-pity, only compassion and tender thoughts for everyone, including me. Perhaps it's kismet or even karma.

The tannoy hails me. Williams is waiting and wearing a fiendish grin. "You're on the move, get packed."

"What took so long? Anyway, it's suppertime."

"This must be your lucky day."

"I've another Combined Ops posting, Chief?"

"Bet your boots. You're ideal for the job." It's an old paddle steamer converted to anti-aircraft ship, with a top speed of ten knots. Ideal target for German dive bombers. Bon voyage, Roberts."

It's no problem. I'm happy at sea, and if Angie shakes her feathers, I'm Williams's worst nightmare come true. Whipping through the routine, I catch the train to London. It's only a short bus trip to Tilbury, and I'm saluting the *Royal Eagle's* quarterdeck at 1200 hours.

"Call me Pop," the quartermaster says, inspecting my notes. It's fitting; he looks my dad's age. Satisfied I'm not a spy, he says, "They're not a bad bunch. The only badass is Gypsy Barnes. Steer clear of him, he's round the bend."

"Thanks for the tip. I'm for the quiet life. Stand my watch, drink my tot and mind my business." Lying comes with the territory.

"I'm your guide," a soft voice says. The owner reminds me of Hughie, though he isn't Scottish. "The name's Jake, from Cornwall," he confirms.

The *Royal Eagle's* promenade deck's ugly. Its twelve-foot paddles jut out like bat's ears and bristle with ordinance. The seating's been replaced by an awesome arsenal of firepower: twin six-inch guns up front, a Bofors down aft, and three banks of four-by-four Canadian pom-poms down port and starboard flanks nicknamed "Chicago pianos."

Leisure areas below paint a different picture. Wall-to-wall royal blue carpets cover wide hallways panelled in oak and walnut that reflect the chandeliers' lights. Some cabins are off-limits, but most are converted for navy use.

After the sweatboxes I've endured, this is luxurious. It feels like hallowed ground and like I should remove my boots. Jake tells me not to fret, and I'll get used to living in a floating hotel.

"There are strict rules, and we're proud of this ship," he adds. "Everyone pulls his weight. The skipper insists on cleanliness. Don't let him or your shipmates down." He pushes open a polished cabin door. "Let me introduce you to the others."

He's lantern-jawed, raw-boned and surly. "I'm Leading Stoker Simms, your watch commander. Most of the men are ashore having a few bevies. We're off at first light on six days' patrol in the Channel. Been to sea before?"

Feeling less than welcome, I give a brief nod.

"You scarcely look out of knee pants. I've a bairn your age." Scotsmen are notorious for being forthright. Unless he's trying to establish his authority? There's something about me he doesn't like. It sounds impossible, but it happens. Lots of old guys regard all kids as idiots. Maybe he's jealous of my youth? It's his problem, not mine.

"Jake will get you settled in and show you the ropes. Stay on your toes and pay attention."

Jake's a mine of information and breath of fresh air after the frosty reception from Simms.

"Our watch commander always a misery or someone pee on his cornflakes?"

Grinning, Jake says, "You've a good sense of humour. This might seem a cushy number, but don't be fooled. It's bloody hard graft."

The sleeping quarters are heart-warming and have oceans of space, with a double-width bunk plus twelve-inch side-rails. I'm impressed.

"You'll need those once we're at sea. The old gal's stable alongside the wall but more than a ripple, and she's a bull in a china shop."

Does Williams have knowledge of this floating museum? I'd not put it past him. Perhaps he knows Simms too?

"Are you all right? You've gone pale."

I shrug my shoulders. "I'm dead whacked."

"Get a good night's kip. You've got the morning watch with me, and though we're on duty, it's rig of the day."

It hits me like a thunderbolt. Whether by chance or sharp cunning, the chief has put me aboard a General Service ship and all the bull one can shovel.

Chapter Sixty-Two

I've had a glorious night's sleep. The lapping of the waves against the dock wall and the hum of generators lulled me to sleep the moment my head hit the pillow.

There's no room for pleasantries with every man at his station. Once she's slipped her lines, the *Royal Eagle's* a fighting ship geared for action. Discipline's tight and there's little conversation, except for relaying and repeating orders. It sounds like Echo Valley. The engine room's worse: telegraphs apart, speech is non-existent. There's an enclave consisting of a gnome-like chief stoker and rail-thin petty officer. Nearby stands Simms with another leading stoker who is gorilla-sized and has a face to match. My money says it's Badass Barnes. Acting on Pop's advice and Jake's comments, I'll play it cool and keep my lips zipped. I don't wish to incur the wrath of Smiley Simms or Badass Barnes.

Sitting at the mess table, I'm pestered with questions. My answers are brief. The less they know the better. My accent confuses them, their interest wanes, but they'll be back. I'm just mopping up the remains of a tasty breakfast when I'm aware there's lots of elbow room. My companions have moved away. I know my manner's not hearty, but I'm not contagious.

My query's answered as two figures sit down opposite. Neither looks fulsome. The usually rowdy mess goes quiet. No one's looking, but everyone's listening.

"So you're the new kid?" Barnes asks. "Saints preserve us, Chief. We can't fight a war with babies."

"Now, Jim, don't be hard on the boy. You can't judge someone by looks alone."

So that's their game? Tease the dog until he bites then punish him. It's old but reliable. They think I'm a rookie, unaware I've been schooled in the art of dirty tricks by some of the Andrew's finest.

"Pretty boy doesn't bother me. A few days under my tuition, and I'll soon lick him into shape."

Ignoring Barnes, I focus on the organ grinder. The monkey can wait. "Permission to speak, Chief?"

He's surprised. A smile twitches his lips. "Feel free, you're among friends here."

I wouldn't bet on it. The beast's getting restless. My next remark could have him beating his chest.

"Leading Stoker Simms assigned me to his watch when I arrived. He studied my papers and decided I was competent for duty. I stood down at 0800 hours, which explains my tardiness for breakfast, Chief."

Barnes is fuming. "I knew that crafty Scottish swine would pull some caper."

Chief Hanson's on his feet and not happy with Simms's antics. "As you were. I gave Jock instructions to sort the watch rosters while we were ashore, and I'm sick of you two butting heads. I want you both in rig of the day and outside the chief engineer's cabin at 1100 hours."

Barnes is stunned. It's not the response he'd expected. He's big and brawny but minuscule in matters of the mind and crossed the line. His function is to instil discipline, not step on his superior's toes. Though the tail sometimes wags the dog, protocol must be observed.

The chief stomps away. Bemused, Barnes trails behind, possibly wondering, "Who's eaten my porridge?"

The boys can hardly wait. None of their remarks fill me with joy, ranging from lighted matches under my fingernails to a full-scale vasectomy.

"It wasn't my fault. Surely he'll see reason."

"The only thing Barnes will see is blood, mate. Yours," one wag says. He and his buddies are having a ball. I ignore them and the jokes subside, replaced by concern. Barnes isn't just hard but a mad dog too. Sailors love to spin a good yarn, yet the nodding heads confirm this man's brutality.

I ask why no one reports the physical abuse. Besides their laughter, there are many theories. The chief has his back? Maybe it's blackmail? They're in cahoots? It's always Simms's word against the whistle-blowers', who are prone to accidents and mysterious falls, which bring silence or quick application for transfer.

There's plenty of advice on what to do. The favourite one is to obey and keep quiet. I thank them, but reading between the lines, know that when the proverbial shit hits the fan, they'll be taking shelter.

Barnes doesn't intimidate me. I'm no hero, but with God's seasoning, a dash of stubbornness and a liberal sprinkling of good luck, I'll survive any calamity.

Thoughts of battle are put on hold at the sight of Simms. He'd told me last night that everyone does double duty. We lend support as spotters for enemy planes. It's no problem. I prefer it to being down below. I accept without grumbling, which takes Simms off guard. He does a double take, before muttering, "Bloody unusual."

Staying in character, I follow obediently in his footsteps. He's been digging. Knowing I've been to sea before has softened his attitude. He's next door to a smile when I confide my experiences on the *Daisy*, including lookout duties. He cannot believe his luck. I'm eager to please. It's hard work, but I need help to survive here.

"What's that big pier?" I ask.

"Southend, the longest in England, boasts a railway over a mile in length and has shops, cafés, even an amusement arcade. The *Royal Eagle* used to run day trips here before the war. It was the East End's treat of the year, the only time young kids had clean feet after a paddle in the Thames." Seeing me smile, he adds, "I'm not joking. Ask any cockney who experienced the Depression."

I chastise myself for my loose tongue. Simms doesn't answer, but he's smart enough to know that I must come from a privileged background. He's filling me in about shifting sand, maverick mines and keeping my eyes on the skies. The navy expects much for its basic six shillings and six pence a day.

We're into the English Channel now and riding the waves like a bucking bronco. I recall bittersweet memories of standing on the bridge, searching for the enemy. Simms is more talkative now and introducing me to the game. "We don't wait for trouble but go hunting. The Luftwaffe avoids our air force seeks easy targets. At ten thousand feet, this old tub looks ideal. Jerry's usually homing in for attack before realising his mistake. Our guns cut them to ribbons. It's dirty work, and we lose many brave men. Six in the last month, but the top brass thinks we're doing a grand job. We've seen off thirteen planes and been awarded a few gongs too. Every single one was posthumous."

Although virtual strangers, we're kindred spirits. I know only too well of what he speaks. Good mates are gone yet will be forever etched in our minds.

Chapter Sixty-Three

Alife on the ocean's waves is frequently fraught with danger, more so when trying to eat. Attempting to control a tin plate loaded with baked potatoes, three veggies and gravy is impossible. You need the tentacles of an octopus plus the patience of Job, and you know what a miserable sinner he was.

Nevertheless, sailors are resourceful, and feeding time is a religion. We're all in the same boat (no pun intended) and rally to the flag. One rating holds the plate steady while a second cuts up the meal into bite-sized proportions.

Many of the crew are seasick; not a pleasant sight. Their faces are greener than the waters on which they sail. Luckily, I've good sea legs, and my approval rate has improved dramatically. Less fortunate souls, unable to stand their watch, are grateful for a go-to man. I've absorbed their thanks modestly while watching the rum accumulate in my bottle. I'm smart enough to know that staying on one's feet is the best cure for motion sickness, which disproves the theory that I slept during science class.

Thankfully, by the fourth day the ailing are on the mend and sadly my breakfasts are smaller, but as David said to Goliath, "You can't win them all, kid."

I'm A-1 in Simms's eyes, and Barnes, while not bountiful, hasn't bothered me. Jake cautions me not to relax. I tell him I'm not expecting a conversion from Saul to Paul.

He's perplexed. I leave before he asks, "Paul who?"

The sea lanes and skies are buzzing with traffic. The enemy's conspicuous by his absence, and aboard the *Royal Eagle*, we're close to screaming boredom. Five and a half days on this whirling dervish is enough to turn a nun into a nymphomaniac. Strangely, a sigh of relief runs through me at the sound of action stations. Anything's better than being battered by this madcap mistress. In fewer than three minutes, we're into protective gear and tin helmets and gazing skywards—nothing! Perhaps the ASDIC picked up a blip from a sub? We scan the waves but more nothing. One thing is certain: we will not stand down for another hour if only a seagull zooms overhead.

Talk's minimal. Orders are issued quietly but firmly. Everyone's functioning with calmness and efficiency. Everyone's done this before—except me. It's like first day at school waiting for the bell to ring. Given a choice, I'd hide behind the bike shed until playtime.

Simms is liberal with advice. "Shove cotton wool in your ears and stay down. It gets loud when the lads open up. We've the advantage and wait for their move."

The wireless operator comes scuttling onto the bridge and hands the captain a flimsy. He reads, smiles, and passes the note to the gunnery officer. "Alert your chaps, Nigel. We've company dropping by. Let's give them a warm welcome."

His manner has less emotion than asking someone to pass him the sugar. I'm surrounded by a bunch of idiots! After dealing with this inconvenience, they'll be breaking out deck chairs and pouring cocktails.

Fascinated, I watch the vast artillery swing into position, and I breathe a little easier, happy to be down here rather than flying through this wall of firepower. My initial thoughts and prayers are for the enemy.

More words of wisdom are being issued. "They attack in two waves. The first strike's conventional, diving from around one thousand feet. The second's at low level, skimming the waves." Simms pats my arm. "Don't fret, lad, our gunners know what they're about."

Any further philosophy's interrupted by the starboard lookout. "Enemy planes sighted, sir, approaching from the southeast."

All eyes swivel to the skies beyond our rear quarter. The Stukas are honing in and easily recognised by their bent-wing design. Possibly can't believe their luck. One plump duck, unguarded and asking to be plucked.

It's difficult getting a head count, as planes peel off left and right. Nobody's perturbed by their disappearance, knowing they'll be back for the kill. The drones change to high-pitched whines as the first sortie begins. Six attack from the northwest, the other half dozen from northeast. The Germans think having the sun behind them will be an advantage. They may be right.

I've not heard a shot from our guns. Even with a half pound of padding in each ear, the noise is shredding my skull.

Risking a glance, I see the bomber coming out of his dive pattern at the same instant that the fo'c'sle's twin six-inch guns open fire. And the plane's gone, blasted into a thousand bits.

There's no time to ponder. A large boot, planted solidly on my ass, sends me crashing face-first to the bridge deck. Mother tells me I'm too inquisitive. Simms agrees, though not so politely. The big guns fall silent, and the pom-poms pick up the challenge. The ferocity and rapid-fire catch me off guard. Even with hands clamped tightly to my head it feels like my brain's crumbling to dust. My heart skips another beat when the clattering Oerlikons join in the chorus. Rolling onto my back, I see the gunner swivelling in his chair, tracking and firing at a plane. Though not seeing the kill, the marksman's huge grin and thumbs up are proof enough.

I feel bloody useless lying here while this turmoil takes place. Yet, when push comes to shove, we'll be needed to plug leaks, put out fires, and, God forbid, bury our dead. It's the longest five minutes in my short life. There's no jubilation, nor time to lick wounds as the drone of engines fade on the breeze. They'll be back before we've time to catch our breath. We've suffered no direct hits, but a couple of near misses have caused some havoc. Thanks to due diligence, there are no major casualties.

We're not kept waiting long. The bombers scream in line ahead, mast high, with machine guns blazing. Their plan's daring and suicidal. Our main artillery's useless at this level, but the small arms are lethal at close range. Jake and I are trapped on the observation deck, searching for damage during the lull, and though not in danger, we have an excellent view of the proceedings. Bridge and wheelhouse are the enemy's main objectives. They may not sink us but could slow the ship down and kill some crew too.

Whether by design or malice, the Germans launch a series of fanatical strikes and seemingly expend every last shell before heading for home. A crippled vessel could make easy pickings next time around. The firing's ceased, and the silence is ominous. Jake's sitting cross-legged, a tobacco pouch in his lap, rolling a smoke. Yet he's shaking! Witnessing the bloodbath on Normandy's beaches, I've convinced myself that I'm fireproof. Watching this man's twitching face shatters that illusion. The battle-hardened veteran's had enough. I can't believe he fears death but is afraid of what life has to offer. It's too late for prayers. Jake's enough is too much.

Chapter Sixty-Four

The clatter of boots down the companionway, and Barnes's appearance does not lift my grief. He's accompanied by two Brummie stokers who are not my dearest friends. "Been looking for you skiving deadbeats," Barnes says. "You're wanted up top. We're short of bodies." He kicks Jake's ankle. Jake looks up, grins and carries on smoking.

"On your feet, and stand to attention," Barnes shouts, drawing back his foot.

Desperate men take desperate measures. "You're wasting time, Leading Stoker. Jake's in shock and requires medical attention."

"Who made you a bleeding expert?"

"Saw it frequently on D-Day."

The Brummies look stunned; Barnes is flummoxed too, but he's foxy. "He's just swinging the bloody lead. It's amazing what a swift kick up the ass will do."

It's too late to back down. "Any further abuse by you, Leading Stoker Barnes, towards Stoker Latimer, and I'll report you."

I'm already putting distance between myself and Barnes. One haymaker could hospitalise me for months, and any help from his minions is out of the question.

Thanks to Trevor Palmer, I'm fitter, faster, and well versed in the noble art of self-defence. The main object is to let your attacker meet his own Waterloo. I've listened avidly to tales of Barnes's exploits. He won't keep me waiting. I recall Trevor's mantra: be quick, cool, and wary.

We're about the same height, but Barnes is twice as wide and reputed to have quick hands and punching power.

He's coming in fast, ducking and weaving, cutting down my space. A vicious, looping left hand smashes into my shoulder, driving me into a stanchion. I bounce off, incline my head instinctively, and feel Barnes's right fist graze my cheek then smack into steel. I hear a horrific breaking and grinding of bones, tissue, and flesh. The stanchion's still standing, but Barnes isn't. He's on his knees, sobbing in fear.

I turn to the stokers. "Get Hooky patched up and remember he wasn't pushed. He stumbled. Say anything more and I'll cut you adrift."

Jake's still smiling, oblivious to the scuffle. "Come on, old son," I say. "It's time for a little bed rest." I gently ease him to his feet.

It's been a bittersweet day. We've downed five planes but lost three brave shipmates. Plus, there're seven walking wounded, not counting Barnes. Jake's been sedated, and it's anybody's guess if he'll recover his faculties.

Rumours are rampant. We've lost half of the port-paddle, and we're going into East India dock for a refit. Most of us are returning to base. I'm the only one pleased. I'll say a special prayer for Angie tonight.

We're hobbling home with our sister ship, the *Queen Eagle*. Progress is slow and good cheer absent. Barnes and his cohorts are giving me a wide berth, and his baleful looks warn me he's seeking revenge.

Halfway through supper, Simms sits down beside me. "Get your cap, lad. The skipper wants to see you."

"Never knew he cared," I answer but receive a cold stare.

Silly me! This is General Service, and the captain's log has to record every fly crawling up every dead light. It's not an ideal finish to an unpleasant day.

The cabin's glittering with gold buttons and scrambled eggs. I feel worse than Cinderella at midnight. I adjust my face to look as miserable as the company.

"Glad you made it, Roberts," Captain Blake says.

There's little choice, I muse, with visions of my sausage and mash getting cold.

"We need to hear your account of this afternoon's incident, just for the record."

Whatever goes in the report, we have to be singing from the same hymn sheet. Judging by the anxious faces of the chief engineer and chief stoker, they're doubtful about information received so far. Hopefully, truth will not come out on this occasion, which reminds me of the fable of George Washington's dad when George admitted he'd hacked down the cherry tree. The popular belief is that he forgave his son for being honest. I've always believed it was because young George still had the axe in his hand.

I'd cautioned the two Brummies, but maybe they've squealed to save their own hides. Barnes is certain to hold his peace. Jake, awakening from his slumber, won't remember anything. Gracefully as a swan on a lake, I sail into action. No one knows that beneath the surface I'm paddling like mad.

"Leading Stoker Simms had ordered Jake and I below on damage-control duty. We were trapped when the second attack took place. Once the firing ceased, we waited for a stand-down order."

Hanson bobs to his feet. "According to previous statements, you were found ten minutes later, sitting down and smoking."

"That's not correct, Chief. Our previous orders hadn't been rescinded, and I do not smoke."

Captain Blake's impressed. Chief Hanson's incensed.

"What was Leading Stoker Barnes's reaction, Roberts?" the chief engineer asks.

"He told Latimer to stand up."

"And you?"

"I was already standing, sir, bending down and looking at Latimer."

Zipping my mouth, I wait for the next question.

"Carry on, Roberts," the skipper cuts in. "We'll be here all night."

"He's ordered to his feet again and told to stand to attention. I advise Leading Stoker Barnes that Jake's suffering from shock."

"You were disobeying an order," Hanson trumps.

"No, Chief. Giving an honest opinion, but the leading stoker wanted to see for himself. I moved away. The next thing I see is Barnes on his knees. The ship was bouncing around crazily. He must have lost his balance."

"Begging your pardon, sir," Simms chimes in. "Things were pretty chaotic with that busted paddle. We were going 'round in circles."

Simms has done a grand job of pinch-hitting. He knows there's a fox running loose in the hen house, and he's not ready to sacrifice one chicken for the ship's good name.

Leaving the *Royal Eagle* will not bother me. They've no room for a renegade. If you lie down with dogs, you'll get up smelling like them.

Mother would sigh, tell me I'm too proud, then give me a big hug.

Dismissed, I wander up top. It's late August and the weather's beautiful. One more year and the war could be over, although at our present speed we may not reach dry land to celebrate the occasion.

I drift back to the mess for an early supper. I'm on second dog watch at 1800 hours. There's cheering when the BBC announces the fall of Paris to the Allies. Even well-disciplined General Service boys sometimes smile.

My two-hour duty crawls by slowly. When it ends, I'm happy to exchange the stuffy engine room for the breeze on deck. It's dusk, and the shadowy Kent coastline indicates that we're skirting the Goodwin Sands, approaching the River Thames. Sailing the sea is fine, but it's always nice to come home.

Somewhere ahead, a loud boom disturbs our reverie. We're into our gear and primed within minutes. There's no sign of the enemy, only a god-awful hush. It takes a few minutes for the truth to dawn. This area's alive with maverick mines. The irony is that these fields are for our protection but often we're the victims. Already the rumours are that the *Queen Eagle* has lost half her stern.

There will be a lot of restless heads tonight.

Fascinated by the ocean from my early days aboard the *Daisy*, I still have flights of fancy alone on deck and can distance myself from this bunch of losers. It's quiet and peaceful, or not, as a big hulk steps from the shadows.

"My boys said you'd be here. We've some unfinished business."

"I've no quarrel with you, Barnes. My concern's for Jake."

"You've made me look a bloody fool."

"You didn't need any help."

"I'm going to teach you a lesson you'll not forget," Barnes says, unbuttoning his watch coat and pulling out a club.

I'd overlooked Barnes's cunning. Even one-handed he could crush my skull like an eggshell with this baton. I can run, but I can't hide. I'm sidling along the fo'c'sle rail, contemplating between the devil and the deep blue sea with Barnes padding after me. A voice rings out loud and clear.

"Drop your weapon, Leading Stoker Barnes, or I'll order my men to fire."

Trooping along the foredeck is a phalanx of officers headed by Captain Blake. With him are two able seamen, rifles at the point.

Dropping the club, Barnes springs smartly to attention.

"You're a disgrace to the service," the skipper says, his eyes just inches from Barnes's. He addresses the coxswain. "Arrest this man and put him in the chain locker under guard until we reach port."

Looking bereft, Barnes is escorted below.

"Captain Blake wants to see you again," Simms says.

"Does he want to kiss and make up?" I ask.

"Life's full of surprises."

He's not joking. The first shock is seeing the two Brummies standing in the skipper's cabin.

"We owe you an apology and explanation, Roberts. The ship's company, myself included, thought you wouldn't make it. Your ability and compassion's amazed us and influenced others. So much so that Henderson and Leach here told Simms what Barnes's plans were. Luckily, the cavalry arrived before he fed you to the fish."

"What will happen to Barnes, sir?" I ask.

"They'll reduce him to the ranks, and he'll spend a few months in Kingston. But he's a damned fine sailor. One might say a warrior. Knowing Barnes, he'll live to fight another day. Mind you, it will not be aboard the *Royal Eagle*," Blake says.

Chapter Sixty-Five

The mess deck is the focal point of a sailor's life. We eat, sleep, and swap tales around the table. This evening, hours from a safe harbour, sadness simmers beneath the surface. Three stokers have perished, Jake's still in limbo, and Barnes is locked away. War's a funny thing but rarely laughable.

Sleep's out of the question. Limping along like a lame dog with mines bobbing around loose is enough to shatter the sweetest dreams. There's a tug on the way to take us into East India docks. It can't arrive soon enough.

After gallons of cocoa, my prayers are answered. I could kiss the tugboat's crew but stifle the impulse. There're still a couple here dubious of my gender.

Once in tow, we'll be able to relax. Think again! General Service bull is back. Everyone's in rig of the day and at duty stations. For three hours we line the decks and pay respects to each naval vessel we encounter on the trip.

Paying off a ship is unpleasant. I've seen wakes with more spontaneity. We hang around waiting for the scribes to stamp pay-books and scribble railway warrants, then we're rewarded with a gruff, "On your bike, lad," from the buffer.

I'm the last to leave. Being the black sheep hasn't helped. Into every sailor's life a little rain must fall. I've just survived a monsoon. I cast a last glance at the old gal. I've been fond of her. It's not a wife's fault, having a drunken husband.

"Where to, mate?" the cab driver asks, loading my gear. "You'll have time for a pint of pig's ear in the Dirty Duck," he adds, learning of my destination.

It's hard to be miserable with these cheery cockneys; he's the right idea but the wrong poison. The second rum and black tastes better than the first.

London North Eastern Railway is the slowest in England. It would be quicker by stagecoach. Though not keen on Europa, the quicker I get there, the sooner I can gab to Angela about my application. Williams will be thrilled to see me, but first I need a kip to get my brain in gear.

While I've been knitting fog, the Allies are foraging across France, Russians chasing Germans back to the fatherland, and Italy is ready to throw in the towel. Add in MacArthur's invasion of the Philippines and Winnie ready to see off the Japanese. I'll have to extract my finger, or Jack will be home before I've my kit packed. Closing heavy eyes, I stretch out tired limbs and feel my brain slowing to a steady beat.

BEING AWAKENED BY A SMILING face is rare. I'm not dreaming or dead and gone to Heaven. The block petty officer's imploring me to rise and shine before the officer of the day's inspection. He's granted me two extra hours since the official rise and shine at 0600 hours. I'd arrived late last night, and he'd found me a bunk after checking my papers. Discovering I'm a warrior, he'd treated me thus. I'm enjoying the experience. Come tomorrow, I'll just be another burden.

The jungle drums will have informed Williams of my return, but he can cool his heels while I take a leisurely breakfast. He's easy to spot as I walk in: the one with the sour face. I'm Dick-be-Quick and hand my docket to Angela before Williams can blink. He doesn't favour an audience when dealing with me.

"Home again so soon," she chirrups loudly. "You must be Captain's best boy."

This young lady doesn't need thumbscrews.

We know the chief's leaving by the slamming of his door.

"You've a letter from Lucy. She's fine though hasn't heard from you."

"I've been up to my ears in alligators, but I'll write her."

"Do it now. It will give her a boost. I'll mail it special delivery."

"You're not just sweet, but smart too. Any more glad tidings?"

"It's nothing interesting, only that you've been approved for the course. You start in two weeks. Now scarper before Williams has a screaming fit."

Sauntering through the routine, writing to Lucy, and dodging duty takes up the forenoon. A tad after 1300 hours, I'm aboard a train heading home.

It's usually a tedious trip. Lucky me, I sleep most of the way.

Physically, I'm good, but I'm still emotionally raw from Barnes's rant and trying to fathom why they blamed me for his downfall. I didn't rat on him. Maybe I'm a salve for their conscience.

The leave will help. Family and friends understand my strange behaviour. It will be nice being normal. I've one small case, and with no gear to slow me down, I skip up the stone stairway. The station clock tells me Dad will be working. I'll surprise Mother instead.

Any stranger could find the Bodega; it's the noisiest joint in town and packed wall-to-wall with GIs. I weave my way to the counter where Mother's dispensing largesse and pints of beer.

My blue uniform amongst all the khaki betrays me. Mother's dazzling smile disappears. "I'm too busy to talk. See you tonight," she says. And is gone!

A dozen words dance in my head, none of them polite. So much for the happy wanderer coming home. I'm wondering why I bothered. Going back to an empty house isn't fun either, so I hop aboard a bus that drops me off at Mr Barrett's garage.

He's working—that's a bonus after my last visit. "We're getting by. Bill's on the road trying to drum up some work."

Lying is hard for Mr Barrett. I know he's hiding something but do not pressure him. Instead, I mention my idea, and we start talking menus. Silver escorts me down the Parade, and the rest is in the oven.

Cheryl arrives home, and instantly the world's a better place.

Anita walks in as the wine reaches room temperature; her greeting's as tepid as Mother's. "We didn't expect you."

I consider saying, "Shall I go out and come in again?" but I let it pass.

Nevertheless, I see Cheryl and Mr Barrett share a glance.

Good food, good wine, and good company always bring out the best in folk. The petulant lady is quickly banished, and my lovely girl's back again. When she hurts, I suffer too.

Troubles are put on the back burner, and we chat about everything that doesn't matter though I bring some cheer with my latest news. Seeing her parents' joy is worth a thousand words, imagining their son will soon be home for good. Only Anita gazes at me stone-faced. I've failed to mention that I'll be overseas for two years. I know she knows but isn't going to spoil her parents' pleasure. Our time will come when I'll brighten my beauty's day by saying I'll be home every weekend.

Tearing myself away isn't easy, but the nodding heads suggest they're ready for bed. Without their dogged determination and unflagging spirits, the wheels of industry would quickly grind to a halt. I decline Mr Barrett's offer of a lift. Five years of strife and struggle have left their mark. Hopefully he'll have a peaceful sleep. The porch light is on, which means Dad's home, and I'm ready for a beverage.

Chapter Sixty-Six

It's bliss being home. Dad and I've spent three hours getting pleasantly pissed and enjoying quiet chit-chat with nothing to prove and with no heads broken. Mother's arrival terminates our mellow mood. She bends our ears with her torrid day on the Bodega's front line. No one's safe when Mother's hackles are aroused. Dad's already reaching for the bottle as she picks on me.

"I didn't need him barging in and being rude."

Mother should study the Parental Guide to Raising Children, which states parents are not allowed to display bad manners in front of offspring. Maturity isn't what it's cracked up to be, and I've answered my own question. I'm stubborn and Mother's too proud. If I'd followed the university trail, might she have relented? I bid a polite goodnight and kiss Mother on the forehead. There's a suggestion of thawing, and they're chatting casually again.

TRACKSUIT-CLAD AT 0630 HOURS ON a chilly morning, I'm jogging the lanes, which Fred (as a Boy Scout) would approve of. "Be prepared" is a grand motto. I intend to be fit for my course. Dad's tickled pink, Mother's dumbstruck, and my brother hasn't surfaced yet. My head has treadmilled half the night, dreaming how I can honour family and friends before sailing east. It'll be small reward for their support.

Accompanying Dad on his trek to the bus stop, I ask, "Are you and Mother at battle stations again?"

He nods. "She's hatching another grand plan. Scrimping and saving every penny that job brings and squirreling it away in a separate account. It's rainy day money, she says."

"Don't worry, Dad. With our weather, it'll be too wet to go and spend it."

"It's not funny, son. Perhaps one of those GIs has persuaded your mother to buy a cattle ranch in Texas."

"True, Dad. You've always said the Americans are full of bull."

"There's one thing on which she and I agree, son. You're definitely weird."

Mother does know best, and it's a wise father who knows his own son.

Mounting my bike, I slowly peddle the quiet, tree-lined streets that link Solihull to Hall Green. It's a different world here. The swish of autumn leaves through my spokes invades my thoughts. I hadn't told the Barretts the rest of the story. Both Anita and Cheryl, though delighted, were preoccupied, and Mr Barrett's shadow-boxing is worrying too. Bill Brown might be able to fill in a few blanks.

I'm steering into Mr Barrett's place when a shiny black limo comes barrelling off the forecourt. Brakes screech as it comes to a shuddering halt inches from my front wheel. The maniac clambers from the car and spits profanity. He looks familiar. His passenger is Anita. Switching back to the driver, I recognise the pale features and Bingley belly. I hate foul language and detest hearing it used in the company of women or children. Reasoning's out of the question, but a hard jab to Junior's midriff might shut his bad mouth.

The kerfuffle's attracted an audience eager to put in their two cents' worth, particularly if someone's targeting kids. My fertile mind's alive with thoughts of a lynching mob and of Junior dangling from a lamppost. More so, when seeing Bill Brown seize Junior's arm. Bill has a heart of gold and detests coarse language too. No one hears his advice, but Bill gives me a solemn wink as he loads the hapless youth back into his vehicle. Anita sits pale-faced with head bowed. I decide against teasing. She's had enough embarrassment, which proves that beneath my brash chest beats the heart of a well drug-up young man.

Bill and I wave them fond farewells. Blowing a kiss, I receive an apologetic smile from Anita. We find Mr Barrett, as usual, underneath a car, but now isn't the time to kick his foot. According to Bill, although they're keeping their heads above water, things are rough and Mr Barrett isn't well.

"But you didn't hear that from me, Eddie. He's a stubborn cuss, and we're not allowed to fuss. Cheryl and yon wee lassie keep him trucking, thank God."

"Not to mention your noble efforts."

"Don't thank me. The true champions are my Maggie and Fred. They came up with the idea, which is something else I didn't tell you."

I stand bemused as Bill joins Mr Barrett to discuss their work. While I'm beating my brains out, the real adults are predicting the future. All things being equal, which they seldom are, I think the war will soon be over and loved ones safely back home and happy. I'm an optimist but have never seen a rainbow after every storm. Then again, I might be letting recent experience cloud my judgment.

Politely yet firm, Bill Brown has reiterated what Fred advised. They'd take care of Jack Barrett's worries, and I'd concentrate solely on his son. Being captain of my own destiny and a burning desire to see the world comes at a high price. I've forgotten what's going on in my own backyard.

One thing's certain: I'm not needed here but for sweeping the floor. Similar to my hammock, when I took off for Normandy, I'm surplus to requirements. I've created a monster, complete with a new identity, during the past eighteen months, and I've learned to live with it. Living the lie is second nature. Friendships, though brief, are warm and genuine. Emotions are kept under wraps and treasured privately. We guard each other by necessity. Home from the battle, we forget it. Time's too precious to waste. There's enough sorrow around without rehashing it, and nobody needs misery.

I'm preparing lunch for the work slaves when Anita arrives. "Glad you're here. I should have told you yesterday, I've a date tonight."

Ignoring the firecrackers in my head, I say, "Never mind. I'll stay home and wash my hair."

It's not a brilliant riposte but creates the desired effect.

"Aren't you curious or concerned?"

"Certainly not. I'm the boy who loves and trusts you, not your jailer."

The question's been asked and answered but still requires an explanation.

Anita's impish giggle is replaced with a cute smile. "I should have said 'appointment.' I have to attend college two evenings a week to learn the whole secretarial and financial business of the bank. My boss is pleased with my progress, and it's a wonderful opportunity."

"It couldn't happen to a nicer person. Instead of taking you around the world on my ship, we can go on your yacht."

How can one be miserable with such a delightful young lady? We sit down to lunch, Silver's big head on my knee. The talk's cheerful, devoid of worry or war, but it's over too soon. The men take off while Silver and I escort my lovely back to the bank. Having all afternoon and nothing to do, Silver and I take a leisurely stroll to the garage. There's a police car on the forecourt and two officers talking animatedly to Jack, while Bill's making hand gestures, instructing us to carry on walking. Silver hates uniforms; I can hear his throat rumbling.

The constable turns to face me. "Your name Roberts?"

He doesn't know. He's asking. Why should I spoil my leave answering damned silly questions? Bill and Mr Barrett have no intention of giving the game away. I shake my head and turn to walk off.

Chapter Sixty-Seven

The peak-capped officer talking to Jack turns around. "Calm down, Constable Simpson, and stop waving your arms before that hound tears you to pieces. We've found our man."

It's difficult lying to a police officer but to Dad's friend, it's impossible. "I've always thought the boys in blue were wonderful, Uncle Bob."

Chief Inspector Wilson grins. "Albert's right, you are trouble. We've been looking for you all day."

"I wasn't lost. I was enjoying my leave until you two arrived."

"Sorry about that, just doing our jobs. Received instructions from Lowestoft ordering you back to base by midnight. Failure to comply will be regarded as desertion and punishable. Do you understand?"

Nodding dumbly, I check my watch. It's 1630. I'm going to be pushed to make the deadline.

"The call came at thirteen-hundred. Desk sergeant phoned your house. No answer. Someone noticed the Christian name differed from the street address, so everyone in the phone book named Roberts received a call. I arrived in the middle of the panic and immediately got in touch with your dad. Hope you get back before the firing squad loads their rifles."

His face will crack if his smile gets any wider, yet it's nice to know a copper's not just someone to ask the time.

Graciously, Bob offers me a lift, which I refuse. I've my own transport. Retrieving my bike, I head for home, vexed and puzzled. Cancelling all leave has ruined my plan. Marshalling a combat force for the Far East is the priority now, which means I can say goodbye to Loughborough too.

I'll bet Chief Williams is already rubbing his hands. There's worse news! If I'm shunted overseas, I'll not see my love for two years! I pound the pedals madly, speeding back to the bank.

Exhausted, I fall out of the saddle, lean the bike against a car, and stagger through the door and up to the reception desk.

"May I help you?" the receptionist asks.

"An oxygen mask would be handy."

A fleeting smile skips across her elfin face. "Do you have an appointment?"

Politeness and big words usually produce results. "It's imperative that I speak with Miss Barrett."

The girl frowns. "Take a seat, sir. I'll see if she's available."

Adjusting earphones and mike precisely, she fixes a serene smile on her face, leans forward to flick down a switch on the keyboard, and softly begins the spiel.

She's done this before, and my task's easier than I'd imagined. Except her serenity's melting into terror, as though she has been pierced through the heart with a poisoned arrow.

I'm rising to my feet when Bingley Senior comes bumbling into view.

"You!" he screeches. "I should have guessed it was you creating havoc. This silly bitch should have shown you the door."

I curb the impulse to punch his lights out. "Mind your mouth and manners in front of a young lady. It's easy to see where your son's picked up the habit. And I'm not causing trouble. I've come to say goodbye to Anita. Your receptionist was trying to help me, proving she has a heart, not a swinging brick."

Bingley's already wagging his big head. "We're running a financial institution here, not a social club. Get lost."

Well aware of where he's going, I make a last-ditch effort. "Suppose I refuse."

He's positively gloating. "You're on my turf. I'll phone the police and have you arrested for disturbing the peace. They're good friends of mine."

Mine too, but I've had my fill of Bobbies for one day.

Hopping on my bike, I push off home. There's no time for farewell parties, hugs, kisses, or booze. I need to put on speed. This is a game of Russian roulette, only more serious.

It's shorter across country, but the trains stop at every station. I opt for the Glasgow to London express, which after picking up in Birmingham travels nonstop to Euston. Catch a cab and have hair-raising trip to Liverpool Street Station and thence on the London to Cromer run, stopping off at Lowestoft. Unfortunately, there are no taxis, and a bunch of tired sailors have to leg it back to Europa.

We arrive at 0030, not too dismayed. Patrol Service isn't as pusser as the real navy, and the guards wave us past the raised barrier. Everyone but me.

There's an able seaman with a rifle motioning me to the guard house. I've always suspected that one day the lunatics would take over this nuthouse. Still, it's been that sort of day, and being a live coward beats being a dead hero. Smiling politely, I quietly acquiesce.

It takes a couple of minutes to adjust to the room's bright lights after the dark, damp exterior I've just left. First glance reveals no one I know among the petty officer of the guard and his minions. Some idiot's having sport at my expense.

"Well well! If it isn't our runaway sailor returned home," says a familiar, gravelly voice.

Spinning around, I see standing in the shadows the bulky shape of Williams, like a latter-day pirate. Why aren't I surprised? My first thought is wishing he was Long John Silver. I'd unscrew his wooden leg and smash his skull. Instead, I display a winsome smile.

"Mother dear, you shouldn't have waited up. Sailor boys are not the same as in your day."

I'm sure my quip gets more laughs than Williams's, which is my sole intent.

Williams turns to the petty officer. "Find our funny friend a nice cell. Mark him adrift by thirty-three minutes and bring the form for me to co-sign."

"What about the others, Chief?" the PO asks.

"They're bottom feeders. Throw them back. We've caught the big one. He's special. I'm keen to see if he doubles round a parade ground with a rifle on his shoulder as fast as he runs his mouth."

He's the only one grinning. Nobody's talking, well aware that he who has the gold makes the rules, even if it's only gold buttons.

Chapter Sixty-Eight

The final strains of reveille have scarcely faded away when some idiot is rattling my cell door. Last night's arresting officer steps over the threshold. "Chief Williams wanted you banged up until Captain's Report, but you don't look dangerous."

"He's just being his normal despicable self."

"You surely know how to bend his nose out of shape."

"We do have a history."

"He's a bad one to cross and intends to cut you down to size."

I stifle a laugh. "He'll have to step lively. I've a feeling my name is already on the next Far East draft. What else can he do? He's cancelled my leave."

"He'll hit you where it hurts. Stoppage of pay."

Keeping my grin fixed in place, I say, "No problem. I'll ring Daddy and ask him to sell one of his yachts."

It's a strategy I'd adopted years ago as a small child. Instead of tantrums, I'd give a sunny smile. It works like a charm. Wrapping your heart in asbestos makes you fireproof.

In a court of law, one has to be proven guilty. The navy works ass-backwards; he accused must prove his innocence. Among this realm of ne'er-do-wells, naysayers, hangers-on, and vipers, that's impossible. And I'm only talking about the prosecution team. Passing a camel through the eye of a needle is child's play in comparison. Following morning parade, I fall out with ratings under punishment or report and am excused working party duties for the forenoon. I skip back to my dorm to dash off a couple of letters to loved ones. I've ample time to make a good first impression, so I shave, shower, polish my boots, slip into Number Ones, and saunter to the guardroom, ready for the fray.

Truth to tell, I've never felt so unready. Williams knows every trick in the book and hates my guts. It's his word against mine. He's probably got the PO wrapped round his little finger. God's my witness, but nobody will hear His word. It's a pity that Spencer's not here. He'd tell a few home truths about Williams.

I remember Spencer often telling me I had a big mouth. He'd say, "Don't worry kid, the truth will never kill you."

There isn't time to cogitate. The chief pokes my shoulder. "On your feet, sailor, it's your turn in the barrel."

He leads the way. I follow, with an armed guard bringing up the rear. It's two hundred yards to the captain's office, yet it seems like the last mile. Matelots gawk as though I'm an axe murderer. We walk many hallways and finally reach a cavernous room, where there're half a dozen other sinners awaiting judgment from the High Priest. They're a scruffy-looking bunch; ranked beside them, I could be the navy's poster boy. Nevertheless, I'm wary. I was adrift, and I expect to be disciplined but will Williams be content with his pound of flesh? Or will he attempt to extract more vengeance by lying?

Crying foul and claiming the chief doesn't like me won't work. I'll have to rely on the roll of the dice, but what happens if the dice are loaded?

A sharp nudge in my spine from my minder revives me as the Officer of the Day, standing in the captain's doorway, calls my name. Marching briskly in single file, we line up opposite the desk. The Buffer reads out the charge then places it at the captain's right hand, and we're off. Almost. He has picked up the document and is studying it closely.

Something's attracted his attention. His pale-grey eyes gaze steadfastly over gold, half-rim spectacles and fix on Williams. His smile matches Dr Gregory's too. "Indulge me, Chief Petty Officer. Why was Roberts placed under arrest?"

"Insubordination," Williams swiftly replies.

Cunning swine; that covers a multitude of sins, I conjecture.

"Was he drunk, abusive, or threaten violence? After all, he'd been recalled halfway through his leave," the captain persists.

Perplexed, the chief shakes his head.

"So you apprehended him for being adrift before you charged him with insubordination?"

Williams has painted himself into a corner with few bristles left on his brush. Content to let the pot simmer a while before adding the final ingredient, the captain says, "Being right isn't always the right thing to do, Chief."

Taking off his glasses, he polishes and then replaces them. "All documents relating to the alleged offence will be destroyed, and Roberts's service record will remain unblemished."

There's no olive branch from Williams as he stomps away. He'd be happy to see me hanging from one. I wasn't expecting a bouquet.

News of small fry vanquishing big chief has spread through the base faster than a prairie fire. Bucking the system's made me an instant hero. Ratings I hardly know are shaking hands with me and slapping my back. Infamy brings its rewards too. I'm offered free drinks, which I graciously accept.

Williams's conspicuous by his absence but makes his presence felt by my inclusion to the overseas draft. He's gotten rid of me. Though I feign dismay, secretly I'm over the moon. In less than a month, I'll be closer to Jack. Tonight will be the last blowout; tomorrow we start our draft routine, and in less than forty-eight hours, we'll be heading for Falmouth and the Orient.

Chapter Sixty-Nine

I couldn't ever remember not wanting to sail the seven seas. Dreams of pirates and buried treasure are now supplanted by a round-the-world cruise on a luxury liner.

It's organised chaos as we're issued tropical kit, inspected and dissected by the medics, marched to the station, herded aboard a troop train, and shuttled to the south coast. Marching down the narrow, rain-drenched cobblestone hill at 0300 hours to be marshalled aboard a ship that is already teeming with a full regiment hasn't lifted my plummeting morale either.

Two days out of Falmouth and well into the vagaries of the Bay of Biscay's viciousness, I'd swear hearing Mother's voice in the rigging warning me, *"Be careful what you wish for, baby boy."*

Fortunately, I'm a good sailor, though simpatico and cautious of those who aren't. Sharing a meal is considered impolite, particularly if your companion's is all over your boots.

Finding space aboard this merchant cruiser crammed to capacity has been difficult, but I've solved the problem with devious cunning. The multitude of seasick steer clear of the ship's bows, which makes things worse. I love the sharp end and watching the porpoises dive and frolic through the waves.

If humans had this much fun, there would be no time for fighting each other.

"Stop dozing, boy, and go stand in the corner."

I look up into a familiar, bearded face. I frantically search for a name. The soulful brown eyes and classroom joke solve the riddle.

"Les!" I holler, leaping to my feet and into his arms, hugging him tightly. "I've missed you mate."

Struggling free from my embrace, he says, "Put me down. You'll have people talking about us." Although he's chuckling.

We sit straddle-legged on the fo'c'sle. War and want mainly forgotten, we relive our childhood which is filled with happy days and boyish pranks that have disappeared over the horizon. However short our reunion, my schoolboy chum, and I intend to enjoy every moment of our passage to India. The voyage to Ceylon's scheduled for sixteen days, where the army boys will disembark. Even for working sailors, this is a long spell without putting a foot on dry land. The soldiers are going berserk, and Jolly Jack's winding them up worse. Bickering and fisticuffs are frequent but the navy, in true pragmatic fashion comes up with an ideal solution. All disagreements will be settled in honourable fashion.

Combatants wearing gloves will box three three-minute rounds under Queensberry rules. They'll be judged and a winner declared. I'm intrigued, though not a fan of the noble art. I see no gain in a fat lip or busted hands; it would hinder my drinking habit. But I do hear the ch-ch-ching of money. Although it's illegal to run a book on the outcome, I've got Les and a weasel-faced army corporal I've recently adopted in my corner. They'll help me clean up without having a glove laid on me. Having a spy in each camp enables me to unearth the big spenders and lay off the odds too. It's worth repeating, "My momma didn't raise no fool."

It's easy keeping the pot boiling and the animosity bubbling. The soldiers, apart from the odd roll call, aren't put to work, whereas sailors on passage are, which prompts much friction and rude comments from the soldiers.

I remain aloof and tight-lipped throughout the sneers and jeers. After all, one has to consider one's financial future. Added to which, it's difficult to retaliate when twenty feet beneath your tormentors and sitting in a cradle a little above the waves with only a red-lead brush in your hand. These extra-curricular jobs are never seen on Royal Navy recruiting posters. Yet I'm here by choice and enjoying the ride. Shangri-La couldn't be better.

Granddad always says, "The world's a beautiful place, only people are ugly."

We'd become close after Mary-Jane, my grandmother, died when I was seven. He was devastated. Mother told me years later that I saved his sanity. Apart from Charlie, the family had little time for a curious child. Every Saturday I was packed off to Granddad's house. It was a match made in heaven. We both needed someone with whom to talk. In my fertile mind, Granddad was Merlin, the wizard who knew the answer to everything. No question was too difficult to answer. Though Mother often scolded him for teaching me things I was too young to know, she was content to see him smiling again.

He's the super optimist and will probably have "Living the Dream" etched on his tombstone, which is what I'm doing as Les leans on the guardrail.

"Keep grinning that way and the white coats will be sedating you."

"Just thinking what a beautiful day it is."

"Sooner be in Brum on a rainy Sunday afternoon."

Surprised, I glance at Les's sad face. Something's bugging him, but I'm his mate not his mother. I'm quick with a joke and can make him laugh, which is useless at the moment. He needs help not humour.

"Need some assistance with your sums again, Les?"

He affirms with a nod, though his trusting eyes speak volumes. I sit on my haunches, waiting for him to gather his scattered thoughts. If there's truth in opposites attracting each other, we're your boys. He cogitates while I cackle.

"Had a letter from Rosie's mum." He pauses for me to digest this morsel. *Into each life a little rain must fall* springs to mind. I ignore it. Les is primed and ready to explode. "She tells me her daughter's pregnant. Once the baby's born, it will have to be adopted, and we're too young to marry without permission."

I'm dumbfounded. "You didn't know?"

"'Course I knew. We planned it. Thought they'd relent and be happy for us. We've known each other forever."

There has to be a first time for everything I suppose. Maybe I'm too refined or possibly too slow, while thoughtful Les has been putting much more than sugar on his Shredded Wheat. "What am I going to do, Eddie?" Les pleads. "I'll lose my girl and my baby."

Sometimes being clever isn't smart, but faith finds a way. "Not a thing. Count your blessings. You've a girl who loves you dearly and in a few months will be free to marry no matter what the world thinks. Your real deal-breaker will be when Granny gets her first glimpse of that wonderful bundle of joy that's impossible not to cherish."

"You make it sound simple. And two years isn't a lifetime, is it?"

"Especially when there are gorgeous girls waiting back home," I say.

It's great to see his sunny smile again. He puts an arm around my shoulder and squeezes tightly. "Thanks a bunch, pal."

Tongue-tied, I think, *Don't blame me. God made me do it.*

Chapter Seventy

A day's wait at the mouth of the Suez Canal has dampened our ebullience and the hooded, hump-backed vultures straddling the miles of telegraph wires, ravenously watching the ship's funeral progress, don't inspire confidence either. The warm sun, to which we'd eagerly lifted pale faces, is now a fireball that peels the skin from our hides. We have to seek patches of shade. It seems that the farther east we travel, the hotter it becomes. More importantly, despite rumours, no one will verify where we're bound. The draft from Lowestoft had been labelled Party 135. Shipped to Colombo, Ceylon initially and detailed for some mission to only God knows where. And he's not talking.

Compounding the situation, the harbour's teeming with traffic, and we've been swinging on a buoy just inside the boom for two days, waiting to get berthed at the quayside; the army brass are seething about the delay. They've a hard day's slog ahead upcountry to Kandy to take over the garrison.

We're weighing anchor and running up the engines as the aircraft carrier *HMS Illustrious* sweeps majestically past us. Bugles and bo'suns' whistles stridently rupture the early morning air.

Our alacrity proves that if you snooze, you lose. Equally, the khaki-clad brigade waste no time getting their act together. Within three hours, the whole regiment, loaded down with backpacks and equipment, is heading for the hills and their new billet.

Having finished lunch, we're metaphorically sticking pins in our master's eyes for denying us shore leave when the tannoy demands, "Naval Party 135 assemble on the fo'c'sle, at the double."

We grab our caps, scramble up top, and are met by a time-worn chief petty officer. He hustles us smartly into line. "Try to look intelligent, boys.

You're about to meet the new boss," he says, with a wintry smile.

Right on cue, the bo'sun's whistle shrieks a welcome. Approaching from amidships is enough scrambled egg to make a wedding cake, headed by a tall, elegant figure in white full dress and medalled uniform.

Hearing Les gasp, I ask, "What's up, mate?"

"Don't you recognise him? It's Dickie."

"You mean your Uncle Dickie?"

"No! Mountbatten, the top dog of Southeast Asia Command. Combined Ops is his brainchild."

I'd guessed he was important by the gold rings nearly up to his elbows, though he's twice as handsome as in the newsreels.

"Order in the ranks," the chief bawls.

"Dickie," as he is affectionately called by sailors, is within earshot now and he's grinning. "Relax, Chief. They're on our side, and you're not on the parade ground. Go and do whatever you do when not badgering ratings while I have a chin-wag with my latest band of brothers."

Pacing off another ten yards, he turns to face us. "Okay chaps, gather round. Let's get down to cases."

He's of royal blood and uses the position to his own advantage and Britain's. Affectionately adored by the masses as a hometown hero, yet abhorred by the white-hairs in Whitehall, he'd captained a destroyer during the early days of the war. He then rose through the ranks and was appointed Supreme Commander of SEAC last year.

Moreover, he's a sailor's sailor. We listen well.

"You're the spearhead of Party 135. It's a dirty job, but someone has to do it." He chuckles. "I thought of you lot right away."

Noting that he has our attention, he continues, "You were specifically selected because of your previous combat experience. Nevertheless, tomorrow morning, bright and early, you'll be en route for Madras and intensive training. It's not a picnic, chaps, but essential. Good luck and Godspeed."

Stepping back a yard, he snaps off a smart salute. Without thought, our squad springs to attention and returns the gesture.

Having completed almost two years of service in His Majesty's Royal Navy, it's nice to feel one belongs. Then again, it might be a touch of heatstroke.

Chapter Seventy-One

Dickie wasn't kidding when he'd said bright and early. It's barely 0500 hours when we execute a sharp left outside the boom and head northeast for India. Two days behind schedule, a lightened load, and putting on some speed, Party 135 are the last of the passengers. The ship's company are anxious to see the backs of us. They treat us as lepers, particularly yesterday's chief-in-charge. He's still smarting from Mountbatten's boot up his backside and boasts of off-loading us onto our nursemaids. The man must be childish. If I find his teddy bear, I'll throw it overboard.

Officially, we're considered in transit, therefore excused work detail. We know our sabbatical's nearly over. Yesterday is rarely mentioned in Combined Ops, and tomorrow's anyone's guess. Today is what counts. One size fits all. Les arrives with two tin mugs of cocoa. It lifts me from the doldrums, which is not unusual, though I never tell him. This gangling, cock-eyed optimist would scoff if I said he'd been my saviour; he idolises me.

Classmates called him stupid and dumb. He's slow but determined. They jeered because he'd no lunch. I told Mother, who sent extra for him. The kids bullied me for talking to him. He smacked their heads. It's old but true: what goes around comes around.

A few light years ago, I'd stepped aboard this ship, unsure if I were on foot or horseback. I was still shaking off occasional night sweats and a shadowy past while looking forward to the next stage of my self-imposed journey. Then, from my childhood, up pops the solution.

Reflecting, I realise that the worst may be behind us. Both the Americans in the Pacific and the British Fourteenth Army in Burma are making headway. By the time we've finished boot camp, it could be all over, bar the shouting.

Spending two years in the sun will suit me, especially if I'm not shot.

"You're the only bloke who's smiling nine thousand miles away from home." My simple friend doesn't miss much. "We've to meet our new leader at eleven. Let's see if he brightens your day any further."

"He will if I get the right answers to some questions," I say.

"Ooh! I love to see you all fired up," Les coos.

I regard him suspiciously, not too sure who's the simpleton.

We muster on the fo'c'sle for a headcount. All present, we're marched under guard to a huge navigation cabin where a captain and several NCOs await us. The sentries take up position outside, and the doors are closed firmly behind them. This meeting's being conducted in secrecy. Everyone who needs to know is here.

The chief petty officer has left his seat and is already prowling the room. He's not trying to scare us. That rolling gorilla gait is his natural walk. Once witnessed, it's hard to forget. Time has fluttered by, though Mr Gordon does not appear to have mellowed.

Kenny always preached, "Deal with the devil you know, not strangers."

Having finished his tour of inspection, the chief is ready to spread the word. He's not acknowledged anyone personally. If his audience expects a warm welcome, they're in for a shock. He's a tough nut. Only par excellence is good enough.

"Welcome, gentlemen," he says. "Remember the words. You'll not hear me utter them again. You've been selected for this operation due to your combat records and previous experience. Once you've passed muster, Party 135 will be disbanded. You'll be deployed on search-and-destroy missions, which explains the secrecy. According to navy records, you never existed. Try telling that to the marines."

"Thank you, Chief," the captain says, rising to his feet. He's climbed the ladder since last I saw him on the Downs outside of Brighton. It's beginning to feel like an old boys' school reunion, minus the happy memories.

"Good morning, men. My name's Barry Stewart, your new Gaffer, and Admiral Mountbatten's gofer. He's been my CO since I was a snotty-nosed sub-lieutenant back in forty-one and believes in calling a spade a bloody great shovel."

No rating questions his words. All the NCOs are nodding too. Lord

Louie's protocol's impeccable. He knows a winner when he sees one. "It's taken three years to persuade the Whitehall warriors to accept Dickie's plans. You, my lucky lads, are the guinea pigs." He holds up a restraining hand to quell the muttering.

"Hear me out before you start asking questions. There's the chance of a little extracurricular activity, providing you stay the course." Stewart pauses, letting the carrot hang in the air.

His words have a familiar ring. It's a different location, but they're playing the same game. Gordon challenged our manhood. Now they're more subtle. This ploy has been orchestrated from the top. During yesterday's visit, Dickie had joked that the mission wasn't a picnic; we'd laughed indulgently. The chief's comments were taken lightly; we believed he was winding us up. Stewart's left to fill in the blanks. He's ideal for the job, a snake-oil salesman has nothing on him.

Shooting up a hand while he gathers breath, I ask, "Permission to speak, sir?"

Stewart's all teeth and charm. "Certainly, old chap. Everything is confidential in here. Fire away."

"Speculation's been rife from day one. Party 135 were a bunch of misfits that no one wanted. Someone suggested we call ourselves the Mushroom Squad because we were kept in the dark and fed a load of crap. Many of us had leave curtailed, courses cancelled, and were stuck aboard this floating coffin for seven weeks. Apart from veiled hints and sneers of not being up to snuff, we've still no clue where our future lies," I finish breathlessly.

There's muttering around me, echoing my words, though not so delicately. Gordon is on his feet, demanding order. The captain smiles and waits implacably.

"Having poked you all with a stick and finding you're awake, I'll tell the rest of the story," he says. "I offer no apologies for the cloak and dagger work. Secrecy is vital to the success of this operation, as you'll discover. Following the successful invasion of the Normandy coastline, similar tactics were expected out east, but it's proved to be a different ball game. There are few natural deepwater harbours to accommodate large ships or beaches on which men and materials can land. Yet, more to the point, Japanese soldiers wish to die in battle and are deemed cowards if they surrender."

Barry hesitates a moment. No one speaks. We're waiting for the punchline. "The Fourteenth Army are fighting the Japs up north, pushing them back too. It'll take two years at the present pace to defeat them, the experts forecast. Explain that to folk back home."

"Thinking about Jack?" Les asks, rubbing my arm. He's the only one who knows.

Nodding, I listen to Stewart galloping on. "Most of Burma is jungle, swamp, and mountains clear to Thailand's border, with villages hidden up muddy rivers."

Nothing changes. The whiz kid still needs a second banana.

"It sounds like the Norfolk Broads," I suggest.

"Exactly!" Stewart trumpets, faster than a moggy on a mouse. "And who knows small craft and streams better than Patrol Service lads?"

Our nagging suspicions are confirmed. The innuendo slots neatly into place. We're not ferrying men into battle. We are the search-and-destroy force, the whole goddamned nine yards.

Puffing contentedly on his pipe while the room settles down, he reassures us that we've two months' training before any sniff of danger, and only then if we qualify.

"Two conditions apply. You sign and swear an Official Secrets Act and be willing to kill a man with your bare hands," he says. "His Majesty's Royal Navy is neither your God nor conscience. Should you successfully complete the specialist and jungle survival courses, the final decision will be yours alone."

Relighting his pipe, Captain Stewart leans comfortably back in his chair, basking in the knowledge of having us by the short hairs. Mentioning the conditions is a master stroke. Signing the Secrets Act before leaving the room forbids us discussing any details, even amongst ourselves. The piece said that we'd been noted as possible candidates for selection, smart too. Passing a course could mean promotion and more pay, which wouldn't create any pain.

All in all, the three musketeers—Dickie, Barry, and Flash—have done a fair job on us, which proves that officers are more than merely a pain in the rear end.

Chapter Seventy-Two

We are corralled into submission by Stewart and his sidekicks then arrive in Madras at the witching hour. Our savaged souls are not soothed. Even the attention of the hausfraus hasn't helped. The POs are having a whale of a time as we dejectedly wait for transport to boot camp. We suffer in abject silence, knowing they're going to be our tutors and taskmasters in the immediate future.

Adrift (as usual), we hurl ourselves and our kit aboard the trucks and hit the road, which contains more potholes than tarmac. We travel twenty agonising miles then wearily tumble from the tailboard on the blackest night in Christendom with bruises on our bums to match our egos. We stare in astonishment.

The petty officers are giggling like schoolgirls. The whole place is ablaze with lights. Dazzling white buildings, manicured lawns, and crushed gravel paths abound. It's the Taj Mahal. The drivers must be lost! Speechless, we follow our leaders through the wrought iron gates to a huge hall filled with tables and chairs. They invite us to sit and relax. Any moment now, I'm going to wake up.

Les is sitting next to me, grinning like the Cheshire cat. I'm still trying to get my head inside this when Dickie and his stooges amble in. Acknowledging the warm welcome, the admiral tells us to resume our seats. "Christmas has come a little early this year. I hope you like the new surroundings. While training, you're attached to my staff and accommodated in a self-contained block with all amenities at hand. The rest of the camp is a rest and recuperation centre for sailors entitled to leave. It's been a long day, and I expect you're shattered, so I'll leave my ADC to be as brief as possible, wishing you goodnight and good hunting," he concludes.

I feel like standing on my chair and cheering. This small boy has become a man and discovered a real-life hero to replace Long John Silver.

Mother will be hopping mad knowing I've been in the company of royalty.

Stewart's savvy enough to cut the cackle and instructs our nannies to off-load us into dormitories lickety-split. We are ten to a room, and someone's already put our gear by the beds.

I strip buck naked then crawl under the mosquito net, spread-eagle on the crisp, cotton sheets and I'm asleep in minutes.

AWAKENED BY A QUIET VOICE encouraging me to show a leg, I open bleary eyes and perceive much more than legs being shown. Ceiling fans are bravely battling, but it's hotter than hell. It's only 0800 hours. Nude male bodies are rarely picturesque, particularly before breakfast. Petty Officer Rabbitz, our latest soothsayer, is clothed in freshly laundered track pants and a sweatshirt. He reads the first lesson as we, still unclothed, listen to his message.

"I want you bunch shaved, showered, scoffed your grub and in the lecture hall by oh-nine-thirty hours, bright-eyed and bushy-tailed. Chief Gordon has wise words, which he wishes to impart."

There are many ways to humiliate grown men. He's found a cracker. We've barely had time to get our knees brown, but I think fun in the sun is over.

"It's like being in school," Les says, sliding into the desk next to me.

"No it's not. There they caned you for talking. Here they shoot you."

"Silence!" the petty officers shout in unison.

The dog handler has his hounds well-trained.

Gordon is off the mark. "Discipline's the name of the game. We talk, you obey. Any infraction, you'll be punished by dismissal and returned to base. Every rating will be subjected to jungle warfare training and instruction in their own trades. After qualification, you'll be formed into squads and deployed behind enemy lines on sabotage missions. It's dirty, dangerous work. Barring a miracle, it's the quickest way to end the bloodshed. So! Let's move our backsides and learn how to survive."

His bedside manner's not the greatest, but I admire his style. I'd wade through a field filled with corpses to follow this man into battle.

Strangely, the only perils we encounter throughout the day are stabs and jabs from injections, plus the ignominy of raising our shirts and dropping our pants and coughing obligingly for the doctors. Drafting routine always takes precedence and with one hundred bodies to be addressed and assessed, this uses up most of the day; the highlight is exchanging white ducks for jungle greens, including a wide-brimmed bush hat. The whole enchilada's cooler and more comfortable.

I pick up Les from his dorm, and we stroll to the cafeteria for supper. The chow's first class, and the daily medication is straight from the keg. Praise the Lord.

"Over here, Roberts," a voice calls.

No! It's not Him, but one who must be obeyed.

"It's delightful to meet you again, Chief Gordon."

"Speak for yourself. Seeing you bothers me. What mischief are you plotting?"

Drawing myself up to a full five and a half feet, I say haughtily, "You disparage me, sir. My motive's are as pure as driven snow. I've come to bury the yellow peril, not to praise him."

"Wrong answer," Gordon says, frowning. "You're a single cog in the wheel. I don't need dead heroes. Each man's a blood brother, watching backs. Read my lips, for expendable read dependable."

Acknowledging Gordon's advice, I keep my mouth shut and beat a hasty retreat.

It's hard for a court jester to laugh when he hears his own head fall into the basket.

Chapter Seventy-Three

We scramble from our virtuous couches at the sight of the baton dangling from the quartermaster's wrist. It's no fashion statement. His "Jump to it!" demands instant respect. Rabbitz promised bright and early, but dawn hasn't cracked yet. I'd thought of sleeping fully dressed, but resisted the impulse. I didn't wish to crease my new jungle-greens.

Mayhem sets in when Rabbitz says, "There are fifteen minutes to clear the area before the enemy arrive." They're armed, yet we've no weapons. I'm beginning to wonder who thought of this stupid game. Then realise it's for real. Gordon and friends are teaching us to survive. One thing's certain: if push comes to shove, I can outrun most of this bunch. Our leader's almost simpering. We're ready, on the move in good time, and adopt the old method of two by two: jog two hundred paces, walk two. It's easy to see that Gordon has informed Rabbitz about me when I'm made pacemaker for the squad.

Puffing alongside me, the PO says, "Ease up, cowboy, you're running these kids into the ground. You've left the chasers in the dust. We'll cut through the jungle and come round behind them."

"Shame, I was beginning to enjoy myself. Shall we eat al fresco while we're here?"

"You're a bloody nutcase. The squad will be dead within a week at this pace."

"I know, but it's nicer than having a bullet up your breeches," I whisper. Deep in the undergrowth and taking a welcome swig from canteens, the squad chuckles. Even Rabbitz grins. "They'd love you in Tokyo."

"Why not go home for supper while the rest find their way out of the woods? It could be hours," I say, hogging the limelight. "Especially if they meet Little Red Riding Hood."

"Tough luck," Rabbitz replies. "We're out here for three days and nights to study the wildlife. Once you've sheltered under the same poncho with your mates a few times, you'll be really close friends."

We live rough for seventy-two hours. We have primitive hygiene, no fresh water or hot food, and it isn't much fun. Equally, being back in school, studying for exams, is frustrating too. I'm flopped on my bed, sweat-soaked and dog-tired after a three-day sojourn up country when Rabbitz tells me to report to the chief.

It's difficult to read Gordon's face. He always resembles the Grim Reaper. "Enjoy your nature ramble?" he enquires.

It's tempting to answer his quick wit with a caustic comment, but I refrain. Since my early roasting, I've been a good boy. I'm determined to pass this course and gain promotion, if possible. Thanks to Les' nurturing, it's working, though it's not easy keeping my fast mouth buttoned.

The chief and his minions are smiling benignly, which in itself is suspicious; wariness is the watchword.

"We've been hearing stories about you," he says, with an expansive wave at his colleagues. "All favourable I'm happy to say. Delving into service records, we discovered you've hidden talents. You've obtained diplomas for fitness and athletic prowess, pre-service days, and during initial training achieved a recommendation for an ERA course, which you never took due to some idiot in Lowestoft screwing up. Captain Stewart has agreed that you fast-track the PTI course and bring the rest up to speed. We need a crack team asap. You know the men, and they like you, though only God knows why."

"Thank you, Chief," I answer. "It's probably my dazzling personality."

"You don't fool me. You're out here for a reason."

"Bet your cassock, as the actress said to the bishop," I respond.

It's scarcely a cool day, yet I sense a tiny tremor. God speaks in many tongues.

Sauntering back to the dorm, I pinch myself a couple of times to see if I'm dreaming. It will be strange having people being nice and fun, taking the wind out of pompous one's sails. Although, having an anchor on my arm may command a little respect. Les will think it's a hoot, though in a few weeks he'll be made up too. He's a wireless operator and pretty hot I'm told. It would be great being on the same team. We battled through junior school together. No sweat! The Japanese will be a cakewalk.

ROAD WORK OR FALL GUY, Les is here every step of the way: from blistering, flat-out five-mile runs in the heat of the day, to five-minute, no-holds-barred brawls using hands, feet, elbows, and dirty tricks. He's a lean, hard man, who's determined to toughen me up or die in the attempt. How could one find a better friend? He's bruised and battered, but he's no bones broken as we celebrate his hook with a couple of cold beers. It's a mixed blessing. The latest buzz is that we may not complete the course. The ancients at the Admiralty are pressuring Dickie to launch his devilish scheme, and we've only three crews prepped at the moment. Gordon declares our supreme leader's language would make a stevedore blush.

We aren't surprised by the hastily convened meeting. We crowd into the hall expecting fireworks. I've witnessed sadder occasions, but not many. Our local hero is standing front stage and centre, ready to deliver his soliloquy. Dutifully, we arrange our faces to suit Stewart's mood.

"We've been scuttled by the bigwigs. After months of dithering, it's now, damn the torpedoes full ahead."

There's a nice touch. I bet he's read that somewhere.

"I know that many of you will be disappointed by not being selected, and to this end, Dickie has reached a compromise regarding your futures," Stewart says.

He can't be serious. The only sadness these bums will feel is the loss of neat rum and drinking filthy, watered-down swill.

Stewart applies the sweetener. "Every rating selected for this course will be a member of the task group and crew aboard the mother ship LST, which is an essential part of the operation."

Naturally, Gordon has to put his boot in. "Everything else remains the same. No one contravenes the Official Secrets Act. Disobedience will get you shot."

Love them, or hate them, chief petty officers are a necessary evil and sure to raise your hopes, even in the roughest ocean.

Chapter Seventy-Four

Strangely, the change in plan causes barely a ripple. During the following days, our friendship bonds tighten. We're no longer competing for top-dog spots but assisting and helping the struggling fraternity.

Four months of togetherness has made us real close. The true lead-swingers have long been sorted and the others, bless them, don't wish to leave. The devils I know can count on my vote every time. My main task is to teach them unarmed combat. Many big men have big ideas. They think their bulk and weight make them invincible. Wrong! It makes them more vulnerable. Speed and agility are paramount.

Following good advice and humbling, teeth-shattering falls, they're offered rifles with bayonets. It's revenge they rarely reject. To me, this is not about heroes and villains, but respect. And while I'm not afraid, I'm not brave. My opponent is just slower with a gun. I put him down, press the bayonet against his chest and maybe place my boot hard upon his shoulder. Usually, I help the victim back to his feet and throw the rifle at the next pupil.

"Who's ready to die?" I ask, deliberately turning my back.

We carry on without apologies or inquests. This is war, not purses at ten paces.

I'm not seeking solace for myself or gratitude from anybody, but as I tell them, "You do not have to love me, just don't forget me." It works every time.

Sailors are suspicious souls. The change in modus operandi had puzzled us but by design, or providence, we now have enough ratings to form seven mobile attack units. Maybe three wise men found juicy carrots to dangle for their willing donkeys.

A fleet of single-decker grey buses roll up to take us to Madras. A brand-spanking-new LST lolls against the quayside. Standing on the quarterdeck, I gaze across the bay at the massive array of ships. Bitter memories flood back. I thought I'd outgrown this stuff.

A firm hand grips my shoulder. "You can't bring them back, Eddie," Les says. "Let's grab some lunch and see the sights."

Granted all-day shore leave—the first in seven weeks—we tour the town. It's an exercise in futility. The place is packed solid with every colour and creed, from lobster-pink to charcoal-black. Service personnel of both sexes jostle for space among beggars, cripples, rickshaws, and bikes, not forgetting the gorgeous, raven-haired girls clad in brilliantly coloured saris. I'm shocked by the vast cultural differences. The Raj casually brushing aside children, whose faces are destroyed by leprosy. They beg for baksheesh. Would Mahatma Gandhi's dreams be realised if India were granted independence?

I don't ask Les's opinion. Being the eldest of nine kids, he might embarrass me.

Trooping back to the ship, we loiter on deck, waiting for the stragglers. Though we're unmarried, there're many who are interested in afternoon delight. Personally, I'm fretting, because my tot hasn't been issued. I'm not the only one. Being polite and loose-lipped has distinct disadvantages. My mates delegate me spokesman in times of need. Rabbitz affords the ideal opening when he asks if I'm enjoying my day. Answering in the affirmative, I do express a little disappointment at missing my mid-day medication. The sun shines brightly on the righteous. The PO says we'll receive our grog back at base.

Tradition and dogma play a huge part in navy life, and if things are going well, it's a sign there're rough times ahead. It's almost four months since we've been true sailors, stood a watch, or witnessed bad weather. Though the course is brutal, we are well cared for and cosseted. Yet, like me, my mates are yearning to get back to sea. It's second nature for Jolly Jack to grumble but feeling the deck dip and lift under your feet and your chest expand with the tangy, salty breeze are exactly why we'd joined the Andrew. I've always believed that sailors aren't born, just launched.

Climbing off the bus, we're told to scrub up and report to the cafeteria in thirty minutes. It appears the axe is about to fall. We wait patiently in the corridor, while a head count's taken. The doors are flung open, and we're greeted by Mountbatten's staff officers and their wives wishing us a Merry Christmas. It isn't December yet.

Customarily, officers serve Christmas dinner to lower-deck ratings. Dickie has gone one better and coaxed the ladies to help out too.

Each squad has its own table. Escorted by our respective leaders, we stand to sing the national anthem, toast the king, and drink everyone's health before sitting down to eat. I no longer think of myself as the bottom of the pole and today proves one doesn't have to be last. It's a shame Mother isn't here to witness my being served dinner by a real live lady.

Stuffed, I need a nap, but Dickie has an agenda. Now that we've eaten our turkey, he wants to talk it. There's a huge map pinned to a blackboard, and he's itemising red dots. "Here's Rangoon, down here southern Thailand, and nearly all jungle in between, but the Japanese have oil depots and ammunition dumps from where they supply troops fighting up north. Your assignment is to destroy them, and God willing, this will be the last Yuletide we'll be parted from loved ones." Raising his glass high, he acknowledges the audience. "My deepest thanks and best wishes to everyone here for a good Christmas and bright future."

There's wild cheering for the boss, and I'm happy to be here, though officially I could be shot just mentioning the matter. Who cares? No one will believe me. Even my own mother calls me weird.

Chapter Seventy-Five

Our exodus takes longer than anticipated, but Gordon and his followers are unconcerned. Maybe, as with mosquito bites, it's part of the job. They firmly shake our hands and give us meaningful hugs. They're like devoted grannies watching us clamber aboard buses. Eons ago, we'd been eager, cocky young kids out to conquer the world. With nurturing, nattering, and occasional sheer bloody-mindedness, these unsung heroes have made us into a band of brothers.

I'm astonished by where life's lessons can be learned.

The normally raucous matelots are quiet as the bus chugs down the gravelled highway to Madras and our new berth aboard *LST-296*. We've the pleasure of being under the watchful eyes of new officers and NCOs, and we're listed as crew. However, men selected for missions are anonymous and will not be recorded in the ship's log. Rumour becomes reality in the first tussle with our taskmasters, including signing another Secrecy Act. Once more, we're ordered never to speak, write, or inform any living soul of our actions. Contravention could result in death.

It would be easy to say, *I haven't read the small print*, or *I heard you the first time*. I find it bloody annoying trying to fulfil a boyhood dream of sailing the world and becoming a buccaneer, but not allowed to breathe a word of it.

I can't help but admire the planning that's gone into this enterprise. The *296* is a depot ship for naval vessels in the Bay of Bengal. Its home base being a secluded island offshore from Madras, complete with sheltered cove big enough to contain seven MTBs already converted into assault craft. There's more heavy lifting to do, and we have to learn boat drills. Everyone's impatient and straining at the leash. All we need is King Richard standing on the bridge, wielding his sword, and yelling, "Let slip the dogs of war!" We do even better, as the tannoy screeches, "All hands on deck! Admiral's barge is coming alongside."

Dickie, tanned and fit, cuts a salute at the quarterdeck and comes smartly striding up to greet us. "Dropped by to give you the latest news. The armchair admirals have finally issued the green light. You've two days to get your ducks in a row, then it's all systems go. We're mounting five attacks on specific targets." He chuckles at our shocked faces. "Don't panic, chaps. It's all sorted. The Burmese fishermen will guide you. They know the swamps blindfolded. Your job is to sneak in quietly, blow the objectives to rat shit, and scarper. The *296* will be waiting offshore to retrieve you. So don't hang about; I don't need dead heroes."

We've learned how to survive in the jungle with little food, sleep in trees while snakes slither across our bodies or insects drink their fill, and learned to defeat an armed man. The question no one asks or answers is, "Are you callous enough to kill with just a stiletto?"

It's a rusty old adage that all's fair in love and war. It vexes me. I'm aware we're expendable volunteers. We are young and single men, but does that mean being completely discounted? If we are never recognised, what we do never happened.

Having skilfully passed the buck and relevant documents to the captain, Dickie spends time glad-handing everyone. I might be overreacting, but he seems reluctant to leave, as though not expecting us to return. Maybe I've been a landlubber too long and become fixated.

There's no time to ponder anything for two days while we rehearse our roles. I'm comfortable knowing Les and hard-nosed Benny Levine are with me. Troubles shared make good companions. The clock's ticking again as we get underway. I'm buoyed by the sight of a destroyer riding shotgun on the starboard bow. Although assured the RAF rule the skies and our navy the seas, we take everything with a pinch of salt. Literally, we're working in the dark, so it doesn't really matter.

Silence is the main order of the day. Only the captain and navigating officer know the destination, though our squad's ordered to standby. I hear the engines decelerate. I'd expected my adrenaline to start pumping, but I feel calm. A sharp glance at my mates reveals their calmness too. Perhaps our superiors have brainwashed us. When they say jump, we ask how high. Whatever's prompted this serenity in my heart, I realise this is where I have to be. I certainly can't afford to miss the boat now.

Chapter Seventy-Six

What a difference a day makes. I've seldom been so underwhelmed, and I'm not alone. The demolition experts clambering back aboard are silent, sour, and don't smell too sweet after crawling along the sewer drains to gain access and plant their explosives. I'd been ordered to stay with Les while he monitored communications. Missing the action's annoyed me. But then again, what action? I've had more thrills playing with my ducks in the bathtub.

Our escorts are already blowing smoke. I crank up the revs and chase after them. We've twenty minutes before all hell breaks loose—not that we'll be able to enjoy the fireworks or read about them. There's a big cheer for Les when he reports contact with the *296*. Despite my dislike of the flat-bottomed bastards, it feels like homecoming. Stinking of garbage but treated royally, we're winched aboard, regaled with a tot of rum, fed, and mustered for debriefing. Conducted by Captain Blackwell, assisted by Jimmy the One, and a scribe to scribble down answers, the questions follow the usual pattern.

"Think carefully, Roberts, then tell me, what did you see?" the skipper asks.

"I saw nothing, sir."

He looks at Jimmy, who says, "Surely you saw something, Roberts."

I shake my head. "Black as pitch, sir. Couldn't see a hand in front of my face, though I was wearing black gloves as instructed."

The writer's hand stops moving. The first officer's face turns pink.

Blackwell steps boldly into the breach. "Engaged on a dangerous mission such as this, you must remember some incident, man."

Frowning, with deep concentration, and milking the moment for all it's worth, I say, "One thing bothered me. When the boys climbed back on board, there was this horrible stench as though someone had stepped in something."

A wintery smile crosses the captain's features. "Thank you for that useful contribution, Roberts. Go and get your head down. You've earned a lie-in."

Occasionally, saying very little speaks volumes. I've a distinct feeling I'll not be interrogated often.

FORTUNE IS SAID TO FAVOUR the brave, but we're not grumbling. The *296* is listed as a workhorse, yet she's been swinging on a buoy for two weeks while our happy band soaks up the sun's rays, swims in the lagoon, and lives the life of Reilly. It couldn't happen to a nicer bunch of loafers, but being disciplined sailors, we know the clock's ticking. We're here on standby, nothing's not for nothing in His Majesty's Royal Navy!

Rumour has it that the next raid's going to be massive and will happen soon. Evidently, the initial one (which never took place) was an outstanding success. Hush my mouth. It's no surprise when Stewart and Gordon come calling a couple of days later. They're looking chipper and pleased with themselves.

"Great show chaps," Stewart says. "Obliterated every target and suffered only two casualties. We've another mission planned three days hence, when all ten squads, with a few exceptions, will participate. Another victory will definitely knock the stuffing out of the Nips, and we'll be able to launch the Big One."

Chief Gordon calls for silence, and Stewart continues. "The British Army aided by the US Air Force has parachuted more troops behind Jap lines and driven a wedge between them, which gives us a great advantage."

I've never before witnessed men about to do battle look so pleased, though a thought strikes me. The captain mentioned exceptions. Omitting a man from a squad is akin to cutting off an arm. I'll probably never meet one of this tribe in heaven, but I'd go through hell for them.

Gordon takes over. "Before anyone starts whining, I'll give the squad changes. We require more tutors. Fortunately, we've men capable of taking on these duties and can promote from within the group. Every job's important in the overall scheme, and the sooner we get at it, the better."

My unspoken question's been answered. Gordon hinted that once I'd passed the course, this was a possibility. He's been trying to railroad me from day one of our reunion. Chiefs possess the memories of elephants, and he's not forgotten being upstaged back on the Downs. Though acknowledging my skill, he insists that I'm too cocky and need watching, whereas I regard him as crafty and carefully study his actions. He's a crusty old sod, but I can't help loving him.

Any notion it's going to be a soft number is quickly snuffed out. Gordon informs us we'll be pulling double shifts. We've one month to get two hundred Royal Marines combat ready. "The lions may sleep tonight, but you lot won't."

His words strike like a dagger between the ribs. Extra duty's no problem, but training marines? *No way!* Apart from marching and music, they're a complete waste of space. No self-respecting sailor would attend a marine's funeral. They would actually, but only to bring a spade. Robbie Burns was right on when he said, "Ne'er the twain shall meet."

Yet! I can't refuse. I'm damned whether I do or don't. Either side could shoot me. On second thought, it might be interesting to see if these leathernecks are as hard as they profess. After all, it's for their benefit.

The chief wastes no time. "Sew this hook on your shirt. You're in charge of all trainees. Many are officers, but their rank doesn't count here. Captain Stewart thinks they'll be pleased to have someone speaking their language."

"Mother will be thrilled to know."

"Don't be facetious, just mind your manners," Gordon replies.

Rabbitz struggles to keep a straight face. He's the unfortunate who has to teach me the ropes. I'm going to enjoy this chore. Soft bed, good food, early morning jogs. Trevor would be pleased.

I've twenty in my squad, all in jungle greens, with no visible pecking order. I introduce myself then spend a few moments explaining the objectives while ticking names off my list. There's always one who's late. "Foster!" I loudly call out for the third time.

"That's me. Sergeant Foster, Royal Marines," the big hunk says, sauntering across the square. He's more than big—try ginormous. One look tells me his ego is jumbo-sized too.

I smile demurely. "We do not use titles here, Foster." I hold up my arm. "I'm the only one with a rank. Please join us. Let's begin at the beginning. Before being able to defend yourself, you must learn how to fall."

King Kong has already pushed his way to the front and is listening intently. I'm not fooled. I remember the drill: man with big stick walk softly. No crystal ball's required to know Foster's a hard case, used to giving orders and being obeyed. This month's sabbatical will be a stroll in the park for him, including having someone half his size to boss around. I've reluctantly taken this position, wanting to stay with Les indefinitely. Maybe God has other ideas. I've been such a good lad lately; he's possibly concerned. Having right on my side and a hook on my arm gives me an edge. I've never been fond of bullies and giving this giant his comeuppance could provide much-needed relief in the busy weeks ahead.

Chapter Seventy-Seven

How's your love affair with Foster?" Rabbitz asks.

"Not sure," I reply. "He grunts most of the time."

"He's complained to Gordon that you're holding him back."

"Take a couple of dray horses to do that."

The petty officer looks serious. "Watch your back, Ed. Rumour has it he's a loose cannon."

"Don't fuss; my plan's foolproof. The madder he gets, the harder he'll work and want to whip my ass. He'll be a human wrecking ball by the end of the month."

"Hope you survive that long."

"Thanks for the vote of confidence. Got to dash now. Here's my team all hyped up for their five-mile trot. It's bound to sort out whiners from shiners."

"You're an evil instructor," Rabbitz says.

"You're an excellent teacher."

Leading the men off at a steady pace, I recall my clash with Gordon and the look of anguish he'd given me as I'd left him in the dust over the final hundred yards. He'd graciously accepted defeat and cleverly turned it to his own advantage, for which I'd admired him. Still do.

And then there's Foster, who seems a nice guy. He's pleasant and popular but has a score to settle before he rips down the Rising Sun. He believes I've humiliated him and seeks retribution. Although no direct threats have surfaced, speculation's rife, and a little spice might wake the joint up. Spats among servicemen happen frequently, seldom amount to much, and usually end with sharing a couple beers in the canteen.

Foster looms beside me. "Be dark before we reach base," he says, stepping up the pace.

Smiling inwardly, I watch him go. He'll soon tire of running solo. His impatience will affect his judgement. The smart ones keep pace with me, aware I'm cruising, not dashing. I've nothing to prove. My job is to make them all winners. Adjusting my headcount, my feet follow suit. Half the men stay, and we're starting to reel Foster in fast! Suddenly this shamble of arms and legs is evolving into a running machine. It's a perfect union of grit and determination. Up front, Foster's losing cohesion. He paddles along like a pregnant seal about to give birth. Our drumming feet must sound fiendish in his ears.

Easing off beside him, I show him how thoughtful I am. "I'll ask the chef to leave your supper on a low light, Foster," I say, then chase after the leaders.

There's no first prize; it's a team effort. The camp guardhouse marks the finish, and a small crowd of officers and ratings cheer home the squads. Every point counts for the Best on Parade. It's Dickie's idea of togetherness and it works. These hard cases would kill for each other. They make the Mafia look like angels.

Pushing ahead, I stage an epic victory for the crowd's pleasure then applaud all the contestants past the post.

Foster finishes a credible fifth. "It's not over yet! We've another three weeks," he crows.

I say, "Good, you'll need every second to lose that fat and replace it with muscle. Imagine you being the Royal Marine's pin-up boy."

It will be snowing in the Sahara before the sergeant smiles.

The lecture hall's a tomb of gloom. There are sad faces in abundance. Two of the teams are twenty-four hours adrift. My mates, including Les, are aboard one of the vessels. Neither prayer nor blasphemy helps and not knowing knots my nerves.

War waits for no one. Men die while we dither. Chief Gordon smartly girds our loins, though he's probably more stricker than most. He threads the needle for us to repair the holes in our ranks. These petty officers really are house mothers. We lower-deck slobs mess up, and they always pick up after us. I'm beginning to wax philosophical. Maybe maturity's taking over. My hook has removed my one foot from the gutter. Once my mates stop messing around in the Bay of Bengal, things may get back to normal.

I hear tempers flaring around me. Tension is high. Suddenly the canteen doors burst open and Les, with the rest of my old crew, come crowding in. They're dishevelled, dirty, and smell similar to day-old Calcutta curry, yet look a beautiful sight. It's taken three and a half days to reach base on one engine. These vessels are supposed to be for light duty only. I'm not sure who was on the tiller, and I'm too happy to ask. Days such as these are precious when we just enjoy each other's company, knowing tomorrow may be too late. Living every day like it's my last works for me.

The morning after finds us less cheerful, and Gordon is chafing at the bit. Dickie's had his chain rattled by the War Office and guess who carries the can? We'd volunteered for this caper, and Dickie's a bloody fine skipper!

There's no cause for debate. We decide that it's past time the Japanese get one almighty ass-kicking. Work rate has improved dramatically, and morale's through the roof. The canteen's deserted. We spend our spare moments devoted to writing home. Naturally, we can't divulge our movements but assure our families that we're well. Days relentlessly tick by. We're becoming jittery waiting for the Off.

"Seems you've escaped a beating," Les says. "Foster's forgiven you."

"I wouldn't bet on it. He'll probably leave a bomb under my blankets."

"Strange. The leatherneck seems a nice bloke. You're the only one he dislikes."

My dear pal is a harbinger of doom. Despite several attempts on my part to make him welcome, Foster shuns me. It's not compulsory to love the ones who lead, but I guess even nice people, such as I, can't win them all.

There're a bunch of us soaking up the sun and chatting when he comes by. "Still feeding the lads that crap?" he enquires.

"Your hands can save your life if skilled and fast enough."

I'm aware Foster's not here for small talk and provoke him with a cheeky grin. I sense he's hell-bent on revenge. I take a step back, instinctively ducking and weaving to the left. My adversary, with lightning speed, throws a looping right cross that crunches into my left shoulder and sends me crashing to the ground. Red-hot pain lances through my arm from collarbone to fingertips, and I'm trying to suck air into my empty lungs.

Foster stands over me, huge arms akimbo, waiting for the audience's approval. He's determined to bask in his sweet victory. I'd been preaching for weeks on how to survive (dirty tricks included), and who's stupid enough to tackle Goliath?

While he's gloating, I've been thinking that if I move my arm or even blink, I'll be finished. But there's nothing wrong with my legs and feet.

The deed's faster than thought. I hook my left boot around the back of his ankle and bend my right leg to place the bottom of my foot against his right knee. Then I smartly straighten my leg and tug on his right ankle while swivelling onto my left hip. I hear a loud crack and a blood-curdling scream. Foster goes down faster than a giant redwood. I swear the ground shakes.

Pain shelved, I bounce back to my feet, whip the stiletto from its sheath, and place the blade flat across Foster's throat. "Next time you decide to play the game, Foster, do it right. Finish the job before taking a bow."

I give him a long, cool, blue-eyed stare, then reluctantly shrug and back away.

Les is hovering. "You frightened the crap out of everyone. We thought you were going to stick him, Eddie."

Gordon and his posse arrive, armed with notebooks and pencils and seeking facts.

The medics have left long since with their latest case "A nice clean break of the fibula in two places," the quack cheerfully announced.

This news doesn't improve the chief's affection for me, which resembles Hardy lambasting Laurel with, "This is another nice mess you've gotten me into!"

Some days it certainly pays to stay in bed and pull the covers over one's head.

Chapter Seventy-Eight

The chief wants to see you in his office," Rabbitz says. "He's not happy and looking for blood."

"How can you tell? Anyhow, vampires only come out at night."

"Cut out the comedy, kid. Get your cap, follow me, and keep your trap shut."

You're a joy, I think, but manage all three. I'd just consumed a large lunch and tasty tot before crashing onto my cot, looking forward to a siesta, when he'd come in, firing on all cylinders. On a good day, he's not a bad sort, but I'm off duty until the next band of innocents arrive, keen to kick the crap out of the Japanese. Experience tells me the sooner this is sorted, the quicker I'll be snoozing.

Trotting after Rabbitz, I'm wondering what's flown up Gordon's nose.

"Come in, sit down. I've news for you," Gordon says. He waves a hand at the PO. "You can trot along." He waits for the door to close before adding, "He's a nice bloke, but has ears that fit his name."

I stay mute, heeding Rabbitz's warning.

"Received a call this morning that you've been disturbing the marines."

Though perceiving a chink of light, I hold my tongue. I still need a compass.

"Lieutenant Colonel Harvey from JAG wants words with you."

"Did I park my bike in his spot?" I enquire, adding a little levity.

"It's not funny," Gordon snaps back.

"Who's laughing? You had my report yesterday. It was a misunderstanding. These legal eagles always want their pound of flesh."

"Nevertheless, he's stirring the pot and wants you available for questioning. I've enough problems without babysitting you."

He lapses into silence. I let him ruminate as the clock in my head starts ticking. Asking and answering his own question, he's provided the solution.

"Why are you grinning? It's a damned serious matter."

"According to records, I'm a member of *LST-296* on a secret mission in Southeast Asia. How can I give evidence if I'm not here? You'll be shot if you disclose my whereabouts. Problem solved," I explain.

Gordon is discombobulated. "But you're an instructor."

"I beg your pardon, Chief. It's only temporary. My prime duty is governed by the Secrecy Act, and I believe sacrosanct."

Gordon's face is of a child swallowing cod liver oil. "You're a devious swine, Roberts. I should be thanking you, but I've a feeling you're looking out for number one."

He's no mind reader but suspects I've an agenda. Too true, he'd be shocked by the stubbornness that's carried me halfway across the world. I wait obsequiously while the chief stares into the distance, trying to figure out my motive for this bonhomie.

Eventually, sighing heavily, he says, "The sooner you're aboard *296*, the better I'll sleep." Coming around the desk, he thrusts his big hand in mine and shakes it fiercely. "Though I'll miss you if only for your bloody nuisance."

Praise indeed from a CPO, I muse, while strolling back to my dorm.

THANKS TO ADROIT SHUFFLING OF the pack by Chief Gordon, I'm back aboard, and it's nice to be among my mates. I endure the jibes of "teacher's pet," while modestly accepting the "giant killer" accolade.

I'm happy to be a sailor again. After languishing in the lagoon for days, we're finally on the move. Destination-wise, we've not a clue. The rumour mill refers to it as the Big One, with five hundred Royal Marines, the main assault force, and ten naval support craft to act as decoys. The whole shebang sounds too simplistic to be true. Though we've had good results from previous hit-and-run attacks, this operation's on a far greater scale. I remind the naysayers that the Fourteenth Army are going great guns but could use our assistance.

Further speculation's averted by the tannoy ordering, "All hands on deck."

Scampering up top, we're jovially greeted by Captain Blackwell. "In two hours we'll be rendezvousing with the rest of the group. The marines will attack Tavoy, while our boats provide diversionary tactics blowing up bridges and roads. Info's all in here," he says, waving a black oilskin package. "Study it, digest it, and we'll have debriefing later."

My sympathy's with Les. As wireless operator, he has to remember codes, signals, co-ordinates, and the whole ball of wax. Whereas I push the gear stick forward or back and I'm done. Sometimes it pays to be stupid, which makes me wonder how I got here.

I'm dreaming of golden locks and blue eyes when Les leans on the rail beside me. "We're not going ashore. Skipper wants us on point in case of emergency."

"Could have stayed in and painted my nails, not played guard dog," I say.

"Be thankful we've touched for a soft number. Spare a thought for our mates."

This kid from the wrong side of the tracks I've never seen down on his knees. Perhaps, standing tall, he notices things better than most people.

Leaving 296 swinging on a buoy a half mile off Tavoy Point, we quietly meander, with the incoming tide's help, towards the tree-lined coastline. Stealth's the name of the game: keep under cover, stay alert, and be patient. We know the drill. It's as easy as falling off a log. Besides, it beats dying. Unexpectedly, the dull boom of a gun makes us instinctively duck. It's followed by rapid fire and explosions. The onslaught's been perfectly synchronised with the garrison town the focal point of the marines and the assault craft concentrating on the outlying areas. Concealed by thick undergrowth, we impatiently wait for the pandemonium to subside. It sounds greater than a skirmish, and we see no sign of our boats, which makes us anxious.

Benny slithers alongside of me and whispers, "The 296 has gone."

"Don't fuss. She's standing off and will be back to pick us up," I tell him.

Seizing my arm, he says, "I mean really gone. She's been torpedoed and sinking. Les has just received a message from the skipper."

"That's put the cat amongst the pigeons. The Japs were expecting us, or we've been betrayed."

Everyone looks crushed by my words, apart from Benny, who declares, "We'll make a run for it again, lads. It's a piece of cake."

Lightning rarely strikes twice, yet most of the crew nod enthusiastically.

"Last time there were no ships searching for you with radar, which will easily make contact and blow us to Old Glory," I remind them.

Their optimism receives another blow when Les adds, "Eddie's right.

I've shut down transmission to avoid any messages being picked up, and without power or engines, we're safe for the moment. For what it's worth, there's a bloody battle being raged and more Japanese soldiers than first supposed. My last order was to look out for my buddies, Swain."

Levine's grinning from ear to ear. "I couldn't have put it better myself. We'll split into watches, keep our eyes skinned and gobs buttoned. Any questions?"

There's no debate; we're of one accord. The hatches are battened down, deadlights firmly shuttered, and the sounds of conflict strangely muted.

We prize open a pack of Pacific rations and feast on cold peaches, baked beans, and sardines. The mess deck table's strewn with bottles and glasses of rum, which magically emerge although it's strictly forbidden on a mission. But any port in a storm. We're living on borrowed time. Grub will last two days, and our weapons consist of one revolver with twelve bullets and ten stilettos. I hope Levine's a good shot. Bows and arrows would have been better. Nudging Les in the ribs, I suggest we spell Benny and Jock Grier up top. Only the odd shot disturbs the night air, and with no sign of our comrades, we're on our own. Concealed in the shadows, we study the shoreline. Inscrutable as the Japanese are, I hope they'll soon tire of this game of cat and mouse. Staring into a well of darkness becomes hypnotic.

"There's one of our boats coming down the estuary," Les says.

I slide round the wheelhouse to join him, and it's certainly a converted MTB. Yet something's screwy. She's not flying battle pennants. We've been bamboozled.

I say, "It's manned by Japs." But Les is already waving. I grab his arm. It's too late. A dazzling searchlight snaps on, piercing the gloom and undergrowth, while the vessel comes barrelling forward. I leap for cover and hear and feel a terrific bang behind me. It feels like somebody's pouring molten metal down my leg.

Chapter Seventy-Nine

It's one hell of a hangover, but I've never passed out before. Needle-sharp memories stab my brain. I go between organised chaos and descending blackness until I awake early in the morning. My right leg's sore. Everything else is hazy, despite having lain puzzling in this cot for the past hour. I'm terrified to open my eyes. Something is out of whack.

"Will he wake up, Daddy? He's been asleep a long time." I hear a young, clear voice say.

"I did pump a hefty dose of morphine into him," a man answers. "He was in a lot of pain."

Surprised I'm among friends, I open one eye.

"It's blue." The girl giggles. "I've never seen one before."

Remembering my manners, I display the other one too.

"Please forgive my inquisitive daughter, Mariana," the tanned, sandy-haired gentleman says. "Apart from me, she's seen few Europeans."

Mariana is dark-eyed and brown-skinned. She is gorgeous. People of mixed ethnicities are reputed to be the most beautiful people in the world. My face must mirror the thought.

"Her mother's Burmese, but I'm from Holland originally. I was a surgeon in Rangoon for many years. When the Japanese invaded, I brought my family down here out of harm's way."

"It's my good fortune you were in the neighbourhood when needed, sir."

"A pleasure, young man. My name's Pieter Vanheyden. I'm in the business of saving people, not killing them."

"Touché," I murmur. I'm delighted to know I'll survive. "How's my friend?"

Looking grave, the surgeon says, "He wasn't as fortunate. The grenade shattered his left calf, which I amputated almost to the knee. Hopefully, we've prevented gangrene from spreading."

Stupidly, I say, "Les will be heartbroken. He's a brilliant football player."

Mariana cuts in. "No, he won't. He's happy, makes me laugh, and talks about you, Eddie, all the time."

I tell Pieter of my longstanding relationship with Les. Pieter and his charming daughter arrange for my cot to be placed next to my mate's cot. Les and I have a pretty nurse changing our dressings twice a day, we have each other's company and no guards to watch over us. Pieter's greatly respected by everybody, Japanese and villagers alike. No one is allowed to interfere with the hospital or his staff. There are only a few patients in recovery, who are transferred to the prison block once they're able to walk. Rumours say the Royal Marines who attacked Tavoy were all killed. The Japanese there have moved north to fight our Fourteenth Army, and the road to town is impassable.

Les and I laze on our cots, act idiotic, laugh too loud, and behave as though these are our last moments on Earth. Who knows?

A visit from Pieter and a Japanese colonel has us speculating. The Japanese man points his cane at Les. "He go."

Vanheyden shakes his head. "No can do. Show the man, Les."

Grinning, Les pulls up his robe, displaying one and a half legs.

Turning sharply, the colonel studies me keenly. *"Ni ashi."*

Baffled, I look at Pieter.

"He's asking if you have two legs."

Les laughs. "Talk yourself out of this one, Eddie."

Satisfied I've both legs, the Japanese colonel leaves smiling. Pieter not so much, which sets my cogs whirring. Thoughts of leaving Les are grim. I need to know the score. Maybe a teenage girl's curiosity will provide the answer.

SEEING THE ANGUISH IN MARIANA'S eyes while delivering the bad news makes me wish I'd cut my tongue out. Our captors have been ordered to leave and move to Thailand. All able-bodied prisoners will be taken under guard to a POW camp. The remainder left at the village will have to fend for themselves. Viewed from any angle, the future's not rosy. We can die here, expire on the journey, or pop our clogs in some camp. Les wants to come with me and is raving at Pieter to make him a prosthesis, but he's told it's not yet possible. I've also upset him by telling him I'm staying here with him.

"You have to go. Jack's been waiting long enough. Who wants to see your ugly mug anyway, with Mariana to keep me company?"

Puzzled by the Japanese's attitude, I quiz Pieter.

"Don't be fooled. They're cunning. They think they'll be treated kindly for not having killed their prisoners. Pray that happens sooner than later. You'll be lucky if you finish the trip."

I'm not offended. He owes no loyalty to Britain or Japan and believes that one who lives by the sword shall die by the sword.

In spite of our angst, the Mexican standoff is halted between Les and I when Pieter discovers gangrene has spread to my pal's knee, which means more surgery. Reluctantly, and recalling my promise to the Barretts, I decide to leave. Walking away, I feel guilty and ashamed, though Les is still laughing and acting the clown. Whatever transpires, he'll always be in my prayers. I've benefitted from two weeks spent in hospital and the constant care by the Vanheyden family, unlike most of the bunch assembled for the journey. We've little baggage to carry but a long way to go.

Rules are simple, cruel, and non-negotiable, as we quickly discover. Everyone walks. Japanese soldiers, prisoners, and native guides march from dusk till dawn and rest up in the heat of the day. Failure to keep pace means being left behind, which happens frequently after the first week. One minute someone is walking beside you, the next moment gone! Burma plays no favourites. I'm sad and missing Les. I revert to my initial routine aboard the *Daisy* and distance myself from the pack.

Rations are running low, tempers high. Some of the prisoners are threatening mutiny and see me as their saviour. Tough! I'm a simple soul, not a raving lunatic. Two dawns later, a guard's found strangled and six prisoners are adrift. Boxes of food have vanished too. Takasartu, the Japanese sergeant, goes berserk. He sends out a patrol to hunt down the renegades then selects three of us for punishment.

Retaliation isn't my wisest choice and completely out of character, but I've seen better men than I lose control. I'm surrounded by five thugs eager to teach me a lesson, which offers me no option of flight. My white-hot anger surges and won't listen to reason. But the Japanese are always polite; a soldier steps forward and bows. My lightning-fast back elbow smashes his nose like it's an over-ripe tomato. I give a sharp kick to a second one's groin. He's screaming too, but suddenly the party's over. A savage blow to my injured leg puts me down. Courteous as ever, they wait for me to stand up then flatten me again. Each time I stubbornly regain my balance; they take me apart with fists and feet. I'm battered, bruised, and almost broken, but I'm not defeated. I'm hurting bad but still breathing.

Maybe I'm dreaming, delirious, or daft, but I swear someone says, "You didn't come all this way to die on a mountain."

The Japanese sergeant's voice stirs me, though the sword he's waving more so. Tired of his goons failing to pound me into submission, he's going to enact the Bushido code. Raising the sword, he brings it down swiftly. Wearing a hideous grin, he touches the blade gently to my throbbing leg.

"You walk now, Inglis?"

Eagerly, I nod, as Takasartu frowns and studies my wound. His shout brings a soldier scurrying up with a first aid kit. Within minutes, I'm sporting a new dressing, and I'm good to go.

The posse returns with most of the food but no escapees. Killing a Japanese soldier is punishable by death, but my companions seem interested only in the extra rations. I'm crushed by the lack of compassion Among such friends, who needs enemies? It was a wise decision to go it alone, though faith has rarely left my side.

We've finally bridged the mountain at the expense of many more deaths, both prisoners and soldiers falling victim to myriad tropical diseases. Clear of jagged rocks and rough terrain, we're into the heavy heat of the jungle again. It's rumoured that once we're through this steaming cauldron, there's a real road. The prisoners are elated, expecting food and rest. I'm doubtful.

We've finally reached Thailand.

Chapter Eighty

It takes another two nights to reach Wampo, which is fewer than ten miles at a snail's pace. At the compound's gates, we're ordered to strip naked, including boots and socks, then dump our filthy rags into a cauldron of boiling water. Next, the remains of Party 135 (all eight of us) are herded into a hut and hot showers. It's my wildest dream and timely too. I'm almost blubbering at the painful state of my comrades. They're zombies, walking dead men. I couldn't prevent their heartaches, but a kind word might have helped.

Outside again, we're met by a gaggle of Japanese and British officers, plus Korean guards. It smacks of Madras and market day at the Medina: while we're being issued clean shirts and shorts and recovering our belongings, the officers are wrangling over our future. The British medical officer's insisting we're too sick to work, and the Nippon major's screaming for bodies to repair the trestle bridge across the viaduct. USAF Liberators bombed it yesterday afternoon.

Strutting past me, the cretin says, "Ah so, he look strong, can do."

Compared to my fellow prisoners, maybe I can. Someone had mentioned I'd not come all this way for nothing. I'll not find Jack standing here scratching my ass.

The MO and Japanese major have reached a truce; the sickest four are shipped to hospital. The rest of us are assigned to labouring, which is fine with me. It affords me the chance to quiz other captives. My mellow mood soon vanishes. I walk among scarecrows, many with just one good leg and a wooden stale for support. And the ritual bowing makes my blood boil. The British sergeant escorting us through the camp has already cautioned me for blowing raspberries at the Japanese.

It's stupid being angry. I have enough demons to tackle, without creating more, but our new billet isn't fit for pigs. No self-respecting hog would put a trotter over the threshold. All huts are a hundred yards long by ten wide with no side walls; the walkways are wooden duckboards. Raised sleeping platforms run full-length on each side, and prisoners sleep on bamboo slats with only two feet of space between them. Apart from a few cadaverous bodies, the place is empty; the fitter ones are at work camps. The sweet-sour smell of death is ever-present.

Averting my eyes in fear of losing my breakfast, I scuttle to the end of the hut, where British Army officers are gathered. Sitting on a rickety orange-box stool, sipping Earl Grey tea from a tin mug has a calming effect on my addled brain. We're being welcomed aboard in true English fashion and discover a brand-new meaning to afternoon delight. Largesse isn't the sole reason for such hospitality. Having been cosseted, we're about to be cross-examined.

"We require proof of identity and your mission," Colonel Pritchard says.

I'm out of the traps fast, shaking my head. "It's private and confidential."

He's miffed. "Dog tags will be fine."

My eloquent shrug doesn't soothe him. "You could be shot for disobeying a direct order."

"You'll have to stand in line, sir. We're sworn not to tell anybody."

Frantically, my fellow travellers are nodding their heads.

"You sailors love playing pirates," the colonel sighs.

It's time to be nice. "True, sir, and you have our deepest sympathy for your plight. Yet, it's not funny marching through the mountains for a month and arriving with only eight survivors from thirty-two starters. Though no documentary evidence, we can provide names, ranks, and service numbers, plus the last vessel served aboard. Everything else is classified."

Placated, and all his ducks in a row, Pritchard replies, "That's jolly decent of you, old chap. Better grab some shut-eye; your hosts will be shuttling you off to work early tomorrow. Still, look on the bright side. You'll get a midday meal."

"One bit of advice," the medical officer cuts in. "Eat whatever they offer you. Don't refuse anything. Along with cruelty and disease, life's a delicate balance."

Nodding, the CO says, "We're improving here, but many camps are rampant with cholera and dysentery."

He's proud of his achievements but putting me in the picture doesn't improve my morale one scrap. After jumping through so many hoops, I'm anxious to land on my feet and find Jack. Everyone thought me mad when I'd boasted of bringing my friend home. I know it's God's will; directly I stumble, He steadies me. There's always someone at my elbow when I'm faltering. My faith took a nosedive when I lost Les. Fortuitously, he found me in the Burmese mountains. It's strange that I taught this boy his sums and now have to count on him. Yet how can I fail with such unselfish loyalty? Bone-tired, with my ditty bag as a pillow, I collapse on the slats.

Following the past month's misery, roughing it is no problem. But sleep is hard to find, with the moaning, groaning, and gut-wrenching screams around me. I barely remember closing my eyes but must have dozed for a spell.

All that makes sense is to escape this abject horror before I go stark raving mad. On wobbly legs, I crash into a Korean guard in the hut doorway. The first rays of dawn illuminate his unlovely face.

Chapter Eighty-One

They're a ragtag gang, not in pristine condition, yet grateful to be on their feet. It's a ten-minute walk to the viaduct, and according to Dan and Stan, my new mates I've befriended, Tucker will be waiting for us. During last night's wee hours, while my dorm-mates were busy castigating our captors, I'd been cogitating. Help's needed by anybody who knows the ropes. These two cobbers from down under seem good prospects, and it's time to off-load my fellow hikers.

Aussies are friendlier than Brits, who think they're superior to foreigners. Moreover, they remind me of Maurice and Jimmy, with whom I'd enlisted.

Dan, the tall, thoughtful one, has broken the ice. "When did you ride in, sport?"

"I didn't. It was Shanks's pony all the way from the Bay of Bengal."

"Blimey! Your dogs must be ruddy barking, mate," the wiry one responds.

"One gets accustomed after a while. It's similar to hitting oneself on the head with a mallet. It's a wonderful feeling once one stops."

"We've found a right nutter, Dan. And he's a bloody Brit, too with a gold-plated gob."

"Fair dinkum, Stan, he's right up our alley if he's bonkers. Give us a couple of weeks, we'll soon have him talking our lingo like a true blue."

Honestly, if a little rain's destined to fall into my life, a sprinkling of stupidity is welcome too. This relationship could prove enlightening, and it's good for my morale.

Everything I've ever heard or read back home pales in comparison to seeing it up close and personal. Details of the march and the cruelty I witnessed defy repetition, but last night's horror-house sickened me beyond what I thought possible of man's bestiality towards other human beings. Even thinking about it is revolting.

Sitting, shovelling this gluttonous rice stew down my throat, my heart goes out to the two hundred souls here who are enjoying a slap-up breakfast. Hollow-cheeked, skin-and-bone ragamuffins with sunken eyes brightly glowing while salivating over their food. Three years of working on the Railroad of Death and its aftermath hasn't crushed their spirits yet.

Once the meal's over, the Japanese will be hustling, and they start saying *Speedo* again.

"It's a quid pro quo situation. We mend bridge, we eat food, also good, everybody happy."

"I never knew you could speak Japanese, Dan," I say.

"And if we're lucky, the Pommies will blow the bugger up again," Stan replies.

"Stay with us, sport, we'll look after you," Dan says. "Keep your trap shut and remember to bow to the Japs. They love a bit of flannel. Also, watch their cook. If he sees you've some flesh, he'll drop you in the pot."

I'm already wondering who's the daftest one of all, but I've no complaints. Picking these screwballs was a wise choice. I've already learned they've been here since day one; they know the right people and the villains. If I keep my ears open, I might hear something useful, though questioning them would be unthinkable.

"How long will it take to repair the bridge, Dan?"

Swivelling his head around for possible eavesdroppers, he says, "The grapevine reckons a month. We can expect another visit by the boys in blue by then."

Noting my astonishment, he says, "Don't ask. There are stranger things twixt Heaven and Earth, Horatio."

"For example, the progeny of a convict quoting William Shakespeare."

"Who's he, when he's about?" Stan demands. "Air Marshall of the RAF?"

"Not hardly, dear chap," I reply indignantly. "He's a neighbour of mine from jolly old England."

"Blimey, Dan, we're hobnobbing with bleeding royalty," Stan says.

"Another bloody fine yarn to tell your sheep back in Queensland," Dan says.

Laughter all the way it's not despite the agreement between guards and captives. Time is of the essence and half the labour force aren't fit for twelve hours of hard graft; by mid-afternoon many are collapsing in the broiling heat. They're whipped back onto their feet. Several fall, but never rise again; they're loaded onto carts, trundled back to camp, and committed to the funeral pyre, which is always well stoked. I'd heard of atrocities while the railway was being constructed, but ignorance is bliss, and I'd thought conditions had improved since its completion.

Combating the conditions and enemy, with tongue-in-cheek lunacy, is the diggers' survival mode. I couldn't ask for better companions. Saving the world is out of reach, but it's possible to save Jack, and my sanity by hanging in here. Dan swears we'll be home for Christmas. Drained but dogged, the remaining prisoners are slaving from dawn till dusk completing the final touches to the bridge. The past three weeks have seen men dropping like flies. The Aussies have been missing the last two days, and I've heard they're both unwell. I'm not feeling too chipper myself. It's been one god-awful day. Trudging back to camp, wet with sweat, I decide to drop in the sickbay to see my mates.

Captain Lowery, the MO, eyes me shrewdly. "You look flushed, Roberts."

"I've been working, sir. It doesn't agree with me."

He keeps staring. "I don't like the look of you."

"I'm not too fond of you either, sir."

He allows a tiny smile. "Seriously man, let me give you a check-up."

Nodding, I sit down. It seems a good idea, and he means well.

"I only came in to enquire about my pals."

"Shush! Be quiet and sit still like a good boy."

Any moment now, he'll hold up a teddy bear and tell me to watch the birdie. I hope he doesn't, I've not combed my hair.

Top to toe, it's a good overhaul. He doesn't miss an eyebrow or a hangnail. Ears, nose, and throat all come under close scrutiny. Apart from a high temperature and a slight case of the runs, I'm in fine fettle. Not quite. I've the onset of malaria and diarrhoea or possibly dysentery.

"The quicker we pull you out of line, the better."

"Great, I'll get to see my buddies."

"You're too late. The Japs shipped them up-country to the Burma-Thailand border to build a road. Don't worry, they're tough nuts and will be back. There are glad tidings for you though. We're sending you to Kanchanaburi, where they're better equipped. You've had a rough spell and need a break."

"Well thanks, Doc! I never knew you cared."

"I don't," he answers. "It's your daft, optimistic smile that intrigues me."

Chapter Eighty-Two

Captain Lowery's been pulling a few strings I reckon. I board the truck with a dozen more walking wounded, bound for Kanchanaburi. Some of these poor wretches will be fortunate to survive the trip, and I've received one smack around the head already for helping one sad soul over the tailboard. Even keeping one's lips sealed doesn't always work.

Yet, for a few weeks I'm free to concentrate on recovery and behave myself.

"That will be the day," I hear Mother say.

Strangely, it's not the first occasion I've heard voices, particularly at stressful moments. Trust me, I'm not alone. Many demented compatriots talk back.

The road trip's short and sweat-laden. My clean shirt's already a dishrag. We're off-loaded and pushed and jostled into line by our sour-faced sullen guards, ready for inspection. Under a blazing sun, the task takes over one hour. Some things never alter. This place looks in better shape than the last one, but the Japanese have the same mindset: we're cowards and deserve to be treated cruelly.

Allied surgeons and practitioners are performing miracles daily, but once men are fit, they're shipped back to work camps for the Japanese's own selfish needs.

"Jock" MacClachan, the base's head medic is spitting blood over the delay, but just receives a polite bow from Sergeant Naguchi as compensation. Three doctors, ably assisted by a dozen orderlies with authority, efficiently and speedily poke, probe, strip, shower, and settle us into cosy cots under clean, freshly laundered sheets. I'd kiss each if I possessed the strength. Sadly, I'm slithering down a long, endless slope.

A cool breeze fans my cheeks. I'm in bed, and the sun's gone down. I must have nodded off. Yet I've the sense of returning from a distant journey. I haven't slept on a real mattress for ages. How did I get here?

The sporran-based voice answers my silent request. "Glad you're back. We were bothered for a wee while, thought you'd popped yon clogs."

Beaming beatifically, sitting at my bed, is MacClachan.

"Sorry, sir, needed a siesta. Feel good to go again now."

"Whist sonny, you're going nowhere until we've put some meat back on yon bones. Ye look like something the cat's dragged in. Still, everybody's happy you're o'er the worst. They've had no rest with the din you've made the past four days. Sorry we had to tie you down, but you wanted to fight the Japanese Imperial Army by yourself."

"No wonder I'm hungry. Please extend my sincere apologies to everybody who witnessed my bad display of manners, sir."

"No problem, lad. They enjoyed the show and said it was unusual to hear blasphemy spoken in such perfect English."

"Mother would be very disappointed."

"Aye, and awful proud of the stubborn wee bairn she's raised," the doc adds.

Getting back on my feet takes a few days, which the medical staff use to their advantage. Sergeant Naguchi monitors the progress of patients and visits the sickbay daily. Without fail, there's always a heated discussion regarding the patients' health. The Japanese are keen to see the sick discharged to huts, and thence to work camps, while doctors adopt the opposite stance. Naguchi's a middle-aged, bespectacled figure, featuring a librarian rather than a soldier. And he's pliable. Recovering mobility is painstakingly slow, but as the monkey said when losing his tail, "All good things come to an end."

I'm shipped to a normal hut, where if you're warm you're fit enough to work. *There has to be a hundred bodies packed in here,* I think. A few steps away, dedicated men are struggling to save lives. Meanwhile, these Japanese jackals are blatantly disposing of sick young soldiers. Finding space to lay my head could be difficult, though many of the men look like merely wasted remains and probably incapable of making it through the night. A sharp nudge grabs my attention. There's a diminutive elderly man staring at me with shrewd, rheumy eyes. He's clad in khaki drill and white clerical collar.

"I've been expecting you for ages. What kept you?"

He's a face one couldn't forget in a hurry. "You have me at a disadvantage, sir," I say politely.

"I couldn't forget your face, seen it a thousand times. Jack said you'd come."

Grabbing his thin shoulders, I shake him hard. "Jack's here! Show me!" I shout.

"Course he's here, been driving me mad for nearly three years waiting for you. We've prayed every night for a miracle. God does provide."

"Take me to him, Father. This is the best moment of my life!" I holler.

Picking my way through the carcasses is scary. I'm afraid I'll tread on one, and they'll crumble into bits. But I'm aware that Jack won't be the strapping man I knew. Once you've seen a few of these emaciated men, they all look the same. God's advocate steers me to the left, where a skeletal figure's waving wildly. There's delight in my eyes, but my heart's heavy. I gently hold this precious man in my arms at last. Only through his mammoth smile can I recognise him.

There's no time for sorrow. Within minutes we're recalling halcyon days.

After his initial rush of excitement, Jack settles down. I bring him up to speed on home, family, and friends, with special attention given to the closeness shared between Jack, Charlie and myself throughout the years. Talking long past lights out, we finally fall asleep, side by side, our arms wrapped tightly around each other. There's nothing stronger than brotherly love. News of a reunion has sparked interest. Space is found for me next to Jack. Besides their reserve, the British are chivalrous when it counts. Father Maxwell returns bearing gifts of extra victuals. It's scarcely enough to feed five thousand, yet sufficient unto the day.

Talking about tomorrow is taboo here. By order of the Japanese Imperial Government, all clocks in POW camps are set to Tokyo time. Living in the moment is all that counts. Whatever fate awaits us is beyond our control. I've travelled this way before, and though totally different, it's exactly the same. I'm a harbinger of death, waiting for a wonderful person to die as I had watched my cherished brother Charlie, short years ago.

How much faith does one small boy possess to keep smiling and be cheerful while his dearest friends are taken to glory?

Chapter Eighty-Three

The bodysnatchers arrive at dusk. I've been expecting them. News travels fast, particularly bad news; the Judas, keen to earn a smoke for his co-operation. I've tenderly nursed Jack in my arms since the 0200 hours headcount, denying he'll desert me. But he's gone, drawn his last breath one hour ago. I gently rock him and babble away like a demented chimp. Now they are here to steal him away.

Naguchi is trailed by two gaunt-featured Korean guards toting a blood-stained stretcher and Lee-Enfield rifles. Silence descends. Each hollow eye's riveted on the group's progress along the sodden boardwalk. The sentries halt by my cot, drop the litter, port arms, and stand rigid but wary. Skipping onto the platform, Naguchi points his cane. I tighten my hold on Jack and scrabble back against the wall.

Frowning, Naguchi studies me for a moment then says, "Is too late. We take him now."

Shaking my head, I kick, swear, and spit at the guards, but it's no contest. They drag Jack away with little effort. I'm still fragile from malaria and dysentery. Stubborn is my strong suit, which I now trump with stupidity. Seeing these pigs pulling Jack by the ankles across these rough bamboo slats maddens me. Can't they show any humanity, even in death? Struggling to my feet, I lunge at the closest guard, intent on taking him down. My frantic fingers never reach his skinny throat. Naguchi's cane smacks my head, and I collapse in a heap. I'm more bemused than hurt. I have taken much worse punishment.

But fools never learn. I push myself upright on wobbly legs. I say, "You'll have to do better than that, Sarge."

Patiently, Naguchi waits for me to regain my balance then goes into action. He's fast. I duck too late. The razor-sharp bamboo slices a paper-thin cut in my forehead. Blood gushes from the gash and down my face. A grey mist's forming; my brain's screaming for peace and quiet. Voices hot with anger jerk it back to reality. Lifting my head, I see the guard's hateful eyes staring into mine and his bayoneted rifle three inches from my bloodied face. He's prepared to kill me in a heartbeat; probably thinks it's his due. Their screaming match does nothing to soothe me. Attacking a guard's punishable by death, and this cretin is seeking vengeance.

For some reason, Naguchi's trying to save my skin. I harbour serious doubts. My would-be assassin's a foot taller than him. Slowly, my brain kicks into gear.

The Japanese's dilemma is clear. My death will create problems. There'll be reports to write, possibly an inquiry but far worse, he'll lose face—great minds, etcetera. He steps between the guard and me, jabbing his cane sharply into the guard's throat. Gasping for air, the mercenary staggers back yet recovers quickly from Naguchi's torrent of abuse and springs to attention. It appears honour hasn't been satisfied, and I watch horrified as the sergeant draws his Luger and points it at the dirtbag's head. The audience is rapt. Only the odd cough and laboured breathing disturbs the cathedral quietness.

The click of the safety catch is like a cannon. Every heart skips a beat. Closing his eyes, the guard screeches with fear. Giggling, Naguchi levels the gun at the quivering man's heart. He'll have no qualms killing this moron. The Japanese hate Koreans with a passion. Having established his superiority, our samurai warrior briefly savours his triumph before sliding the weapon back into its holster. Everyone relaxes, except me.

Pride intact once more, he's the professional soldier. Prodding me in the ribs, he demands I sit against the wall. I obey tout de suite. I'd jump through hoops for my captor.

The guards dump Jack's remains onto the stretcher and fold his wasted arms across his skeletal chest, hands together in prayer. I'm shocked that they have feelings. Dream on! They leer and place their rifles at each side of his frail body. There's ample room. Naguchi's harsh voice stops their cackling. Lifting the body easily, they move off but are halted by Naguchi's shout. Hopping off the platform, he tugs Jack's bush-boots from his matchstick legs. Retracing his steps, the sergeant stares at my raw feet and tattered shoes.

Dropping the boots, he says, "You stupid fool, but good friend," and points at the stretcher. "He not need now. You wear, make him happy."

Bowing, I attempt a smile. It hurts like hell, but this man holds my life in his sweaty palms.

His glance is bestial. He pushes the cane hard against my chin and says, "I not forget you, I come back after."

Tucking his favourite toy under his arm, he struts off. The guards follow at a slower pace on the slippery boards. I watch closely. Prayers for a broken leg go unheard. God's not listening—again!

Jack's left, though that bundle of bones is scarcely him. He's been gone since 10 December 1941, when the *Prince of Wales* was torpedoed. It's bloody heartbreaking. He's survived three and a half years and dies when I eventually find him.

Kicking off my ratty shoes, I pull on Jack's boots, wiggle my toes, and revel in the lambs-wool caress. "I'll walk many a mile in these," I crow.

"You'll be lucky to walk at all once that guard cuts you down to size."

It's easy recognising Corporal Watkins. He's the manners of a ferret with face to match, and he's accompanied by more vultures. They never take long to gather.

"Much too big for you anyhow," another smart-mouth suggests.

"All the better for kicking your fat ass, Granny," I reply.

These losers don't scare me. Most have one foot in the grave already. Anyhow, I'll soon be back in Wampo. This cesspit's for the sick and dying. Work, and there're two bowls of rice a day, not one. Trust me, brother, survival's the name of the game.

Backing off a tad, the parasites continue their taunts. "We won't have to wait long, Corp," someone sneers.

Watkins agrees. "If Naguchi doesn't kill him, that guard will mark his card."

I think it's strange, when push turns to shove, how friends become enemies. I raise a hand checking for damage to my head. White-hot flame sears my throbbing head, and I find massive swelling over my left eye. However, on a brighter note, the bleeding's ceased though my face is caked in dried blood.

Needled by my lack of response, the buzzards are discussing the sharing of our kit. They already consider me dead!

Scrambling to my feet creates panic among the predators, who scurry for the shadows like cockroaches caught in bright light. I hurl my discarded shoes at them. One ricochets off Watkins's shaggy head and into the rafters. "Banzai! That will make you keep your heads down. As for these boots, I'll burn them first." I'm breathless but beaming. "Should hold you SOBs for some time," I cackle.

Some folk think me nice. Many believe I'm nuts. I'll settle for the middle. Feeling totally exhausted, I sink down on heavy haunches while battling the floodgates of fast-rising emotions. These birds of prey will pick my bones clean at any sign of weakness. Placing Jack's kit bag behind my head and the drawstring around my wrist, I huddle into a foetal position. The trick is to switch off. Forget the derelicts, ignore their screams of pain and endless gibbering, grit my teeth, and watch the shadows lengthen while willing myself to wake up to a brand-new day. Now there's a greater incentive to survive. Who else is going to tell the Barrett family about their son's demise in this godforsaken hole?

I AWAKE ALERT. The boots adorn my feet, the bag is still safely anchored to my wrist. Stretching arms and legs and waggling my head, I try a few press-ups. No bones are broken, just slightly bent.

They're here before daybreak—Naguchi and the same pair of gargoyles. Their haggard faces and creased uniforms are in sharp contrast to the sergeant's, whose bush shirt and pants look freshly pressed. He sports an oilskin cape around his shoulders, slick with rain, the only blemish being mud on his polished jackboots. Wasting no time, he crooks a finger at me. "Come! We go now."

Ready, though not willing, I jam on my bush hat, grab my kit and Jack's, then stare at Naguchi. He ponders briefly before nodding and shrugging his shoulders.

There are some disappointed scavengers, and Naguchi is smirking; perhaps humour is universal. Shouts of *Good luck!* echo in my ears as we squelch down the boardwalk into a weeping, pearl-grey dawn. Even close to death some of those poor bastards were rooting for me.

A prod from the guard's rifle reminds me there's a date with destiny ahead. Crossing the parade ground, the thick mud sucks at my boots. I scrunch my toes. Nothing is parting me from these heirlooms. Better served than most camps, this one has a cemetery for all denominations situated at the edge of the jungle. I can smell the damp, dense foliage. It's ambrosia after the death stench of the huts.

I pant up the slope behind Naguchi, who stops short of the brow. "Go! Now, say goodbye to friend. We wait here."

Off-loading the gear slowly, I sense something's wrong. Next to Jack's plot is a freshly dug pit, and it's obvious why Naguchi had said, *"After."*

They're cunning. "Prisoner escape into jungle, so sorry had to shoot him." Very convenient. I'll be dead and buried, no questions asked.

Digging the cane into my spine, he says, "Hurripoo, I tell you."

Taking a few steps, I glance back; both guards are already unslinging their rifles.

I've no fear, just a serene calm. After all, they can only kill me. "Up yours," I shout, presenting a two-fingered salute and turn my back. "Coming Jack. We've got the last laugh. Those poor sods have to walk back in the pouring rain."

Does one hear the rifle's crack or feel the bullet first? Why worry? I'll be dead. Reaching the mound of rich brown soil, I fall onto trembling knees. Cold sweat mixed with warm rain trickles down my bare back. My hands are shaking; my heart's pounding. So this is real courage? Perhaps God is making house calls after all.

Smoothing out a plateau in the pungent earth, I write *Rest in Peace* in tiny, round pebbles, jabbering nonstop, only ceasing at the sergeant's command. Taking a moment for a final word and inspection of the colourful display, I slope back to my captors and bow formally, thanking him for his kindness.

"We not heathens," he snaps.

The thought never crossed my mind.

He studies me briefly, turns, and mutters to the guards. All three stare then burst into laughter. I'm sure it's not good news. Maybe a bullet's too simple? I've offended them and have to suffer. Well, I've dignity too; let them do their worst.

My fears are compounded by Naguchi saying, "I say again, British have many strange customs. They will die for friend. Japanese warrior only die for their God."

He raises the cane, and I immediately shut my eyes, expecting a blow. I wait. Nothing happens. Risking a peek, I see his smiling face and his cane still held aloft. Flicking back the bush hat, he points at my sun-bleached hair and puzzled blue eyes. "Is untrue, not all same-same. You different. Naguchi never forget."

The mercenaries are giggling, whereas I'm serious and suspicious too.

Enough already! Let's get this show on the road. By the expression on his face, he's reached the same conclusion.

There's a touch of sadness in his voice. "I think we not meet again. You go now with soldiers."

I'll be lucky to survive a beating; they're experts at inflicting torture.

"Don't tell me it will hurt you more," I say, staring into his pensive eyes.

Naguchi's nonplussed. He presents a charming smile. "Inglis no understand. You go to hut, sleep good, then work camp."

He hesitates, then moves closer and executes a deep, courteous bow. "You fine, honourable man. *Sayonara.*"

Matching his politeness, with equal dignity, I echo, "*Sayonara.*"

Dumbly, I watch him strut out of sight and hopefully out of my life for good. The sun's rays and white hair might have given the samurai warrior cause to wonder. Or possibly the Son intervened.

Chapter Eighty-Four

Didn't expect you back so soon," Captain Lowery says as I enter the room.

"Sergeant Naguchi's idea. He thought I was having too much fun."

"I'm sorry to hear about your friend."

"Only the good die young."

"Glad to see you've not lost your sense of humour."

"I'd rather die with my boots on at a work camp than in a charnel house."

"God willing, it won't be for long. According to our radio, the war in Europe's nearly finished and the Fourteenth Army has recaptured Rangoon."

Blessing his optimism, I visit the hut and search for friendly faces. I discover it's half empty. I expect there're many more suffering or likely dead. Despite some believing that it's all over, bar the shouting, I've grave doubts the Japanese and mercenaries will discard their cruel mentality for human decency. There have been rumours circulating of plans to massacre all prisoners in the event of surrender, which sounds more their style.

Grieving apart, returning to Wampo is crucial. I can go to the work camp, get paid, eat better, and even meet Dan and Stan again if I'm lucky.

Lowery thinks me mad yet laughs when I ask about the Aussies. "They're probably the most villainous highwaymen in Southeast Asia," he says.

Watching the Liberator bombers heading for the bridges over the river and the marshalling yards at Kanchanaburi stiffens my resolve to flee up-country to the safety of the jungle rather than be blown away by friendly fire. A few months won't kill me—hush my big mouth.

"Count your blessings, son. You'll be getting a lift most of the way," Lowery says. "It's altered since my day. We had to march over two hundred miles from Ban Pong to Sonkurai, and those Japanese bastards told us we were going on holiday. True, thousands made it right to the Pearly Gates."

The sorrow in his eyes stops me pursuing the matter further. I've no words to offer. Silence is golden.

Mother's always insisted, "It shows that you really care."

IT'S WONDERFUL CLIMBING INTO A truck outside the barbed wire. There's a fleet of them waiting to whisk us away from the walking dead.

Our journey will take most of the day, and we're excited as kids despite the early morning rain. But be cautious with your wishes. Saddle-sore and weary after three hours of nonstop driving, we've another ten miles of jungle to negotiate on foot, and glory be, or harsher words, it's still persisting down. Chivvied and bullied by brutal Korean guards along elephant tracks oozing with ankle-deep mud, we arrive bedraggled and chastened, the charred remains of No. 2 Camp failing to raise our hopes. There are only four habitable huts, and these are overcrowded. A cholera epidemic's decimated both captive and native workers ranks, medical staff are overwhelmed, and within a few weeks more than three-quarters of the local workers have died, plus four hundred prisoners from the six hundred drafted two months ago.

Our captors issue us with tents and order them pitched next to the natives' quarantined camp. Erecting tents in a monsoon is not recommended, and fires are forbidden. By the time we've stopped the raindrops falling on our heads, everything is waterlogged, including blankets.

Nevertheless, I wrap mine around my body. Sleep's out of the question and also prayer, which sets me wondering. How long is it since I last prayed, and is anyone listening? I've been fence-sitting since Jack's died, achieving the long-held ambition of rescuing him crushed in the blink of an eye. I've travelled a rocky road and ridden rough seas to reach this brutal country, believing wholeheartedly in His salvation.

I'm no holy roller, yet, my faith once strong is wavering, and this Hell on Earth is the last place to find pastoral care.

Soul searching's put on hold by reveille and another fun-filled day is here. The monsoon's playing havoc with railway embankments and bridges. Following a breakfast of rice stew, the guards count heads. Then we're off on a ten-mile hike to Three Pagodas Pass with the prospect of at least twelve hours of hard graft ahead. Scores of these men worked at building this railroad and remember the Japanese brutality with their 'speedo' tactics. They are scared it might happen again.

However, we've a choice. Stay here and die from cruelty or remain in camp and succumb to disease. I've set my goal, in spite what the poem says, and decide I'm not dying in a far-off foreign field. There's lots of walking left in Jack's boots too. Anxious to finish the repairs, the Japanese have reached the same conclusion as I have. Why not keep work crews on site instead of wasting time marching them to and fro each day? They've lots of tents available too. Pleased by their ingenuity and the prisoners' obvious pleasure, our masters also increase the food allowance. We're now given a midday meal break, but with Bushido logic, the work shift is extended to fourteen hours. The boost to morale's astonishing. Even pessimists are smiling; crazy as it sounds, everyone's happy. Vanquished and victor are coexisting and working for the common good.

The euphoria's brief, thanks to the monsoon's unrelenting onslaught. Labouring and living knee-deep in water, leaking tents, and damp clothes have taken a toll. Within six weeks, three-quarters of the group have been struck down with diphtheria. Japanese losses are severe too, and the dire situation requires a difficult decision: with little food and impassable roads, the only answer is flight. It's a long haul over mountains and through jungle. They say we're going south. That's something I've been doing for years.

Chapter Eighty-Five

There's been little rejoicing by the remaining forty "fit" prisoners at the thought of going walkabout, but we agree it beats staying here and dying of malnutrition, disease or cruelty. Anyhow, with the Fourteenth Army on the way, it may be only a short hike.

We set off for No. 2 Camp. We carry positive thoughts in our hearts and bawdy songs on our lips, which creates a cameo of proud men, not beasts of burden.

Arriving at Sonkurai has us whistling a different tune. Dreams are swept away by keen monsoon winds. All the camp's personnel, both prisoners and guards, are formed up waiting and anxious to join the exodus. The main problem is many of these men are suffering all sorts of ailments and are scarcely capable of raising a smile, never mind their feet. There are two dozen stretcher cases brave enough to join the march. Breaking camp earlier, we'd boasted on making the journey in a few weeks. Having this bunch of wretches in tow will take us twice as long but being selfish will not buy baby a new dress or get us home. If these invalids are willing to try, we'll be bloody proud to carry them.

Times may be changing, but Japanese tactics aren't. Cruelty's still their game, but we face greater peril: hacking a path through humid, rain-sodden jungle. It's back-breaking, soul-destroying work. We're advancing five miles a day and losing as many men. I'm saying hail and farewell to a new face each morning, though I've begged off burying dead sparrows. Infection's the only thing that's thriving, while the marrow's being sucked out of our bones. Trying to live on one meal a day is virtually impossible, with the staple ingredient being rice and anything that will fit inside the pot such as rat, cat, dog, or snake. A chicken by any name tastes as good when you're starving, trust me.

Learning that we're just one day from Wampo brightens our day. Then it's ruined when we're informed that there's no room and it's another forty miles before we'll reach Kanchanaburi. Showing rare generosity, the Japanese lay on extra food and a complete day's rest. We're unimpressed but eat every crumb, rest our weary bones, and prepare to "stiffen up the sinews and summon up the blood" as the Bard of Avon might say. My heart's racing, knees are creaking. *Take it easy, you're almost there,* I tell myself, but my legs aren't listening, and there's a loud buzzing all around me.

"Sailors are like stray cats, do ye see, Father? Feed them once, and they'll keep returning," a fruity voice says.

"You should be asking for an offering as we do in church—that will keep them away."

Opening my eyes, I see MacClachan and Maxwell grinning.

"He sleeps a lot too. Had me troubled for a wee while."

"He's luckier than many of the poor boys," the Padre answers. "At least he made it through the gates."

"What happened?" I ask, still fuzzy-brained.

"You collapsed from sheer exhaustion. Yon ticker was going nineteen to the doze, and you're so thin, we didna need to take an X-ray."

"I'm feeling better just listening to your Scottish twang and Irish brogue."

"There's nae thing wrong with yon funny bone, though you're not out of the woods yet, lad. Ye sorely need rest and recuperation."

"Amen to that," the cleric adds piously. "It'll take more than five loaves."

I lean back against the pillows; knowing I'm in capable hands relaxes me. It's a comfort receiving such attention, for my physical and spiritual well-being. Entitlement's brief. Within two days I'm back among the walking wounded and discovering little has changed. Every hut's overcrowded, food's tightly rationed, and the Japanese's conduct as vicious as ever. They're the masters; we're the slaves.

Each morning the guards come for workers. Should the hut leader protest that a man's unfit, he risks a beating or is put in the "no-good hut" for a spell. Playing the game gets me out of camp, engaged in clearing up the rubble created by Allied bombings, plus I hear progress about the war from the local Thais. I've also struck up a dialogue with a winsome young beauty who promises to bring me freshly baked goodies each time we meet. I'm unsure if frailty or my ash-blond hair's the magnet. It's amazing what I'll do for grub. Fraternising is forbidden, which means I'll have to deal with the foe. Hiding the treats inside my bush shirt's easy, enticing a guard to assist much harder.

Magically, there's a simple answer. Greed's a great motivator. Japanese soldiers are neither highly paid nor well regarded. I've already noticed one hungry-looking shark. The deal is he (Yosuke) ensures me free passage past the camp's sentries, and I'll introduce him to the finest confectioneries in the world.

Shaking his head vigorously, the guard says, "So sorry, no can do." Falling at the first hurdle's a bitter blow, might even be fatal. I turn to leave. "Hey Joe! Don't go," Yosuke calls. "Is no problem, can do Monday, Wen'day, and Friday. My friend on gate also. You tell young lady, all good."

Inscrutable Japanese be buggered. We're all suckers for a pretty face.

Keeping the operation low-key makes sense. The treats are scarcely a feast, but after the diet to which we're accustomed, it's perfect. One can almost taste the compassion and kindness in Rose-Elana's baking.

Escaping the camp at every opportunity's essential. Death constantly hovers there. The lazy ones sneer and call me "Jap lover." But returning at night, I find many already on the highway to Hell. Work is hard, though the hours are not so long, and the guards not as cruel, at least not outside. Misconduct is handled in-house either by beatings or time spent in the no-good hut.

Night-time's the pits. Maxwell keeps me company after supper; without him, I'd be hitting my head against the wall. He brings the drinks: cocoa for me and something more potent for himself. We play chess and talk; we have an understanding. The Padre's never preachy, and I don't mention drunks. God has strange disciples.

Despite rumour and speculation, I'm still here after six weeks in this sewer, hoping and praying for freedom. The Father has arrived and is setting up the chessboard.

"Heard the latest?" he asks. "A couple of Korean guards are claiming that the Yanks are dropping huge bombs on the Japanese people."

"Hardly seems fair picking on women and children," I reply.

Frowning, Maxwell says, "Needs must my boy. If these tactics bring peace, then surely goodness has prevailed."

Unsure of my ground, I remain silent. Goodness is something to which

I've paid scarce attention lately. Survival creates demons from angels; God knows. Even a conscientious choirboy sometimes sings off-key. Enough said.

"Place is quiet tonight," I say, looking around the almost empty room.

"Everyone's uptight and restless, waiting for news. It's been this way for days." He speaks too hastily, as a host of prisoners comes storming through the door, followed by the hut commander. It takes a while to silence the uproar, and then we're informed that Japan's finally thrown in the towel. Everyone goes crazy and charges outside again to join in the mass hysteria.

There's a sudden lull in the racket then a timorous voice begins singing "God Save the King." The soloist could use some help, and I don't need prompting; within moments the whole camp's joined in too. I've never heard the British national anthem sung so loud, for so long and with such fervour. It's a grand night of celebration with familiar songs, laughter and good cheer from every quarter; yet small beer for three and a half years of harsh captivity.

Starting on my quest, I'd never imagined being marooned. Perhaps it's part of becoming a man. But I don't exist. I've no pay-book or dog-tags to prove my identity. There's only the CO at Wampo in whom I'd confided, and he might be long gone. Freedom's knocking on the door, but I'm afraid to answer. Blabbing could get me shot. The war's over but not the military emergency.

Lying here in the dark, I decide panicking will not solve the problem. What would Les have said? There's a ten-second pause. "Sleep on it," he says.

Really! I swear it on my mother's life as the words echo around in my head and I close my eyes.

Chapter Eighty-Six

Waking bright and early, little has changed. Suing for peace is easy; gaining one's freedom is harder.

We remain on the inside looking out, while the Japanese generals are dithering whether to surrender or commit hari-kari. The guards still carry arms, and the death rate through disease and malnutrition is increasing among the prisoners.

Hitting a brighter note, Allied planes are parachuting in food and medical supplies. Also, there're dozens of British Army red caps supervising proceedings though mostly our boys want repatriation not revenge.

Dwelling on the lack of urgency makes me mad, but what really pisses me off is seeing the gaggle of colonel blimps that are coming out of the woodwork. Where the hell were they when we needed them?

Dickie Mountbatten soon gets things moving with the help of rescue teams. Leaflets are dropped in the camp, both in English and Japanese. Ours tell us to stay put, theirs tell them to cease fighting. You need a good man at the wheel to steer a straight course. I'd liked Dickie from day one, with his firm handshake, and I knew he wouldn't let me down. Learning there's a naval attaché here lightens my load considerably. I do hope he's gentle with me.

Commander Allen takes his time relighting his pipe. My tale of woe has him baffled. "You could be charged for losing your pay-book," he begins. "What was your last ship?"

"She was sunk at sea with the loss of all hands," I reply.

"Where were you ashore?"

"Sorry, sir, but I'm not allowed to say."

"What damned idiot gave you that order?"

"Admiral Mountbatten, Supreme Commander, Southeast Asia

Command, sir. I was seconded to Combined Ops and on a special mission. No identification was to be carried, per his orders."

"Why the devil didn't you say so initially?"

"I'm governed by the Official Secrets Act, sir, and though not super smart, I would prefer a week in cells rather than being shot."

"We're not that harsh, Roberts. There's a base in Singapore we can send you for convalescence. Both your brain and body need bringing up to snuff. Meanwhile, I'll get cracking on the paperwork, maybe drop Dickie a line too."

Pleased at clearing the first hurdle, I go searching for the navy personnel the commander has informed me are here. It will be nice to hear mess deck gossip; I've been a wallflower too long. The next two weeks fly by while waiting for passage south with my new pals. It could take a few months to recover full fitness we've been told. Looking at some, I'll not be surprised to see them on the first available ship back home. There are no navy uniforms in situ, so we gather up our remnants and stuff them in bags and climb on the truck wearing our everyday rags of the day. We're taking the train to Bangkok and then by sea to Singapore aboard a frigate, hoping we've our sea legs under us and that rice isn't on the menu.

CONTRARY TO OUR SCRUFFY APPEARANCE, we're warmly welcomed and applauded by the ship's officers and crew, as all fourteen of us stumble up the gangplank.

Truly, the Royal Navy does look after their own; for the next two days we're treated as heroes and handled with gentle care by these hard-nosed sailors. All too soon, we reach Singapore and weave a path through a massive array of sea power from aircraft carriers down to tiny bum-boats selling fruit. Bugles and bo'sun's whistles herald our arrival. We drop anchor, and *HMS Sultan's* whaler is already alongside to escort us to the main naval base.

"Step lively, you dozy shower," a sour-faced petty officer bawls from below.

I could never run a business or mind my own. "We need a hand. Some of these men are unsteady on their feet," I holler.

"My duty is to ferry you lot ashore. I'm no nursemaid," he yells back.

Before I can mouth a suitable answer, a brawny arm brushes me aside. "I don't want your dirty boots soiling my ship nor any assistance. I'm the coxswain here, and my men and I will deal with these brave souls. Sit down on your skinny ass and keep that gob shut. One wrong word and you'll be swimming back."

"Couldn't have phrased it better myself, Swain."

"Actually, it was the skipper's idea, but I won the toss."

Once safely seated, the journey to Clifford Pier is short and sweet. The PO's antics don't bother us. We've seen the Bushido boys at work. A five-minute ride in the liberty bus brings us to the opulent, refurbished base, and it's easy to see where the coxswain has acquired his swagger. Everything's pristine; the place oozes BS wherever I look.

Waiting outside the Drafting Office to be appropriated by a higher being is making us nervous. All we need is a bed, three meals a day and our tot and we're happy. Saluting anything that moves, and painting it if it doesn't, isn't a problem.

Arriving at a gallop, the bearded chief petty officer's words do nothing to brighten our day. The tirade includes such plums as, "You're a disgrace to His Majesty's Royal Navy. Who sent you here? You're not in rig-of-the-day."

Finally, breathless, he stands, hands on hips, with spittle running down his chin and our destruction on his mind. Naturally, we're taken aback. We look at each other and burst out laughing. Japanese methods never included explanations. Their bamboo sticks said it in spades, or cuts and bruises. Douglas Cameron, a pugnacious Scot relays this information to the troubled chief. Omitting the Glasgow lad's invective, there is nothing much left to say. Naval police have appeared at the double, plus interested spectators, including a fresh-faced, young Officer of the Day.

Good, honest, upstanding sailor boys would and could have informed the chief of his folly, but compared to the real bogeymen who've kicked and beaten the crap out of us countless times, this dick's an amateur. Nevertheless, he's going the whole hog and instructing the naval police to arrest us.

"Hold your horses, Chief Petty Officer Baxter," a firm young voice rings out. "Have you asked for any explanation before passing judgement?"

Astonishment clouds the chief's face. How dare a boy just out of naval school challenge his experience? Yet the boy does outrank him.

I can't help thinking, *This could have been me.*

Pointing my way, the officer asks, "You've something to say, blondie?"

Receiving the nod from the mob, who say I talk proper, I begin. "Actually, sir, it's a complete faux pas. We're en route to Johore from Thailand, and the base apprised of our arrival to provide transport forthwith." Having produced the bolts, I proceed to screw down their nuts, metaphorically speaking. "Our dishevelled appearance must be a grievous shock to everyone, inasmuch that good manners and common sense have flown out of the window. We're not here to destroy your old-world dignity nor to be bullied and verbally lashed by ignorance. We've been there, done that, every tatty-assed one of us. Please do everybody a favour, Chief Petty Officer, and get on that phone."

I'm surprised by the applause. The crowd must think there's safety in numbers. Subbie is not concealing his glee, and the chief's taking defeat like a gladiator. He's already smiling and shaking the urchins' hands.

Marvellous how straight talk can alter one's mindset, or as my granddad would say, *"That man knows on which side his bread is buttered."*

"Don't rush off, Chief," the officer calls out. "I've a special duty for you. See these men settled in. Find them a quiet billet, get some chow inside them, and most important do not forget their rum issue."

It's worth repetition. Without CPOs, the Royal Navy would run aground. We'd missed both victory celebrations due to being otherwise engaged, but the party staged in the chief and petty officer's mess on our behalf is a real humdinger.

You can't beat a happy ending. Maybe they know something we don't know.

Chapter Eighty-Seven

Cruising Singapore's busy streets, heading for Johore's base is hazardous. The road's barely wide enough for one vehicle yet crowded with chickens running every which way. Two unscrupulous mates are discussing grabbing a couple for supper. Jungle habits are hard to break. Our nurses tell us there's plenty to eat, even a menu.

Compared to Sultan, this place is palatial, stretching right to the river's edge, adjacent to the causeway joining the island to Malaya. Custom-built pre-war, it includes outside swimming pool, bar/restaurant, and theatre, with no expense spared. Having been introduced to some of these delights, and expressing our delight at the right moments, we're now seated on cavernous couches surrounded by white coats, listening to the head honcho's welcoming words. Dr Andrew Hardy's a dapper man, plain spoken, and with few pretensions. I'm sure we'll get along fine.

"Most of you are due to go home, and once you're strong enough to travel, off you'll go. The rest will be our guests until fully fit in body and mind. There are no wonder drugs or miracle cures, but we're winners, right?"

Rarely have I seen so many nodding dogs, except at "Crufts." Hardy's methods are unique. He's giving us time to catch our breath. We're still in the jungle not his world, but time's a well-known healer.

Strolling in the sunshine, selecting new uniforms, swimming in the pool—the days of Speedo are fading fast, and I'm sleeping better. Naturally, there are some grumbles. We're not allowed shore leave, the grog's watered down, and in one bittersweet moment, eight of the lads are shipped home for demobilisation.

We're due to begin solo therapy sessions, which are rumoured to be make or break. We've tried to discover the facts, but everyone's clammed up. I'm gaining weight when this news hits me, and a light clicks on.

"No! You can't go back to sea," Hardy barks. "You've not been declared fit. There are still your mental capabilities to be assessed."

"You think I'm mad?"

"Must be, making such a daft request. I've your medical records and know how you've suffered. Believe me, your head needs looking into first."

Despite my ire, I laugh. "You're in the wrong business, doctor."

"You're definitely nuts if you think I'm joking."

Mortified by the blow, I survey my options and reach an obvious conclusion: when you can't beat them, join them.

Dr Hardy's the expert and has found a crack in my armour. It's time to banish the clown and play the game their way. A strange thought creeps into my cranium. Perhaps the devious doc, while perusing my medical history, also glanced at my service record. Starting with my career in the cadets, taking in the Naval College success and trials and tribulations to date, it may prove excellent character material, if needed.

As my boyhood pal Kenny often said, "You go with what you've got, kid."

Trying to fit round objects into square holes, even as a small child, never lit my candle. I quickly bored of them in nursery school, and I'd whack them off the radiators. After two sessions with the shrinks and conspiratorial chats among my fellow sufferers, I unearth the doctors' little secret: they're testing our patience with variations on the same theme. Blow your top, and it will convince them that you're unstable. It's easy to see why everybody's close-mouthed; I'll have to be extra couth.

Behaving like a pusser sailor for two months is hard graft and it created gossip. I've a consultation with Dr Hardy today and am expecting eruptions.

"You're a persistent sod, Roberts, banging in another request for sea duty."

"I've been a landlubber for almost a year, sir. Reckon I'm due."

"I'll tell you when you're ready to haul anchor. You're my responsibility."

"I've wanted to sail around the world since I was a child. I was gutted when my mother refused to sign the entry forms," I say, turning away to hide my smile.

"You're in the wrong business too. You should be on stage with that performance, sweeping it, not acting. If it's any consolation, you'll have no problem being recommended for duty. We need well-trained, able-bodied men, and according to your service record, you're not as dumb as you make us believe."

"Thank you, sir, I'll try to live down to your expectations, and don't take this personally, but I hope to never see your face again."

Shaking his hand, I leave while I'm still ahead. I've a feeling there won't be many future opportunities. Packing my gear two weeks later is long and tedious, after months of travelling light. Fortunately, the trip's only a half hour to Singapore then onto a diesel-powered, motor minesweeper affectionately called a Mickey Mouse.

"Bon voyage, mate," the driver says as we finish unloading my kit onto the jetty.

Though the craft was moored in two banks of three less than a hundred yards inside the dockyard, he'd insisted on this courtesy. Bless his heart.

Taking the rifle off his shoulder, the QM points it at my chest while inspecting me from top to toe. "The navy must be getting desperate, recruiting kids from kindergarten."

My new uniform's confused him. He thinks I've arrived on the last banana boat. One choice word would clarify the situation, but I decide to be pleasant. "Excuse me, old chap, could you tell me the whereabouts of minesweeper *2236*? I've been told to report for duty."

"Blimey, we've being invaded," he says, almost dropping his rifle. He turns round and shouts, "Maury! Get your ass up here! There's another one of your mob just come aboard."

I'm still translating the sentry's words when this blond giant comes galloping along the deck and sweeps me into his brawny arms.

"Praise the Lord!" Maurice shouts, hugging me tightly. "It's Choirboy, back from the war to serenade us again."

Breathless, I ask, "Who are us?"

"Me of course, you dimwit," Jimmy says, arriving at the double. "This baboon would be lost without me."

Unashamed, we celebrate our reunion in gay abandon. I'm so happy I could cry. Such joy after the crap I've endured for a year doesn't seem credible.

"Are you okay?" Maurice asks while holding me tightly. "You're trembling."

"The world's stopped turning. Some idiot's pulled the plug."

"You've had a busy day and need to relax. We'll get you sorted post-haste."

Befuddled I may be, but the look my pals exchanged seemed strange.

Chapter Eighty-Eight

D ewy-eyed optimists believe the ancient folklore that good luck comes in threes. Being a pragmatist and following on the heels of Dr Andy Hardy's expertise, plus the miracle of meeting my erstwhile buddies, I'm not expecting any more goodies coming my way.

Having finished stowing away my gear on *2236*, Maurice and Jimmy return to their own vessel, while the chief stoker introduces me to my new shipmates. I've a nodding acquaintance with some from earlier days in Patrol Service, particularly one tall, nice-looking lad, possibly because he's offering me a drink.

"Welcome aboard, man. I'm Brian Liddell, though better known as Geordie from Newcastle, where the best footie players are born."

Ten minutes later, we're talking like old mates, and this canny lad strongly reminds me of Jack. Cynical me thinks, *Maybe the old saying is true?*

"Eddie— May I call you Eddie?" Geordie asks.

"I've been called worse names."

"I see why those guys like you. I remember you in Europa's NAAFI years ago. You had the place in an uproar."

"Some folk haven't forgiven me, said I was insubordinate, but I've never been home that early."

"Are you always this silly?"

"No way," I protest. "On a good day, I'm much dafter."

Geordie does a quick survey for any snoopers and whispers, "Your pals are planning a quiet run ashore tomorrow. We're sailing for the Andaman Islands the next day on a sweep for three weeks."

"That will be a first. They usually return under escort."

"We're the flotilla's flagship and have to set a good example, but don't sweat it, the skipper's Harry Tate's Navy too," Geordie tells me.

His answer solves a burning question. The commander of this flotilla wants the best men available, hence the preference for Patrol Service personnel. We may be rough, but we're always ready.

I'm duty watch tonight, from midnight to 0400 hours with Geordie as my mate, and he's bringing me up to speed regarding protocol and routine matters. Now that I've a regular berth, contacting family and friends is urgent to tell them I'm alive. I cannot divulge any information until I learn how much they know of Jack's death, if anything. Officially, I wasn't with him and haven't mentioned the cruel degradation I'd spent in captivity to anyone since I've left Johore. The nightmare's too poignant to consider, let alone speak.

Wise men say, "There's no cure, but time heals." How do they know? They weren't there. There have been enquiries into my adventures, but it's well known that sailors rarely tell sad tales, only the funny ones. My skeleton's in the cupboard aren't for public display.

Letter-writing marathon finished, Geordie takes me to see the sights. Everywhere is neat and tidy, truly Bristol fashion—ultrasound machines, radar screens, ASDIC detectors, and the whole ball of wax for mine-hunting. Though only the length of a corvette, there's tons of space, even in the thunder room. After three years as a matelot, I've found a ship where the mice aren't humpbacked. I'm so chuffed, I could kiss Geordie. Perhaps not!

Quaintly, my comical friends are also caring but emphatically deny the fact. Promises of a quiet night ashore prove to be just so. A select restaurant with excellent supper, complemented by a pleasant wine and gentle stroll along the Padang beach to the dockyard, a mug of cocoa and an early night. Prettier faces have shared my table, yet never with such concern for my welfare.

We're up and away before dawn's barely cracked with *2236* leading the trio of minesweepers through the Malacca Straits. I'm up the sharp end, with the deck undulating beneath me and the spray lashing my cheeks, reviving boyhood dreams too long buried by jungle terrors. Once more I'm free to sail oceans, see wonderful countries, meet beautiful people, and have a fun-filled life. I feel deliriously excited.

I can imagine Charlie saying, *"Go for it, kid. The world is your oyster."*

Yet it's just Geordie nudging my arm. "You look like a little boy opening presents on Christmas morning."

My moment's worth sharing. "It's a fairy tale come true, Geordie, though there were a few dragons too."

He's the good manners and moxie to let my words simmer a few seconds. "It's nothing a bright young man couldn't handle though," he finally concedes.

"Whatever cranks your handle," I answer casually.

Sun's nearly over the yardarm, which spells grub and, more importantly, tot time. We're spanking along at fifteen knots and should make landfall before it's dark. We'll find a nice sheltered bay in which to anchor overnight, and we'll be hot to trot at dawn. Three weeks of searching, contacting, and destroying magnetic mines is monotonous. There's no glamour but ample danger. Our working day finishes at dusk. Operating equidistant at five hundred yards in a V-shape formation, we blanket one mile in length by one thousand yards in width and make three passes. If all's clear, we move into another unswept section. Myriad multicoloured fish are having more fun.

Everybody's happier, including the wardroom cat once we weigh anchor and head for Bangkok. A life on the ocean waves is great but better with a bar in sight. Needless to say, the joss-sticks at The Blue Lagoon were burning late last night, while counting their takings.

Commander Douglas Blair, no pun intended, looks half-seas over as we head out of the bay with the sun scorching our throbbing heads. It's a hard life, but we'll be back later for more suffering. The buzz is this will be the last kick of the can. After this sweep, we sail south for the Maldives and finally the Seychelles islands, without shore leave. We'll return to Singapore and prepare the flotilla for pay-off in the Philippines. If the tales are true, most of the crews will be finished with their time and due for repatriation to England. Though I've not completed my two years, there's a chance I may slip under the wire, all things considered. Making the most of freedom is essential. We're taking no prisoners in Bangkok. Aware of our monastic future, there's no time to snooze and losing my friends' company is unthinkable. So party on! It's amazing how tempus fugit when one's having fun. I keep confusing the Thai barman by asking if he's on Tokyo time.

Arriving in the Maldives, following the Blue Lagoon caper, is definitely going south in every sense of the word.

My mates think me mad when I say, "I'm pleased we're not allowed ashore. Who needs drunken sailors spoiling such a beautiful place?"

Fulfilling a childhood dream, at last, becomes reality when I see waving palm trees, crystal-blue water, silver-sand beaches, and gorgeous, stunning sunsets.

Relaxation to the majority of the crew, once the daily grind's done, consists of hobbies, writing home, and personal care, whereas my favourite pastime is on deck observing, fantasising, and absorbing nature's marvellous panorama. Maurice is simpatico to my cause and tells me the Seychelles are more beautiful, having spent holidays there as a child with his parents. Aside from Jimmy and me, no one else knows of his privileged background.

Dropping anchor at fifty-yard intervals in a small inlet, the crews use a dinghy to visit each other. Commander Blair's a true diplomat and treats everybody as one big happy family.

"We're all in this together, men, be it a blessing or a bollocking," he insists. Beating boredom takes art and craft, which is no problem. Our flag officer's both artful and crafty. Simple solutions satisfy sailors. The Maldives weren't so tedious after all, we figure, hauling anchor and heading west.

There's much to be said for sailing the ocean and being paid too. Duty watches apart, it's a delightful two-and-a-half-day cruise.

Maurice speaks the truth. Seychelles is fantastic. If God has built a better spot, he's kept it well under wraps. It seems sinful to disturb the serenity of this utopia.

Nevertheless, when the devil drives, we finish the job and hie back to Singapore. I mail my glad tidings home and wait anxiously with fingers crossed.

Mother always said good things happen to good folk and I feel sated. Less than a year ago I was wallowing in misery. Now I'm king of the hill again, surrounded by friends and looking towards the future. Keeping a lid on my emotions crucial. Two months without a break is crippling, but until I receive news from home, everything's on hold. Finishing this last leg and paying off these ships are my priorities.

Watching other people work is a hobby I enjoy. Having completed a forenoon watch, had my lunch, and enjoyed my tot, I'm down aft watching the technicians paying out the pulse cables. Jimmy comes hurtling past, yelling frantically, "There's a bloody great mine up against the stern!"

He's not joking, as the stampede confirms. Everyone heads for the bows. Alone and aloof, I consider my options but realise there are none. Snatching up a boat hook, I push the hook-end through the eye bolt on the mine's top edge while leaning heavily against the pole. Miraculously, the canister stops swaying and swings up vertically. With most of the mine submerged, there's little strength required. Slowly, agonisingly so, the ship's momentum pulls her clear of any immediate danger. Unfortunately, the pole's only ten feet in length. Literally, whatever happens next is completely out of my hands. Reaching the end of my tether and my arms, I retreat tentatively and pray that we're not running with the tide. Restarting the engines isn't possible until we're farther away, as turbulence could set off the mine. Even if crew and ship were saved, all the underwater gear would be kaput. Sometimes being the monkey isn't bad.

Smiling faces look down from the wheelhouse and bridge, signalling Panic Stations is over. The skipper, chief engineer, plus a few hangers-on are flocking along the deck to greet me.

"Damn fine job, Eddie. Cool head when needed, eh!" Blair says, casting a long, disparaging look at his entourage.

"Truthfully, sir, I was too terrified to run."

"Besides being weird I've heard," the captain replies.

"Guilty as charged, but could you grant me a small request, sir?"

"Anything's possible, though I'm not your fairy godmother, lad."

"It's worrying me you may discipline the rating who left that boat hook lying around when we should be thanking him for saving our lives," I say.

Chapter Eighty-Nine

I t's impossible to please all the people all the time. The crew's blaming me for spending another day at sea.

"Be grateful you're not under it," I say.

The Royal Navy never allows minor incidents to deter obligations. Once we're at a safe distance, the skipper dispatches another sweeper to blow up the mine while recovering our gear from the ocean and ensuring all's well. Abandoning the sweep for the afternoon, Captain Blair makes it clear that tomorrow's back to normal. Hence, the ugly faces in my direction. Seven weeks of sobriety has turned my shipmates into Devil's Disciples.

I'm so dismayed, I need to get below for a drink to soothe my jagged nerves. Sometimes, wishful thinking creeps up on you. Imagine my delight, stepping over the mess deck transom, and seeing my mates with raised glasses, waiting to drink my health and happiness. *Silly, suspicious me,* I think, lifting my tumbler. *After all, what's not to love?*

Despite the usual moaning, everyone's relaxed and cheerful on the two-day run back to Singapore, which isn't surprising, knowing most will be homeward bound shortly, following farewell parties. Sadly, there's one task we've to perform first—ferrying the minesweepers to be paid off at the US Naval Base Subic Bay in the Philippines. Worse yet, every vessel, including equipment, is inventoried before departure and again on arrival; menial jobs for menial workers. Guess who gets lumbered? His Lordships at the Admiralty really enjoy their pound of flesh.

There are no high spots in Captain Blair's final briefing. "It seems the bigwigs have saved the bitter pill till last. We've the dubious honour of taking our ships to their graveyard, including towing a disabled duck. I feel it's a very poor ending for the arduous job you've performed, of which I'm very proud. Thank you all."

He's worth three rousing cheers. We rarely find officers of this type anymore.

Choking down our chagrin, we get plastered each night before sailing from Singapore and heading northeast at a plodding seven knots an hour with a stripped-down minesweeper in tow. Lashing the helm amidships and securing the rudders should keep the vessel's bow forward, providing the water stays calm. Anything rougher than a millpond will spell danger.

Two days at sea and our worst fears are confirmed when the weather turns rough. The tow line snaps, and the ghost ship veers right, heading for Borneo. All the crew starts to cheer, which brings the skipper down around our ears.

"We've to catch that damned ship or sink it!" he hollers. "It's breaking maritime law to leave her floating free."

Realising the "we" means "us" immediately wipes away our smiles.

Signalling the rest of the flotilla to steam on, the *2236* comes about and chases after the runaway.

"Getting aboard her is impossible in this weather, and there's no one to catch a line," the captain says. "Uncover the Bofors, we'll sink the bloody thing."

Good thinking! Except these ships have wooden hulls. It could take days to fill up with water. It's wiser to keep still my tongue my in head. Blair's paid the big bucks.

Within minutes, the superstructure is ablaze from end to end, and there're dozens of rats leaping overboard, which signifies the flames must be below decks too, but she's only listing slowly. We'll be here for hours!

Typhoon-force winds and rough troughs are making staying on station difficult and going round in circles is no laughing matter. Ten hours later, battered but not quite broken, we watch our comrade, wraithlike, slide silently beneath the waves. We stand quietly, staring down for a few moments, as sailors always do.

Arriving in Subic Bay mid-afternoon, we find the rest of the crews have gone ashore. Following a hectic, sleepless night, we crash our weary heads. Refreshed and ready for hijinks, I receive the bad news. We've a daily allowance of just four American dollars with no other currency accepted.

"Enough for two beers, without sex or sandwiches," Jimmy says.

"No problem," Maurice adds. "The Yanks and Aussies go crazy for navy rum."

"And we have a goodly supply, Ollie?" I ask.

"We certainly do, Stanley," Maurice answers.

"I presume you've arranged the itinerary, James?" I ask.

"Not really, but I know where we're going," he grins.

"He's learning, Maurice. We'll soon be able to let him off his leash."

Breaking for lunch and a well-earned tot, we saunter down the quay, do a deal with an Aussie tug-boat crew then stroll along to the US Naval Base as the USO's opening their door. Protocol demands that guests are not allowed to buy drinks, but once it's known we're here for business as well as pleasure, there are eager hands to assist us. Naturally, a little subterfuge is required, but it seems every American sailor has a slim flask in his back pocket for such emergencies.

Promptly at 1700 hours the canteen's closed. Everybody's ushered outside, and that's it. Nada! There's nothing to do. Correction, there's an outside movie theatre and, would you believe, John Wayne. Palatial it's not, but with a few drinks inside you and a bottle or two tucked in your shirt, what the heck!

Today, before allowed ashore, we'd had to dress in white, full duck suits and be inspected. It's been a hot afternoon, and we've had a few jars plus there's a bottle of gin in my hand, from which I've taken a few sips. The wooden seat's a tad hard on my cheeks, I'm tired, and everything's gone black. I must have closed my eyes, but I haven't. They're wide open, yet I can't see. Maurice laughs when I ask if the film's gone off, though the sound's loud.

Panicking, I yell, "I'm blind! I can't see a thing, Maurice. Help me!"

A big arm comes around my shoulder and pulls me close. "Sit quiet for a few minutes. You're out of kilter. I've never seen anyone really blind drunk before."

"Thank you, Maurice. I've never felt more sober in my life than I do right now."

"Owe you that, Eddie. You saved me when I sat shaking on that navy bus."

"That's what friends are for. Hey! The film's back."

"Glad you are, buddy. You're overtired. Probably a delayed reaction. We should get you to bed right away."

"Cheeky! You sailors are all the same, I'm pleased to say."

"Nothing wrong with you now," Jimmy adds. "Great to hear you're back to your normal daftness."

"Well done, James. You must have met Mother," I answer.

Geordie who'd been duty watch this afternoon has saved us supper, and we spend a couple of hours in idle chatter without mentioning my incident. He's a worrier and remembers my frailty when I'd first come aboard.

Whatever ogre's been running barefoot through my brain has taken flight, and I'm as fit as a butcher's dog, which is not the plight of my frazzled mates.

Testing our drinking prowess isn't brought into question. Confined to the dock area and doing a final inventory takes up the next two days. Then we're packing our kits and shuffling on board another flat-bottomed tin-can, Singapore-bound. It's a dreary, four-day trip, and we're packed to the gunwales. I'd forgotten how cramped the accommodation is on these floating coffins.

Back at the ranch, watery rum, tiger cub cat pee, and studying the draft board comprises the day's entertainment, with squeals of joy or blasphemy. Farewell parties are nonstop, as the lucky ones strike gold. Personally, I'm spitting blood when my three amigos are selected for repatriation, but not me.

Putting on a brave face, while helping them pack for the off, I hear my name called on the tannoy. "Knew they wouldn't forget me!" I shout. I return five minutes later, thoroughly pissed off. "I'm out of here too, but not to England. The bastards are sending me to Sumatra on an MTB, as escort for Dutch troop ships."

Chapter Ninety

Y ou're late," the crusty voice complains as I study the sleek lines of the armed motor launch. I'd been expecting an MTB, not the admiral's barge. Admittedly, all the guns are covered, but it's hardly a job for a real sailor. More like putting training wheels on your first bike.

"You could have started without me!" I yell, instantly regretting my angst. It's not the quartermaster's fault that my buddies took off without saying goodbye.

He's not perturbed. "Hop aboard, mate. Mad Pat's anxious to get away and busy laying down the law." He waves a calloused thumb. "He's down aft."

It's tempting to say, "I know my aft from my elbow," but save wit for later.

Mad Pat, the skipper, is easy to spot. He's the one wearing a shirt and an officer's cap. The shirtless ones are standing around gossiping.

Captain McGrath bellows for silence, smiles at the deathly hush and addresses me. "Thought you'd gone AWOL, lad. Ever been to sea in one of these?"

"Yes, sir, they're virtually unsinkable."

"Thank God someone believes me. I've been trying to educate this dumb lot," he replies, nodding at the blank faces. "Let's get below for some grub. The boys will be back from the base with the mail and grog soon, and we've a long trip."

That's not good news, especially with an inexperienced crew. The skipper's staring me down and slowly wagging his head. Our paths haven't crossed, but I know him by reputation, and I don't possess a death wish.

He's a living legend, been decorated and demoted many times. His latest fall from grace was due to the vicious beating he gave a Japanese sergeant, who'd boasted of beheading a British prisoner in Java for causing him to lose face. The victim had been Mad Pat's brother, and by the time three naval police had pulled McGrath off the sergeant, he'd little face left to lose. Though saddened that he hadn't demolished the enemy completely, the skipper knows he'd honoured his brother's life. Once the medics patch the Japanese sergeant back together to stand trial for his war crimes, Pat will have the satisfaction of seeing him hang.

I've been dreaming instead of scheming and wondered why the mad rush. Squeezing thirteen bodies into a space built for eight solves the equation.

The captain launches into action. "Grab your tots and listen up. You've heard the good news, touched for a soft number, but first you have to arrive, and judging by your faces, the majority couldn't paddle a canoe up the River Thames, never mind sail this baby to Sumatra." Scanning his audience with a look that would make Frankenstein shiver, he continues, "I need men I can trust and vice-versa. Anyone at odds, stick up your hand and I'll willingly boot you ashore. No questions asked."

Mad Pat hasn't been officious, he's spoken softly and apologetically, words straight from the heart.

"No need for a vote, Skipper," a voice calls from the shadows. "Engine room is in safe hands."

"So I've been informed often from Duncan and yourself, Dick. Your exploits aboard the *198* were notorious, Choirboy."

"Is nothing sacred in the Andrew, Skipper?" I ask as Tracey, grinning madly, steps into view.

"Not on my watch, sailor," Mad Pat laughs. "And you pair can save the kisses and cuddles for later. We've to slip our moorings by 1500 hours. So, step lively. I want this vessel spick and span, fit enough for the admiral's inspection, with you slovenly mob dressed in your best bib and tucker. Understand?"

The lapping of the sea against the keel is the sole response.

"You all got cloth ears? I said do you understand?" the skipper thunders.

Frantically and loudly, we answer.

Nodding and grinning fiendishly, he says, "We're the British Royal Navy, and still the finest in the world. Find me some Brasso and a couple of rags, Dick. I'll make a start on the ship's bell."

Leading by example has the desired effect, and the dour become the doers. It's dangerous telling Jolly Jack he can't do something; he'll move heaven and high water to prove that he can.

It's taken less than three hours for both vessel and crew to undergo an outstanding transformation. The launch is festooned with coloured pennants, thanks to the ingenuity of the bunting tosser and the ratings decked out in their best number one ducks. Twenty-four hours ago, I'd not known of their existence. Noting their campaign ribbons, I realise that we're not a crew, but brothers who belong together and know the score. Added to which, we've a boss who believes in us. I'd come aboard full of misery. Yet it could be a good move. Mad Pat's a man true to his word. The inspection's thorough, and he greets each of us personally. He's not interested in past deeds, but wants to know what we can contribute now, though I've a feeling he's already picked Dick's brain.

Scrutinising vessel and personnel might be finished, but Mad Pat isn't, despite Sub-Lieutenant Woods insisting that the pilot's getting antsy.

"Go tell Won Hung Lo to sit in a bucket and cool his assets. I'm not done yet. I've words for my men. You lot make me damned proud," he says. 'The craft's immaculate, and you're all a credit to the Service. From the moment we shove off, I want you to stand tall and show these wharf-rats how real sailors act." He cuts a smart salute, about turns and heads for the bridge.

A short while ago, we'd been cursing our luck, but now this epitome of naval discipline is hailing us as hometown heroes.

The glare of the hot sun is affecting my vision. Through the haze I see real, brave men like Jack, Jim, Hughie, and dear Les, plus many more who never made it.

"Shake a leg, lad!" Woods rants. "We're on the move."

Aroused from my torpor, I scramble back to my station amidships as we glide steadily in the pilot boat's wake to the harbour entrance. My despair's quickly dispersed by the salutes and goodwill messages from the ships at anchor. This spontaneous acclamation of bon voyage always fills me with pride.

Maybe Mother's right. Despite her best efforts, I'll always be a little boy.

Chapter Ninety-One

The skipper's sitting at the mess deck table when we arrive.

"Time we had a heads-up and I brought you up to speed. Woods is plotting a course through the islands down Sumatra's eastern coastline. It's smoother sailing with few trade winds, and apart from smugglers, not dangerous, and if they spot our white ensign, they'll quickly scarper."

Mad Pat's final words ease my mind. Going back into the jungle has made me jittery, without blood and guts to disturb my slumber. Seeing Tracey again makes it easier. He'd been my mentor, and a strong shoulder to lean on in my first, shaky days aboard the *198*; without fuss, or a foul word, he'd guided and guarded me against the tragic loss of my friends on the *Daisy*.

I'm sitting on the engine hatch cover, sorting the bunch of mail I've received this morning, when he comes by.

"Lots of letters from those scream-age girls who think you can sing?"

"These letters are a year old, been halfway around the world, and just arrived." I wave a blue airmail, and say, "My girlfriend's left me."

"You've lost that pretty blonde girl with the gorgeous mum? Thought you were childhood sweethearts. She must be crazy."

"Idiot, Anita hasn't left me, her family's left town. Sold their business and gone to live in Wales. I should have known you'd remember Cheryl."

"Honourable petty officer only married, my son. I'm not blind. And look on the bright side. Wales isn't bad. There are ten thousand Welshmen at my local pub in London every Saturday night, singing 'Land of my Fathers.'"

I look up anxiously as the launch veers sharply starboard.

"Don't panic," Tracey advises. "Woods's found us somewhere to lay up overnight. The skipper wants us well rested. It's a long way to Pladjoe."

"Tipperary too," I moan. Unlike my shipmates, I'm still not enamoured by the cushy number we've inherited. "Does the captain enjoy playing Boy Scout?"

"Watch your mouth," Tracey snaps. "Skipper's not playing. Listen well to the last of a dying breed."

Feeling severely smacked, I hold my tongue, grateful that the break gives me time to sort my mail. Anita's letter has made me think. It's no billet-doux and extremely cool. She's not heard from me since December of '44, despite writing several times. Her letter's dated 10 September 1945. A quick memory check reminds me that I was in therapy fitting square blocks into round holes back then. Two months previously, with the war in Europe finished and Japan ready to quit, the Barretts were making plans for Jack's return when they were told of his death. Cheryl suffered a nervous breakdown and had to be placed in a nursing home, which took Mr Barrett's business into bankruptcy. Anita's right; her dad had no choice. He'd grafted hard for love of family, only to see it crash and burn due to man's stupidity and greed. Selling out and running away must have seared him deeply, but why Wales? Surely my parents or business friends could have helped? And what the hell happened to Bill Brown?

I've a thousand questions but not a single answer.

Now my mail's arriving in Singapore, I might receive up-to-date news. I'll dash off another letter to Anita, and better yet, a missive to the font of all knowledge: dear Mother.

CAPTAIN'S ON THE BRIDGE AND the ball at first light. He'd said bright and early, as Tracey warned. Mad Pat's for real. His logic's simple: he's twice our age and if he can do it, so can we. He's not hanging about, wringing fifteen knots an hour out of the twin diesel engines and singing bawdy songs. Blow a gasket at this speed, and we will be cleaning up the engine compartment with a brush and pan.

Following a restless night, I'd risen in a foul mood and with a bleak outlook. Once more I'm back on Lonely Street, and even super-sleuth Tracey would find it difficult to solve my problem. Thankfully, he respects my privacy and allows me to wallow in peace.

We've eased off speed, and whether by chance or design, as we're crossing the line, Up Spirits, is piped. We're seated around the table, waiting for our medication, when the skipper and Tracey stagger in carrying rum-fannies.

"Sorry we're late," Mad Pat says. "Had to be careful not to spill any. Normally, we'd be celebrating this occasion but haven't enough men to act as jury. Most of you are pollywoggers, but tradition says you've to perform special tasks. Therefore, as King Neptune, I command that you all drink one extra tot of rum as punishment and on completion, I will then present each with a royal deed."

Since childhood, I've dreamed of sailing the ocean blue, searching for pirates, and to the true believer, they certainly exist, even if Captain Patrick McGrath, RN is back in command and hell-bent for Sumatra.

Though well-versed in mechanics, sometimes I forget the first lesson: make sure the brain's engaged before operating mouth.

Suddenly, the day's brighter. Maybe it's the rum or lack of bull and brass. Whatever, Tracey nails it. "Sit back and enjoy, you're a long time dead."

Scarcely poetic but apt, and it gives me an out with no embarrassing apologies.

Still, our perfect day's ruined when reaching the the main channel to Palembang, Musi River, and we're told we've another two-hour trip. While most of the crew lean on the rails soaking up the scenery, I disappear down to the engine room. I've already had a bellyful of tropical forests.

Stepping ashore at Pladjoe, we're given a warm welcome by Royal Marines and matelots, especially by the sister ship's crew, who've been pulling double duty and are anxious for our arrival. Furthermore, the boot-necks' generosity puzzles us when they fling open the canteen's portals. Luckily, sailors are not too proud to drink with anybody, even marines, if unavoidable. Naturally, we promise to be good boys. And the band plays on.

We're not allowed off base and while on duty, not even ashore. It's not hard work, just boring. Five or six hours on the river at tortoise pace is not breathtaking. The end of this caper seems as far off as Mars, and our sole hobby is getting paralytic every other evening. Surreptitiously, tragedy descends one dreary, rain-swept afternoon.

"Stir your stumps, lads, we've been called out," Joe shouts down the mess. "Skipper's already on the bridge."

Despite foul language and the usual grumbling, within five minutes we're away into the main channel and heading for the Java Sea in the gathering gloom. Caution is mandatory. In addition to the fo'c'sle spotlight, many of the crew up top are extra eyes. The Musi River is Sumatra's lifeline and teeming with traffic.

I'm lucky down in the engine room, out of the rain. Yet it's a mixed blessing. Even at half speed, it's like a sauna; ten minutes is sufficient. I've pleaded with Tracey to keep Mad Pat away from the controls, if possible. The sudden surge in revs grabs my attention. It seems my plea was in vain. Someone's in one a hell of a hurry. The levers register full ahead, tappets and valves are screaming, and the cacophony's pounding my brain to mush. Stuffing my ears with cotton waste, I scramble for the hatch, preferring death by drowning to being barbecued. The bloody thing's stuck!

Pushing frantically eases it slightly, and I hear Mad Pat's dulcet tones. "Stay at your station sailor, that's an order."

No sweat (bad choice of words). Wherever we're heading, it will not take long at this speed, providing we don't explode. Bongo drums are still beating a steady tattoo inside my skull as we make fast, and eager hands haul my parboiled remains onto the deck. I'm not damaged but thoroughly wrung out; something's drastically wrong. Marines with stretchers and body bags verify my suspicions.

Cornering Joe, I ask, "What's gone down, mate?"

"Cunning sods set us up. Knew we were coming and used their own kids to fool us. The bumboats were selling their stuff when two junks came roaring out of the trees with guns blazing, one port-side, the other starboard. The youngsters thought it great fun and took off soon as the shooting started. Our boys were slaughtered."

Familiar faces are missing. "Who bought it?" I ask.

Joe's distraught. "Woods and Tracey were killed in the first salvo. We've lost half the crew, which explains why Mad Pat's back. He needs replacements."

"We're going out again? It will take all night in this weather."

"You tell him, mate. He's bitten my head off once," Joe moans. "Acting strange and saying there's a job to be done and promises to keep."

"It's nothing personal. The skipper's carrying everyone's pain," I say, as Mad Pat troops aboard with half of the other launch's crew. "He's chomping at the bit and anxious to push off," I add.

Orders are terse yet implicit. Stealth and silence are essential, and except for navigation lights, the launch is blacked out. Thanks to the marines, the night-vision glasses are a godsend in this gloomy, dank swampland as we quietly drift on the tide. Mad Pat's plan is simple but smart. I've to run the engines as slowly as possible until we're past the village, then he'll take over. Believing the marauders have gone into hiding, Mad Pat doesn't wish to spoil the broth for a halfpenny pinch of salt.

Crouched behind the rev counters, my eyes glued on the flickering needles, I'm nervous yet proud to be regarded as man enough for this job.

Caught off guard by the boat's sudden surge, I'm sent sprawling full length a split second later then I hear a loud bang and the rising crescendo of the engines. Buffeted and bruised, I do the only thing possible: pray! How long I lay there, only He knows. I'd had emotions from sorrow to joy—the naked truth of loss of friends, especially Tracey, and the insane glee that we've left those murdering bastards something to remember.

Undoubtedly, the loud noise I'd heard had been the Bofors gun. Further good news reveals that I'm not dead. I feel pain in every muscle. Sadly, there's little time for tea or sympathy. Though we've arrived unscathed, there's still work to perform. At first light tomorrow, we've four thousand eager Dutch soldiers to deliver. I wouldn't miss this gig for the world.

Chapter Ninety-Two

The morning after starts badly. Lacking a good night's sleep, everyone's tired and tetchy. A vow of silence exists, per Captain's orders. Our progress is slow, and the river's almost devoid of traffic. News of a troopship normally has the bumboats swarming around.

"Place is like a graveyard," I comment. I'm surprised by the lack of response. I study my boots. Maybe I've trodden in something.

Joe's already on the fo'c'sle, badgering Cookie and giving me black looks.

They think I'm daft. Never shy, I ask, "When were you going to tell me?"

"Skipper's sworn us to secrecy, said he'd break the news," Cookie replies.

"Probably told you what I don't know won't kill me either. Yet it's hard not to notice that he's blown the whole village sky-high."

"Mad Pat says we were obeying orders and not accountable." Joe adds, "Though we backed his decision one hundred per cent."

"Bet that made him smile. He loves teamwork," I say.

Palembang's on the horizon and seeing the ship safely anchored takes priority. We're thankful to be back in Pladjoe by noon, though there's more gold braid on the jetty than I've seen since leaving Singapore.

Speculation is rife, but the Royal Navy with its usual efficiency reacts fast. The captain is relinquished of his command after suffering mental distress and is under medical supervision. The whole operation's suspended with all personnel being returned to base.

It's a short and sinister message, and if Captain Patrick McGrath's mad, I'm a monkey's uncle.

RETURNING TO SINGAPORE UNDER ARMED guard's embarrassing. I'm told I may have to attend a board of inquiry which is annoying, but to be sent on another draft is soul-destroying! I'd dreamed of being halfway home, yet here I am about to board a landing craft gun anchored in the Johore Straits. Furthermore, it's never been in action. Along with two dozen other unfortunates, I've joined a care and maintenance crew. Polish and oilcan are all I need.

Dear Lord, have mercy on this poor sinner.

I've been here before, straight from Thailand to have scrambled brains reset. They've done a good job with the base; I'm not sure about my head.

Leaning over the side of *LCG 108* is a face easy to dislike.

"What do you want?" it demands.

"Not you, dear heart, you're not my type."

My remark falls on stony ground. A hook and chain with wire basket attached comes squeaking down, and a cockney voice advises, "Bung your kit in there, and get your ass aboard smartly."

Mother always insists, "Manners make the man." It's been an awful day, and no loud-mouthed slob from the smoke is going to disparage me. I'm zipping up the gangway prepared for battle.

He's big, brawny, and beaming. "Got your attention didn't I, mate?" he says, extending a huge paw.

Nodding numbly, I inspect my hand. I still have five fingers.

"I'm Leading Stoker Sidney Payne, and you're not what I expected when hearing that north and south," he says studying me closely. "Thought we'd got royalty come to visit."

My swift appraisal assures me I've run into a real pro. He's at least thirty years old, knows it all, but still needs someone to bully. Unless he's winding me up. I'll play him at his own game. "Sorry, old chap, you caught me at a loss. It was a culture shock being posted to this old rust bucket. I much prefer sailing the ocean."

Puncturing Payne's pride and denting his dignity in one sentence is no mean feat. I wait with bated breath for a response.

He doesn't deliberate long. "I'd a good feeling the minute I clapped my mince-pies on you, son. Reckon we'll scrub along together nicely, better once I've taught you to talk proper, like what I do."

Surprised, yet delighted at our instant rapport, I suggest, "Why not take me on the tour and we meet the other inmates, Leading Stoker?"

Introduction to "the brotherhood," as the C&M party call themselves, is a pleasant surprise. Expecting unshaven, hard-faced characters, I receive a hearty welcome from young men with a common goal—all are anxious to go home.

Shamefacedly, my rant concerning the ship's unfounded too. She's immaculate inside and out. Perhaps mine has finally come in.

LCG 108 is our pride and joy. Every day the crew works to keep her in prime condition from black and green camouflage paint to remote-controlled gun turrets. Despite never firing a shot in anger, she's battle ready. Sid and I take tender care of the powerful diesel engines and generators, even to changing their gaskets.

Meanwhile, my burgeoning relationship with Sid has gained me admiration from shipmates, who've noticed his change from surliness to smiles. Thrust together by work has brought us closer. We find it easy to talk, and I've learned that listening is an important part of conversation. Labour intensive, the job is not. Three hours graft each morning; make and mend each afternoon; drinking and/or debauchery thereafter, depending on your choice.

Many of the crew believe they've discovered the life of Reilly; oh really? Any which way one swings in the Royal Navy is their own business. Initially derided, I am now admired for my abstinence, even envied by some who've visited Rose Cottage.

Seasonal gloom's setting in. Many of us will experience our third Christmas away from home. By tradition, the officers play Santa Claus for the day and wait on the crew. There'll be no snow or mistletoe. We'll sing songs, old and new, reminisce, and get pleasantly pissed. Savouring the moment when Jack's as good as his master, if not better.

Good fortune comes in threes: the arrival of grub, grog, and mail lifts spirits greatly, news from home being number one. Sandy Shaw, our mailman, is loaded down with goodies, and we nod sympathetically as he groans, "I'm knackered."

Sailors are like kids with presents. We open the big ones first. Usually, letters are tucked under plates, to be read later in private. Parcels are different, and everyone is eager to view the contents. The humongous, globular, brown-paper parcel that Sandy deposits in my lap stirs curiosity among the crew. Speculation ranges from sublime to ridiculous, and the sheer size, with Yuletide nigh, suggests it may be something we can share.

"Open it! The suspense is killing me," Sid pleads.

Five minutes later, snowed under by string and heavy-duty brown paper, I've uncovered a huge tin. Slashing away the sealing tape, I ease off the lid. Atop the waxed paper is a letter in Mother's bold script, which I quickly remove, and frantically strip off the final shroud. The heady perfume is reminiscent of a distillery. Instinctively, eyes glaze over, nostrils twitch appreciatively, and taste buds salivate with fond memories. Necks crane forward for a closer inspection.

Merry Christmas, Everyone, the scrolled, red icing proclaims, etched boldly into pristine-white icing, interspersed by all things festive, including Santa, complete with reindeer and sleigh.

Hard-faced drinking men are transmogrified into small children. Their eyes are agog at the wondrous sight.

"It's a bloody great Christmas cake, look you!" Taffy Evans shouts, stating the obvious.

"You're wrong," Sid says. "It's a work of art. Your mum deserves a medal, Ed."

There're loud cheers when I say, "Mother tells me to ensure all my friends receive a slice of cake and choose a decoration as a gift."

Mother is a born diplomat.

I take the chance to slip away. I've stacks of mail to read and questions to answer.

I'm sitting on a deserted gun deck pondering when Sid finally tracks me down. "You look glum, chum. Thought you'd be over the moon."

"There's trouble back at the ranch. Everything's changed in the past couple of years."

"That's life, mate. Happens to the best of us. I'll tell you a secret. Came up from Portsmouth on a weekend pass to see my family. Walked down the street, and half the houses were flattened. The Germans dropped a bloody great landmine. I lost my wife, five-year-old son, parents, and twelve more relatives. Only my old granny survived." Staring across the Straits collecting his thoughts, Sid continues, "I sat in the gutter and sobbed, became a miserable, selfish swine. Probably still would be, if you hadn't come along and made me laugh with your daftness."

Unaware of Sid's beliefs, I opt for safety. "Perhaps Granny's on the touchline?"

It's an honour to be trusted and reminds me of Les. Unloading his own tragedy has been Sid's way of proving the triviality of my situation.

"Whatever's altered while you've been gone isn't your business, Eddie. That pretty girl's no doubt blossomed into a beautiful lady. Just say you love her and leave the feuding to the families."

"But they're not talking to each other."

"So! You'll have a quiet honeymoon."

Ten years Sid's been in the Andrew and never stuck for a reply, drat him, though I'm glad he's here. There're only him and three others left from the bums I'd inherited. Times have changed. The replacements drink milk and like to be between the sheets by 2100 hours; their own, not someone else's. Sprawled around the table are the real sailors, hungover from last night's farewell party, sipping rum while waiting for the grub to arrive. Thankfully, our lips are in good working order.

Prissy in their blue work-shirts and matching pants, the new boys are arguing about who's serving food.

Leading Stoker Payne has his beady eyes on them. Any second, these delightful ducklings will be receiving one hell of a roasting. He lumbers to his feet, ready to break hearts, even heads.

"Enough! You're the biggest shower of nancies I've ever seen—" He's interrupted.

"As you were, chaps," a voice rings out. "No one's walking the plank."

My fiendish hopes are dashed. Standing in the hatchway, on one of his rare visits, is the skipper. He's a good-humoured man; he's a tad peculiar, but among friends.

"I bring glad news and not-so-glad news," he kicks off. "You five vagabonds will gather your goods and chattels together and journey forth from Johore unto Singapore, on the morrow." Frowning and reflecting a moment, the captain adds, "Let's pray you are not set upon by thieves of any description."

Listening to this man's eloquence is a joy, and his version of the sailor's sermon on the road to damnation, pure whimsy. Sadly, it's lost on most of his captive audience, who stand with glassy eyes and open mouths.

"Excuse me, sir," one of the newcomers says. "You mentioned bad news too."

"Ah! Yes, but only the idle and dim-witted have anything to fear, young man. Your sojourn in the sun is almost done. Starting tomorrow this vessel becomes a training ship. There'll be hard-nosed instructors determined to make sailors out of you. Judging by your performance today, they face a Herculean task, and so do you. Changing from selfish brats into team players will be extremely difficult."

Pausing in his litany, the skipper beams benignly round the mess, and says, "Hardships you bastards, you don't know what hardships are."

Undoubtedly, there's no riposte to such eloquence.

Chapter Ninety-Three

A Chinese proverb says "a journey of a thousand miles begins with a single step." The trip from the LCG to cruise ship is one gigantic leap. Excitingly packing our gear, we've forgotten naval customs and for three days are subjected to stiff tests of physical and mental strength, including a search-and-destroy project (shades of the nit nurse). Happily, there are no machines to inspect my brain. My thoughts are sacrosanct.

Two more days are expended installing five thousand members of the armed services onto this ocean-going liner. By His grace or astute thinking, we've been segregated onto separate decks. Though willing to fight a common foe, we're not overfond of each other. It's not the pleasure trip we've imagined, sailing into a becalmed Indian Ocean with the late afternoon sun beating down. Yet God is in His Heaven, and things are right with the world as we head for England's pleasant land.

My fascination with the sea's never waned, and most waking hours I'm up top, unlike the landlubbers, who are in their bunks at the first quiver of the hull. Sid's the ideal soulmate, and we've endless conversations concerning grannies and girlfriends. He's kind, considerate, and doesn't pull his punches but is truthful. We've known each other briefly, though I feel I'm an old mate. Soon we'll be parted. I'll miss him, not with sorrow, just fond memories.

Rationed to one beer per day, adulterated rum, and little money makes Jack a dull boy, including the square-bashers and fly boys. There are not many fiddles; though my duty-free cigarettes pluck at some heartstrings, it still creates a sour note. Luckily, the meagre pickings allow the purchase of a few cans of beer, which keep my mates smiling.

Reaching Port Said has taken fifteen days. We stopped at Colombo and Bombay, and anchored in the big lake for a full day, waiting for access to the Suez Canal. Passengers are becoming fractious. Only whispers of an overnight stay at Malta and shore leave soothe the savage beasts. Six until midnight isn't utopia, but at the witching hour, every reveller's back aboard and sound asleep; the infamous Gut has survived another onslaught.

Recognising Gibraltar's easy, the bowls and buckets by numerous bedsides signals our crossing of the Bay of Biscay.

Portsmouth's on the horizon when the buzz goes round that the customs boys are coming on board the moment we drop anchor, searching for contraband. There's wholesale panic, as we hunt through kits. I've a couple of Lugers plus magazines, which I'd bought in Bangkok way back. I'm calmer once the Japanese knock-offs are wrapped in a towel and dropped in the harbour's murky depths.

We've just finished our final meal together. It certainly feels that way. Solemn faces around the table suggest we've reached the last mile. All that's missing is the firing squad, ready to escort us to the execution chamber.

Yet, rarely does the sailor say goodbye. It's *See you later*—never uttered in despair, always in hope.

"Granny won't know me, sounding my H's and not saying *ain't*," Sid says.

Letting him have the last laugh, I smile politely, turn away before sniffling, and join the Chatham crowd. It's a warm, sunny afternoon, but there's a sudden chill down my spine. It must be the English climate or a harbinger of things to come.

CHATHAM BARRACKS ISN'T AS REPUTED but is twice as bad. There are petty officers hiding in shadowy doorways, ready to tell us what horrid little ratings we are. Their evil intent is to nab us for some minor infringement.

Anyone is fair game, particularly a newcomer. The main purpose is to inflict the fear of God into their victims. It's not a cruel joke, but a way of life.

Discipline reigns supreme. The Parade Square is hallowed ground. Walking is forbidden. A whistle blast followed by, "That man there! You dozy sod, double up. You're not on Daddy's yacht," plus invective to which no mother's child should be subjected.

Escaping this Bastille's my solitary thought. Keep my head down, mouth buttoned, and powder dry until the train is well north of Watford.

It had taken the money-changers two days to figure how much they owe me, but ahead stretches six weeks' leave and good times are coming!

Faster than a speeding bullet, I'm out of the station, across New Street and zipping into the Windsor Bar and Grill, as Lou lifts the towel off the beer pull.

I've hardly drawn breath from Dad's hug before the landlord's sliding a glass in front of me. "On the house, Ed. Glad you're back," he says, nodding at Dad. "It'll stop this old bugger moaning."

I'm surprised when Dad declines a second beer yet notice Lou's slight shake of the head and curb my witty response. I'll quiz my host later.

There's more silver in Dad's well-groomed hair, and he's a gear slower too. It's no surprise—the old fellow's getting up there.

He left school at fourteen, and including four years' service in World War I, hasn't missed a day's work through sickness for forty years. The devout vow is that God grants each person a special gift. Should that be true, having the world's best dad suits me fine.

Normally reserved, his chatter on the way homes is infectious, and we're still laughing as Mother's crushing me in a fierce embrace.

After the first frenzy's passed and following dinner, we relax in the drawing room with cups of tea and amiable conversation. Mainly, I sit back, listening to my parents avoid mention of the Barrett family. Without the roof caving in, I know something's wrong.

Tonight's not the time for inquests. Besides being travel-weary, it's wiser to establish a better rapport with Mother before opening that can of worms.

Yawning, I say, "Sandman's calling. Be nice to sleep in my old bed, unless the Pope's dropping by."

I'm halfway down the hall, when Mother says, "He gets quainter every day."

"Expect the sun has fried his brains," Dad mutters.

It's heart-warming to know your parents care for you.

Rising early, refreshed from a grand night's sleep and having consumed a huge breakfast, I'm helping Mother unpack groceries, for which I'd supplied money and ration coupons. Largesse apart, my adroit move may help to loosen her tongue.

Jumping in the deep end I demand, "What's happened between you and the Barrett clan?"

Mother isn't smiling. "We're not talking," she snaps.

"That's your problem. I'm off to Cardiff to see Anita."

"Wasting your time and money. Her mother's threatened to call the police if you visit. She blames you for Jack's death, which is why we quarrelled. Someone wrote and told her you'd watched her son die and walked away."

Pain's etched deep in her sad hazel eyes. The chin's stubborn and firm, though her lips tremble.

"Why didn't you tell me you'd been captured?" Mother whispers.

To lie by omission is easy, but face-to-face, it's impossible. "Too ashamed. I'd boasted of bringing Jack home and failed. I've never told anyone, didn't want you to worry. Though I promised Jack, before he died, I'd deliver his love and final wishes to his family."

"You've always been obstinate, but you have a good heart. Just be warned: Cheryl isn't the lovely lady we once knew and loved. Losing Jack's sent her crazy. The booze and breakdown are taking a heavy toll."

"Perhaps seeing me will help," I say optimistically.

"I wouldn't bet two pence on it." Mother sniffs.

Plainly, there's no more information coming, so filling my flask with rum and slipping into uniform, I sally forth. It's only one and a half hours by train to Cardiff, and I have the address. Any cabby worth his salt will know the way.

Shortly after 1400 hours, we're stopping in front of a modern, three-storey office block. "You want the main office or house, sir?" the driver asks.

Looking up, I see emblazoned in huge, black and gold letters across the front fascia, Bingley & Bingley Enterprises: Commercial, Residential, and Industrial Developers, Inc. Suddenly, the pieces drop into place.

Despite the tragedy that's befallen the Barretts, they've a nice roof over their heads, I figure, gazing at the red-bricked, Tudor-style mansion. Whatever deal Bingley has conned, it seems Mr Barrett's fallen onto his feet, though the pallid-faced figure opening the door is a shadow of the man I'd once adored.

He's courteous and soft-spoken, explaining Cheryl's taking a nap as we walk to a study where Anita's seated and surrounded by paperwork.

I'm mesmerised by her beauty. The dimpled, cheeky grin has been replaced by a cool glance of appraisal. "It's kind of you to come. Father mentioned it, but I said you're much too busy."

I'm tempted to give a round of applause for her well-rehearsed speech. I'd not expected her to leap from a cake half-naked, blowing a bugle, but a warm hug would have been welcome. Selfish motives apart, I'm here on a mission, and remembering Mother's words, have been formulating plan B on the journey.

"My visit's more important than a social call. It's to honour a pledge I made to Jack shortly before he died," I say.

Aware I've my audience's full attention, I'm about to plead my case when the door bursts open, and swaying precariously is a wild-eyed, dishevelled woman who looks at least a hundred years old. She's wailing like a banshee.

"Get this vile creature out of here before I call the police, Jack," she insists, staggering towards me.

Drunk as a skunk and it's only mid-afternoon. Some might find it amusing, but I feel her anguish. It takes one to know one. Mr Barrett and Anita promptly intercept Cheryl and quickly subdue her, wrestling a glass from her tenacious grip. She's still muttering and shooting me venomous looks, but she's remarkably docile under her daughter's strong handling. Whereas Jack was gentle, Anita's inherited her mother's feistiness. There are no prizes for guessing who kicks ass in this house.

Taking to the floor, I say, "I'm here today to deliver a message and clear my name. First of all—"

"Lying toad will say anything to get my child back," Cheryl interrupts.

Nonplussed, I look around desperately. If no one's willing to listen, I'm scuttled.

Salvation comes from an unusual quarter. "This young man wouldn't tell a lie to save his life," Mr Barrett says quietly.

"That's a wicked thing to say, Mother," Anita scolds. "Eddie's the most honest person I've ever met, and I need to hear what my brother had to say."

I'd love to run over and kiss her but bravely resist. "The father's wrong. I went to hospital for treatment and met Jack two weeks prior to his death. We talked incessantly of you and home. He told me not to write but to visit and give everyone his love, and apologise for letting you all down. I didn't desert Jack—he died in my arms. They carted him off, buried his bones in the jungle, allowed me to visit at his grave, then sent me back to the work camp," I say without pause.

"I returned three months later, but the whole site had vanished," I add.

There's an ominous, blank silence while they digest my words.

Unsurprisingly, it's Cheryl who breaks the lull. "You were always a silver-tongued charmer, and why would a man of the cloth speak falsely?"

It's an astute question from a drunkard, which deserves a truthful answer.

"We all need a crutch to lean on. Father Daniel was a Roman Catholic priest and an alcoholic. He accepted confessions from many debilitated prisoners, and also gave them to the Japanese guards to satisfy his craving. It wouldn't surprise me if the booze didn't make him delusional too."

"Your fancy words and prissy ways don't fool me," Cheryl hits back. "I want you out of my house now, and Anita certainly doesn't need you either."

Exhausted from my diatribe, I sit down, though swearing not to dwell on past calamities. I've reneged and let her poison affect me. Yet, somewhere in Cheryl's babble, there's a grain of truth.

Anita's sharp voice gets my attention. "Correction, Mother. It's not your house. It's owned by Bingley Enterprises, and I'm the tenant."

Magically, a thousand light bulbs illuminate my sluggish brain. It's similar to a Christmas pantomime, where the fairy godmother floats down, taps Cinderella on the shoulder with her magic wand and says, "One day, child, all this will be yours."

Foolishly, I'd thought Mr Barrett was manager and Anita his girl Friday. How wrong can one be? This gorgeous creature's running the show. One gives credit where it's due. The Bingley cowboys, with superb business acumen, a fat checkbook, and a goodly supply of altruism, have hit the jackpot. Outbidding Bill Brown, Dad, and numerous friends (who likely made valiant efforts to save Jack's empire) was sheer genius, and why they're hopping mad. For my part, I'm proud of Mr Barrett for having the guts to turn his back on the world when the welfare of his family was at stake.

Switching to Cheryl, anticipating eruptions, I see she's nodded off and has unwittingly furnished the final piece to the puzzle.

Now is the ideal moment to strike. Timing is of the essence. Rising to my feet, producing my flask with a flourish, I pop the cork and take a hefty slug. Anita looks flushed and angry; Mr Barrett's too tired to care.

Forestalling any acrimony, I hold my hand high, palm uppermost, signifying peace. It worked for Geronimo. "Your mother, in her befuddled state, has summed up the situation perfectly. You don't need me, darling. You've more than enough emotional cripples to handle, and a brilliant future lies ahead. My sweet girl has blossomed into a beautiful, talented lady with the world at her feet, which makes me very proud."

"You were the one who taught me how to fly and were an excellent teacher," Anita says.

Struggling to stay calm, I reply, "Maybe so, but Peter Pan's only flying on one wing and has some growing up left to do. I'm not leaving through lack of love, it's because I care too much, for all of you."

"I love you, Eddie, and want you to stay, whatever the rest think or say," Anita protests.

"You and your family will always be in my heart, darling Anita, and you know that's no lie."

Lifting my empty flask, I turn to Jack. "Take good care of each other, and tell your lovely lady the minute she surfaces, like the Bedouins of the desert, I've gone in search of another oasis. She'll know exactly what I mean."

Wobbling unsteadily, I'm out of the house, down the steps, and opening the taxi's door as Mr Barrett reaches me.

Seizing my shoulder, he says, "You have always been stubborn and too bloody proud. That's your trouble, son."

"I know, and it takes lots of practice, but forgetting is a damned sight harder than forgiving."

Forlornly, Mr Barrett sighs. "Believe me, lad, I do understand."

"You do?" I demand bitterly. "I wish to dear God I did."

Waving wildly and yelling, "Goodbye," "adios," "sayonara," and not forgetting "up yours," I collapse onto the seat as the cabby zooms away.

Softly, yet clearly, I hear a voice: "Don't let the bastards screw you down."

About the Author

E.R. Rhodes was born and raised in Warwickshire, England, and served in the British Royal Navy from the ages of sixteen to twenty-one. After fighting in World War II, he told himself that he'd never speak of the experience. But his passion for writing and a promise to his late wife, Vera, made him break his silence. And so his debut memoir, *Tears Before Bedtime*, was born.

Rhodes began his love affair with words at a young age, working on short stories, articles, and speeches for dignitaries and politicians in England. Having now turning forty (twice), he plans to continue writing from his current residence in Delaware, Ontario, Canada.

You can connect with E.R. Rhodes online at EddieRhodesBooks.com.